W9-BIA-197

Am Anfang war die Tat.

—Goethe

To ingenious attempts to explain by the light of reason things which want the light of history to show their meaning much of the learned nonsense of the world has indeed been due.

—E. B. Tylor

οὐδὲν χρῆμα μάτην γίγνεται, ἀλλὰ πάντα ἐκ λόγου τε καὶ ὑπ ἀνάγκης.

—Attributed to Leucippus

The Genesis of Plato's Thought

BY ALBAN DEWES WINSPEAR

New York
RUSSELL & RUSSELL

LIBRARY OF CONGRESS CATALOG CARD NUMBER 55-10273

Manufactured in the United States of America

Preface

For several years now it has been my pleasant task to read the Republic of Plato with students of Greek at the University of Wisconsin. When I first undertook this work I did so with the conviction that a study of Plato's masterpiece was one of the supreme educational adventures of the Western world. Experience has served only to strengthen this conviction, though the reasons I should now give are somewhat different. It now seems clear to me that nowhere can the social roots of philosophy be more sharply seen and more firmly apprehended than when one is dealing with the origins of Western philosophy among the Greeks. This book contains, therefore, the body of information which in my judgment a student should have if he is to approach Plato as a historical figure.

In order to make the book useful to as wide a circle of students as possible, I have adopted the excellent suggestion of my publishers and given brief biographical identifications for the various figures of Greek life introduced in the text. I trust that more advanced students will not regard this as a deliberate insult to their intelligence. Translations have been taken either from Jowett or from Shorey in the Loeb Library edition. In either case I have done my best to protect the reader against the loving distortions of discipleship.

The author is conscious of a multitude of thronging obligations. It is only the generous help of students and friends that has made it possible to produce this work in the busy interstices of a heavy program of teaching. I have used in several places the results of Mr. Edwin Eagle's doctoral dissertation on "Aristocratic Bias in the Writings of Plato." Many of the ideas advanced in the first half of Chapter Four on the Pythagoreans result from pleasant discussions with Mr. Edwin L. Minar, Jr., at a time when I was directing his thesis on "Early Pythagorean Politics in Theory and Practice." Mr. Minar has treated the evidence for these views more fully and systematically than would be germane to this book. His work seems to me much too valuable to merit the oblivion which seems to be the fate of typed dissertations. I very much hope that it will soon find publication in its own right. Mr. Norman O. Brown has worked out in some detail ideas that I suggested to him on Hermes and Dionysus. I have availed myself in one or two places of facts contributed in seminar papers by Miss Jane Machlis and Mr. Richard Drummond. Funds from the Federal N.Y.A. have enabled me to have the valued assistance of Miss Jeanne Smith and Miss Jane Halbman, the former working on the identifications and assisting me to check footnotes, the latter assisting with bibliography and indices. Mr. Frank Jones has kindly volunteered to read proof. My wife has toiled nobly with the preparation of the manuscript.

Two others I can not pass by with a perfunctory acknowledgment. Prof. Karl Heinrich Niebyl of Carleton College has read the work in manuscript and made fruitful suggestions, several of which I have incorporated in the text. Particularly in the first few pages dealing with Oriental society, where I am on relatively unfamiliar ground, I have relied heavily on his judgment as a specialist in economic history. Mr. Tom Silverberg, too, has been unremitting in his willingness to help. At least three sections of the book owe much to his patient work and intellectual acumen.

Several colleagues have read the work in manuscript and made valuable suggestions—Profs. W. R. Agard, W. E. Leonard, Howard Selsam, and Meyer Reinhold. Mr. David Erdman has labored manfully with commas and tenses. My thanks, too, to Mr. William Kirsch for making available to me the work of the Russians on this period.

I am indebted to Mr. Leonard E. Mins for many useful suggestions and criticisms.

Thinking that the recent history of psychological theory might powerfully reinforce the central theme of the book, I asked Prof. Lynn Baker of the department of Psychology at the Milwaukee extension centre of the University of Wisconsin to prepare a condensed account of this movement of scientific thought. Three pages in the sixth chapter of Part Two are a result of his kind acquiescence.

Nor can I forget that in the summer of 1936 the special research fund of the University of Wisconsin gave me a period of precious leisure. Part of the material for this work was collected at that time. To all these and others who have helped with their interest and their encouragement the author wishes to express his deep and sincere sense of obligation and gratitude.

Madison, Wis.
August, 1940.

PREFACE TO THE SECOND EDITION

IT IS GRATIFYING to learn that a new edition of the *Genesis of Plato's Thought* is called for. In this edition nothing has been changed but a new chapter on the Academy and the later dialogues has been added. I have made no changes in the original material because the loving care of many critics has not convinced me that any change was necessary. The analysis of Greek philosophy as a function of the social relations of Greek society is still in its infancy. In the words of Magalhaes-Vilhaenna it is still at the stage of *Tatonnement*. There will inevitably come a period of more intensive discussion by scholars who have departed from the present abstract approach to the history of philosophy. When that day comes this book may be modified in detail but I do not think that its fundamental thesis will be overthrown.

My thanks are due to the University of British Columbia, and in particular the staff of the reference department for making available to me the books I needed both from the library and from interlibrary loan. Professor Malcolm MacGregor of the University of British Columbia has from time to time made available to me the fruits of his superb scholarship. To both of these my grateful thanks.

North Shore College,
North Vancouver.
January 20th 1956

CONTENTS

PART ONE

The Approach to Plato

1. From Oriental to Occidental Society 13
2. The Spiritual Revolution 37
3. The Great Age of Athenian Democracy 65
4. The Conservative Philosophy 75
5. The Progressive Philosophy 112
6. The Life of Plato 161

PART TWO

The Republic of Plato

7. The Argument with Thrasymachus—What Is Justice? 187
8. The Social Contract Theory of the Origin of the State 195
9. The Sociology and Psychology of the Platonic Virtues 203
10. The Education of the "Guards" 218
11. How the "Guards" Were to Live 240
12. The Philosophy of Plato 269
13. The Academy and the Later Dialogues 303

APPENDIX

Suggested Reading 343

List of Abbreviations 346

Footnotes 351

Index 373

PART ONE

THE APPROACH TO PLATO

CHAPTER ONE

From Oriental to Occidental Society

To understand Plato we must understand his times. Many readers who will accept without question this dictum of historical criticism may wonder why we should think it necessary to begin our enquiry as far back as Homer and beyond. It would be almost as though we were to say that in order to understand John Dewey one must first make a careful study of the Italian Renaissance. Even this latter judgment is not entirely absurd. In the last analysis any historical figure can not be isolated from the total context of ideas and forces that have gone into his making. But in the case of Plato there is an even greater need to pursue the argument back into the very beginnings of the historical period. And it is quite impossible to understand the genesis of Plato's ideas without understanding the profound change that Greek society underwent in the post-Homeric period. It is, in brief, the change in social structure which created mercantile, progressive Greek society and laid the foundations for all the subsequent history of Europe and the West.

The unified tribal order represented in its latest stage in the Homeric poems broke up under the influence of changing technical and economic organization; great inequalities appeared in the possession of property; there were consequent clashes of political factions, and a new form of political organization arose—the city-*state*. Too many of our historians have treated this period under the influence of the prejudice that all historical evolution proceeds in an unbroken series of gradual and imperceptible changes—that nature and history do nothing "in a leap." (*Nihil per saltum facit natura.*) In our view it is impossible to appreciate fully the development of Greek thought without understanding how thoroughgoing and revolutionary was the change that came over Greek society in this period. For most of the leading ideas of Plato make their appearance, at least in embryonic form, in the changing relations of man to his environment as shown in the transition from the tribe to the state. To this process we must devote considerable attention before we even approach Plato's philosophy.

Let us first then characterize, though very briefly, the social organization of an Oriental type which lies in the dim and shadowy background of Greek thinking. Civilization seems to have developed first in the great river valleys of the world—the Ganges, the Tigris and Euphrates, and the Nile. (We can here disregard Aztec culture, where another factor was operative.) This early development, we can suppose, was due to one major factor—the availability of water for purposes of cultivation. More concretely, in these favored regions, man early in his career learned to control the water supply either by means of a system of irrigation or else by a system of conservation. This factor was of decisive importance for social organization. It meant, in the first place, that everyone who took part in the processes of primary production, namely agriculture, must be a member of the communal society, alert and responsive to its sanctions. The whole system of control of the water supply, its use as needed for cultivation, was much too delicate to be entrusted to slave labor. Slaves, as we shall see in a few moments, were used for quite different purposes. Moreover such a system of agriculture made necessary a directing group—we might even describe them as a bureaucracy if that word had not come to acquire so many invidious connotations. These men were needed to co-ordinate the work of communal production and to ensure exactitude in the carrying out of assigned tasks. Moreover these men had to develop certain bodies of knowledge. They had to know something of weather and the seasons; they had to develop astronomical investigation. They had to manage the distribution of the land; this led them to discoveries in the science of geometry and mathematics. At first these technicians, directors, and research workers seem to have been elected from the tribe. But as it became necessary to provide this group of people with sustenance, though they took little or no part in direct production, as, in other words, they had to live from a tribute paid in kind, they naturally hardened into a caste, one degree removed from the work of primary production.

It is important for the technique of analysis that we shall use in this book to notice that this "bureaucracy" of technical and intellectual workers was in no sense parasitic. On its stability and continuity depended the very life of the community. And yet it was necessary to invoke sanctions for their privileged position. And this was the social function of ancient religion in Oriental society. Arguing from the analogy of Polynesia, Prof. Karl H. Niebyl suggests that primitive taboos and totem cults, originally developed to safeguard biological reproduction, became a system of sanctions to safeguard the executive and directive tasks of society. The guarantor of procreative relations—the *mater familias* in primitive agricultural societies, the *pater familias* in early hunting societies, became divorced from their particular representatives in a concrete human individual just as the need for stability and continuity in "executive" functions became divorced from actual production. Hence arose ancestor cults, and, as society matured, a deity, who became the responsible executive in charge of the direction of communal affairs. Hence, too, the need to develop magnificent cult objects for the greater glory of the directing priesthood. For the construction of these cult objects, temples, say, or pyramids, slaves were used. And this is the social function of slavery in society of an Oriental type. The children of Israel in their Egyptian captivity, let us remember, were set to work collecting straw and making bricks under the lash of an Egyptian taskmaster. Slavery in such a society could not, let us repeat, be used in the actual labor of production, which required a high degree of social responsibility in all who took part in the work. Carelessness or malice could do profound social harm, and every worker on the land must be included within the sanctions of the tribe. This will explain why, in the famous code of Hammurabi, a provision was made for the instant freeing without compensation of a slave, who by accident was sold back to his native land and tribe.

The point is quite central for the developing theme of this

book. We shall observe later that in Greek society and the classical world generally, slaves were used for a very different purpose:—they took part in production, on the land, in mine and workshop. We can, therefore, hold that *classical* society was based on slave labor. By this we do not mean that all who worked in the production of goods in such a society were slaves. We mean rather to contrast classical society with Oriental society, which had not yet developed to the point where slaves could be used for productive purposes and, say, modern society based on the free laborer and the machine. To this point we shall return in a few moments.

As Oriental society succeeded in solving its primary problems, as agriculture became efficient and the bureaucracy entrenched, we find a relative and temporary pressure of population, a need to expand, to bring into cultivation all possible irrigable land. The tendency to expansion and a kind of mobility within Oriental society was enhanced by two other factors. One was the growth of the semi-independent farm unit, a development which was encouraged by the bureaucracy in order to make more simple and efficient the collection of tribute in kind. The semi-independent farm made possible the use of metal tools and permitted the domestication of animals. At this point there emerges the development of husbandry as a derivative of the agricultural life of the river-valley cultures. Animals were exchanged for the food surplus which these cultures were beginning to develop. But husbandry presupposed a continuity of food supply, and this could not be found within any single oasis. As a consequence the family units engaged in husbandry began a regular series of migrations from oasis to oasis. At this point contact between the river-valley cultures became established and an exchange of products on the basis of barter became possible.

The bureaucracy and priesthoods, by now thoroughly congealed into a caste, thus found a usefulness for surplus tribute. As the volume of this tribute gradually outdistanced the consuming power of the officialdom, there developed the increasing exchange of unconsumed surpluses and the consequent pressure to have exportable produce replace goods for home consumption.

But this pressure in turn increased the exploitation of those engaged in agricultural work. This pressure, however, had to reach a limit, for the productive capacity of the peasants was objectively limited by the available water supply. Here then, we can suppose, was the fundamental factor which broke up the relative stability of Oriental society and forced the great period of migrations which characterized the second millennium before Christ. But let us notice that Oriental trade, which fostered the increasing importance of crafts and handicraft articles and tended to undermine agricultural production and create a relative shortage of food, was not yet a function of society that had released itself from communal relations. Trade or barter was still the prerogative of the priesthood and the bureaucracy.

Into the details of the migrations we need not enter. We shall see later that the entrance of the Greeks into the Hellenic peninsula laid the basis for two quite different types of historical development which we shall describe, roughly, as the Spartan and the Athenian. Moreover, the period of migrations increased immeasurably (as we shall see) the importance of the military leader and laid the basis for a specialization of function as between priest and "king." Increasingly the relative scarcity of foodstuffs gave rise to piracy as well as barter, and certain well-defined "trade routes" begin to appear—particularly the Black Sea. This development is reflected in literature in the famous voyage of the Argonauts and the quest for the Golden Fleece, i.e., wheat. This is, in spite of the golden aura of its literary and mythological setting, simply trade in the form of piracy—a direct outgrowth of this relative scarcity of foodstuffs.

As the migrant Greeks settled in their new homeland, conditions were ripe for a new and profoundly important advance.

One was the increasing importance of the vine and olive tree in the "economic" life of these peoples. Perhaps the development of cults and worships to which we have already referred was an important factor in this situation. Oil too, as we shall observe, was important for the toilet of the body and the manufacture of clothes. The use of wine may have been fostered by the relative scarcity of drinking water in Greece. At all events, the culture of the vine and olive became increasingly important in Homeric and post-Homeric times.

Other factors conditioned the development of Grecian economic life—the small size of the valleys and the difficulty of resuming agricultural production on the large scale of the river valleys. What is more, the climate of the Aegean was more suitable for agriculture, rainfall was fairly abundant, and there was no need, therefore, to depend on elaborate techniques of irrigation.

All this meant one thing. Agricultural production took an entirely new form, and the use of slaves in production became possible for the first time. This tremendous advance quite revolutionized the basis of society, broke up once and for all the gentile structure, differentiated agriculture from trade, and led to the "progressive" society of Greek antiquity. Nonetheless, slavery was slow to develop, and it took several centuries for the implications of these new institutions to work themselves out.

The reader may forgive this rather breathless survey of a great deal of social development. For an understanding of these factors is entirely necessary in order to comprehend the life and thought of classical Greece.[1] We can now examine the transition from Oriental to Occidental society in some detail.

For the society of the Homeric period we have the evidence of Homer's poems, now abundantly supported by the findings of archaeology. And within the structure of the two poems we are able to trace several important social advances which rest in turn on technical improvements, as well as the more fundamental development of the institution of slavery. First, then, in our brief examination of Homeric society let us notice that slavery in the period under review seems to have played an increasing role in economic and social organization. There is much more mention of slaves in the Odyssey than in the Iliad. But even here their numbers are not large. Alcinoüs and Odysseus each boast of fifty[2] (and this may be a poetical round number), but these are female slaves and do not figure much in primary production. They weave and tend the loom, and "work at the mill" (grinding grain), but these household tasks are the economic tasks of that day. There is no example of either of the words used in Greek for slave—

doulos or *andrapodon*. Male captives seem to have been for the most part slain; women were taken "to walk to and fro before the loom and tend the couch." Slavery is still patriarchal slavery, and the kind of social organization that bases itself on slave labor is still in the mists of the future. Moreover, relations between slave and master (or mistress) seem to have been close and cordial. Nausicaä, the king's daughter, washes the linen together with her handmaidens; then they bathe, anoint themselves, and play with a ball together, almost as equals. The scene is one of great charm with not a hint of the more brutal and oppressive slavery of a later day. Patroclus, when entertaining one of the heroes, gives commands to his companions (presumably free) equally with the domestic slaves.[3] Achilles does likewise when the aged Priam comes to visit him.[4] The handmaidens of Andromache are addressed by the complimentary title "fair-tressed maidens."[5] Moreover the lord and master works alongside his slaves. Even the great Odysseus walks behind the plow and constructs for himself a raft with his own hands. His father Laertes worked in the fields and orchards along with his slaves. Master and slave were very close together; the slave frequently sat at table with his master, shared in his joys and griefs, was buried in the common burial ground.

Of the later system when numbers of male slaves will engage in large-scale production we have only traces and foreshadowings. Eumaeus, the swineherd of Odysseus, seems to have had slaves working under him to perform subordinate tasks.[6] We hear of male domestics.[7] In the poignant lament for her dead husband, Andromache expresses her fear lest the little son Astyanax should end as a slave.[8] The poignancy of her foreboding should make us hesitate before we describe Homeric slavery as entirely humane. Nonetheless, compared with the later development of the institution, slavery in its inception does not exhibit the gross cruelties of its later development.

But even in this relatively simple and relatively humane type of slavery the relations of master and slave as developed in later Greek society are already present in embryonic form. The master, even at this early date, has the power of life and death over his slaves. Odysseus treated the goatherd, Melanthius, who took the side of the suitors, with great brutality, putting him to death by torture; the twelve female slaves who sided with the suitors were hanged.[9]

It is, in some ways, a matter of surprise that the invading Greek tribes were so slow to recognize the potentialities of their new environment. The institution of slavery developed very slowly, and it was several centuries before all the implications of this profound social change were fully worked out.

The process was assisted by the fact that the invading Greeks had in the period of their wandering learned the usefulness of iron. In the Homeric poems we notice the gradual substitution of iron for copper as the basic metal for implements and weapons.

As between the Iliad and the Odyssey there is indicated an important economic fact, a significant technological advance, the beginnings of a change from the Bronze Age to the Iron Age in Greece—the increasing use of iron as the basic material for weapons and implements. Bronze still keeps its dominant position, particularly in the earlier poem, the Iliad; in the Odyssey it occurs much less frequently. Iron is mentioned slightly more often in the Odyssey than in the Iliad.[10] Even in the Iliad, however, iron is beginning to come into use both by herdsmen and farmers who buy their iron implements in the neighboring city.

> Though his rich fields live very far away, the winner will have them five revolving years to serve his need; for not through lack of iron will his shepherd or ploughman fare to the city; nay this will supply them.[11]

We find in the Odyssey an incidental (and, therefore, highly significant) mention of iron as a commodity, used in trade and transported in a ship.[12]

> "Therefore of a truth will I frankly tell thee all. I declare that I am Mentes, the son of wise Anchialus, and I am lord over the oar-loving Paphians. And now I have put in here, as thou seest, with ship and crew, while sailing over the wine-dark sea to men of strange speech, on my

way to Temese for copper; and I bear with me shining iron."

Even more significant, perhaps, is the fact that the adjectival form comes into use as a descriptive epithet; we hear of "iron endurance" and the "iron hand"; the sky, which in the Iliad is the "bronze sky," in the Odyssey is described as "iron."[13] But even so, iron in the Iliad is still an article of luxury, and even in the Odyssey bronze is mentioned four times as often as iron. Moreover archaeological evidence indicates very certainly the gradual transition from bronze to iron as the basic metal in the period from around 1100 B.C. to 700 B.C.[14]

The advance from bronze to iron accompanies and to some degree induces a progressive improvement in farming methods. This is bound up with an increase in the importance of agriculture itself, contrasted with the earlier stage of pastoral and migratory life based on the possession of flocks and herds, a condition which prevailed during the period of migrations, several centuries before Homer.

> During the period of migrations Greece was continually traversed by peoples who brought their flocks and herds trailing along with them and could not have a taste for agriculture. Thucydides describes in sober brief terms these distant centuries in which each worked the ground only enough to live, without possessing a surplus or even planting, and "the best land changed masters often."[15]

This last phrase must be understood not as a change in ownership, but as a redistribution within the tribal structure.

There are many indications in the Homeric poems that this transition is a recent thing; men looked back to the day when in a different setting* livestock had become the chief form of wealth; perhaps such memories are reflected in legendary folk like the Cyclopes, who do not eat wheat. And in the earlier poem, the Iliad, the wealth of the nobility is still comprised primarily of

* By different setting we mean, e. g., the Danubian valley as an instance of those river valleys from which the Greek tribes had come and in which they had developed some of the rudimentary agricultural techniques they were now employing.

herds. Livestock and particularly horned cattle are the fundamental standard of wealth; one female slave is regarded as equivalent in value to four oxen, another, to twenty; a tripod is matched by twelve oxen; bronze armor, nine, gold-ornamented armor, nine.

> And then from Glaukus did Zeus, son of Cronos, take away his wits, seeing he made exchange of armor with Diomedes, son of Tydeus, giving golden for bronze, the worth of a hundred oxen for the worth of nine.[16]

Brides were purchased and captives were ransomed with oxen, and so a young girl was given the epithet "she who brings in oxen."[17] Mules, like oxen, were valued for field work,[18] goats, pigs, and sheep as food. Horses seem to have been used only to draw the chariot in warfare and as mounts for cavalry, not for economic purposes at all. But it is characteristic of this society that the breeding of horses should be held in high esteem. For the horse was used for warfare, for hunting, and for sport. As a symbol of the esteem in which these animals were held, we may cite the gentle and nobly born Andromache, wife of the knightly Hector. She herself brings wheat and wine to feed the steeds of her husband.

> Now pay me back your tending [Hector shouts to his horses], wherewith in abundance Andromache, daughter of great-hearted Eëtion, set before you honey-hearted wheat, and mingled wine for you to drink when your souls bade you, sooner than for me that avow me to be her stalwart husband.[19]

The land on which cattle are pastured seems to be held, at least in the Iliad, as the collective possession of the tribe. Shepherds lead their flocks wherever they will, i.e. of course, within the territorial possessions of the tribe. But in the Odyssey the advance towards private control, if not ownership, of the land is well under way.[20] Increasing migrations as well as the development of pirate trade had created warlike situations. Greek tribes were brought into conflict among themselves, as well as with the cities of Asia Minor. The period of constant warfare had increased the importance of the military chieftain and had made necessary more continuity in his tenure of office. Continuous tenure made it possible for the chieftain to translate his military pre-eminence into economic advantage. This, at first, was expressed in booty, movable goods like caldrons, tripods, oxen, female slaves, and the like, captured in war. In the Odyssey there are definite signs that this pre-eminence is beginning to express itself in the control (and perhaps the possession) of land. The ruler of the island of Ithaca possesses forty-eight herds on the mainland, and on the island the estate of the lord is so vast that a stranger needs a guide in order to traverse it in safety. The ranch of Odysseus is described in the Odyssey.

No chieftain, remarks his swineherd, Eumaeus, owns so much wealth, neither on the mainland nor on Ithaca, and twenty men would not own so much. It is described in detail—on the mainland, twelve herds of cattle, as many sheepfolds, as many droves of pigs, as many roving herds of goats, all tended by strangers or slaves.[21] In Ithaca, seventy-two herds are mentioned and the total wealth of Odysseus in flocks has been estimated[22] at seven or eight thousand head. To tend them forty hands were required: to protect them from wild beasts and marauders, to clean and tend the folds, to store fodder for the winter, and to prepare the beasts for slaughter. In the account of the cave of Polyphemus we have an interesting picture of a Homeric dairy farm.

> The crates were laden with cheeses, and the pens were crowded with lambs and kids. Each kind was penned separately; by themselves the firstlings, by themselves the later lambs, and by themselves the newly weaned. And with whey were swimming all the well-wrought vessels, the milk pails, and the bowls into which he milked.[23]

Hunting still retained some economic importance in the Homeric period, and hunting scenes are familiar, particularly in the Iliad.[24] Fish and small game are despised by the nobility. They will use fish only in an emergency.[25] But such food satisfied humbler folk, and in later times fish becomes an important article of diet. It has been suggested that such dietetic prejudices developed during the inland sojourn of the Grecian tribes and remained simply as taboos when the tribes migrated to the Aegean littoral. The prejudice, we may well conjecture, dissolved most rapidly among the poor, who were nearer to the pinch of hunger. But for an upper class (and, as we shall soon see, we can now begin to speak of an upper class emerging) the defense of such taboos is bound up with a defense of its own pre-eminence.

Oxen and mules were valued for plowing; this, too, points to the increasing importance of agriculture. There is frequent mention of the primary cereals, like wheat and barley, "the marrow of men." Plowing is a well-known activity in Homeric society, and we hear not only of the simple plow made of one piece of wood, but also the "fitted plow" made of three.[26] Certainly, agriculture cannot be dismissed as entirely primitive and undeveloped. We learn that the field was usually plowed three times,[27] and there is even a reference to the process of manuring the soil,[28] a practice which could hardly arise until after centuries of trial and error in primitive farm management. The harvest was reaped with sickles,[29] threshed on a primitive threshing floor of baked clay by oxen or the even more primitive flail, winnowed by the wind, as chaff and wheat were thrown together into the air, then ground in hand mills or, even more simply, in pestle and mortar.

Two other crops seem to have been regarded as primary in importance—the vine and the olive:

> Toward the end of the Homeric period Greece becomes covered with vineyards and lays the foundations of the olive groves, which will one day be its adornment and fortune.[30]

Out of piracy, trade was gradually evolving between Greece, Asia Minor, and Egypt. These latter countries produced barley and wheat, which the Greeks needed. The Greek terrain, on the other hand, was ideally adapted to the cultivation of the vine and the olive, both of which products were in increasing demand for cults as well as handicrafts. This simple geographical fact goes far to explain the differentiation in the development of progressing Greece.

On the shield of Achilles was depicted the gathering of the grape and the gay scenes of festival that accompanied it.[31] The poet of the Iliad describes a gardener carefully tending the shoots of the fruit-bearing olive tree "in a secluded spot where there is spring water in abundance."[32] Olive oil was prized not only for consumption, but also in the manufacture of linen clothing—"well-woven tunics faintly glistening with olive oil";[33] olive oil, too, was used to anoint the bodies of heroes[34] and as an aid in the toilet of lovely women.[35] Orchards, an object of devoted care, were highly valued. The gardens of Alcinoüs grew rich with pears, apples, pomegranates, and fig trees; he had olive groves and vineyards and a vegetable plot.[36] The garden of Laertes, the hero's father, where the old man and his slaves worked, was rich with olive groves and vineyards as well as fig trees and pears.[37]

In the matter of technological accomplishment, therefore, the Homeric poems depict the slow and painful progress of mankind toward an improved agricultural technique. But in spite of the very considerable advance here recorded, the economic structure of Homeric society remained undeveloped as compared with that of classical Greece. We are still almost entirely at the stage of agricultural self-sufficiency. Nearly every case of exchange known to us in this period was, in its primary essential, barter; thing exchanged for thing, product for product. The conventional symbol that we call coined money had not yet appeared. Nor, unlike contemporary societies of the Orient, was metal used as a standard of value; long-horned oxen still served as a standard of exchange with all the inconveniences and qualitative differences that such a system entails. There is practically no hint of a currency. The one or two references to talents may be later in date and a result of influences from the East.

Crafts were few in number and relatively unspecialized. We hear of artisans in a few crafts; blacksmiths, saddle makers, carpenters, potters, and goldsmiths; we hear of the queerest (from the modern point of view) of all "craftsmen": physicians and town criers.[38] The very fact that doctors were placed on the same level with the artisans proves how slight was the differentiation into trades and how abundant the supply of slaves relative to the numbers then needed. Nor was there any hint of specialization within the craft; the tanner must himself attend to every process, from the treatment of the hides to the finishing into shoes or shields; the carpenter himself did all the work in building a house, from preparing the timber to applying the decorative finish. For the most part craftsmen appear as wandering artisans usually working on their customer's material within the customer's own lordly hall. Thus, when Ajax, son of Telamon, the great lord of Salamis, had needed a shield of bronze with sevenfold bull's hide, Tychios, "he that was the best of the workers in hide," had been summoned from far off Hyle in Boeotia.[39]

In the Odyssey the geographical horizon has widened; Sicily[40] has now come within the Grecian ken. Merchants, a class unknown in the Iliad, now make their appearance. And with merchants, we find markets, harbors,[41] and trading voyages. Iron is more frequently mentioned in the later poem, and slavery is now a developed institution. Yet what trade there was seems to have been mostly barter: the exchange of slaves for commodities, wine, or articles of luxury. There seem to have been no fixed and accepted standards of value and there is similarly little sign of a merchant class. The *pater familias* was the merchant. Those we meet in the poems are usually Phoenicians; in the Odyssey there is only one reference to a Greek trader—that is, as an independent functional occupation—the one swallow that heralds the summer but can hardly be said to mark its arrival. Nor can it be said that the Phoenician merchants stick too closely to trade. The line between piracy and trade was not sharply drawn. The early seafarers were not above making slave raids and even drawing a king's son, like Eumaeus, into captivity. Nor did piracy invoke any great social disapproval, as Plato remarked long ago.

It is quite clear that these changes were having an effect on the organization of society. The old system of landholding is in transition toward something new. There are many traces of the older communal system of landownership. But the process by which individual nobles, like Odysseus in the example that we have quoted, came to own or at least to use for their own purposes the collective lands of the community is already well under way. "In the very bosom of collective property, private property is formed."[42] With the gradual emergence of private property in land we find more and more signs of a social differentiation into rich and poor, landed and landless, free and slave. The old type of family organization begins to break up. Family ties are loosened: "Younger sons and bastards protest against a vexatious inequality; young men of adventurous spirit cannot resign themselves to dull work; criminals are driven out."[43]

Both the Iliad and the Odyssey contain pictures of a king's household—those of Priam and Alcinoüs. Here there are slaves who work, but always alongside their masters, preparing to supply every household need. The king and his family and his slaves weave in a workshop and grow produce in the orchards and kitchen gardens, importing no staple products from the outside. Odysseus, coming to the land of the Phaeacians, found the daughter of the house washing the household clothes in the "fair-flowing" stream.[44] The primitive life described by Homer indicates the distance that Greek social organization was to have traversed by the time of Plato, to whom all work with the hands was menial and unworthy of freemen.

The women described in the Homeric poems also worked with their slaves. Clothing was all made at home, the wool combed and carded, spun, woven, and made into garments.

As to the system of landholding, it is difficult to be absolutely certain just what the situation was. Homer's use of the word *klēros* (share or plot of land, strictly allotment) points to the system which originally prevailed, tribal or clan ownership of land. In the word *"temenos"* (from *temno*, to cut)* there is a reference to "allotments" given over to the user, i.e., in most cases the family, for lifetime cultivation. In addition there remain "commons," "indivisible plots" which were given to individual families with the right to graze livestock under stipulated conditions. In this respect, too, Homeric society manifests all the characteristics of a transitional period. There is individual use of land

* Cf. the German *Abschnitt* and the Russian *Otrezok* as cognates.

on the one hand, and strong traces of communal ownership on the other. (By individual we mean the family and, increasingly, the head of the family.) Nor does it seem that private ownership of land was unconditional as it has been in recent European and American society. In post-Homeric Greece the right of bequest seems to have been strictly limited to the family and, failing that, to the clan. It was only in the time of Solon that the right of free bequest was granted and then only where there were no children in the family to inherit the property.[45]

Closely bound up with this system of landholding is, of course, the organization of the family. The development of husbandry and agriculture, the transition from bronze to iron, the development and increased extent of private property, the growth of slaveholding—all these furthered the growth and consolidation of the patriarchal order of the family, and particularly in the households of the kings and nobles, the families distinguished by their wealth. The normal type of Homeric family is more and more the small monogamous group, and it is highly significant for the development of the concept of private property that a high value was placed on feminine constancy—as in the story of Penelope. At the same time—and here again we see a society in a stage of transition—there are strong traces of the older stage—the polygamous family. Of this remnant, the household of Priam serves as the classic example. The old man seems to have kept with him in the common house his fifty sons with their wives and families, as well as the husbands and offspring of his twelve married daughters. It has even been suggested that there are traces of a still more primitive arrangement of the family—the matriarchal—in the poems. Matriarchal relations tend to remain as legal arrangements, though active economic functions were increasingly being usurped by the man. Even at a later date the story of Clytemnestra in Aeschylus' *Oresteia* (significantly taken from Homeric times by the poet) indicates the conflict between traditional taboos and actual social functions. This conflict was solved, as Aeschylus shows, only in the fifth century with the emergence of Athena and the state. But whether the family was large or small, the head of the family and lord of the household was the man. The *"megaron"* or men's hall was the main part of the Homeric house where guests were received and banquets given, while the women's apartments and rooms for household functions were located in the rear. The wife became a kind of household manager, in charge of the slave women, mistress over her husband's concubines, and guardian and protector of his children. Her whole activity centered around the household. Economic activity, whether war, piracy, or agriculture, was the function of the man. He became in effect the owner of the family property. Women might, on marriage, bring a dowry of cattle, but this, too, passed into her husband's possession. The economic, and hence social, subordination of women was well on the way.

Strong traces of an actual tribal order remain in the references to later social organization.[46] We hear mention of the family (*genos*), of the clan (*phratra*), of the tribe (*phylon*). There is some evidence in the Odyssey that the family is coming to be associated with a definite geographical location, as when Odysseus says, "I am an Ithacan by family (*genos*)."[47] But in general the arrangements by phratries and tribes is a military one. Regarding this we may take the advice of Nestor to Agamemnon as typical when he urges the "supreme commander" to separate the men by tribes and clans, so that clan may bear aid to clan and tribe to tribe:

> Thou wilt then know who among thy captains is a coward and who among thy men, and who too is brave; for they will fight each clan for itself.[48]

There is reference in the poems to the blood feud, but more evidence that the older system is beginning to break up, displaced by exile for involuntary homicide;[49] or a money fine levied as atonement. In the trial scene on the shield of Achilles the dispute between families seems to have been tried before the council of elders—a significant foreshadowing of the development of criminal law, and a court like the Athenian court of the Areopagus.

In general the structure of Homeric society is strongly aristocratic in tone and temper. The common people hardly figure at all; only twice in the two poems do we have mention of individuals outside the charmed circle of aristocratic heroes and chieftains.* In one case the swineherd, Eumaeus, turns out to have been a king's son carried off years before by Phoenician slave raiders; the other, Thersites,[50] is depicted in a very unfavorable light, physically deformed and temperamentally a brawler and a troublemaker, to be beaten into deserved submission by Odysseus amid roars of discomfiting laughter.

The aristocracy seems to have possessed relatively generous shares of the land. They are called the "much-allotted" or "many-shared" (*polykleroi*) and we hear frequently of "rich shares" and "broad fields." Much here may be laid to the poet's romantic imagination. There is no indication in the Iliad that any individual possessed more than 20 acres of land. We may consider movable property much more important economically as a source of basic wealth: cattle, weapons, valuable objects of bronze (sometimes iron), and slaves. The Homeric hero set an inordinate value on such booty taken in war—notice for example the negotiations that Agamemnon makes (in Book IX): seven tripods untouched by fire, ten talents of gold and gleaming caldrons and twelve strong horses that have won prizes for speed, seven women of Lesbos skilled in handiwork.[51] Also, in describing the palaces of Alcinoüs or Odysseus, for example, the poet dwells with relish on their rich adornment—the bronze walls and the cornice of *cyamis*, the golden doors and silver doorposts in a threshold of bronze; the silver lintel and the golden handle, the gold and silver dogs that guarded the doors and the rich embroidery that covered the seats.[52] The terms by which wealth is described indicate that this is an era before the stage in social evolution at which the *possession* of land becomes all-important. Chieftains and leaders

* The word chieftain—used here for lack of a better term—must be used elastically—with enough play in its meaning to cover both the *actual* tribal kings, the *basileis,* who are chiefs in a titular sense as well, and the military heroes, whose status is more or less that of *primi inter pares*. This distinction is of some importance; for the military aristocracy in Homer rank very often on the same plane with titular kings. In fact, both groups contributed a great deal to the formation of the Homeric nobility, and the final product, the landed aristocracy, appears to have been a blend or an amalgam of the old tribal chiefs, or "kings," and the more powerful military leaders.

in the Iliad are addressed with such epithets as "possessed of many cornlands,"[53] or "many flocks,"[54] or "much gold,"[55] or "many possessions."[56] In the Odyssey none of these epithets occurs as applied to individuals; on the other hand, the epithet *polykleros* (of many allotments) occurs only once and that in the Odyssey:[57] "I married a woman from among men of many allotments," i.e., a daughter of the wealthy. Too much weight cannot be given to this rather scanty evidence, but in general it serves to confirm the impression which we get as we examine the person and position of Odysseus—the trader, chieftain, pirate is beginning to evolve into a wealthy landowner. What is at least certain is that in the course of the following two centuries, the economic pre-eminence of the Homeric tribal chieftains, which in the "heroic" days had been based on booty and movable property, had by the seventh century become transformed into the pre-eminence of landed families, who then called themselves "eupatrids," i.e., having "good" fathers.[58]

Work on the land seems to have been performed for the most part by peasant farmers. There is no evidence in the Iliad that slaves worked on the land as they did on the great estates of later antiquity. Nor is there any evidence of serfdom or of the economic subordination of the small landowner to his lord. The analogies between Homeric society and feudalism are in this respect quite misleading. But even so there is already the beginning of inequality as between members of the small landholding group. We hear (once) of *polykleroi*, possessed of many shares, and once of the *akleroi*,[59] or shareless. We also hear once of *thetes*,[60] or farm laborers. These may have been "peasants" with small farms who were forced to eke out a livelihood by working on the lands of their more prosperous neighbors. And so, we may safely conclude, a number of factors tended to foster inequality within the structure of gentile society. The period of migrations and consequent war tended to entrench the military chieftain. This pre-eminence soon reflected itself in economic terms as he gained control of a larger share of movable goods. With the growth of slavery this economic pre-eminence increased by geometric progression. It now became increasingly possible to use the labor of others. The "king," as a consequence, gained possession of the best and largest sections of the tribal domain, which he was now able to till and pasture with slave labor.

Odysseus possessed land not only on the island of Ithaca, but also on the opposite mainland. In time of war the "king" received the choicest booty; presents came to him, too, from the people. "To be a king is no bad thing," said Telemachus. "Riches accumulate rapidly in the house of a king."[61] Here are the factors which will hasten the breakup of gentile society and create the state. The tribal chieftain does not yet represent the state, but the process is well under way.

And not only was the king or chief gradually set apart from the tribes; the same process created nobles and wealthy families, as distinguished from the "common herd." The position of chief, while still in theory elective, comes to be more and more a prerogative of a few wealthy families.* They use their positions in peacetime to amass more wealth; in wartime they engage in single combat and provide fit material for the songs of bards. The reverse side of this process is the growth of a class of dispossessed; there is mention of this group both in the Iliad and in the Odyssey, and in the former poem the young and brilliant and heroic Achilles imagines himself working as a day laborer on the land of a portionless master; he would prefer even *that* to ruling as king over the hosts of the dead.[62] Odysseus himself seems to the suitors such a wandering laborer. Appearing in the guise of a beggar after twenty years of absence he is addressed by one of the suitors in the following terms.

* Cf. A. J. Tyumenev, *History of Ancient Greece* (ed. Kovalev), I, 130. "In so far as the kingly power, elective in principle and partly, as we see, in actual practice, bears the character of the rule of the tribal leader, it is not yet a state in the strict sense of the word. The state as an organ of coercive authority does not yet exist. The kingly power, as such, does not have at its disposal any means of influence, not even the simplest administrative apparatus. Even the town criers who assemble the folk, who are present and who keep order in the folk assemblies and, in the times of the court of law, hand the staff to the one speaking, are not in any way governmental organs and are not considered as such by their contemporaries, but as *demiourgoi* as persons similar to craftsmen who serve some public need or other."

> "Stranger, wouldst thou have a mind to serve for hire, if I should take thee into service on an outlying farm—thy pay shall be assured thee—gathering stones for walls and planting tall trees? Thus would I provide thee with food for the year through, and clothe thee with raiment and give thee sandals for thy feet."[63]

In the Homeric age there is already present in germinal form all the elements of the class structure of later society; the tribal nobility, the small peasant proprietor, the day laborer, and the professional craftsmen. While this developing order of society has not yet destroyed the older political structure, important modifications have, nevertheless, already begun.

Thus, if we speak of a political organization (in strictness we should not, for the state is so far merely embryonic) the society of the Homeric period represents the twilight of a primitive system of tribal democracy. In the Iliad the mention of an assembly of the folk is rather frequent. Any of the "kings" seems to have had the right to "call the folk of the assembly." And "when they were assembled and met together," the lordly kings engaged in high debate over policy or strategy and the things of gods and men. Only once do we hear of a member of the common folk daring to lift up his voice—the unhappy Thersites—and his experience is not such that many would care to follow his example. In the Odyssey, the assembly is much less frequent—pointing, perhaps, to the decay of the system; in fact, during Odysseus' twenty years of absence the folk assembly of Ithaca never met. But perhaps this may be explained by the chaotic condition of the island during the absence of its king.

Side by side with the assembly of the folk is the "council" of elders (the very name points to a tribal origin), the heads of families gathered in solemn conclave. When we meet the institution in the Iliad, the tribal aspect has begun to fade; the council is now a group of patricians, young and old. In fact, the aged Nestor is an exception; he exhibits a rather comical senile garrulity—romantic nostalgia for the distant past. Most of the "elders" are young and brilliant and "like to the gods." Yet the assembly had great power. The "will or voice of the people" is still decisive. The assembly could decide all-important questions, but the power of the king was encroaching upon it.

At the head of the entire political structure stood the *Basileus*, the king or tribal chief. And here it is necessary to shed most of the associations that cluster around our notion of modern kingship. The Homeric king was by no means an absolute monarch. Others might be braver or wiser than he and would be so regarded by the council of the elders. On occasion an individual chieftain could oppose the "wide-ruling king" or hold him up to mockery. The king could do nothing unless the council concurred, and the council could enforce its will against his. Moreover, when his days of military usefulness were over, the king could be deposed. Laertes, the father of Odysseus, had been retired to private life and seems to have worked his own farm.

Yet the "king" is still the military chieftain, the commander of the host, as well as the representative of his tribe in their relations with the divine. But even here we note the coming of a change. The old priest-king is forced to yield to the beginnings of specialization and we find a prophet-priest, devoting himself to the business of religion, becoming the mouthpiece of a god, or gods, specializing in the interpreting of omens and coming to know "the present, the past, and the future."

Of this simple society with its strongly aristocratic tone, its delight in external things and external rewards, its joy in warfare, in wealth and acquisitiveness, the Homeric poems are in spirit a perfect reflection. It remains for us to observe how the religion of the poems reflects the changing society of those times.

Unquestionably certain elements in the Homeric pantheon reflect a much earlier period. The sky-god, the sun-god, the earth-goddess, and the god of the sea go back very far in the experience of early man. What is of interest in the Homeric world is to notice the tendency to make of the pantheon a heavenly replica of the patriarchal family, to make of Zeus the "father of gods and men" and to subordinate the rest of the family to him, except in so far as they can cajole or outwit him. The process may reflect the growing necessity that the Greek tribes with their emerging city states felt to "federate" in order to protect their "life-line" to the Black Sea. Zeus has not yet become an eternal principle of justice; that role he will come to assume as the conflicts between rich and poor become sharper and the need concomitantly becomes more pressing to give inequality an eternal sanction. The Homeric Zeus is more the irresponsible lord of natural forces and possessed of a very human if kingly personality. The code which Zeus enforces is still for the most part tribal. He punishes those who fail to respect their parents or mistreat them.[64] He is harsh with those who commit perjury,[65] and to decide the issue (in one case) a trial by ordeal is arranged under his supervision.[66] He is the lord of hospitality and in particular takes under his protection strangers and suppliants.[67] On one occasion he is said to punish those "who give crooked judgments in the market place and drive out justice, heeding not the vengeance of the gods."[68] This exceptional reference foreshadows the function which (as we shall see) Zeus comes to assume in the post-Homeric period. From the point of view of a later system of morality Zeus' conduct is frequently scandalous. Yet even Olympus reveals the germs of a significant later development.

In summary, then, we can see in Homeric society an example of the decay of the tribal order. The older system was destroyed by a number of factors. The development of the paternal right of inheritance made possible the accumulation of property within the family and thus gave strength to the family head over against the head of the tribe. Out of this accumulation developed the rudiments of aristocracy and monarchy. The growth of the institution of slavery, too, though embryonic and still confined to captives taken in war, will continue into a subsequent phase of development without scruple, until members of the same tribe, even of the same family become enslaved. The growth of family and individual wealth and the *relative* scarcity of natural as well as reproducible foodstuffs fostered pillage, plunder, and warfare, setting tribe against tribe in order to gain booty, slaves, treasures, and cattle. Already we begin to see riches being regarded as an end in themselves, as justifying any adventure and any risk, as affording an excuse for the most violent deeds. When a social organization is devised that will give absolute sanction and complete protection to the right of private and individual property, devising elaborate rules to protect a man's holdings against fraud and theft and individual violence, as well as against the organized protest of the poor and dispossessed, the state will be born. The process which the Greeks called *synoikism* (literally living together) is the birth of the modern state.[69]

In a subsequent chapter we shall have to characterize briefly the politics of the fifth-century Athenian city-state. At this point, however, let us content ourselves with observing the major consequences of the development from tribe to state. In fifth-century Athens we have, although on a small scale and in extremely simple terms, an example of a governmental state, complete if miniature; tribal consciousness had been replaced by civic consciousness; every Athenian citizen played some part in the daily political life of the *polis*. His loyalties were no longer to the close in-group of the family, but to Athens, the "democratic state." Wealth and property were no longer simply land and the primitive objects and animals of Homer's age. Trade not only had been introduced, but had become a prevailing force in economic life. The whole machinery of law, accounting, and administration now existed to enforce the sanctity of property and contracts. The metropolitan, mercantile democracy is a far cry from the rugged agrarian simplicity of late tribal society. In the next chapter it will be our main concern to survey the reflections in human thought and feeling of these great changes in environment and social organization.

CHAPTER TWO

The Spiritual Revolution

THE PERIOD which followed the age of Homer is one of considerable intellectual and social creativeness. In some senses it might be difficult to find another period in which so many advances were recorded and in which so significant a foundation was laid for the brilliant flowering of a subsequent epoch. For over two thousand years men have looked back with gratitude to the creative achievements of fifth- and fourth-century Greece. There is hardly (it is no exaggeration to say) a subsequent generation which is not profoundly indebted to the men of that period. And yet the great age of Greece was made possible only by the intellectual achievements of the post-Homeric centuries. One need only list some of these great achievements to establish this point.

This is the period in which man invented coined money (as opposed to mere representative symbols) and so made possible not only extensive trade, but also the primitive beginnings of a banking and investment system. In this age the mortgage was first devised in the Western world, an invention to which we may or may not look back with gratitude. In this period, too, we have for the first time in the Western world the development of writing as an easily managed technique, no longer confined to account books on clay tablets and the recording of political treaties, but now a more facile instrument for the creation and transmission of literature. In this period we note, too, the emergence of new religious cults or at least new emphases given to old ones. This is the age of the ascendency of Apollo, the far-darting lord of pestilence, the god of the silver bow; the golden-haired radiant sun-god of the Homeric poems becomes the god of prophecy, the lord of temperance and the herald of an ethical system, the aristocratic code of "Nothing too much." Zeus, too, undergoes a transformation. The father of gods and men, the all-human tribal father of the Homeric poems, has now become moralized, and is associated in men's minds and thinking with the "eternal" principle of justice. Athena, the flashing-eyed goddess of the Homeric poems, has become queen of a civic cult, the divine wisdom which protects the city; religion has become nationalized, or more exactly, civicized, as it would become in the northern European states at the time of the Reformation. In this period we find developed the germs of drama, both tragedy and comedy, lyric poetry, the beginnings of historical writing and of serious prose in general. But above all, it is in this period that we witness the birth of philosophy.

Philosophers with a very natural impulse to magnify their own cult have tended to claim for it a divine or at least heroic ancestry. It is gratifying to the self-esteem of philosophers, and particularly of professors of philosophy, to think of their vocation as the disinterested speculation of remote and lofty men. "Philosophy," said Plato, "was the child of wonder"; and around this birth there has come to cluster something of the mystery and the glamor of a divine incarnation and a miraculous parthenogenesis. The sceptical temper of our age leads us, however, to look for a more earthly paternity.

The period which fostered this great series of intellectual advances—the period from the ninth to the sixth centuries—was marked by profound social change caused by shifts in social structure more thoroughgoing and more significant even than the change from a slave-owning to a feudal society which we call the decline and fall of the Roman Empire, or than the destruction of feudal society which we call the Renaissance, or than the triumph of the bourgeoisie in the French and American revolutions. For this is the period of the final destruction of tribal society and the creation of the state. The "city," *ptoliethron,* of Homeric society is a tribal headquarters; the "city," *polis,* of the fifth century is in every respect, though on a small scale, a state.

We need only recall the results of our last chapter to recognize the major social factors involved in this change.

As we pass from the poems of Homer to those of Hesiod* we almost seem to be changing worlds. The bright and worldly optimism of Homer gives way to the bleak, discontented pessimism of Hesiod—"the earth is full of woes, of woes the sea." Hesiod, as has long been recognized, represented that group which had failed to profit by this social change—the small peasantry, who were being squeezed more and more by the new economic forces, had not yet been organized, as they were later under Peisistratus,† for political action, and had not yet wholeheartedly made a change from agriculture to trade. Hesiod, as was to be expected in an age that had as yet produced no systematic reflection on economic processes and social change, quite misunderstood the forces that were making life increasingly difficult for himself and his class. He personalized the whole process, presented it to himself in terms of individual guilt, and blamed the "gift-devouring kings" for giving "crooked judgments" and for cheating him and his fellows out of their rights. In other words he felt that he was suffering from *injustice.* But what is justice and where is it to be found? For the first time in the history of Greece the problem of justice was sharply raised. Here is one of the germs from which philosophical thinking developed.

We can put this same point in another way—using a philological rather than a sociological method. In the passage of time from Homer to Hesiod the meaning of the word *diké* (which later we translate justice) was completely transformed. (*Diké* is most probably derived from the verb *deiknumi,* to show, to point out.) In

* HESIOD (fl. eighth century B.C.)

Hesiod, the Boeotian genealogical poet, was born at Ascra near Mt. Helicon. His father migrated from Cyme in Aeolia (in Asia Minor) to Boeotia. After the death of his father, Hesiod charged his brother with bribing the lords in order to obtain a greater share than half. His brother's farm fared badly and Hesiod wrote a poem, the *Works and Days,* to teach the principles of economy and agriculture. He portrays miserable social conditions in Boeotia, which he ascribes to the oppression of corrupt judges and lords and "gift-devouring" princes.

He treats the beliefs and traditions of the common people and expresses nostalgia for the Golden Age of happiness—a tradition which, of course, recalls the comparative security of conditions in gentile or tribal society then passing away.

† See below, p. 69.

its most primitive meaning *diké* referred to the "way of things" or more generally the "way of the world," the natural processes and regular course of the whole universe or any part thereof.[70] There are many remnants of this more primitive usage remaining in the fifth century; *the way of,* i.e. after the fashion of, an unconquerable mountain-beating torrent;[71] *the way of* a colt, i.e. like a colt;[72] *the way of* a wolf, i.e. like a wolf.[73] One aspect of "the way" is the way things are done in society; human custom, the pattern of behavior accepted by the social group. At this stage there is little distinction between social and natural law; each is equally regarded as the "natural" way of doing things. And so in the Homeric poems *diké* is simply *mos* or custom. We hear of the *diké—the way—*of high-born kings, to hate one man and love another.[74] Or again, this is *the way*, i.e. *this is what happens* when a man is away from home as long as I am.[75] There is the *diké* of servants—they are always afraid of new masters;[76] and the *diké* of mortal bodies in death—the sinews no longer hold flesh and bone together.[77]

But there is also discernible another shade of meaning: custom involves obligations; and *diké* begins to take on an "ethical" shade. It is important to notice that this does not derive from any abstract notions of an ethical code, nor from a concept of religious sanctions as laying down a system of right or wrong in human behavior. The custom of the tribe determines what is due, and transgression is simply departure from an accepted norm of conduct. *Diké* expresses this concept. We read of the *diké* of old men—to sleep gently after taking food and a bath.[78] Here the meaning is transitional. It is both the "custom" and—because a recognized custom—therefore the "due," or "right," of old men to sleep. In another passage the "ethical" reference is becoming clearer.[79] The suitors devour the well-fattened hogs, heedless in their hearts of the wrath of Heaven or of pity. "But," says Homer, "the blessed gods do not love deeds of recklessness; they honor *diké* and the upright deeds of men." In the *Iliad*,[80] too, Odysseus advises Achilles to demand from Agamemnon a feast of reconciliation as his *diké*. Here the emergence of ethical obligations out of tribal custom has become very distinct.

The sense of legal obligation involved in the word had a similar origin. The customary procedures of the tribe, "what is done and what is not done" and, therefore, "what should be done and what should not be done," came to be embodied in the *dikai** of kings. Similarly among English "public school" boys, to say that a thing is "simply not done" is equivalent to saying "it isn't right." The *dikai* refer to the judgments given in arbitrated disputes—they may be the decisions of kings or accepted leaders. They are always specific, concrete, and of immediate application; they suggest an interplay of reciprocal rights in a highly integrated social context. And they never fail to derive their sanction from custom. Mr. Tom Silverberg's summary of this stage is worth quoting:

> It seems safe to say that in the tribal and family organizations of society the term *diké* embraces a number of notions and attitudes which are organically connected into a total pattern of a primitive nature. The origins of the word are rooted in a social monism that identifies human practice and custom with natural process, the way of the world. And to a large extent the early identification persists—i.e. a clear distinction is never developed between custom and nature. Custom is considered as natural law, and even with the advent of ethical and legal notions which creep into *diké*, custom holds its place as the real authority. The term *diké* itself comes to take on more than one meaning. But neither the ethical nor the legal aspects of the word become separate, independent offshoots; they remain within the shadow of the basic meaning, habitual custom, which fixes the emotional loyalties of the group and resists the disintegration of its sanction.

The change which comes over the meaning of *diké* as we pass from Homer to Hesiod is a measure of the depth of the change which has transformed the very bases of society. As the tribal organization of society came to be more and more superseded, as communal possession of land died out, as social inequality based on ownership or lack of ownership of the land came more and

* *Dikai* is plural.

more to displace the old "military democracy" of the tribe, as the landowners found it necessary more and more to band together for mutual protection in the process that the Greeks called *synoikism*, as the relationships between men became governed less by blood ties and increasingly by geographical contiguity and, within that contiguity, by common economic interests; in other words, as the tribal or gentile order gave place to the state, so the word which expresses the primary relationship of man to his fellows, the word *diké*, came to take on an entirely new meaning.

To the perplexed peasant-mentality of Hesiod, the process which had destroyed the tribe and fostered inequality is quite incomprehensible *as process.* His point of view is personal and subjective. Inequality and injustice, he thinks, arise among men because of evil strife and the "crooked judgments" of "gift-devouring kings." (He makes an interesting distinction between evil strife or conflict and "good strife" or competition. Both notions are foreign to Homeric society; the latter notion, of course, develops with the idea and the practice of craft competition. The growth of slave labor, too, tended to heighten the sense of competition among free peasants.) The famous allegory of the five ages of man expresses the poet's dismayed nostalgia for a society that has passed away—distress at the loosening of family ties, the corruption of oaths, and the disappearance of reverence.[81] "*Diké* shall be in the strength of a man's hands, and reverence shall be no more."[82] The relation of landholder to peasant is mirrored in the fable of the hawk and the nightingale. "A far stronger than you holds you in his grasp; and you must go wherever I take you, well though you sing. I will make a meal of you, if I please, or let you go. He is a fool who strives to withstand the stronger."[83] Justice as once understood—the old interplay of equals hallowed by custom and fortified by oaths, has gone; in the fifth age, the iron age that now has come upon the earth, its place is taken by the justice that rests in the strength of a man's hands. But at the same time the poet is conscious that "justice through strength" does not exhaust the tale. Somewhere there must be a court of appeal against the "justice" of the strong, which is injustice for the weak. Where is this court of appeal to be found? The poet takes refuge in faith—the "substance of things hoped for, the evidence of things not seen." *Diké* becomes an eternal principle, the maiden daughter of Zeus;[84] justice has made the long and toilsome ascent from earth to heaven. It is no longer a function of social relationships, it is an eternal principle standing *outside* human relations. Bound up with this change there arises the concomitant notion of rewards and punishments for the just and unjust.

> But you, Perses, listen to right [*diké*] and do not foster violence; for violence is bad for the poor man. Even the prosperous cannot easily bear its burden, but is weighed down under it when he has fallen into delusion. The better path is to go by the other side toward justice[85] [literally "just things"]; for Justice[86] [the personification] beats outrage when she comes at length to the end of the race. But only when he has suffered does the fool learn this. For Oath keeps pace with strong judgments. There is a noise when Justice [the personification] is being dragged in the way where those who devour bribes and give sentence with crooked judgments, take her. And she, wrapped in mist, follows to the city and haunts of the people weeping, and bringing mischief to men, even to such as have driven her forth in that they did not deal straightly with her.
>
> But they who gave straight judgments to strangers and to the men of the land, and do not go aside from what is just, their city flourishes, and the people prosper in it; Peace, the nurse of children, is abroad in their land, and all-seeing Zeus never decrees cruel wars against them. Neither famine nor disaster ever haunt men who do true justice; but light-heartedly they tend the *fields which are all their care.* The earth bears them victuals in plenty, and on the mountains the oaks bear acorns upon the top and bees in the midst. Their woolly sheep are laden with fleeces; their women bear children like their parents. They flourish continually with good things, *and do not travel on ships, for the grain-giving earth bears them fruit.**
>
> But for those who practice violence and cruel deeds

* Emphasis ours.

far-seeing Zeus, the Son of Cronos, ordains a punishment. Often even a whole city suffers for a bad man who sins and devises presumptuous deeds, and the Son of Cronos lays great trouble upon the people, famine and plague together, so that the men perish away, and their women do not bear children, and their houses become few, through the contrivings of Olympian Zeus. And again at another time, the Son of Cronos either destroys their wide farm or their walls, or else makes an end of their ships on the sea.

You princes, mark well this punishment, you also; for the deathless gods are near among men and mark all those who oppress their fellows with crooked judgments, and reck not the anger of the gods. For upon the bounteous earth Zeus has thrice ten thousand spirits, watchers of mortal men, and these keep watch on judgments and deeds of wrong as they roam, clad in mist, all over the earth. And there is virgin Justice, the daughter of Zeus,[87] who is honored and reverenced among the gods who dwell on Olympus, and whenever anyone hurts her with lying slander, she sits beside her father, Zeus the Son of Cronos, and tells him of men's wicked heart, until the people pay for the mad folly of their princes who, evilly minded, pervert judgment and give sentence crookedly. Keep watch against this, you princes, and make straight your judgments, you who devour bribes; put crooked judgments from your thoughts.

He does mischief to himself who does mischief to another, and evil planned harms the plotter most.[88]

The supreme problem for Hesiod, therefore, is the relation between force and "justice." Social strife is the cause of injustice (in the world of nonhuman life there is no justice, only force and strife). Justice is in danger of being reduced to mere force; and yet this cannot be all. From the realm of bleak force man can appeal to the transcendent principle of justice which is now becoming personalized as a deity—the daughter of Zeus. The old unity of justice and natural law has broken down. The dualism of human law and divine justice makes its first appearance. The monistic conception of justice, conceived in relation to a natural order and the social life of the tribe, gives way to the dichotomy which reflects social conditions in an age of bitter conflict.

By the sixth century the social forces which we here describe had developed very far; the rise of trade and commerce, the increasing concentration of the best land in the hands of a small group of landholders, and the growing discontent of the peasantry induced sharp social conflicts in the progressive Greek states and particularly in Attica. Nor were the landholders united in opposition to the laments and disquiet of the peasants. The rise of usury had fostered a group of "liberal" patricians whose wealth came from mortgages and trade rather than from direct possession and exploitation of land. Such a man was Solon,* who became by common consent the arbitrator between the contending factions

* SOLON (640-559 B.C.)

Solon, son of Execestides, was born at Salamis. Chosen one of the archons or magistrates in 594 B.C., he introduced many important and unprecedented political and social reforms. When the Athenians lost the battles with Megara for claims to Salamis (his birthplace), they decreed death to any man who should advocate renewal of the war. Solon, feigning insanity, aroused the Athenians to renew the fight; they did, and were victorious. He also succeeded in having the Athenians acquire the Thracian Chersonese.

One of his first proclamations scaled down debts, annulled mortgages which pledged the debtor's person, and declared that all men who had become slaves through debt default were now free. This reform, called the *Seisachtheia,* was publicly celebrated. To secure the enforcement of the latter, he decreed that debtors could not be enslaved.

Following these, laws were passed which limited the amount of property a single person could possess; forbade the exportation of all products but oil in order to ensure a sufficient domestic supply.

Solon introduced Attic (Euboic) coinage, which accelerated trading relations with other states. Some regard this measure as a kind of currency inflation.

His reforms of the judicial structure: instituting democratic "people's courts," admitting members of the lowest economic class to membership in the Assembly, and rendering the Council of Elders impotent in matters of administration and legislation, gave him the approbation of the people to continue these and other reforms. The Council of the Four Hundred, comprising members of the four tribes, took over functions which had previously been the business of the Council of Elders. His reforms were in essence compromises between the very rich and very poor in the state, but did lay the groundwork for the increased democratization of the Athenian constitution.

In his eightieth year he resisted the attempts of Peisistratus to usurp the rulership and establish a tyranny. He died at the age of 80 in Cyprus.

and undertook the task of revising the constitution.[89] His work has been summarized by Plutarch:*

> Solon deceived both sides in order to save the state. To the poor he secretly promised a division of land, to the rich —to recognize their debts.[90]

His own account of this work is a little more idealized.

> To the common people I have given such a measure of privilege as sufficeth them, neither robbing them of the rights they had nor holding out the hopes of greater ones; and I have taken equal thought for those who were possessed of power and who were looked up to because of their wealth, careful that they, too, should suffer no injustice. I have taken a stand which enables me to hold a stout shield over both groups, and I have allowed neither to triumph unjustly over the other.[91]

Notice that justice here becomes once again involved with social relations, but this implication is on a much higher level than the social monism of the Homeric poems. The legislator and the state are now thought of as standing above the strife of factions and "holding even the scales of justice as between class and class."[92] Here is first enunciated the theory of the neutral state, and the function of the legislator is here first described as a neutral impartiality. In the account in Aristotle's *Constitution of the Athenians*, Solon is made to boast that he had *brought force to the dictates of justice*. Justice and violence, which for Hesiod stood in opposition to each other, are now again brought together in the prescriptions of a legislator and the coercive authority of the state. In one sense we may say that Solon has brought justice down to earth again. But not completely. Solon's social position is not

* PLUTARCH. (*c.* 46—*c.* 120 A. D.)

Plutarch, a Greek of Chaeroneia, in Boeotia, is one of the greatest of all biographers. He studied and travelled in Egypt, visited Italy and taught there. His chief works, "Parallel Lives," are studies of character of illustrious Greeks and Romans in pairs, from Theseus to his own time. In all, there were some fifty lives. Unfortunately, fourteen are lost, including those of Epaminondas, Scipio, and the early Caesars. Plutarch was an enlightened and pious polytheist—an aristocrat by sympathy and an enthusiast for Hellenic tradition.

sufficiently unambiguous for any such clear-cut formulation of justice as is embodied in decree and statute law. He also speaks of justice as a divine principle—"the unshaken rock of holy justice."[93] The ambiguous attitude of Solon foreshadows the two opposing schools of a later date: the idealistic school of the Eleatics, Pythagoreans, and Plato (which will see in the state the reflection of a divine harmony and divine idea); and the relativistic and materialistic school of the Sophists (which will see justice as purely relative to a series of social situations).

Although not contemporaneous, Hesiod and Solon represent very interestingly the two opposite phases of the great transition of the post-Homeric period—the patrician landholder and liberal statesman, and the poet who gives articulate utterance to the point of view of the dispossessed. And in general, as we might expect, the views of men displaced and robbed of the comfortable sense of security that tribal life afforded hardly could in the nature of things often find systematic expression in literature at such a period. In order to get even a faint sense of the feelings of such people, we have to examine the half-articulate longings and hopes that are dimly reflected and refracted in the utterances of their religious teachers. The post-Homeric period was an age of great religious activity; the seventh century B.C. has been called the "most mystical" of the centuries. Alongside the Homeric deities, a surging tide of new cults, new teachers, new ideas, and new aspirations found expression. Or, if we must abuse the spatial metaphor, we should say "below" instead of "alongside." For these cults, like all valid religious movements, were of popular origin; they came welling up warmly from below, giving concreteness to the half-formulated aspirations of the nameless and unknown multitude. And this welling up of new mystery cults is certainly not unconnected with the great social change that we have already described.

The Orphic cult, which is the best known and which we can regard as typical of this whole movement, was, as has long been recognized, a popular movement. It will not, therefore, surprise us to find that the mythical and legendary singer and religious teacher, Orpheus, holds the same general attitude to *Diké* that we have examined in Hesiod. In strictness we should perhaps have treated the Orphic expression of this outlook before Hesiod; it probably arose earlier in time. But for clarity of exposition it was necessary to examine the transformation of this concept when its expression had become more articulate.

Diké, then, in the Orphic fragments has achieved all the new functions that she has assumed in Hesiod's poem. She is closely related to Zeus; in an account preserved in Plato's *Laws* she is said always to follow him.[94] Yet again she is described as "*Diké* the severely punishing, who succors all, who follows Zeus."[95] In the passage that we have just referred to from Plato's *Laws* the function of *Diké* as the fountain of retributive justice is clearly apparent, although Plato (characteristically) tones down her function so that she punishes those who transgress the *divine* law.

> Justice always follows Him, [i.e. Zeus] and is the punisher of those who fall short of the divine law. To that law he who would be happy holds fast, and follows it in all humility and order; but he who is lifted up with pride, or money, or honor, or beauty, who has a soul hot with folly, and youth [this was written when Plato was an old man], and insolence, and thinks that he has no need of a guide or ruler, but is able to be the guide of others, he, I say is left deserted by God.[96]

Now although Plato, in using this quotation, has a special and different purpose, we are able to discern through it the important fact that Orphism stressed the function of *Diké* as the guardian of social justice; she performs, in other words, in Orphism a similar function to that in the poems of Hesiod and reflects similar social impulses.

But Orphism goes much further and is even more germinal for the evolution of Greek philosophy. As is easily recognizable, the analysis of forces so subtle and intangible as religious feeling cannot in the nature of the case have the same rigor of demonstration that we have been able to achieve in analyzing the changes which come over the word *diké*. We may, however, safely conjecture that two elements, each arising from the nature of social arrangements, contributed to the matured doctrine of the separation of body and soul. It has long been recognized that primitive fertility rites lie in the background of much traditional Greek religion, particularly the cults of Dionysus and Demeter and the Orphic religion. By sympathetic magic and mimetic ritual early man seeks to compel the powers of nature to grant him sustenance and abundance. When the returning spring seems to be the response to his inarticulate longings, he strives by rejoicing and communion to identify himself with the earth's awakening.[97] It is significant that cults such as that of Dionysus and its Orphic offshoot become important in this period of the Greek world. The changing structure of Greek economics actually decreased the importance of homegrown products. The expansion that the peasantry might have hoped for did not take place. The growing need for agricultural products was met by an expanding import trade. Hope and feeling, therefore, tended to cluster around the recurrent "miracle" of the grain of wheat (or barley) that falls to the earth and dies; that goes, as it were, underground and after a period of death and decay, rises again to triumphant new life in the spring of the year. That is, the poor peasants tend to focus attention on the hoped-for miracle of tomorrow's revival. We can, therefore, very well imagine it was believed that the grain held within itself the kernel of immortality, and that, although the body died, the "soul," as it were, of the wheat remained alive, to take to itself a new and glorified bodily life and to bring forth fruit in abundance.

In an age when an increasing proportion of mankind in human society found no hope and no place for themselves in human society, and when the majority of Greek mankind found itself cast adrift with the breakup of the unity and comparative security of tribal society, the landless and hopeless, cast adrift and tossed about on the tide of social process that they did not at all comprehend, would (it is not hard to imagine) have equated their own hopes and fears to the grain of wheat and formed the expectation that, as the wheat could in the end triumph in spite of apparent death, defeat, and dissolution, so they, too, by communion with a god, Dionysus, could rise again and ultimately find release from their miseries. The development of these "spiritual" notions will thus relate itself to the great transformation of society which we have described. St. Paul centuries later will bespeak (though more articulately and eloquently) the central thought of the Greek mysteries of fertility.

> But some will say, How are the dead raised up? and with what body do they come?
>
> Thou fool, that which thou sowest, thou sowest not that body that shall be, but bare grain, it may chance of wheat, or of some other grain:
>
> But God giveth it a body as it hath pleased Him, and to every seed his own body . . .
>
> So also is the resurrection of the dead. It is sown in corruption; it is raised in incorruption; it is sown in dishonor; it is raised in glory; it is sown in weakness; it is raised up in power; it is sown a natural body; it is raised a spiritual body. There is a natural body, and there is a spiritual body.[98]

Such a doctrine must have proved a powerful compensation for frustration and hopelessness, and not least in the great period of transition that we have under review.

In thus applying to human life notions derived from vegetative cults and mimetic ritual, the Orphics completely transformed man's concept of himself. In the Homeric poems there is no notion of the opposition of soul and body. There is the "self" (*autos*) and a shadowy replica of it, a pale, thin, unsubstantial wraith (an eidolon) living a poor and unsatisfying life which no living man in his senses would for a moment choose. "I would rather," remarked the shade of Achilles to Odysseus in the underworld, in a passage quoted with disapproval by Plato, "serve as a plowman on the land of a portionless master, who had only a scant livelihood, than rule as king over all the dead in the world below."[99] Plato, in fact, chooses several such passages and expresses indignation that Homer should paint so unpleasant and uncompelling a picture of "the other" world.[100] The Homeric eidolon is like the ghost in medieval fancy, a shade haunting a churchyard or moving majestic through an ancient castle. And though this ghost has frequently been identified in popular superstition with the "reason" or "consciousness" or "personality" which is thought to survive after death, it is by no means the same thing. In Homer, then, we have the ghost or eidolon; in the Orphics, taking over the notion of "the kernel of immortality" from the grain of wheat or barley, we have the full-blown opposition between soul and body and the notion that the "body is the tomb of the soul."[101] The mood is very much like the scriptural "O wretched man who shall deliver us from the body of this death." It is easy enough to imagine that to the lowly of the earth in this period (just as in the first century A.D.) there should be a great longing to escape from wretchedness and misery. The belief in immortality gave satisfaction to this longing.

In noting this development from Homer to the Orphics, we are of course, enunciating no new doctrine. In the book which has become something of the classic exposition of the development of Greek notions of the soul, Rohde writes,

> This, then, is the keystone that completes the arch of Orphic religion—the belief in the divine, immortal and abiding life of the soul for whom union with the body and its desires is a thwarting hindrance and repression —a punishment from which its one desire, as soon as it is awakened to a full knowledge of itself, is to escape in order that it may belong entirely to itself in full enjoyment of its powers. The contrast between these ideas and those of the Homeric world is complete: *There,* the soul released from the body was credited only with a poor shadowy, half-conscious existence, so that an eternity of godlike being in the full enjoyment of life and its powers was only thinkable if the body and soul, the twofold self of man, were translated in undissolved communion out of the world of mortality.[102]

The second aspect of the transformation of the wraith-body antithesis into the full-blown antithesis between body and soul and the immortality of the latter is not so speculative. It lends itself to a more documented demonstration. As is well known, the

Pythagorean school found much in the Orphic creed that was profoundly attractive to it. The general position of the Pythagoreans as the intellectual spokesmen of landed conservatism will be discussed in a later chapter. We may be forgiven, perhaps, for anticipating that discussion to the extent of noting their concept of the soul and something of the social motivation for these ideas.

The Pythagoreans first developed the parallelism, afterwards to be taken up and elaborated by Plato, among the cosmos, the state, and the individual. In each there is the same conflict between chaos and anarchy on the one side, and the ordering, ruling, limiting, harmonizing principle, on the other. In the case of the human individual, because of the chaos of impulses, desires, appetites, and passions, we need a guiding and ruling principle. This is provided by the soul or reason—the two now come to be equated, and the meaning of *psyche* is transformed into its later sense of *"Geist,"* reason or personality. When this action develops, then the doctrine of the soul has come to full maturity. It is the ruling principle, the reason, an immortal spark within the human individual, striving to escape from the trammels of the flesh. The body is the "tomb" of the soul and the soul can realize its full potentialities only in so far as in this life it subdues the body and its strivings, and in a life to come prepares itself for the blessedness of the best possible reincarnations in an eternal cycle of fresh appearances in new bodily forms.*

From the mythical cosmology of Orphism, Greek philosophy took its start. Here we have the origin of the conflict of oppositions ever going from the primal "One." In Orphism, of course, this is put in mystical, poetical, religious terms. The idea is expressed by means of a myth, imaginative and symbolic, and perhaps even unclear.

When the Ionian philosophers voice the same notion in cold formal prose, stripping away the anthropomorphisms that arise from the primitive and basic oppositions of sex, Greek philosophy as a formal science will be born.

The problem of oppositions and their reconciliation was, in a

* Cf. below, p. 86.

certain sense, one important dividing line in philosophy. We shall see how in the development of the two great rival philosophic schools this was a perennial bone of contention: for one group—the materialistic, sophistic thinkers—it became a cardinal point to stress opposition as a principle itself; while for the Pythagoreans and, earlier still, for Solon, the *reconciliation* of warring oppositions became a keystone to systematic thought. To the consideration of Greek philosophy as a total development we may regard these two themes as complementary—point and counterpoint. This is not to suggest that the whole broad pattern of Greek philosophy can be reduced to the simplicity of two themes alone; there are, of course, other themes, subordinate or even equally important, which fit into the total picture of "symphonic completeness."

With the early Orphic mysteries we were dealing with a primitive religious offshoot of popular origin which caught up the notion of cosmic oppositions under the obscurity of a religious cloak. Now it will be necessary to take some measure of the main and older strain of Greek religion, the traditional family of Olympian deities.

For the purposes of this book, it will be sufficient to notice chiefly only two or three examples of the changes in function that come to a few of the family of gods in the period that follows the Homeric poems.

In Homer, Apollo is by no means the socially powerful deity that he is later to become. He is not yet an ethical teacher. Only the slightest trace of the ethical doctrines of "Nothing too much" and "Know thyself," for which Delphi comes later to stand, is found in the fifth book of the *Iliad*, where Apollo exhorts Diomedes to "think mortal thoughts."

> Bethink thee, son of Tydeus, and give place, neither be thou minded to be like of spirit with the gods; seeing in no wise of like sort is the race of immortal gods and that of men who walk upon earth.[103]

His functions in Homer are more modest. He is the son of Zeus and Leto,[104] born at Delos[105] and worshipped as a local cult god at Cilla, Chryse, and Tenedos,[106] and having a temple on the Trojan acropolis.[107]

He is a warlike god and a passionate partisan of the Trojans in battle.[108] He is the lord of pestilence, the "far-darting king" whose arrows slay man and beast alike;[109] but he is, also, conversely, the lord of healing, he averts the pestilence and heals a hero's wounds.[110] He is patron of music and the arts, the god of the lyre, and is closely linked with the Muses.[111] He has also learned prophecy and exercised his art in "holy Pytho,"[112] an art which he transmitted to his priests: Calchas,[113] Demodocus,[114] and others.

All this is sharply different in many respects from the later Apollo. It is interesting to notice that the shrine of Apollo at Delphi had a meteoric rise and a period of splendor in the seventh and sixth centuries B.C.; in the fifth century Delphi was more or less in eclipse and such cults as that of Athena and Dionysus claimed a warmer allegiance in the hearts and minds of men.

Now the period of the Delphic ascendancy is precisely the period of the dominance of the aristocratic and landholding class. And the god at Delphi, who was in a position to exercise a very considerable influence on the course of Greek politics, did not fail to throw the weight of his great prestige behind the aristocratic and landholding faction in Greek politics; he particularly favored states like Sparta, which represented the political center of the landed reaction.[115]

But it is also important to observe that the famous Delphic maxims, "Nothing too much" and "Know thyself," represent a thoroughly aristocratic ethic. Here again it is not fanciful to revert to one of the major themes in our symphony—the increasing development of oppositions within the framework of Greek society and the reflection of this social fact in religion and thought. The Delphic ethic represents one way in which a governing class endeavors to deal with this problem—to moderate itself and its own conduct, carefully to refrain from the abuse of wealth or power, not to go to excess, for excess promotes a violent reaction, and (to put the point in theological terms) the god is ever waiting to punish "insolence" and the "intemperate" use of power, position, and privilege. This is, in a sense, the whole theme, to take an obvious example, of the histories of Herodotus:*

> Thou seest how God [the god] strikes with thunderbolts the creatures which stand above the rest and suffers them not to make a proud show; while those which are small do not provoke him to jealousy; thou seest also how he hurls his darts ever at those buildings which are the highest and those trees likewise; for the god is wont to cut short all those things which stand above the rest.[116]

This is the spirit of Herodotus' history, even though he puts these actual words into the mouth of a Persian. (It is interesting to note that in a very different period of history, as the poet Horace comes to identify himself more and more completely with the governing group around the emperor Augustus, he recurs to this teaching of the Delphic oracle in its original sense, and constantly advises the "golden mean."[117] The psychology of a governing group in a period of social unrest is well exhibited by the poet in his "Ode to Fortune."[118]

> The mothers of barbarian kings and tyrants, purple-clad, fear thee O goddess, lest with envious foot thou should'st kick over the standing column, lest the people throng together and arouse the laggards "to arms, to arms" and overthrow their rule.

It is particularly important to grasp firmly this aspect of the Delphic teaching and its early social significance, in view of the fact that much later than the great days of Delphi, Aristotle used the doctrine of the "golden mean" for a quite different purpose—the defense of the "middle class").

While the Delphic Apollo gave expression to the ideas, aspira-

* HERODOTUS (484-425 B.C.)
Herodotus, son of Lyxes, was born at Halicarnassus in Caria. Early in life he began to travel, and visited almost every city in Greece. Since he did not possess citizenship, he was unable to pursue a civic career. Consequently he joined the colony which had set out in 445 B.C. to found Thurii in Italy. Here he remained, writing the history of the relations between the Greeks and the oriental powers, until his death.

tions, hopes, and fears of the aristocrats, other classes in society found or developed gods more suited to their purposes and their needs. In particular, there seems to be good evidence that the emotions of the mercantile and trading classes tended to cluster around the god Hermes or Mercury. At all events, in the period under review, Hermes developed an entirely new set of functions, and the impact of social forces on theology becomes almost startlingly apparent.[119]

In Homer the task of Hermes is to carry out the will of Zeus as messenger,[120] as an Olympian herald (counterpart to the earthly heralds at the court of Agamemnon[121]), as the conductor of souls,[122] and as giver of sleep and dreams.[123] (It is probable that in an even earlier stage he was a god of animal fertility, and he still keeps some epithets which recall his past;[124] in this capacity he is honored by the swineherd Eumaeus.[125])

Even in Homer, Hermes is known as a liar and a thief, but because he reflects a state of society in which the tribal unity has not yet broken up, in which, therefore, fraud is welcome as a weapon of the tribe, legitimate enough when used against outside groups, Hermes' talents in this regard (like the similar talents of Odysseus about which Plato complains) were held in no little esteem. In other words he shows the talents of a servant, a minister, an executor of the will of another; he gets results by cunning and quickness rather than by strength, as do Apollo, Poseidon, and Heracles. He is in Homer, generally speaking, a colorless personality, modest and self-effacing (as befits a good servant). But in two passages in the *Odyssey* we find significant additions to the portrait, important hints that foretell his later development. In one passage it is suggested that he is a little loose in his moral standards, a little lacking in reverence as compared with the other gods;[126] and in the other passage Hermes confides to Calypso that he is tired of running errands for Zeus;"[127] he has nascent aspirations for an independent career.

> "It was Zeus," says Hermes, "who bade me to come hither against my will. Who of his own will would speed over so great space of salt sea water, great past telling?

> Nor is there at hand any city of mortals who offer to the gods sacrifice and choice hecatombs. But it is in no wise possible for any other god to evade or make void the will of Zeus, who bears the aegis."

In the "Homeric" *Hymn to Hermes,* a document of somewhat later date, we begin to see these aspirations taking form, and Hermes is in a period of transition. Just as the craftsmen, his early counterparts, are beginning to play a more significant and independent role in society, so Hermes begins to achieve an independence of function and a restlessness of character that will fit him to be the god of the entrepreneur. He is no longer the loyal servant of Zeus; his ambition is to make his own way in the world, "to get rich quick."[128] It has even been suggested[129] that the emphasis on the precocious strength and preterhuman ingenuity of the infant Hermes refers to the "sudden rise of a commercial class no longer content with a subordinate position in society and now aggressively demanding a place at the banquet table."

At all events Zeus explicitly puts Hermes in charge of "the works of exchange," i.e., commerce,[130] and this becomes in the fifth century his most important function. In this context we must view his skill in theft.[131] It is possible that we have reflected in the Homeric *Hymn* two contradictory attitudes to the famous exploit of his infant theft of the cattle of Apollo (it may be that the work of two poets has been combined into one poem): on the one hand, the poet who glories in Hermes' shocking exploits, to whom "thief" and "agile" are adjectives of praise; on the other, the poet who in pompous and unhumorous style makes Hermes accept a very bad bargain in the controversies with Apollo over the possession of the lyre and the art of prophecy.[132]

What is certain is that we find reflected in the *Hymn* a very sharp conflict between Apollo and Hermes; there can be no doubt that this is a transference to Olympus of an important fact of social life on earth and in Greece, the clash between the landed proprietors and the rising mercantile class. The two gods struggle for the possession of the lyre (i.e., education) and the art of prophecy.[133]

> At one point Hermes threatens to sack Apollo's sacred shrine at Pytho; and twice in the *Hymn* does Apollo bind Hermes in chains.[134]

The penetration of a new class into old sanctuaries is well illustrated by a passage in Aristophanes' *Plutus*. Plutus, the god of wealth, has come to stay with Chremylus, and Hermes characteristically wants to join the household of Chremylus and share his good fortune. He offers his services in various capacities and is finally accepted as "the god of games."

> For wealth is alway highly sympathetic
> With literary games and games athletic.[135]

Hermes' penetration into the sphere of athletic contests is in other words the reflection of an emerging social fact—the penetration by the "new rich" of the old preserves of Greek gentlemen.

This point of view is very interestingly confirmed for us by Plato himself.[136] Hipparchus, son of Peisistratus, the "tyrant" (i.e., democratic leader) of Athens, desiring to educate the country people, set up statues of Hermes in the Attic demes and had them inscribed with wise words in elegiac verse. His purpose, says Plato, was that

> his citizens should not admire the wise words inscribed at Delphi, "Know thyself" and "Nothing too much" and others of the same kind, but should regard rather the words of Hipparchus as wise.

The implication is inescapable. The "mercantile" cult of Hermes was deliberately fostered by the democratic tyrant in opposition to the eupatrid and aristocratic cult of the Delphic Apollo.

In the third period, the fifth century, the position of Hermes as the god of the commercial democracy and particularly of the trading lower middle class becomes indubitably established. His particular home is the market place, and he is especially honored by the "clerks" of the market place[137]—the officials who superintended trade. He is credited with the invention of weights and measures,[138] and Plato, who dislikes the mercantile democracy, sums up his character in a few contemptuous words, "the embodiment of thievery, of verbal deceit, and the life of the market place."[139] Aristophanes, who was equally unfriendly to the mercantile democracy, draws in two plays, the *Peace* and the *Plutus*, a charming if hostile picture of Hermes. He is the typical craftsman,[140] the "servant" (the Greek word is *diaconos*, a deacon), the doer of dirty work.[141] He is an avaricious man[142] and always open to a bribe, particularly a bribe of gold.[143] Now we have in full career the notion foreshadowed in Homer—that Hermes is tired of running errands for Zeus. In the *Plutus*[144] he is ready to revolt and justifies himself by summing up in classic epigram the viewpoint of the man of commerce: "Where most one prospers, *there* is one's fatherland."

In the light of all this we can better understand the feelings of the Athenian democracy when, on the eve of the sailing of the great armada against Syracuse, every statue of Hermes was found to have been mutilated and suspicion fell on Alcibiades,* one of the men entrusted by the Athenian democracy with the command of the fleet. To dismiss the episode as pointless sacrilege or a drunken prank would be unfortunate. It would imply a failure to enter into the feelings of the merchants and the democracy as they contemplated the horrifying possibility that their dearest hopes and wildest dreams were in the hands of one whose opposition to the democratic principle might (and in the event did) go so far as treason to the Athenian state.

We can thus in a sense counterpose Apollo, as the god of the landowners, to Hermes, as the religious symbol of the mercantile democracy. Dionysus[145] represents an extremely complex problem, but there seems to be enough evidence to permit us to conclude that he was originally the god of the peasantry and that he

* ALCIBIADES (450-404 B.C.)

Acibiades, son of Cleinias and Deion, the political *enfant terrible* of his time, was born at Athens. He was closely related to Pericles, who later became his guardian. He had an incredible capacity for deception and opportunism, and became prominent in Athenian politics during the Peloponnesian war. His debauchery and impious revels, especially his instigation of the mutilation of the Hermae, were notorious. After numerous escapes to foreign cities to escape prosecution, he finally died in an attempt to overcome the Spartans who had burned his house.

achieved increasing prominence with the rise in economic importance of the independent peasantry.

For our purpose in this book it is sufficient to notice that Plato has no sympathy with Dionysus and tends always to exalt Apollo. He derives the name of Dionysus from "thinking one has mind," because Dionysus fostered this grave illusion.[146] In the *Laws*, which represent in some sense a modification of his earlier conservatism, a concession to some of the Athenian ways, Dionysus is admitted into the state but only after tremendous misgivings and with strictest limitations.[147] In the *Republic*, Plato bans all art which stems from Dionysus, as well as comic and tragic drama.* He is outspoken in his denunciation of the Bacchic dance.

> Certain private cults practice it, but it is good neither for peace, nor for war, nor for the state; let us have nothing to do with it.[148]

Yet Dionysus' services to the development of art, and particularly the drama, were too great to be entirely ignored. He is admitted in the *Laws*, but only as presiding over men's leisure hours, and as the third of a group, after Apollo and the Muses.[149]

And so we counterpose Apollo to Hermes and (less confidently) to Dionysus. But in Greek religious thought there is not only the strife of opposites but their reconciliation. We have seen that in sixth century theory, as developed by Solon,* the function of reconciliation for the strife of classes is lodged in the state. This in its religious form is reflected in the worship of Athena.

The period of germination between the late Homeric age and the flowering of the fifth century, was, as we have seen, the period that created the state and the first primitive attempts to theorize about the state. It is not surprising, therefore, that we should find in this period the rise of a religious cult of the state. This was associated with Athena, and in the late sixth and throughout the fifth century the cult of Athena became one of supreme importance to the Greek world and particularly to the progressive states like Athens. We see no good reason (in spite

* See above, p. 45.

of the labors of critics) for rejecting the view, which antiquity attributed to Aristotle, that Athena was a moon goddess[150] and that Tritogeneia means very simply "born from the sea"—a view of her origin that would come naturally to a maritime people like the Greeks. Even in the Homeric poems she is (though very infrequently) mentioned as "guardian of the city."[151] But as the importance of the state increased and in particular as the theory evolved of the state as an impartial agency "holding even the scales of justice as between class and class," the function of Athena as city guardian correspondingly increased. It is highly significant that Solon, who, as we noticed above,* first put forward the theory of the impartial state, should appeal to Athena as performing exactly this function.

> Such a watcher holds her hands above our city, Pallas Athena, the great-souled daughter of a mighty sire.[152]

By the fifth century she had acquired two other functions in the course of her evolution. She is pre-eminently the goddess of thought. In the Hesiodic myth she is the daughter of Metis or Thought; Zeus swallowed Metis and Pallas Athena sprang full-grown from his head.[153] Naturally connected with her function of thought was her gift of invention. She gave men the olive and for this gift deserved unlimited gratitude and reverence.

The cultivation of the olive is so important a factor in the development of Athenian commerce and is the physical basis for so much of Athens' glory that the giver of the olive would naturally come to occupy a very prominent place in the religious imagination of the Athenians.[154] But she also taught men crafts and was frequently associated with Hephaestus. As goddess of the arts she is mentioned in the Homeric poems,[155] but in the fifth century this function increased in importance; she became the patron of the potter's art and "at Colonus and Academia she was worshipped in union with Prometheus and Hephaestus, the fire gods."[156]

All these functions of Athena made her ideally adapted to be the patron, friend and protector of democratic Athens. And it is

* See above, p. 45.

precisely as the cult of Apollo began to lose its pre-eminent position that (in Athens) Athena rose into even greater prominence. She was the protector of the city,[157] the giver of victory,[158] the giver of peace.[159] But she is, above all, the incarnation of political wisdom and represents the functions of the state as standing above the chaos of faction and the strivings of change. It is no exaggeration to say that the religion of Athena, the architecture of Ictinus and the Parthenon with its chryselephantine statue of Athena, the sculpture of Phidias, the philosophy of Anaxagoras, and the politics of Pericles all express this same central idea. In the Parthenon the idea is even suggested architecturally in the "reconciliation" of the Doric and the Ionic orders. It is the idea which had been developed in germ by Solon and carried to its perfection by the moderate democrats under Pericles—the idea of the impartial state and of a right and justice that stand above the clash of the conflict.

We may now summarize the results we have reached in this chapter. The march of social forces in the post-Homeric period led to a sharp conflict of political interests in the Greek city-states. Influenced by this developing condition, Greek thinking and Greek religious feeling were profoundly transformed. The gods took on new functions—Apollo at Delphi becoming the god of the aristocrats; Athena symbolizing the state as an organ of reconciliation; Hermes, the god of the merchants and the patron of commerce. The needs and protests of the dispossessed tended to take a religious form in the Orphic mysteries, and the reflection of the political and social conflict may be seen in a growth of dualism—the felt opposition between the body as wretched and the "soul" as potentially capable of happier things. This opposition has hardly yet taken shape on a cosmic scale as the antithesis of soul (god) and body (matter). The Zeus of the Orphics is still neither and both.* At the same time the spokesmen of the distressed transformed the notion of *diké*, giving it ethical and legal content, making it a symbol of a program of reform, and transforming its meaning from simply

* See below, p. 129.

the "way" (its meaning in the monistic tribal order) to "justice," the cry of the oppressed.

Homer, Hesiod, and Solon reflect the important social tendencies of their day. The ordered unity of the tribe has broken up into the contention of opposing classes, the strife of the eupatrids and the dispossessed. Man's concept of himself has become in a similar fashion dualistic; now for the first time there develops the concept of soul as an entity separate from the body and in opposition to it, striving to master the carnal appetites and impulses by the power of reason. Here are clearly in germ the great antitheses of the Platonic philosophy: soul and body, matter and spirit, the one and the many, permanence and change. The "strife of opposites" in society sets reflective man to thinking about the strife of opposites in nature. At this point philosophy —as systematic reflection about the nature of the universe and man—comes to birth. The old naïve and pictorial cosmogonies, represented last of all by Thales, give way to a primitive kind of theorizing.* That this is a precise account of the process is demonstrated by the first fragment of formal philosophy which has come down to us. It is Anaximander's account as preserved for us by Simplicius. He said:

> The first principle or beginning of things is the unlimited: from which coming-to-be is, for things that are, and passing away into these same in accordance with necessity. For they give *justice* and *retribution* [*diké* and *tisis*] to one another for the *injustice* committed according to the ordered process of time.

Unfortunately, Simplicius did not use the modern technique of quotation marks, so we cannot be sure what part of this fragment actually comes from Anaximander and how much is a

* This is not to deny that Thales was in some sense a philosopher or that he was moved by the social currents of this stirring time. The story preserved by Aristotle that Thales foresaw a bounteous olive crop and made a fortune by cornering the supply of presses is evidence that he fully shared in the speculative mercantile life of the Ionian cities. But his philosophical achievement was simply that he stated in words of sober prose the age-old cosmologies of the poets and put forward the dogma that all things come from water. Anaximander first raised concretely the problem from which philosophy arose. (For Thales and Anaximander see below, Chap. V.)

paraphrase of his views as later commentators understood them. I incline to the view that only the part from "in accordance with necessity" can be regarded as a direct quote. The earlier part seems too much influenced by the technical terms of later thinkers to be convincing except as a paraphase. But the unquestionably authentic part contains a valuable and very revealing insight. From the infinite oppositions develop. These oppositions in the ordered process (or arrangements) of time commit injustice, one against the other. They, therefore, are subject to "justice" and "retribution" in the temporal order which is the law by which these injustices are removed. And governing the process is the law of necessity: the strife of opposites, the injustice they commit and its removal, are all part of the nature of things. These views of Anaximander are not mere poetic fancies, as the scholar Simplicius would have us think. Approached in a historical light and with a little intellectual sympathy, they reveal the penetration of a gifted mind into the forces which could appear, at that period of social development, to be shaping the world. The same could be said of the other early Greeks. In the fragments of their work which have come down to us the main intellectual and social currents of a great transitional age are plainly revealed.

CHAPTER THREE

The Great Age of Athenian Democracy

PLATO GREW to manhood in the brilliant climax and devastating catastrophe of fifth-century Athenian democracy. Without question his thinking was profoundly influenced by his experience; and so, to understand Plato, it is supremely necessary to know something about the democracy that his thinking so brilliantly criticized.

To the relatively "organic" and unified society of the tribe (even in its disintegrating Homeric stage) we must counterpose the "progressive" society of Greek antiquity, torn by deep rifts, tortured by instability, yet with profound contributions to make to the history of the progressive West. The tendencies of classical Greece came to focus and maturity first in Athens. It is Athenian society, therefore, that we must first characterize. This is an easier task because Athenian society bears, in some ways, a striking resemblance to the society to which we have become accustomed in the past three hundred years. To appreciate the significance of Homeric society requires an effort of historical imagination, a determination to see its problems in their historical context, which has not always been forthcoming.

Athenian society, like our own, was characterized by production for the market. Mining became an important industry: silver and lead at Sunium, copper at Chalcis in Euboea, iron in the Peloponnesus, Boeotia, and the Cyclades. A system of handicraft industries developed, producing in fairly substantial quantities such articles as pottery, armor, and clothes. Olive oil and wine attained an increasing importance as exports. Grain was brought in more and more from abroad.

Production for the market brought growing trade. The society of fifth-century Athens was strongly mercantile, and Athenian ships and Athenian commercial arrangements dominated the Aegean. The greater use and wide diffusion of coined money forms an important indication of the extent to which commerce was diffused and flourished.

These developments had their necessary impact on human relations. Whereas the tie between man and man in tribal society had been a tie of blood and kinship, it was in Greek progressive society *contractual,* i. e. based on law, contract, and a cash nexus. This means a great growth in the legal and administrative function of the state. A whole apparatus of law and administration had to be devised or evolved to protect and enforce contracts and to give sanction to individual property. This was true not only between individual citizens within the *polis*, but also as between state and state, and between individual citizens of the various states of the empire. A code of international law, both public and private, evolved and found its symbol and enforcement in Athens, the "imperial" city, and the Athenian fleet.

Again, as a necessary consequence the development of Athenian history was marked by sharp political conflict—between landowners and dispossessed, great landowners and small peasants, great landowners and wealthy merchants, landed patricians and the democracy, merchants, usurers, peasants, and artisans. The alliances and quarrels between these various groups constitute the warp and woof of Athenian political history.

The changing political relations were reflected in the facts of military organization. Whereas the armor of the Homeric hero had been the long shield, covered with oxhide, protecting the whole body and well-adapted to single combat, the rise of the landed oligarchy as an organized class was marked by the rise of the organized tactic of the heavily armored soldier, the hoplite, and the rise of the mercantile democracy gave increasing military importance to the fleet, increasing political strength to the sailors.

Ancient society, we may say, was based on slave labor, in contrast to Oriental society, which could employ slaves only to build cult objects like temples and pyramids, and feudal society, based on the free peasant. This does not mean that all who worked for a living were slaves. It does mean that ancient Greece evolved (for historical reasons) a set of institutions which made possible the use of slaves in the basic means of production—on the estates of the country and in the handicraft shops of the towns. The position of helots in Crete and Sparta we shall discuss later.

> Slave labor, extensively used by small employers, held an almost exclusive place in those industries which were organized in workshops and factories. In Socrates' day the miller Nausicydes, the baker Cyrebos, the chiton-maker Demeas, and the cloakmaker Menon made their fortunes without employing one free man.[160]

The state employed many slaves; many were used (and cruelly) in the mines. Moreover, expansion in the Greek world was largely conditioned by the need to keep up a supply of cheap slaves in order to permit their economy to function. A fall in the supply of slaves was the ancient equivalent of a fall in the rate of profit and involved serious crises both in the sphere of economics and in the interrelated spheres of thought.

In the late sixth century and all through the fifth century B.C. Athens became the center of a great commercial "empire" that stretched its tentacles from the Black Sea to Egypt, from Ionia to the Adriatic Sea. At the time of its zenith the volume of trade that passed through the Piraeus was enormous. Commercial pre-eminence passed over into political control under the name of "alliance." The "allies" of the Athenians stretched from the coast of Ionia to Sicily and included such great and important islands as Samos and Lesbos. These "allies" paid heavily in tribute to the imperial city; it has been estimated that in one year (425-424 B.C.) the total tribute paid amounted to the huge sum of some fourteen hundred and sixty-eight talents.[160] With this, the democratic leaders of the city maintained and extended the power of the state and consolidated the pre-eminence of the democratic class. Out of this sum they built and maintained a fleet, built the magnificent temples on the Acropolis, and distributed pay for service in the fleet, the assembly, and the jury courts. For these bounties, of course, only full Athenian citizens were eligible. Never was there a clearer case of a "democracy" of special privilege, based upon the miseries of slave labor (the hardships of slaves in the silver mines at Sunium must have been very great) and the political subjection of the allies to the "tyrant city." (On at least two occasions, in Melos and Mytilene, this overlordship was exercised brutally, cynically, and with calculated cruelty.[161]) It is almost as though the inhabitants of the District of Columbia or the Borough of Westminister, rich and poor alike, should hold a monopoly on the perquisites of political privilege, all the rest of the United States or the British Empire paying tribute for their upkeep. A very brief historical sketch will make these points more intelligible.

We have observed that in the late seventh and early sixth century the clash of contending interests within Attica became very bitter. Aristotle's brief portrait of Attic development reveals distinctly and precisely the main lines of conflict.

> After this there was a prolonged and sharp class struggle between the many and the distinguished. For the constitution was in all respects an oligarchy, and the poor were enslaved to the rich, they and their wives and children . . . All land was in the hands of a few men. If anyone failed to pay his dues, he and his children could be delivered into slavery. And all loans were made on the security of the person up to the time of Solon. He was the first "champion of the people."[162]

We have already noticed that at the beginning of the sixth century Solon came forward with a program of reform. We are told that he turned the attention of the people toward handicrafts, seeing that a people that would import must export too.[163] Solon's reforms did not abolish strife. The discontent of the needy peasantry was beginning to be reinforced by the beginnings of a mercantile class. Against this combination landed nobles were relatively helpless and Peisistratus* and his sons, putting themselves at the head of the democratic movement, were able to establish a "tyranny" lasting (with interruptions) from 560-510 B.C. This was a period of tremendous national advance, the age in which the foundations of Athenian mercantile power were laid and Athens became a "great power" in the Aegean. (When later we find Plato inveighing so bitterly against the tyrant, it is well to recall that these "tyrants" were early leaders of an anti-aristocratic coalition.)

The "democracy" grew and prospered. Late in the century a liberal nobleman of the great family of the Alcmaeonid clan, one Clisthenes, put himself at the head of the democrats (the political maneuvers were particularly complicated in the period of his rise to power) and in 508-7 B.C. promulgated a new constitution giving effective power to the *boulé* (or senate), the *ecclesia* (or assembly), and the popular jury courts. Clisthenes was in a constitutional sense the founder of the Athenian democracy.

The Persian invasions attacked a Greece that was by no means unified, either among the city-states into a firm confederation or internally, within the several states. There seems good reason for the suspicion, for example, that in the campaign of Marathon

* PEISISTRATUS (605-527 B.C.)

Peisistratus of Brauron, son of Hippocrates, was one of the generals who helped conquer the disputed island of Megara, and the port of Nisaea, thus enabling the Athenians to occupy Salamis. On the strength of his popularity resulting from this expedition he executed a *coup d'état* and established himself as dictator of the state. Solon fought bitterly against the tyranny of Peisistratus. Shortly after Solon's death in 560, Peisistratus was driven out of power by a coalition of two parties. Megacles, leader of the Coast party, helped Peisistratus to resume his former place on condition that the latter wed his daughter. However, since Peisistratus hoped for a dynastic rule of his sons Hippias and Hipparchus (sons by his first marriage), he neglected his first wife and incurred the wrath of Megacles, who succeeded in exiling him for the second time. During his ten years of exile, Peisistratus formed alliances in Macedonia, Naxos and Thessaly; he accumulated a large amount of gold from the mines and formed a force of soldiers in order to retrieve his former position at Athens. When he arrived at Marathon (540-39), his followers joined him and defeated the opposition in the battle of Pallene. This second *coup d'état* was successful.

He died in 527 B.C., and his eldest son Hippias succeeded him.

(490 B.C.) the Alcmaeonids were ready to open the gates to Persia, in order that those forces in the city which were in opposition to the rule of the landed aristocracy might be ensured the supremacy. And as early as Marathon Sparta was manifestly playing the part that she was to play all through the century as the protagonist of the principle of oligarchy and the defender of the landed conservatives.

But by 480 B.C., when the Persians came again in great force, the growth of Athenian trading interests seems to have thrown the democratic party, now representing largely the mercantile interests, into conflict with Persia. The resistance at Salamis was inspired and led by a democrat, Themistocles,* and from this time forward the democratic or mercantile party comes forward as the party of expansion and of the overseas empire: nor do the oligarchs give much resistance to this policy so long as Athenian expansion does not conflict with Sparta or the Spartan allies. Under the aggressive leadership of the democratic factions at Athens, and as Sparta showed herself unwilling or unable to play a leading role, the league against Persia becomes gradually transformed into an Athenian hegemony over a great part of the Aegean sea. The tribute that the "allied" states paid into a common treasury for protection against the menace of Persia came to be regarded increasingly by the Athenians as part of the public treasury of Athens to be used for specifically Athenian purposes: the beautification of the imperial city with superb works of art, and the payment of her citizens for taking part in civic functions. As this misuse of funds and the general organization of the empire as an Athenian political and economic hegemony evoked resentment in the minds of the "allied" states, Athens was forced to take ever-stronger measures to prevent this resentment

* THEMISTOCLES (*c.* 514-449 B.C.)

Themistocles was a soldier, statesman, and democratic leader. He advocated naval expansion and made Piraeus a magnificent harbor and consequent trade center in Greece. To induce foreign commerce he remitted the aliens' tax, and many business men settled in Athens. He was ostracized between 476 and 471 for allegedly taking bribes. At Argos, the Spartans accused him of treason with Persia. He fled finally to Asia Minor, was proclaimed a traitor at Athens, and most of his property was confiscated. He died at Magnesia at the age of sixty-five.

from breaking out in armed revolt; or if it did so break out, to suppress these outbursts. The revolt of the "allied" states was a constant threat throughout the fifth century, particularly when Athens was herself in difficulties with external enemies. In the latter part of the century Sparta and Persia both exhibited an increasing willingness to assist the states "allied" to Athens to revolt against her leadership.

But nothing seemed to check the exuberance of the Athenian democracy under the leadership of the great Pericles.* Her fleets and her troops were to be found in every corner of the Aegean and in all the lands that bordered that sea. We possess one inscription that refers to Athenian armies fighting in Cyprus, in Egypt, in Phoenicia, in the territory of the Halieis (the southern Argolid peninsula), in Aegina, and in Megara—all in the same year.[164] Not only was Athens to be supreme on the sea; she even felt strong enough to challenge Sparta on land and make the attempt to build up a land empire. Checked in this latter enterprise, Athens decided that her manifest destiny was on the water: the magnificent enterprise of the "Long Walls" joined the city to the port of the Piraeus. When Athenian energy and ambition finally, in the last third of the century, did bring Athens into conflict with Sparta and her allies, Pericles exhorted his countrymen to disregard their Attic hinterland and behave as though the city were entirely an island and naval power.

All through this period of rapid and triumphant expansion the oligarchic opposition was reduced to comparative impotence. The development of democratic institutions (confined, of course,

* PERICLES (495-429 B.C.)

Pericles, the son of Xanthippus and Agariste, was the leading statesman and orator of Athens during the period when she reached her highest power and greatness. His father had also been prominent in Athenian politics, and he was related to the aristocratic family of the Alcmaeonidae on his mother's side. He was well instructed in music and dialectics, and it is said that Anaxagoras influenced his thought greatly.

In the line of political reform he abolished most of the aristocratic institutions and established liberal and democratic reforms in their stead. He cherished the proposal of a federate union of Greece, but the plan never materialized. He was still in power when Athens entered the Peloponnesian war and delivered a magnificent funeral oration for the war dead after the first year of the war. He died during its third year.

to free Athenian citizens, excluding resident aliens, the "allied" states, and, of course, slaves) gave supreme power to the mercantile group and its leaders, the liberal patrician family of the Alcmaeonids. The Olympian Pericles, the leader of the *demos*, seemed to be, and in fact was, all-powerful. Toward the end of his life, however, he began to find himself enfiladed by a political crossfire from two quarters. The oligarchs kept up their futile and somewhat spiteful opposition; but on the other side something like a left wing began to develop in the democratic party—all those, whether wealthy or poor, who felt that they might profit from a more vigorous campaign of expansion and a less cautious, more forthright, program of imperial advance.

Men began to dream of even more intoxicating adventures for the imperial city: Sicily, Italy, Carthage—who knows? These territories *had* to be forced to accept Athenian trade supremacy if Athenian trade were not to stagnate. This meant challenging the Peloponnesian league, and at last, under pressure from the extreme expansionists and perhaps reluctantly, Pericles was forced into war. The war that then ensued (431-404 B.C.) was the greatest that Hellas had yet known. Pericles' death in the great plague in the early years of the war gave an opportunity to the extremist wing of his party. The excitement of the war years enabled the most persuasive of the demagogues to put forward intoxicating plans for expansion. Sicily, the Greek colonies of that island, and Southern Italy proved an irresistible temptation. The conservatives opposed in vain: the brilliant Alcibiades strongly urged the expedition, and the greatest armada that the Greek world had yet seen sailed from the Piraeus.

A combination of circumstances proved, however, disastrous. The well-founded suspicion of the democrats that Alcibiades was not to be trusted was only increased by the famous episode of the mutilation of the statues of Hermes on the very eve of departure.* Nicias,† the conservative leader, who was opposed

* See above, p. 59.

† NICIAS (d. 414 B.C.)

Nicias was a soldier and statesman in Athens who became the leader of the aristocrats upon the death of Pericles. He was prominent as a philanthropist, having inherited a lucrative silver mine from his father. In 421 to the whole project, was influential enough to prevent the one strategical maneuver which might have held out hope of success—the direct attack on Syracuse before the Syracusans had time to prepare. The great armada wasted its time in irritating and futile demonstrations up and down the coast. The recall and desertion of Alcibiades proved a serious blow. At Sparta he explained that the loyalty of a sensible man was not to a particular state but to an international principle of government: democracy was demonstrable nonsense. On his advice the Spartans sent out a general to organize the defenses.

There is no need to dwell on the catastrophic sequel. The destruction of the fleet and of the army (the latter made a despairing effort to escape over land) was a shattering blow to the hopes and ambitions of the proud mistress of the Aegean. For a few years she struggled on against great odds, her allies in revolt, faction and treason at work within the city, none knowing whom he could trust. For a time the hopes of Athens revived while Alcibiades, repenting, perhaps, of his treachery, led the Athenian fleet. But what loyal democrat could trust a man with a past like his? The first reverse (though due to a subordinate who failed to obey orders) was interpreted as treachery. In exile again, Alcibiades warned the Athenian generals of the folly of their dispositions at the mouth of Aegospotami. The generals refused to listen to his advice. If they were loyal, they felt they could not trust him; or, more probably, there was treachery at the head of the Athenian fleet as, the democrats suspected, had been the case at Arginusae in the previous year. At all events, Alcibiades' advice was not taken, and the Athenian prisoners to the number of three or four thousand were put to death. The news came to Athens and "that night no one slept."

This great disaster gave reaction its opportunity at Athens. A small group of extreme conservatives, led by the infamous "Thirty," were able to seize power in defiance of all constitu-

---

he helped arrange the "Peace of Nicias" which ended the first decade of the Peloponnesian War. Three years later, he was appointed with Alcibiades and Lamachus to command a Sicilian expedition. When Alcibiades fled and Lamachus died, Nicias was left in sole command and was killed in the disastrous outcome of the expedition.

tional provisions, and the oligarchs supported by a Spartan army were in control of the city for about eight months. The proud city was humbled to the dust, deprived of her fleet and walled port; the sacred heights dominated by her bitterest enemy, and fifteen hundred of her finest citizens, men imbued with the strongest democratic fervor, put to death. Although the domination of Sparta lasted but a short time, and although without a Spartan garrison the oligarchs were unable to hold power in Athens, men never forgot the nightmare of the ascendancy of the "Thirty." They felt, fairly or unfairly, that in this brief reign of terror the opposition of the conservatives and the oligarchs had reached its logical conclusion. It is important to bear in mind this resentment, because Plato came forward first to defend Socrates who (as we have explained in another place) was held responsible by the Athenian democrats as the intellectual leader whose program of thought had led to its logical consummation in the oligarchical terror. And later, when Plato came forward on his own account as the intellectual spokesman of the conservative faction, not all his persuasive writing could dispel the suspicions that recent events had created in men's minds.

CHAPTER FOUR

The Conservative Philosophy*

We have described in outline the movement of events in Athens and Attica because Athens was the most progressive state of her day, the focal point for the whole Greek social economy, the

* The most important representatives of pre-Platonic idealism belong to two closely related schools—that of Pythagoras and that of the Eleatics. The leading representatives of the Pythagorean school are:

a) Pythagoras, who will be discussed in the text of this chapter. Although it is impossible to be certain how much of the Pythagorean teaching actually goes back to Pythagoras himself, it will be convenient to regard him as symbolical of the views of his school in the early fifth century.

b) Philolaus, born around 480 at Tarentum or Croton, who is said to have been intimate with Democritus and was probably responsible for the Pythagorean tinge in the early thinking of Democritus. There were reports current in antiquity that Plato bought the works of Philolaus and used them extensively. This points at least to the strong influence of Philolaus on Plato.

Philolaus taught philosophy and mathematics as well as engaging in political life. When the activity of the Pythagorean order became intolerable to the democracy, the order was ousted and Philolaus fled first to Lucania and then to Thebes for refuge. A short time afterward some of the Pythagoreans were able to return to Italy, and Philolaus is said to have accompanied them. He seems to have been interested chiefly in developing a theory of numbers and a concept of geometrical law, which he used to interpret man's purpose and place in the state and the universe. He is credited with the view that "soul" is a mixture and harmony of the parts of the body. The fragments attributed to Philolaus have been wantonly challenged by modern scholars on the grounds that he wrote in the Doric dialect.

c) Archytas of Tarentum, a distinguished philosopher-politician of the fourth century, the son of Mnesagoras (or Histiaeus) and a leading teacher of the Pythagorean school. (He is credited with being the eighth leader of the school.) He was for many years practically a dictator in Tarentum, was elected general seven successive times, and brought Tarentum to a high state of military power. Equally distinguished as a mathematician, he is said to have been the first to distinguish harmonic from arithmetic and geometrical progression. He is also credited with the solution of the duplication of the cube. As we shall see later, he was an intimate friend and supporter of Plato; Aristotle wrote a treatise on the philosophy of Archytas. It is said that he invented a kind of flying machine, and in general he seems to have been a patrician of very considerable versatility. According to state in which the economic and social events moved most rapidly toward their logical outcome. But in surveying the influence of social forces on formal philosophical thinking, it is important to notice that Greece developed very unevenly. Some states, like Athens, produced a great mercantile movement, and the landed oligarchs were left for over half a century relatively powerless. Other states, however, less favored by geographical position and natural gifts, developed slowly or even found their nascent growth stunted. Sparta, for example, because of a peculiar historical development that we shall later characterize, was unable to take part in the great expansion of trade that favored her rival Athens. *Her* destiny turned in the direction of landed conquest, and Sparta was successful in subduing her neighbors. The result was to increase immeasurably the power of the landed aristocracy; but the enslaved populations proved always a disquieting factor in the internal relations of Sparta. In order to retain their position of ascendancy, the nobles were forced to create a highly disciplined warlike state and live almost like an occupying garrison in a perpetual state of siege. Sparta, as a consequence, failed to develop an independent school of philosophy. Her function was a little different—to provide a model, an ideal, and an exemplar to romantic conservatives like Plato, who never ceased to dream of supplanting Athenian democratic, with Spartan aristocratic and servile, institutions. The colonies of Sicily and Southern Italy, too, able as they were to draw on broad plains and rich land, evolved in an aristocratic direction, though not to the degree that Sparta did. The strength of the landed nobility in these regions made the growth of democracy a relatively slow process.[165]

The cities of the Ionian coast, however, were forced by their geographical position into trade at a much earlier date. The possession of land was less important. There is less evidence for a stage in which the landed proprietors dominated the state. It

---

a tradition suggested by Horace, he was drowned on a voyage across the Adriatic and buried at Matinum in Apulia.

The most important representatives of the school of Elea—the Eleatics Parmenides and Zeno—will be discussed in the text of this chapter.

was more frequently the case that as the tribe decayed, chieftains evolved directly into a class of wealthy merchants.

We shall find that the various schools of philosophy, as they developed in the fifth century, show an interesting parallelism with the geographical conditions and the social evolution of the states in which they grew. In Ionia and the Aegean islands, philosophy tends to be materialistic and "dialectical"; in Italy and Sicily idealism flourishes; while in Athens the ascendancy of the liberal patricians in the democratic movement is reflected, as we shall see, in the compromise between idealism and materialism that characterized the position of Anaxagoras. Let us take notice, then, of this great bifurcation of philosophy as it developed in sixth- and fifth-century Greece, reflecting the very sharp difference of political outlook between the slave-owning landed proprietors and the slave-owning "democracy" of usurers, merchants, and artisans. Wherever the democracy triumphed, as in Athens, and during the period of its ascendancy, the dominant philosophy tended to be materialistic-relativistic, as with the early sophists, or dialectical, as with the Ionians. Wherever the landholding class held a dominant position, but not so strongly as to crush all opposition, as in Sicily and Southern Italy, or wherever democracy overreached itself and ran into crisis, the strongest tendency was idealistic.

In this bifurcation of philosophy the fundamental problem which divided the schools was that of justice. It was as they answered the problem "What is justice?" that thinkers found themselves in one camp or another. To the idealists, concerned as they were to defend inequality and the rule of the few, as *just,* justice became an eternal principle, a transcendent authority, a divine self, speaking through semidivine teachers and prophets. To the sophists, concerned to defend the right of democrats to overthrow the rule of a favored few, justice was a historical arrangement, relative to the growth of the society that produced it and claiming no greater validity than the sanction of custom and social agreement. To put it in another way, the institutions of the state and the code of justice that they embody are to one group of thinkers natural, part of the necessary, *eternal* nature of things. To the other group of thinkers, the sophists, these same institutions are *conventional,* a *human* arrangement, valid so long as they evoke agreement, subject to change if they fail to accomplish it. The famous *nature-convention* argument dominated a great deal of fifth-century thought, and in one sense we might argue that the whole magnificent structure of Plato's *Republic* is intended to refute the contention of the sophist Thrasymachus, that justice is simply the interest of the class in power.

Using the problem of justice as a starting point, we must now consider how the particular attitude of each camp was built up into a systematic philosophy—a whole cosmological, logical, and metaphysical structure intended to guard the central position—the affirmation of the thinker about the meaning and nature of justice. The Pythagoreans will serve to typify the idealistic position; the sophists, the materialistic. The opposite positions first developed coherently in these two schools.

In spite of the attempt of Hegel and many of his followers to remove Pythagoras and the Pythagoreans from politics and to set them above the political struggle, it can scarcely be denied that they were warmly interested in politics and deeply concerned with the political struggle. Most of our information about Pythagoras himself is of doubtful value. He seems to have lived many years on the island of Samos at the period when the development of commercial capital had destroyed the power of the landowning aristocracy and led to a mercantile ascendancy under the lead of the "tyrant" Polycrates.* Finding this state of political affairs uncongenial, Pythagoras is said to have migrated to Italy in 532 B.C.[166] In Croton the arrival of Pythagoras seems to have led to a rallying of the aristocratic faction, not only in

* POLYCRATES (?-522 B.C.)

Polycrates became master of Samos (probably in 535 B.C.) by *a coup d'état* while the rest of the city celebrated Hera's festival outside the walls. He represented and led the growing mercantile and commercial forces in the island of Samos, recognized the value of sea-power to the Greek state and succeeded in mastering the Aegean basin. The Persian satrap of Lydia, having failed to conquer Samos, lured Polycrates to the mainland and crucified him. Polycrates was a patron of letters and erected public adornments, aqueducts, and temples.

Croton itself, but throughout the Greek towns of Sicily and Southern Italy. According to our authority, who represents the situation from the point of view of the Pythagorean union, he "freed" Croton, Sybaris, Catana, Rhegium, Himera, Agrigentum and Tauromenium (Taormina).[167] The program of the Pythagoreans was clearly proclaimed. "We must avoid in every way and remove, by fire, knife, or any other means, sickness from the body, ignorance from the soul, a love of luxury from the belly, class struggle from the city, and disagreement from a household."[168] It need not altogether surprise us that this program of blotting out the class struggle by eliminating entirely the power of one faction did not appeal to the democrats. The well-meant effort of the Pythagoreans to "free" their neighboring cities was met by the Sybarites who, under the lead of one Telis, drove the aristocrats into exile, concentrating particularly on the Pythagoreans, and confiscated their property.

From Croton came assistance and armed intervention led by the Pythagorean Milo. Intervention was successful; the fair and prosperous city of Sybaris was levelled to the ground. But the victory had an unexpected sequel. The democrats in Croton rebelled in turn, led by Cylon, who is described by our philo-Pythagorean sources in highly unflattering terms—a man hard to get along with, violent, quarrelsome, and tyrannical by temper.[169] This description should not disturb us too much. It is almost a standard aristocratic account of a "democratic" leader. The Pythagoreans were exiled from Croton. The house in which the most prominent of them were assembled was burned along with its occupants. The Pythagorean clubs were broken up, not only in Croton, but throughout Magna Graecia.[170]

The very credible evidence for the political role of the Pythagorean union has met with violent scholarly prejudice, particularly in England and Germany. Hegel, for example, strove mightily to lift Pythagoras and his followers above the political struggle:

> He settled in Croton and was there in an independent and private capacity, not as statesman, or as military leader, not as a legislator regulating foreign affairs, but

as a teacher of the people, with the distinction that his teaching was not satisfied with persuading its hearers of its truth, but that he also organized well the whole ethical life of individual people.[171]

In order to maintain the myth of Pythagoras as the detached recluse, the contemplative sage, half saint and half scientist, Burnet and others are forced to dismiss some of the most credible evidence that we have.[172] This quite arbitrary effort is probably the result of two factors (which are not, however, entirely disconnected)—the perennial disinclination to countenance any identification of the Greek philosophers with practical politics, and a passionate belief in the Socratic myth and the Platonic legend. Anything which in any sense conflicts with the evidence of Plato, or even facts which Plato passes over in silence, are in this view *ipso facto* suspect. The whole argument of this book as well as of *Who Was Socrates?* challenges these assumptions. It can be shown quite clearly that Plato, for example, was by no means a detached "scientist," but an alert citizen of his time and therefore a political partisan; and that he was not above using distortion and innuendo in order to gain his ends. In particular, what possible reason is there to dismiss Aristoxenus* as a witness for the history of the Pythagoreans? He was a pupil of Aristotle, a native of Southern Italy, and an intimate personal friend, as well as an ardent admirer, of the "last of the Pythagoreans" of Phlius.[173] He represents his accounts of the history and doctrines of the Pythagoreans as derived from the oral accounts of these friends; they ought, therefore, to have the authenticity of a traditional account as

* ARISTOXENUS of Tarentum (*fl.* late fourth century B.C.)

Aristoxenus of Tarentum, the Greek peripatetic philosopher; his father was a pupil of Socrates. He completed his studies in Athens under Aristotle and is reported to have been angered when Theophrastus succeeded as head of the school after Aristotle's death. Of his 453 treatises on philosophy, ethics and music, the only ones extant are three volumes of *Elements of Harmony* and an incomplete musical treatise. He studied with the Pythagoreans, and he represents his account of the Pythagoreans as derived from the oral tradition of the school; there is no reason to suppose that this is not substantially accurate.

developed inside the Pythagorean school and as believed by the Pythagoreans themselves.

The political interest of the Pythagoreans is so important to an understanding not only of Pythagoreanism, but also of Platonism and the development of Greek philosophy, that one may be pardoned for dwelling on it at what may seem disproportionate length.

It is true that Pythagoras himself seems to have held no elective office in any Greek state. His function was rather to organize political clubs which busied themselves with practical political affairs and developed a general intellectual *apologia* for aristocratic rule.[174]

> The Pythagoreans met in caucuses and gave counsel about political affairs. With the passage of time, it came about that the young men not only took the lead in domestic matters but in public too; they came to govern the city, forming a great political club. For they were more than three hundred in number.

It is in this connection not without significance that Pythagoras himself held (according to one authority) that all income should come from agriculture.[175] Here we have a hint of that same prejudice against the merchants and the democracy, that defense of the position of the landed proprietor which so constantly recurs in Greek idealistic thinkers.[176]

Once this point is understood, the philosophical teachings of the Pythagoreans become intelligible. A passage in Iamblichus* (which goes back to Aristoxenus) gives their point of view very clearly, and we must connect it with our previous discussion about the importance of the problem of justice.

> Pythagoras thought that the most efficacious device for the establishment of justice was the rule of the gods, and

* IAMBLICHUS (died *c.* 330 A.D.)

Iamblichus, born at Chalcis in Coele-Syria, was the scion of a rich family. He studied under Anatolius, and later with Porphyry, a pupil of Plotinus. He wrote commentaries on Plato, Aristotle, theology, etc., but none of his manuscripts is extant. He was the chief representative of Syrian Neoplatonism. According to Fabricius, he died before 330 A.D., during the reign of Constantine.

> beginning with that he established the state and the laws, justice and the just.[177]

In this interesting passage we have a long step forward in the theologizing of the concept of justice. The contemplation of divine things, thought the Pythagoreans, instructed by Pythagoras himself, was *useful* for mankind. The reason was that we need a *master,* some ruling principle against which we do not dare to rise in rebellion, and this is provided by the divinity. Our animal nature, he argued, is subject to *hybris* (we may recall that the ethic of Apollo was directed against *hybris*—insolence, excess) and is "diverse" and chaotic, subject to control by a variety of impulses, desires, and passions. There must be a power which by its superiority and its "threatening eminence (*epanastasis*)" will introduce prudence and order into chaos.

It is interesting and important to notice the sense in which Pythagoras uses the word "justice." It is not, as it was with Hesiod, an appeal from the *status quo*, but rather its justification, the undergirding of a particular set of social relations and a traditional form of social organization by an appeal to the divine. It need hardly be emphasized that to the political opponents of this school, the "justice" that it upheld and for which it invoked the divine sanction would appear as "injustice"; just as the "liberty" which they gave to Croton and the other towns of Magna Graecia would appear as the very denial of freedom. The tendency which Pythagoras initiates to give special recondite meanings to a simple word, to speak of justice or social justice when those who use the word mean precisely social injustice, is one which was destined to have fruitful consequences in the history of thought and the development of rhetoric. We shall see later how Plato is able triumphantly to "prove" that justice is something quite different from what the vulgar might suppose; is in a fact an ideal principle, uncontaminated by anything so earthly as the distribution of material goods.

Here two tendencies which we analyzed in the second chapter are coming into focus. In order to preserve law, order, and justice (as it was understood by the conservatives), a ruling principle was necessary. This in the universe is the divine; in the state, the aristocracy; in the individual, the soul. Just as our animal nature, because of the chaos of its impulses, needs a ruling principle—the soul, so the state, because of the tendency of democratic and individualistic elements to rebel, needs the ruling principle of "law" and the ruling instrument of the wise. And, in both the individual and the state, the eminence of the ruling principle is guaranteed by the existence of the divine who himself rules, and supports and fosters rulers.

In order to guide men on earth and interpret the will of the divine there is need of prophets able to interpret the will of the gods.

It is interesting to note that in the ideal commonwealth of the Pythagoreans these are not kings but nobles, the *kaloi kagathoi.** Honor, no doubt, must be paid to Pythagoras himself, but as a semidivine being, halfway between man and god,[178] perhaps even an incarnation of the Hyperborean Apollo himself. The Hyperborean Apollo seems to have been revered by the Orphics as an oracle.[179] (The process of "turning inside out," as it were, early popular religious beliefs and using them against the people is one which we shall notice again.)

Next to the voice of the divine, the Pythagoreans valued tradition—one's allegiance to one's ancestors and the laws.[180] (It is interesting to note a confusion inherent in the Greek word *archē* between the *prior in time* and the *ruler* or ruling principle. In Homer *archē* means always the beginning or origin.[181] It is particularly significant that Homer never uses the word in its later meaning of first principle or ruling power. In this later sense it is first used by the aristocratic lyric poet Pindar who speaks of the *archē*, or rule, of Zeus. It is possible that the transition from first to ruler arose from military practice. He who went first into battle led the way, was the leader, and evolved into the commander. The implication in the Pythagorean use of these terms is that the prior in time should rule, which is a useful assumption for a conservative intellectual position.)

Important for an understanding of the Pythagorean psychology

* For discussion of the implications of this word see below, p. 215f.

is their shrinking from what they call *anarchy*. "There is no greater evil than anarchy." And Aristoxenus goes on to make clear exactly what the school means by anarchy. "For man is not by nature to be saved unless someone governs him." Anarchy, therefore, is self-rule, democratic rule, the reverse of the Pythagorean ideal of a hierarchically arranged society. Aristoxenus goes on immediately to give this notion content. "They thought it important to remain true to the laws and customs of old time, even if they *are* a little inferior" (an interesting concession).[182] For to abandon readily the existing laws and to be agents of revolution is by no means either advantageous or safe.[183] The Pythagorean Xenophilus answered someone who asked him how his son might gain the best education by saying, "If he lives in a well-policed city."[184]

The antithesis of ruler and ruled and the "natural" subordination of the latter is a cardinal principle of their thought.

> They declare that everywhere the *archē* [beginning or ruling principle, see above] is the most valuable element, whether in knowledge or experience, or process, or again in a household, a city, or a military expedition, or in all such relations. But the nature of the *archē* is in all these fields difficult to know or see. For in the various fields of knowledge there is need of no common talent to examine properly the subdivisions of the subject and discover just what this is . . . Nor can a house or a city be well administered unless there be present a true ruler and he rule over willing subjects.[185] There is in every system a *naturally* prior and superior and a *natural* follower and inferior. The first should rule and be benevolent, the latter should obey and be grateful. They said that rulers should not only be wise but also lovers of mankind: the ruled must be not only obedient but devoted to their rulers.[186]

Friendship (affection, *philia*) *is due* to benefactors and parents and was a virtue on which the Pythagoreans laid much emphasis; and particularly within the confraternity of the ruling elect (one is tempted to compare the Christian principle—"as much as lieth in you do good unto all men, *but especially unto them that are of the household of faith*").

Government, they thought, should *normally* be over willing subjects and, we can assume, would be, so long as the philosophical propaganda "took hold." But failing this it might be necessary to renounce "friendship." Hatred, they argued, was justified against the "completely bad," i.e., we may conjecture, stubborn and stiff-necked political opponents who refused to submit. When once it was assumed, hatred was to be unrelenting, unless the "malcontent" reforms (and submits). And when carried on against "unregenerate rebels," war became a sacred task. "One must fight not with words, but with deeds; and war is a lawful and holy thing if one fights as man to man." [187]

In this brief exposition of the ethical and political views of the early Pythagorean school we have deliberately confined ourselves almost exclusively to the account of Aristoxenus, evidence that can hardly be successfully impugned. If the work of Hippodamus* were admitted in evidence (scholars are reluctant to do so for reasons that do not commend themselves to us—largely the close resemblance between the exposition of Plato in the Republic and the ideas of Hippodamus; there is ample ancient evidence for the view that Plato derives his ideas from the Pythagoreans rather than the Pythagoreans from Plato[188])—but were this given due credence, the primacy of ethical and political ideas of an aristocratic kind in the Pythagoreans would be even more striking. One part of the argument seems to point very sharply to fifth-century or early fourth-century thinking, namely, Hippodamus' criticism of the sophists as socially dangerous.

They should observe the sect of the sophists and consider

* HIPPODAMUS (fifth century B.C.)

Hippodamus of Miletus was a Greek architect of fifth-century Greece. He planned the port of Piraeus at Athens for Pericles, and when the Athenians founded Thurii in Italy, he acted as architect for the colony. He was noted for his broad straight streets, cutting one another at right angles. In 408 B.C. he superintended the building of the city of Rhodes. The fragments that have come down to us from Hippodamus are particularly valuable because they represent a tradition that goes back to the middle of the fifth century B.C. and must therefore reproduce the views of the early Pythagoreans.

> if their discourses are useful for the laws, public decrees, and the administration of property by individuals. For the teachings of the sophists induce great evils in the souls of men, since they dare to press for novelty in religion and human institutions, contrary to received ideas.[189]

Nowhere is there a clearer short statement of the issues involved in the argument between the conservative Pythagoreans and the radical and skeptical sophists.

Once the concept of Greek philosophy in its relationship to social conflict is fully grasped and, in particular, the position of the Pythagoreans as the spokesmen of landed conservatism, it is very easy to see how the rest of their system falls naturally and logically into place. The importance that the Pythagoreans attached to traditional taboos in dietetics and to magic will be altogether explicable once we appreciate their position as defenders of the old, the established, and the governing against innovation and anarchy. We can understand, too, the importance that they attach to the conception of "soul" as something like an *ens simplex*, a ruling principle whose function is to govern the chaos of physical impulses, just as the aristocracy in the state embodies the principle of order and "law." We can appreciate as well something of their feeling that the soul cannot develop its full potentialities as long as it is hampered by the body and its strivings, and their development of Orphic ideas in an aristocratic direction and toward a fullblown belief in personal immortality. "In Pythagoreanism the body is evil, in Orphism only wretched"[190] is Minar's brilliant summary. Here again we notice how the ideas developed in popular religion are taken over and turned in an aristocratic and antipopular direction.

We can appreciate also the shrinking of the Pythagoreans from "anarchy" in their speculation about the universe, the feeling that the "unlimited" was as distasteful and baffling to thought, in its sphere, as the uprising of "lesser breeds without the law" against the beneficent rule of Pythagorean aristocrats was in the realm of politics. The antithesis between the "limiting" of law and the "unlimited" of chaos reflects on a cosmic scale the antithesis that these men felt with such an immediacy of emotional recognition in the realm of politics. This point is made very clear in a passage cited by a very late collector, Stobaeus. Here is outlined the educational system that Pythagoras advocated, which in many ways bears a striking resemblance to the system of Plato's republic; and in that context we must return to it. Here we notice the underlying assumption: "order and symmetry are fair and expedient, while lack of order and symmetry are degraded and inexpedient."[191] No man should be allowed to go without direction, we are told,[192] and there must be an authority to which every citizen is subject. And just as an animal left alone will fall into evil, so man left alone will be the slave of his desires and be the slave of his bodily impulses. (The conviction in Pythagoras of the essential depravity of man gives a very "Augustinian" cast to much of his thinking.[193]) The connection between "political" and "cosmic" harmony is suggested in a speech preserved in Iamblichus, which, if not attributable to Pythagoras himself, must reflect the ideas of the school in the fifth or certainly the early fourth century.[194]

> "The Pythagoreans exhorted the elders of the city to build a shrine to the Muses as the patron deities of Harmony. Every man has a duty which it is his peculiar task to perform (*oikeion*), and he will by performing it preserve the harmony of the universe."*

The concept of "sympathy" and harmony of all that is reveals the link between the political and cosmological ideas of the Pythagoreans. It is a most vital concept for the development of an aristocratic philosophy, and its significance will become more apparent as we meet with it once again in Plato. Nor should we suppose that the long and respectable tradition of language about the "music of the spheres" has its origin in any abstract contemplation of "beauty bare" rather than in the practical need to demonstrate the rationality of the rule of a particular group.

If we are to regard the cosmological views of the Pythagorean school as related to their political interests and subordinate always to somewhat practical ends, what of mathematics? The same

* Cf. p. 208.

derivation can, we think, be satisfactorily demonstrated, and this is a matter of some importance, as it will help us to clear away the confusion that has arisen because of the tendency of commentators, particularly Burnet, to discuss Pythagorean mathematics in terms of the thoroughly nineteenth-century opposition between science and religion. That Pythagoras and his school interested themselves in mathematics is well attested. Aristoxenus, in a passage preserved by Stobaeus, says that

> "Pythagoras seems more than all other men to have valued attention to numbers and carried this study forward, removing it from the needs of the merchants."

Exactly how mathematical interests developed in the Pythagorean school is well demonstrated by a passage which probably may be safely attributed to Aristoxenus.[195]

> Pythagoras, wishing to demonstrate that, in the midst of the unequal, the asymmetrical, and the indefinite, justice was present as a principle of limit of equality and symmetry, and at the same time, wishing to teach men how to practice justice, said that it [justice] was like that figure which alone of geometrical diagrams, though it has an infinity of shapes and is formed of sides unequal in their mutual relations, always preserves the demonstration of the right angle.

There can be little doubt that the figure to which he refers is the right-angled scalene triangle, the sides of which may be of unequal length and may vary infinitely both in length and mutual relation, which nevertheless always exhibits the same mathematical law—namely that the square on the hypotenuse of any right-angled triangle is equal to the sum of the squares on the opposite sides. This is in other words an account of the famous "Pythagorean theorem." Its relation with social problems, and in particular the problem of justice, is very clear.

> It is the task of justice to introduce equality, proportion, and a limitation [it would be better to translate "a limiting principle"] into the elements of society, elements which by nature are lacking, because of inequalities of

> wealth, of talent, of functions and of numbers among the citizens.

It is important to notice that in Pythagoras' use of this mathematical demonstration of the nature of justice, it is not, in his view, any part of the function of justice to remove inequality. The proposition is useful to the conservative intellectual position just in so far as it demonstrates how justice subsists in the midst of apparent injustice, equality in the midst of an apparent inequality, and a principle of order and limitation in spite of the apparently infinite variety of forms, variations, and mutual relations in which the scalene rectangled triangle presents itself.

At this point we must pause to note that in democratic thinking and democratic practice the concept of equality was of supreme importance. Moreover, to some democrats, equality was not merely abstract or legal. A demagogue in Syracuse exclaimed:[196]

> Equality of wealth is the beginning of freedom, as poverty is the beginning of servitude.

This makes it very certain that to him and his hearers equality meant literally an equal distribution of material goods.

Thucydides, in describing class conflict and civil war at Corcyra,[197] reported that the two factions each put forward a specious slogan—the oligarchs, a "temperate"[198] aristocracy, the democrats "political equality." Herodotus[199] also lays great stress on "equality" but regards it as something already attained in Periclean democracy. Here, of course, it could not mean economic equality and must mean simply equality before the law. A brief history of the concept might be of interest.

Homer uses the word "equality" in the simplest and most literal sense, in the division of booty,[200] in the distribution of a man's patrimony,[201] in determining the allocation of land.[202] Homer also uses the term to imply equal status among individuals, and in this sense it is used (almost adverbially) by Hesiod.[203] Solon, the liberal reformer, still uses the word in its simpler sense and rejects the concept, saying:

> Nor should worthy men have an equal share of the rich earth of the fatherland along with base men.[204]

Needless to say, Solon is using the words *worthy* and *base* with no moral connotation, but rather with a social bias—i.e., rich and well-born, as opposed to poor and lowly.

Characteristically, Anaximander uses the word with a cosmological significance and speaks of worlds being at an equal distance away from each other.[205] Alcmaeon of Croton, as we shall see later, uses the word for his medical investigations, clearly, in so doing, marking himself off from the Pythagoreans.[206]

From about the middle of the fifth century on, the words "equality" and "equality of distribution" (*isonomia* from *ison* and *nemo*—to distribute) have almost lost their economic significance and mean rather generally "equality before the law." In Aristotle, the word has been quite completely sterilized, has lost any possible usefulness as an expression of economic discontent, means simply "the fair," and is by Aristotle equated with "the legal" or the "lawful."[207]

Xenophon, a good patrician, of course makes Cyrus querulously reproach his political opponents, i.e., the democrats, with agitating for equality:

> First of all, then, I came to learn what this equality was which you achieved. *You never kept quiet.** [208]

But Democritus, whose sympathies, as we shall see, were definitely democratic, sums it all up in a sentence which reads almost like a political watchword, "A fair thing in all matters is equality. Excess and deficiency do not commend themselves to me."[209]

The manifest connection with practical democratic and political programs (in the time of Solon, redistribution of land, abolition of debts; in the time of Thucydides, political equality for all free born citizens), helps us to understand why the Pythagoreans brought all the resources of philosophy, mathematics, religion, and even poetry to refute the view that equality had anything to do with justice.

We are in a position to pursue a little further the connection in Pythagorean thinking between political speculation and arith-

* Emphasis ours. Excessive talk, contention, turmoil were frequently charged against the democracy. They debated issues instead of leaving laws alone.

metical investigation. And the problem of justice will again give us a clue. There can be very little doubt that the earlier Pythagoreans defended the notion that justice is "reciprocity." By reciprocity they meant the old law of retribution, the *lex talionis*, "an eye for an eye and a tooth for a tooth," the more primitive code of the tribe and the blood feud.[210] But the development of the democratic movement, the uncomfortable insistence that justice is equality, made a more exact definition necessary. Fortunately, the process by which their notions of justice were refined has been preserved for us in unimpeachable authorities. In the *Magna Moralia* (written by Aristotle or an early member of his school) we are given an interesting account of Pythagorean speculation on the relation of justice with number. And it is extremely interesting that "Aristotle," contrary to his usual cautious custom of speaking of the Pythagoreans, attributes this to Pythagoras himself.

> Pythagoras then was the first who attempted to speak about moral virtue, but he was wrong. For in assimilating the virtues to numbers he did not investigate the peculiar qualities of moral virtues. For justice is not a square number [a number "equally equal"].[211]

This is a most valuable passage. Let us note first that in Aristotle's view Pythagoras himself was the founder of the science of ethics and was the first to speak about the virtues. This is true if we confine our attention to formal philosophers. It is equally true, however, that the stimulus came from the demands of the people for justice, demands that were voiced by poets and religious teachers. The hard common sense, too, which so often marks Aristotle and his pupils is refreshing: "justice is *not* a square number." A scholar of antiquity who wrote commentaries on Aristotle (Alexander of Aphrodisias, third century A.D.) explains the transition from justice as meaning the *lex talionis* to justice as determined by arithmetical proportion.

> Thinking that the mark of justice is "reciprocity" [the *lex talionis*] and equality and discovering the application of these principles in numbers, the Pythagoreans put for-

> ward the doctrine that justice is the first number produced from equal factors.[212]

For some, the number was four, the square of the first even number, for others, nine, the square of the first odd number. The details of the formulation differ widely, and perhaps there was a profound difference of opinion within the Pythagorean school itself. Another later writer thinks that the Pythagoreans' number for justice was eight.[213] At all events, it is very clear that the early Pythagoreans were led to consider the relations between justice and proportion, and in so doing they defined the three main kinds of proportion—arithmetical, geometrical, and harmonic. This is confirmed by many ancient writers. Plato in the *Gorgias* (speaking of the Pythagoreans and Empedocles) writes as follows:

> The wise men say that a community (sharing) and affection and orderliness and temperance and justice hold together sky and earth and gods and men. On this account they call the whole the cosmos . . . You do not seem to me to have paid attention to this, though wise in these investigations. You have failed to notice that *geometrical equality* is very important among gods and men.[214]

It is confirmed too by the treatise *"on law and justice"*[215] which can safely (we believe) be attributed to Archytas.*

* The reader may be diverted to note in passing the kind of argument which led one scholar to conclude that the work was apocryphal. (O. E. Gruppe, *Ueber die Fragmente des Archytas und der älteren Pythagoreer*, Berlin, 1840.)

I. The allusion to the theory of forms shows Platonic influence. (But the theory of "forms" was developed, at least in embryonic form, by the Pythagoreans, and in any case Archytas was well acquainted with Plato.)

II. The expression "reciprocity" applied to "Right" tends to give the text a Pythagorean coloring. (This is very ingenious of the forger.)

III. The magistrate is identified with a father. This conception is specifically Jewish (in the writer's defense we might observe that he was writing before scholars had any conception of the meaning of the dissolution of the tribe and the patriarchal family); Plato contents himself with comparing the two. And so, the author ingeniously concludes, the work is a forgery of an Alexandrian Jew of the first century A.D.!

For our purpose now it is very certain that the author of this treatise, whose sympathies are clearly aristocratic and conservative, throws his weight to "harmonic proportion" because that justifies the distribution of political pre-eminence and economic power in accordance with merit rather than with any principle of bare equality.[216]

A passage from Plutarch will serve as a powerful confirmation of the view that we have here taken of the meaning of geometry to the conservative philosophy in the late fifth and early fourth centuries. In one of his dinner-table conversations Plutarch propounds the question: What did Plato mean when he said that God always plays the geometer? In the whole conversation the sense of the political relations of mathematics is very much to the fore, and both Pythagoras and Lycurgus are named as men who have influenced the thought of Plato. Then, to continue in Goodwin's translation, which, though somewhat old-fashioned, will reproduce very well the sense of the discussion:

> For Lycurgus, I suppose you know, banished out of Sparta all arithmetical proportion, as being democratical and favoring the crowd; but introduced the geometrical, as being agreeable to oligarchy and a kingly government that rules by law; for the former gives an equal share to every one according to number, but the other gives according to the proportion of the deserts. It doth not huddle all things together, but in it there is a fair discretion of good and bad, everyone having what is fit for him, not by lot or weight, but according as he is virtuous or vicious. The same proportion, my dear Tyndares, God introduceth, which is called Diké and Nemesis and which teacheth us to account that which is just equal, and not that which is equal just. For that equality which [the] many affect, being often the greatest injustice, God, as much as possible, takes away; and useth that proportion which respects every man's deserts, geometrically defining it according to law and reason.

Such an attitude to mathematical problems is, in other words, not something that a modern interpreter is reading into ancient thought, but rather something which the ancient tradition itself regarded as basic and causal.

There are indications that the theory ran through ancient philosophy until the very end. Boethius, the last of them, the man who found consolation in philosophy when ancient society in the fifth century of our era was in collapse, reproduces the same view. In his *Institutio Arithmetica*[217] he speaks of the parallels between various constitutions and mathematical proportions—arithmetical proportion to oligarchy, geometrical to the "popular state where equality rules," harmonic to an aristocracy. This may or may not reproduce Pythagorean thinking. What is quite certain is that the earliest Pythagoreans rejected arithmetical equality in favor of geometrical or harmonic proportion as the clue to the meaning and nature of justice.* And although later on they may have granted a certain "validity" to arithmetical proportion, that, too, is in the interest of a conservative social position. The later Pythagorean school grew more subtle in its rationalizations, and one of its members[218] even argued that the ideal state was a blend of monarchy, aristocracy, and *democracy*, using as an example (of all places) Sparta.

We can summarize this problem as follows. Stimulated by the challenge of the spokesmen of the dispossessed, who argued that justice bore some relation to equality, the Pythagoreans turned to mathematical investigations in an effort to suggest that justice was really a subtle and a recondite kind of equality, that had nothing to do with the straightforward meaning of the word, as superficial and democratic thinkers might suppose. In the fifth century, probably, this aversion to equality took the form of a preference for geometric or harmonic proportion rather than arithmetical. Later (in the fourth century) Pythagorean thinkers found that they could do lip-service to equality as they did to

* It may be of interest to note that Aristotle, in the fifth book of the *Nicomachean Ethics,* examines the relation between "corrective justice," i.e., the justice of rewards and punishment, of the law courts and "distributive justice," i.e., justice in the distribution of external rewards, and uses similar mathematical language to explain his concept. He, too, comes to the conclusion that justice is a geometrical proportion.

democracy, and at this stage arithmetical proportion as a key to the nature of justice achieved some favor among them.

In thus indicating the social affinities of Pythagorean mathematical interest, it is not intended to suggest that the school made no advances in the science of mathematics. On the contrary, it frequently happens, as in this case, that a thinker makes an important scientific or philosophical discovery just because of his political interest and his deep emotional attachment to a particular kind of social organization—concepts which then show themselves socially useful and win recognition on other grounds. At the same time, to treat these ideas without any regard for their origin has too often led to a distorted interpretation.

Another passage from Iamblichus (also, in all probability, going back to Aristoxenus) illustrates very clearly the same genesis for Pythagorean mathematics.

> And in general they say that he was the inventor of the whole science of politics, saying as he did that nothing in the world is pure, but that earth partakes of fire (i.e. contains within its own substance a portion or measure of fire) and fire of water, and wind of these, and these of wind; and moreover good partakes of evil and just of unjust and so on; from this position reason takes its impulse to go in either of two directions, for there are two motions proper to both body and soul, one irrational, one proceeding from choice. And he put together three lines to represent the constitutions of states in such a way that their ends conjoined and formed one right angle, one having the nature of the epitrite [i.e. the proportion of 4:3], another five such parts, while the third is the mean between these two.[219]

A modern writer has well elucidated this passage by quoting another from Porphyry:

> If everyone were a king, life would be difficult, and yet we must not reject monarchy. And if all were good, it would be impossible to find a constitution since all would preserve their worth through their goodness; and yet no

> one would be so mad as to believe it inadvisable to inspire in all the desire to be virtuous.[220]

We can interpret their thought on this point in this way. There is mixture everywhere: in nature, mixture of the elements; in the state, the orderly and the disorderly; in the individual, good impulses and bad. It is the eternal "fact" of inequality, therefore, that makes constitutions necessary and justifies all social institutions. The "eternal" validity of these institutions can be demonstrated both by cosmological speculation and mathematical enquiry. In their zeal to demonstrate the objective validity of their constitutional arrangements and the *status quo,* the Pythagoreans are launched into both types of investigation.

Pythagorean arithmetic bears clear traces of its social origin. We have seen how vital for Pythagorean thinking was the concept of the ruling principle which governs the chaos of impulses in the individual, which guards against anarchy in the state, and which acts as a principle of order and limitation in the universe, keeping in check the chaos of the unlimited. Number for the Pythagorean school—quite certainly by the end of the fifth century—was invoked to play such a part. We are told of Eurytus, a disciple of Philolaus,[221] that he gave number to all things, such as horses and men, that he demonstrated these by arranging pebbles in a certain way. It is these views of the Pythagoreans and the contributions which they incidentally made to the study of mathematics that have led many commentators to think of the Pythagoreans as "scientists" and their school as a center of scientific research. And in one sense the discovery of mathematics as a ground of explanation for phenomena and the importance of quantitative formula for the control and prediction of change is potentially a great and fruitful discovery. Unfortunately, however, the principle seems to have been used by the Pythagoreans, and was certainly used by their disciple Plato, in a quite different way: not as a formula to explain process and change, but rather as a static and conceptual "ground of explanation" underlying isolated and atomic appearances. To put the matter concretely, the discovery of numerical principles in the genetics of horse breeding might be a great and important discovery, enabling the scientist by his knowledge of "genes" and "chromosomes" to control and improve over a number of generations the breed of horses with which he was concerned. In other words, it might enable him to understand and so control process, change, and generation. But that is a very different thing from assuming that there is one particular number which *explains* a horse, another which *explains* a man, and so on. The first leads to science, the other to a thoroughly senseless number-mysticism, a contemplation of pure form, a turning away from change and reality, and a passion for the static and the *changeless,* of which number is regarded as the pattern and the archetype.

This Pythagorean number-mysticism is of immense importance in the development of Western thought because out of it (and other elements) evolved Plato's theory of ideas. The bearing and implications of the notion are put very sharply by Aristotle[222]—he is discussing the origin of the theory of Ideas or Forms, and after mentioning Socrates' contribution says:

> the Pythagoreans at an earlier date had arrived at definitions of some few things—whose formulae they connected with numbers—e.g. what "opportunity" is, or "justice" or "marriage"; and he naturally inquired into the essence of things; for he was trying to reason logically, and the starting point of all logical reasoning is the essence.

We may summarize the development of early Pythagorean thought, then, as follows. Justice is not equality; justice is geometrical rather than arithmetical equality. There is a number (four) which "explains" justice. Justice is realized through a "harmony" of "opposites." The most primitive oppositions are those of sex. To these we may give numerical principles of explanation. The active principle (the male) is the number one; the passive principle (the female) number two. The number for marriage is the union of the two, namely, three. Somehow—the relation is not clear—the study of the number will explain the fact. And the study of the number will lead us past "opinion" and "appearance" to reality. There is no fully developed doctrine as yet (so far as we can judge) that the mathematical principle is the *real*; the fact, only appearance endowed with a secondary or derivative reality. Nor is there any notion that the principle is unchanging, the "phenomena" transitory and short-lived. This notion (though implicit in Pythagorean thinking and welcome when it appears) seems to have been developed by the "heretical Pythagoreans" (the Eleatics) whom we must next discuss.

It is interesting to notice, also, that the distinction between "opinion" and "knowledge," which will prove so important for Plato, is already present in germ to the early Pythagoreans.

> They say that they [i.e. the early Pythagoreans] spoke as follows regarding opinion: "It is foolish," they said, "to pay attention to every opinion of every one and *especially to that of the many*; for to form correct opinions and to understand belongs to the few only. For it is clear that this means "those who *know*," and they are few in number. Thus it is clear that such a power would not extend to the many.[223]

Another branch of the conservative philosophy as it developed in Italy and Sicily will give abundant illustration of the social implications of this kind of thinking. The school of Elea was regarded in antiquity as a kind of heretical group of Pythagoreans, and from this standpoint it will be convenient for us to regard them.[224] Students who have painfully followed the argument of scholars whether the "Being" of the Eleatics is to be regarded as ideal or material may have some difficulty in dismissing a question which is, after all, incorrectly posed and would, if answered, add little to our understanding of the Eleatic position. A much more fruitful approach will be to enquire what answer the Eleatics made to the problems that we have been discussing—the nature of justice, the meaning of change. For it should require little argument to establish that one's attitude to change is as much an emotional as a purely intellectual attitude and is to a degree conditioned by one's position in the social structure. A member of a dominant, ruling, possessing group will naturally tend to shrink from change; to feel that any change must be a change for the worse. The poor and downtrodden and dispossessed will welcome it, however, turn to any Messiah who will only promise action; they will feel that any change must be a change for the better.* Fortunately when we put these questions to the men of Elea, we have important fragments from the poem of Parmenides to give us the answer.

A word or two first about the life of Parmenides: he was a citizen of Elea, a town on the western coast of Italy south of Posidonia or Paestum. We learn from an unimpeachable source[225] that he established order in his city with the *best* laws (*aristois:* a word which was half technical in its significance, cf. *aristocracy*), so that the magistrates each year made the citizens swear that they would abide by the laws of Parmenides.[226] The attitude to change thus manifested in his political arrangements is reflected in his theoretical system. The poem of Parmenides[227] deals with the "two ways"—the way of truth and the way of opinion. By this time it need not surprise us that the guardian of the sacred portals which leads to the eternal, the unchanging, and the true is the goddess *Justice*. She it is who welcomes the enquiring philosopher to her abode and assures him that it is not evil fate but *right* and *justice* (*dikē* and *themis*) that have led him to travel on the way of truth.[228] The goddess explains to him the difference between the two paths of enquiry—"the unshaken heart of well-rounded truth," and "the opinions of mortals in which there is no true belief at all." She praises him for pursuing the former and exhorts him to neglect the latter.

* This observation is not new. We got it from Lucretius.

Nam gaudere novis rebus debere videtur
cui veteres obsunt; sed cui nil accidit aegri
tempore in anteacto, cum pulchre degeret aevom
quid potuit novitatis amorem accendere tali?

De rerum natura V. 170.

† LUCRETIUS (TITUS LUCRETIUS CARUS) (99 B.C.-55 B.C.)

The personal history and main facts of the life of the great Roman poet Lucretius are doubtful or quite unknown. He is said to have come from an old Roman family and lived the life of a recluse. The one work of the famous Epicurean, *De Rerum Natura,* is a philosophical poem in hexameters extolling Nature and attacking superstition and religion, arguing that everything is controlled by law, i. e. cause and effect, and that, granted the postulates of atoms and the void, everything in the universe of nature can be explained.

> "But do thou restrain thy thought from this way of enquiry, nor let habit by its much experience force thee to cast upon this way a wondering eye or sounding ear or tongue."[229]

The "way of truth" leads to existence or being—thought and existence are the same.[230] He developed a kind of verbal dialectic of the transitory or the finite, demonstrating, at least to the satisfaction of any temperament that shrank from change, that movement, alteration, change were impossible.

> One path only is left for us to speak of, namely, that IT IS. In it are very many tokens that what is, is uncreated and indestructible; for it is complete, immovable, and without end. Nor was it ever, nor will it be; for now IT IS, all at once, a continuous one. For what kind of origin for it wilt thou look for? In what way and from what source could it have drawn its increase? I shall not let thee say nor think that it came from what is not; for it can neither be thought nor uttered that anything is not. And, if it came from nothing, what need could have made it arise later rather than sooner? Therefore must it either *BE* altogether or *BE* not at all. Nor will the force of truth suffer aught to arise besides itself from that which is not. Wherefore, Justice doth not loose her fetters and let anything come into being or pass away, but holds it fast. Our judgment thereon depends on this: "IS IT or IS IT NOT?" Surely it is adjudged, as it needs must be, that we are to set aside the one as unthinkable and nameless (for it is no true way), and that the other path is real and true. How, then, can what IS, be going to be in the future? Or how could it come into being? If it came into being, it is not: nor is it if it is going to be in the future. Thus is becoming extinguished and passing away not to be heard of."[231]

In the pictorial language of the poet-philosopher a new task for justice emerges—"Justice doth not loose her fetters and let anything come into being or pass away, but holds it fast." The task of the legislator in politics is to express justice in unchanging laws—laws which ensure the state against "anarchy," the rule of a democratic leader. The task of justice in the universe is to prevent "anything from coming into being or passing away, but to hold it fast." The parallelism is very exact, and the psychological and social genesis of this longing for the unchanging should now be clear. As for the world of change, *that* is illusion:

> And there is not, and never shall be, anything besides what is, since fate has chained it to be whole and immovable. Wherefore all these things are but names which mortals have given, believing them to be true—coming into being and passing away, being and not being, change of place, and alteration of bright color.[232]

The other part of the work of Parmenides deals with the way of opinion; this is the world of process and change, and its relation to the real world at which man arrives by the way of truth is obscure. Whether it has a kind of subordinate and derivative reality (whether, in other words, we have here the famous antithesis of Plato's *Republic* between knowledge and opinion and the respective realms of reality and of a world which rolls around uneasily between being and not being, and is never known but only surmised) or whether, alternatively, this world of nature and nature's processes is entirely illusory, the realm of the strife of opposites, of "the fire of heaven gentle, very light, in every direction the same as itself, but not the same as the other; the other is just the opposite to it, dark night, a heavy and compact body"[233] —whether this realm, though accepted by mortals, is altogether unreal and accepted by mortals only because of the blindness of mortal hearts, this in the present fragmentary state of the poem as it has come down to us, it is impossible certainly to decide. We are inclined to think that the realm of opinion has a kind of derivative validity and that we have here in germ the Platonic opposition of "Being" and "Becoming." One fragment, at least, points to speculations about human embryology and this is confirmed by the tradition of a later writer.[234] In any case, this is not the important point. More significant it is to notice that his reference to the "way of opinion" contains something of a polemic against Heraclitus,[235] and if we recall the central argument, namely the function and place of justice, this polemic will be easy to explain. To Heraclitus, as we shall see, the very meaning and essence of justice is to be found in strife, the struggle of oppositions, in accordance with which everything comes to be.

> One ought to know that war is the common element, that justice is strife, and that all things come to be in accordance with strife and necessity.[236]

For Parmenides, on the other hand, it is the function of justice to lead the mind of man above and away from strife; just as it is the function of the lawgiver to remove it by enjoining a universal submission to the laws he has laid down. Here, coming ever more sharply into view, is the developing antagonism between the conservative philosophy, idealistic and static, and the liberal philosophy, dynamic, relativistic, and materialistic. It is the Heraclitean view of justice and the changing world that Parmenides feels called upon to refute. His problem is to *establish* permanence and not to *describe* it as either material or ideal.

The further development of the Eleatic School in the works of Zeno need not detain us long; in general his system is simply a reinforcement of the main arguments of Parmenides. He, like his predecessor, took a leading part in politics, actively opposed a "tyrant"; a later historian gives him some of the credit for the "good government" of Elea.[237] Zeno's particular anxiety was to prove that motion, change, (and as we should say), progress are impossible, that the only real thing is the changeless, and that this changeless is one. The apparent multiplicity of things, the apparent movement and alteration of things, is accordingly pure illusion. To prove these views, Zeno put forward a number of highly ingenious arguments, all striving to show that any opposing theory involved itself in logical contradiction.[238] It is for this reason that Aristotle calls him "founder of dialectic"—i.e. dialectic in the sense of a clash of *logical* oppositions, based on the *logical* law of contradiction. (The student should clearly distinguish this from the clash of material forces that characterizes, as we shall see, the "dialectic" of Heraclitus.)

The paradoxes of Zeno were highly ingenious, but in terms

of our greater mathematical knowledge they now seem somewhat ridiculous. One is the famous example of Achilles and the tortoise. Achilles (in the Homeric poems he was usually introduced as "swift-footed Achilles") could never overtake the tortoise. Suppose that he starts a thousand feet behind and runs twice as fast. In one period he will be five hundred feet behind, in another two hundred and fifty, in another one hundred and twenty-five and so on, reducing the gap until it is infinitely small but never overtaking the tortoise.[239] Now, in terms of a more developed mathematics this perplexity seems very childish. We are perfectly familiar with an infinite series that adds up to a finite sum. It is even hard for us to imagine why some of the greatest minds of antiquity should have perplexed themselves with such riddles. But this is the kind of strait into which men get themselves if they want to deny the self-evident fact of change.

By considering the flight of an arrow he arrived at the same result. If in one separate moment the arrowhead is standing still, then it is standing still the whole time and motion does not exist. But if it is moving each separate moment so that, for instance, its end moves from point A to point B, then this is immediately not *one* moment but *two*. And so movement, change, alteration cannot exist.

We may sum up the argument on the question of plurality and the many as follows:—Let us imagine that a given body be divided into two parts; then each part again. Finally we come to very small bodies and the division may be continued indefinitely. But each of these infinitely small magnitudes cannot be equal to zero or the whole would be equal to zero. But if it is not zero then we have an infinite number of small magnitudes. But the sum of an infinite number of small particles would add up to a whole infinitely great. But we started with a finite thing, and so our assumption must have been faulty. The hypothesis that a body can be divided must be wrong. If, then, it is impossible to divide "things," then it is impossible to divide the universe; and we must think of "the real" as a completely uniform, homogeneous "one."[240]

A sack of grain in falling makes a noise; one grain in falling does not. Therefore, the grains in reality do not exist.[241]

To pursue such arguments is tedious; it is clear that they make science impossible and they represent the *reductio ad absurdum* of this abstract kind of dialectic. For our purpose the interest of such views is twofold: it seems that by an examination of this argument Leucippus and Democritus were led to the famous atomic theory. Using the same assumptions, they argued that if we keep dividing a body, we must finally arrive at "uncuttable" substances, or atoms, not infinite in number, but very great. Each atom is very small, but it is not zero, and the sum of the atoms is not equal to zero. This is the first formulation of the "atomic theory" which has played so influential a part not only in ancient, but (recurring), even more so, in modern science.

The other interest for us is this: Plato, who shared the prejudices of the Eleatics against change, process, the many, and democracy, was moved to argue like his predecessors that we cannot know the changing, that if a thing is changing in every part of itself, it is unknowable even as changing.[242] This position, too, is a negation of all that we today call science, the function of which is to find formulae which will enable us to predict and control change, motion, and process, and not deny to them reality.

Zeno, then, like Parmenides, was a partisan of the one, the changeless, the static. Like him he was, in practice, a stalwart conservative politician; with Zeno, as with Parmenides, there is the same difficulty about the two parts of his system—the way of truth and the way of opinion. And Zeno, like Parmenides, launches a bitter attack on the "philosopher," i.e., in all probability, Heraclitus and his followers.*

* Burnet thinks that the attack was directed against the Pythagoreans. This is most unlikely. Burnet is forced to dismiss the explicit statement of Strabo that links Zeno with the Pythagoreans. In another place (p. 194, n. 2) Burnet says of Strabo: "The statements of Strabo are of the greatest value; for they are based upon historians now lost." Pythagoras is said to have been the first to call himself a philosopher,[243] and although the list of authorities that repeat this legend seems impressive, they all stem from Heraclides of Pontus. The context in which the story appears seems to

With Parmenides and Zeno, like the Pythagoreans militant defenders in practice of aristocratic constitutions, arises an important element that will afterwards be fused in the Platonic amalgam—the passionate conviction that only the static and the eternal are the true, the denial of any validity, or even reality, to novelty and change, the half poetical, half literal association of the changeless with the just.

We have so far indicated two aspects of the development of conservative philosophy in the Greek world, aspects which are really complementary phases of the same movement of thought and feeling in articulate response to the development of Greek society. And both aspects, as we shall see, will find an even more systematic, more adequate, expression in the writing of Plato. To complete and round off the survey one more aspect must be mentioned—the *conceptualism* of Socrates. There is no need to repeat the account that we have already given of Socrates' evolution from social obscurity, sophism and materialism, to social distinction, idealism, and absolutism.† But one or two points in the developed ethical idealism attributed to Socrates are important for our purposes here. Socrates insisted that in examining any virtue and particularly the virtue of justice, it

---

make it rather suspicious. Heraclides is discussing the attribution to Pythagoras of the famous theory of the three lives. In this theory life is like a festival:

> "Some came to contend for the prizes, others for the purpose of traffic, and the rest as spectators; so also in life, the men of slavish dispositions," said he [i.e., Pythagoras], "are born hunters after glory and covetousness, but philosophers are seekers after truth."[244]

The speculative life is praised, as it afterward was by Aristotle, as superior to the life of practice or of honor. But as long as philosophers were actively engaged in politics it is unlikely that they would make the distinction between the practical and theoretical life. It is in the early fourth century—i.e., in Heraclides' own time, when philosophers are beginning to feel their divorce from politics—that their sense of futility tends to be rationalized into an excessive valuation of the detached and philosophic life. On the other hand, the attribution of the term "philosopher" by Heraclitus to himself and his own work can hardly be impugned. (Diels *Vors.* 22B35. See Diels' note *ad loc.,* where he describes the word as "certainly Ionian, perhaps Heraclitus' own creation.")

† In *Who was Socrates?* (New York, 1939).

was not enough to examine particular examples of justice, but to enquire "what it is in itself." The particular example, in other words, does not exhaust the meaning of the definition of the universal. This principle is so important for the history of science and thought that Socrates has been given immeasurable credit as an important innovator in the history of western philosophy. Without seeking to minimize in any way the importance of the principle suggested, it is also important to notice that in its specific, historical context the principle was used by Socrates as a weapon of antidemocratic polemic. In Socrates' mind the importance of his discovery was precisely this:—not only did the specific example of justice fail to exhaust the meaning of the principle, but the principle was important, in practice and in fact, precisely because it contradicted the particular and reduced what men—democratic men—in their naïvete thought to be just to the level of the meaningless and the untrue. And unless one had grasped the *principle,* as an eternal truth and as an objective fact, one was ignorant. Only such a grasp of ethical essence, of eternal truth, was of any intellectual value. All else was ignorance—a kind of blind rule of thumb. And so democratic statesmen like Themistocles or Pericles, because they could not transmit to their successors a grasp of principle, of an ethical universal, of a moral law, were—in any philosophical sense—ignorant men, and all that they stood for was worthless. The obvious corollary of this conviction was that only the wisest and best should rule, and in practice one is inclined to believe the wisest and best were to be found among Socrates' own friends and disciples, the young men of wealth and good family who alone, *as it chanced,* had leisure to devote themselves to philosophy; just as in Magna Graecia, the rule of law, order, and harmony could only be discovered by the prolonged and painful *askēsis* of the Pythagorean apologist of conservatism. It is important, in other words, to examine Socrates' philosophy not in the abstract, but in the concrete. In the abstract, the emphasis on moral principle and ethical law seems to be merely a quite valid insistence that the example or the particular does not exhaust the nature of the definition. But viewing it in the concrete we can observe that the emphasis on the universal means a denial of any validity to the *actual* justice of a democratic state, an appeal to a higher court which can be depended on in advance to reverse the decisions of the lower.

When viewed in this way, we can begin to appreciate the main difference between the position of the early Pythagorean school and that of Socrates and Plato. The Pythagoreans, living in states in which the landed aristocracy was still in possession of power, called in the eternal and the divine to reinforce the decisions of the actual. Socrates, living in a state in which the landed aristocrats had lost power to the democracy, called in the universal to reverse the actual and to make it of no account. In either case this germinal philosophy of idealism was made into an effective instrument for the criticism of democracy, and once the idealistic presuppositions were granted, democracy was bound to lose the argument. It is no wonder that (to quote Professor A. E. Taylor) philosophy, i.e. idealistic philosophy, and the *demos* were set over against each other like god and mammon, as two masters whom no one man could serve.[245]

The position of Socrates in this development is so important that it is worth dwelling on a moment longer. Friendly critics of *Who was Socrates?* have argued that though his affinities in later life with political reaction have been sufficiently demonstrated, the book tends to overlook the great positive contributions of Socrates as a moralist, as, in a sense, the first man of profound moral insight in the history of Western thought. Such critics quote a sentence like "It is better to suffer than to commit injustice," compare it with the Christian principle, "It is more blessed to give than to receive," and paint Socrates as a kind of pre-Christian teacher of a quasi-Christian ethic. These critics are trying to explain by the light of reason what needs the light of history for its elucidation. They neglect entirely the difference in specific social context between the two teachers—Socrates, the protagonist of landed reaction in a small city-state, and Jesus, the spokesman of the poor, the outcast, and the lowly in the period of breakdown of a "universal" civilization. Such criticism, too, is dogged by a kind of verbalism. The very name "justice" rings so fairly in our ears that we neglect to ask ourselves what particular content the notion has. But by this time it is clear that "justice" had many meanings to the Greeks. And to Socrates, inescapably, justice has little to do with what we should call "economic justice," the distribution of economic goods, what Aristotle called "distributive justice." Nor does it have anything to do with social or legal justice, equality of status before the law, as some sophists argued. It is purely individualistic, to commit or refrain from committing acts of violence and pillage within the framework of society, the inequalities of which are accepted as axiomatic. And in so far as we can give any social context to the dictum, we must remember that for Plato (and in all probability for Socrates) the very type and exemplar of the "unjust man" was the tyrant, i.e. the democratic leader, the man who like Peisistratus, for example, put himself at the head of the dispossessed and gave articulate, and sometimes violent, expression to their demands.

At this point it may be well to say a word or two about Aristotle's evaluation of Socrates. Aristotle treats Socrates as an innovator in the science of logic; he credits him with "inductive reasoning" and "universal definition" in the field of ethics.

> Socrates busied himself with ethics, and not at all with nature as a whole. But in this field he sought for the "universal" and first fixed his mind on definitions.[246]

And in another place:

> Socrates busied himself with ethical virtues and first sought to give a universal definition of these . . . For these are two things which one might justly credit to Socrates: inductive reasoning and universal definitions. Both of these deal with the starting point of knowledge. But Socrates did not make universals "separate" nor the definitions; while "they" [i.e. the Platonists] separated them and regarded them as "ideas" of existing things.[247]

Aristotle's concept of the contribution of Socrates is thus quite clear. He credits him with the invention of the inductive method and with the technique of definition, but only within the sphere of ethics. This is, of course, an invention of enormous importance in the history of thought. But we have had reason to see that Socrates' method was used for social purposes which were not entirely beyond blame, or so at least Athenian democrats believed.

Two important questions immediately arise. Was it necessary that inductive reasoning should have arisen in this close connection with reactionary social thought? Was it inevitable that the concept of the universal which dominated the human mind for so long should have been the abstract universal, the universal which negated and, in a sense, falsified the particular? Or could the Greek world have developed a true scientific definition which could in Aristotle's phrase "save the appearances" and give coherence, meaning, and significance to all particulars within a given field of enquiry? The answer to these questions will depend on an analysis of Greek science and particularly of Greek medical science. For the present it will be sufficient to invite the reader to compare the Socratic "ethical" questioning with the magnificent fifth-century medical treatise entitled *On Ancient Medicine.*[248] As A. E. Taylor well points out,[249] most of the logical notions which we have come to think of as specifically Platonic are there raised to be dismissed in favor of an experiential and experimental treatment of specific cases of disease.* It is, therefore, not inevitable, it would seem, that the invention of induction and the definition should have been so much blended with a semi-religious mysticism and with reactionary political and social thinking. But that the Socratic rather than the "Hippocratic" way of thought prevailed is of course an historical fact with explanations that, as we shall see in the next chapter, were very deeply rooted in the structure of ancient slave-owning society.

We are now in a position to summarize some results in the history of the conservative philosophy among the Greeks and to see some of the contributions that Plato's predecessors made to "Platonism." To put the matter bluntly, most of the leading ideas of the Platonic dialogues are to be found in the thinking of the Pythagoreans and are familiar matter of debate in the late fifth century.[250]

* See below, p. 157.

The Pythagoreans were concerned first of all to defend a conservative social position—the dominance within the state of a group of landed proprietors. For this purpose it was essential for them to demonstrate that justice was not a simple equality manifested in the distribution of economic goods, but a much more subtle thing, geometric equality. For the Pythagoreans the important struggle is that against anarchy; this, in the individual, takes the form of a wrestle between the semidivine "soul" and the debased and debasing passions of the body, the struggle of the soul to escape from the "tomb" of the body; in the state, this takes the form of a struggle to preserve the old and tried, the ancestral customs, the rule of a landed class. In the universe, this takes the form of a struggle of the principle of the "limiting" against the "unlimited" of chaos. In order to establish these principles they developed a fairly elaborate system of education, dividing man's life into four parts and at each stage stressing submission to constituted authority as the supreme task. Similarly, in order to demonstrate their views about the nature of justice and harmony, they busied themselves with arithmetic and geometry, holding that things or particulars could be "explained" by number. And though they seem to have applied this notion to only a few kinds of particulars (Aristotle mentions "opportunity," "the just," and "marriage" as sets of particulars for which they connected the formula with numbers[251]), still they enquired into the essence of things. In so doing they dismissed the opinion of the many as relatively valueless and proclaimed the need of "knowledge" of the "essence" as the important thing. From the confluence of three streams of influence within the conservative philosophy: the Pythagorean conviction of the mathematical nature of essence, the Eleatic affirmation of its timelessness and its unchanging nature, and the Socratic emphasis on the concept of the universal in the realm of ethics and politics, the full blown "Platonic" theory of ideas will emerge.

At this point it will be well to say a word about the vexed question of the "philosophical" relation of Socrates to the Pythagorean school. The writings of Taylor and Burnet on this subject have provoked a lively scholarly controversy. But the thesis of these two scholars has been weakened and much of the criticism of their opponents vitiated by the attempt to make the "influence" and the "affinity" a purely intellectual one. One can hardly refrain from commenting on a most extraordinary scholarly phenomenon—that Taylor, for example, though anxious to present as a thesis the affinity of Socrates with the Pythagorean school, neglects the most important evidence for his own view and clings to the traditional prejudice that Aristoxenus was a "singularly mendacious person." The reason for this, we have suggested, is that Aristoxenus seems to detract from the "moral grandeur" of Socrates and perhaps gives some substance and weight to the suspicions of the democracy that condemned him. Once it is fully realized that the affinities of Socrates with the Pythagorean school were *social* rather than abstractly intellectual; that Socrates presented a new and alternative method for the defense of conservatism, then the puzzle completely disappears. It seems clear that Pythagoreanism was regarded by the democracy as a very formidable force, perhaps because of its "international" ramifications by contrast with the purely Athenian aristocratic "clubs." So that Socrates, closely bound in friendship with leading Pythagoreans, criticizing democracy as they had done but in a new, effective, and startling way, must have (as we have argued elsewhere) seemed to the democracy a singularly alarming portent.

The failure (almost complete) of scholars to recognize this basic aspect of the whole problem is another phase of the "metaphysical prejudice." Philosophers are conscious of their own philosophical strivings; of their own social prejudices, and the springs of hidden bias, they are conscious too rarely.

CHAPTER FIVE

*The Progressive Philosophy**

IT SHOULD OCCASION NO SURPRISE that the philosophy of the Greek progressive movements was by no means so articulate or so coherent as that of their conservative opponents. The explanation

* The leading representatives of Greek materialism, several of whom will be discussed in this chapter are:

THALES (*c.* 640-546 B.C.)

Thales seems to have been in his prime in 585, the year of the eclipse which he is said to have predicted. He was an interesting and distinguished example of the rising mercantile life of the Ionian cities. He is said to have visited Egypt and to have made a fortune through "his philosophy" by foreseeing an abundant olive crop and cornering the supply of olive presses. His political activity seems to have been fairly considerable—he accompanied Croesus on the disastrous campaign against the Persians and advocated a pan-Ionian confederacy with the capital at Teos. He was regarded as one of the seven wise men and is credited with the introduction of geometry from Egypt to Ionia. His philosophical doctrine, clearly reflecting his mercantile interests, was that all things come from water. He believed that the earth floated on a sea of water. He made no distinction, however, between matter and spirit, arguing that all things are full of gods. The sense in which he used the word "god" may perhaps be understood by considering his doctrine that the magnet was endowed with soul. Soul, in other words, is simply the power to move things.

ANAXIMANDER(610-547 B.C.)

Anaximander, the son of Praxiades, was a citizen of Miletus. Theophrastus described him as an "associate" of Thales; he was however, about a generation younger than Thales. He was profoundly interested in the sciences of astronomy, geography, and biology, and drew maps intended probably to be used in the Milesian venture in the Black Sea. Here again the influence of the rising mercantile life and the interests that it dictated is very pronounced.

ANAXIMENES OF MILETUS (*c.* 560-*c.* 524 B.C.)

Anaximenes, son of Eurystratus and a native of Miletus, was a pupil of Anaximander. He was a contemporary of Thales, and succeeded him in popularity after the latter's death. He wrote a book on philosophy and was absorbed in the study of astronomy.

XENOPHANES (*c.* 570-*c.* 480 B.C.)

Xenophanes was born in Colophon and died in exile in Elea. He was lies to a degree in the nature of Greek democracy. Democracy in Greece was, in the first place, a slave-owning democracy with all the tremendous weaknesses, intellectual as well as moral, that

---

probably a younger contemporary of Pythagoras and may have been a student of Anaximander.

HERACLITUS (*c.* 536-*c.* 475 B.C.)

Heraclitus of Ephesus, son of Bloson, flourished about the time of the Ionian revolt. An aristocrat by birth, he refused to hold his hereditary right of King. He expressed great disdain for the "people" and for democratic government. Only fragments of his philosophic works, in his characteristically "obscure" style, are extant. His philosophy will be discussed in the text.

ANAXAGORAS (500-428 B.C.)

Anaxagoras was a wealthy aristocrat and Greek philosopher, born in Clazomenae, Ionia. He was popular during the Periclean reign and instructed Pericles in logic and reason. His heretical opinions about the divinity of the sun and the moon led him to trial for blasphemy, but after the intervention of Pericles, his sentence was commuted from death to exile from Athens. He migrated to Lampsacus, where he taught philosophy and wrote books. He died there at the age of seventy-two. His philosophy is analyzed in the text.

ARCHELAUS (*fl.* fifth century B.C.)

Archelaus of Miletus was a pupil of Anaxagoras, but rejected the static and idealistic elements in Anaxagoras' philosophy and developed his views in a materialistic direction. His primitive matter seems to have been similar in substance to air but, like his Ionian predecessors, with mind intermingling. His views on history and human institutions seem to have had close affinities with those of the Sophists.

PROTAGORAS (*c.* 481-411 B.C.)

Protagoras, a Thracian born at Abdera, was one of the greatest of the Sophists. He occupied himself as a teacher at Athens and was a good friend of Pericles, for whom he later framed the laws of the new colony at Thurii. His philosophical treatises expressing "atheistic" tendencies led to his conviction on a charge of impiety. To escape imprisonment he fled to Sicily and was lost at sea.

PRODICUS (*c.* 465-*c.* 395 B.C.)

Prodicus, a distinguished member of the early school of the Sophists in Athens, was a native of Ceos and served in an embassy in his native town. He was known as a teacher of rhetoric and his semimaterialistic views on the universe and on the vortex, which he seems to have regarded as the cause of all process, excited the derision of his conservative contemporaries.

DEMOCRITUS (460-370 B.C.)

Democritus, a disciple of Leucippus, was born in Abdera, Thrace. A large inheritance from his father permitted him to travel extensively throughout Greece, Egypt, Persia, Chaldaea, India, and Ethiopia. When he returned to Abdera, he began teaching and soon developed a school of disciples. He wrote extensively on physics, astronomy, biology, psychology,

such a society inevitably induces. Morally, the progressives had little that they could oppose to the high-sounding ethical "idealism" of the conservatives. They were prevented by the very limitations of their social position from opposing the rather limited ethical vision of Plato and the Pythagoreans with any more universal ethic, solidly founded on the inherent rights of man as

---

ethics, and mathematics. Most of his works have been lost, and others which have been attributed to him are considered doubtful.

ALCMAEON OF CROTON

Alcmaeon, an important figure in the history of medicine, seems to have flourished at Croton in the sixth or early fifth century. It is our view, which we shall discuss in the text of this chapter, that Alcmaeon developed his scientific technique and his philosophical outlook in opposition to the dominant Pythagorean order at Croton.

HIPPOCRATES (*c.* 460-*c.* 359 B.C.)

Hippocrates was born on the island of Cos near the Carian coast of the distinguished Asklepiadae family, which had practiced medicine for many generations. Heraclides, his father, taught him medicine, it is believed. He introduced a new spirit into medicine by denying the divine origin of disease and dissociating it from the priesthood and superstition. He refused to use amulets, charms, and prayers in the cure of disease, and based his practice on principles of inductive philosophy. Since rational explanations of physiological processes were impossible in the fifth century B.C., Hippocrates recorded the symptoms and progress of the diseases he observed with remarkable accuracy. In *Prognostics* he stressed the forecasting of the course of the disease. His *Treatise on Air, Water, and Places* was an extensive study of climatic conditions—and *Epidemics*, a compilation of case histories of diseases in Thasos in relation to the character of the season. Other works were: *Regimen in Acute Disease* and a treatise on *Injuries of the Head*. Finally, he is purported to have framed the Oath of Hippocrates on which our modern physicians base their ethics.

He died at Larissa in Thessaly.

EMPEDOCLES (490-430 B.C.)

Empedocles of Agrigentum, the most distinguished representative of Western materialism, was born of a noble family but took part in political life on the democratic side by helping to overthrow an oligarchical government in his native town. His utterances in hexameter verse are of great historical interest for the influence that they exercised on the Roman poet Lucretius. He was equally distinguished as a teacher of rhetoric, a physicist, a medical man, and a democratic statesman. He held to the theory of the four elements, earth, air, fire, and water, and seems to have regarded change and process as the problem that needed explanation. Change was caused by the opposite forces of repulsion (strife) and attraction (love) acting on the various elements. None the less, with this quasi-scientific and materialistic cosmology he succeeded in combining much that was mystical and much that was simply grotesque.

man. The insistence on ethical universalism, in other words, is one which the democrats of the fifth century cannot put forward; it will appear only when, in the course of history, the slave-owning society of antiquity begins to decay, and then it will be put forward only by the representatives of the lowly, the slaves and the oppressed—"there is neither Jew nor Greek, male nor female, bond nor free, but a new creature." In default of this possibility earlier progressive philosophies constantly degenerated from dialectics into sophism; and within the sophistic movement there was a constant tendency for the objective relativism of historical process, as put forward, say, by Thrasymachus, to break down into the pure subjective relativism—the worship of brute force—exemplified by Polus or Callicles.

This, too, is a reflex of the ambiguities of the democratic position, particularly in Athens. It must be remembered that Athenian democracy, unlike modern popular movements, was predatory and expansionist to the utmost. During the Peloponnesian war it was the extreme "left" under Cleon* and Hyperbolus* which represented the "imperialistic" wing of the democratic movement. It was the proletariat of the city, the recipients of pay for service on jury or senate, the sailors of the fleet, and other "democratic" elements which combined with certain elements from the mer-

* CLEON (died 422 B.C.)

Cleon, son of Cleaenetus, was one of the outstanding politicians whom the advanced democracy produced. He was the leading opponent of Pericles during the latter's popularity. On the death of Pericles, he became more prominent and was the unofficial leader of the Assembly. Under his influence this body decreed death to the Mytilene revolters. Cleon's speech defending, and Diodotus' speech opposing, this decree are among the most famous debates on the theory of justice. The Mytileneans who had been sent to Athens to plead their cause (30 in number) were placed on trial and summarily executed.

* HYPERBOLUS (died 411 B.C.)

Hyperbolus was a politician of the *demos*—or progressive democratic party in Athens. His background and ability were about the same as Cleon's and he led the opposition to Nicias. When Athens was subjugated by Lacedaemon, Hyperbolus called for a vote of ostracism directed at Nicias, who had "sold out" to Sparta. He reasoned that Alcibiades would be regarded as more dangerous by the Nician supporters. Alcibiades, sensing this, broke with the democratic party and joined Nicias. Ironically enough, Hyperbolus was ostracized and banished for ten years.

He was murdered in exile by the oligarchs of Samos.

cantile class, usurers chiefly, and wheat speculators, to form a great pressure group for overseas adventure, making the moderate policy of Pericles (toward the end of his life) seem safe, sane, and unadventurous.

These social ambiguities are clearly reflected in progressive Greek thought. Beginning as it did with a profound interest in change and process, the philosophy of the progressives endeavored to build up a philosophical opposition to the conservative emphasis on the changeless, the static, and the eternal. But unable to build up any organic and all-embracing ethical universalism which it might oppose to the Pythagorean defense of an earlier and more primitive concept of organism and organic harmony, the movement of progressive thought was more and more forced to fall back on an unbridled individualism. In ethics this culminated in the hedonism of the Cyrenaics, and physics, with the atomism of Democritus. The two systems, each in its respective sphere, have this in common, that they begin with the atomic, isolated individual and endeavor to build up a picture of cosmic or ethical truth by a sheer process of combination. We might notice, I think, an interesting parallel with the opposition in the nineteenth century of Hegelians and utilitarians. There is, however, an important difference. Thinkers like Bentham and Mill, though essentially representative of middle-class thinking and the rise of an industrial bourgeoisie, yet live in a society which is *formally* based on the free laborer and not the slave. They are thus in a position to put forward, if only abstractly, the doctrine of the greatest good of the greatest number; the psychological hedonism of classical antiquity is transmuted, in other words, into utilitarian hedonism and becomes the watchword of progressive forces in the nineteenth century.

The problem, too, for ancient materialists is somewhat differently posed. *Their* success in the world (at this period) did not depend upon defending their vested interests against the assaults of a vigorous, rising, opposing class. Their problem was rather to control more fully the external world, to increase trade, and to extend their own opportunities for investment. They were thus inexorably driven toward material speculation, to an interest in the working of material things. But by no means completely. They were democrats living in a slave-owning society, and they shared to a degree the aversion for manual labor as banausic and vulgar. This means inevitably a shrinking from the whole experimental basis on which science must inexorably rest. There is very little in the Ionian physical school and their successors, Anaxagoras, Leucippus, and Democritus, which points to valid controlled experimentation. Experiment, interestingly enough, seems to have been best developed by the Hippocratic school of medicine at Cos; it is equally interesting that the best sociological analysis of the period—perhaps of all antiquity—that of Thucydides, seems to lean very heavily on the methods and the categories of the Hippocratic school.[252]

Perhaps it will not be amiss to quote Plutarch's characterization of Archimedes; though he is of a later period, he is still the best engineering mind of antiquity.

> And yet Archimedes possessed such a lofty spirit, so profound a soul, and such a wealth of scientific theory, that although his invention had won for him a name and fame for superhuman sagacity, he would not consent to leave behind him any treatise on this subject; regarding the work of an engineer and every art that ministers to the needs of life as ignoble and vulgar, he devoted his efforts only to those studies, the subtlety and the charm of which are not affected by the claims of necessity.[253]

The subject has, of course, another aspect. The problems posed for science are, in the last analysis, those raised by the particular stage of material development. When this is at a primitive level, as it was in classical antiquity, the scientific problems which its thinkers set themselves to solve must be equally simple and primitive. And a scientific philosophy based on any such science is bound to be somewhat thin.

All this can have but one result: that the brilliant system of a thinker like Heraclitus, in spite of its profundity and its suggestiveness, is after all a series of brilliant guesses; its scientific reference is very slight. The attempt to derive everything from fire—the way up and the way down, is arbitrary, even capricious.

There is little evidence of any appreciation of the almost infinite complexity of science and nature. To make this point, one has only to contrast the richness and variety of the scientific information and factual analysis now available to a philosopher, as philosophy, after twenty-four centuries of bifurcation, begins once again to transcend the profound dualisms of the Pythagorean-Platonic age. It was therefore good that in order to enrich its scientific content, in order to study reality on various levels, the philosophy of progressive Greece should move away from the primitive dialectics of Heraclitus to the atomistic position of Democritus, even though in so doing progressive philosophy overdeveloped its atomistic individualism, overemphasized detachment from the political struggle and became (as for example in Lucretius) the ethics of the ivory tower. Let us go back to Anaximander and follow through this movement of thought in greater detail.

Anaximander, then, to summarize, went far beyond the results of Thales. He stripped the anthropomorphic elements from the Orphic cosmogony and put into sober prose the fundamental insight of that creed: the primal unity, the separation of strife and opposites, the whole process governed by the law of *diké* or (as we must now begin to translate it) justice. (However let us be careful to separate this clearly from the Pythagorean "justice" as an ideal, static principle. This is the law of the process.)

The world picture of Anaximander was amazingly mature. In general, the Ionian physicists adopt a point of view about nature and matter that is the direct opposite of that of the Pythagorean school which we discussed in the last chapter. For the Pythagoreans, the only "substance" that can be said to be fully important is "soul." Matter possesses only a secondary and derivative importance. It is an inert, formless mass, that exists only to restrain the soul, to form its prison house and tomb. The Milesian physicists, on the other hand, know only of matter. When they do use the word *psyche* (which we translate "soul"), they mean by it something quite different. For them the soul is *simply the innate capacity of bodies for change and movement.* A peculiarly potent example of "soul" in body is the magnet which can move iron.[254]

It is a matter of great importance to notice the different direction which the notion of the separation of opposites took in the sixth century. For the Pythagoreans, the strife came to be one between body and soul, between god and the universe, (i.e. chaos and the limiting principle) between the ruling and ruled in the state, or, to put it socially, between the "better" and the "worse." For the materialists, the strife is a strife within the unity of *opposing material forces*. For the one school, the problem will be to exhibit justice as the law of strife, and the conflict of opposites as the explanation of all change and process. The one notion leads to idealism and philosophized religion; the other makes possible, and in a sense *is,* the development of science.

These considerations will help us to explain the extraordinary maturity, even modernity, of Ionian cosmological notions. There were, of course, older explanations in the Greek world of what the cosmos was like. The earth floated—a circular disk on the waters of ocean. Above was the iron vault of sky with the silver stars like nails. That this iron vault might not sink into ocean or crush the earth beneath it, Atlas supported it on his shoulders.

The views of Anaximander were quite different. For him (we are told) there was an infinite number of worlds.[255] Each world was bounded by a solid firmament having the shape of a hemisphere. These worlds were produced by immanent physical forces at work.

> He says that something capable of begetting hot and cold was separated off from the eternal—at the origin of this world. From this arose a sphere of flame which grew round the air encircling the earth, as the bark grows round a tree. When this was torn off and enclosed in circles, sun, moon, and stars came to be.[256]

A passage from Aristotle which in all probability refers to Anaximander describes how the continuation of this process of separation produced sea and land. At first, all was moist, but as "it was dried up by the sun, the portion of it that evaporated produced the winds and turnings of the sun and moon, while the portion left behind was the sea."[257]

The sun, he thought, was twenty-seven times as large as the earth, the moon eighteen times as large.[258]

The earth, he thought, was cylindrical. What then supports this cylindrical earth of ours? What is to take the place of Atlas in the old mythical cosmology? Here, again, the answer of Anaximander shows remarkable maturity. There can be no falling, because there is no up or down in the structure of the world; as the earth is situated in the center of the heavenly sphere and equidistant from all points, there is no reason why it should fall to one side rather than another.[259]

His theory of the origin of animals and man is brilliant and is, moreover, founded on observation. He (or some predecessor) had noticed that the maggots of dragonflies live in the water and breathe water. But as they grow to maturity, they go out on to the dry land, the chrysalis bursts, and a new creature emerges, flying and breathing air. So the first animals were produced.[260] Moreover, he observed that the human infant requires a longer period of suckling than other creatures; this prolonged infancy and immaturity would have made survival impossible. We must believe, therefore, that man evolved from the other creatures, and he assumed that they developed from fish and were nurtured like the young sharks, finally being cast on the dry land.[261]

Anaximander's picture of the world, we might remark, is the view of an individualistic entrepreneur. Sea and land are put forward as the central realities, notions conforming with the experience of himself and his fellows: the great rise in productive capacity and markets. It is interesting that the earth, which, we may conjecture, corresponds to Ionian mercantile enterprise, is "in the middle" and in equilibrium. His observations of nature are symbolical expressions for a social reality.

It is impossible to admire too much this first draft of historical materialism. Anaximander, though on a very primitive level and with little of the great store of fact that the modern scientist has at his command, still has a general theory of the universe that is comparable with that of Darwin, and which contains elements which even Darwinism lacked—the unity and strife of opposites, and the alternation of slow and imperceptible change with the "cataclysmic moment." The student may be tempted to reflect on the great price that science has paid for the domination through more than two millennia of philosophical idealism. This reflection may lead him forward to discover why, within the structure of ancient Greek society, the rise and the domination of idealism was a necessary historical development.

In the next great representative of the Ionian school, Anaximenes, we notice what seems at first sight a retrogression to the cosmological position of Thales—the endeavor to explain all process as an evolution from one primary physical substance, substituting air for water as the first element. But it is cosmology with a difference, for the positive contribution of Anaximander has been caught up in the system of his successor. Within the infinite first substance which is air the primary oppositions of heat and cold are *separated out:* "The compression and condensation of matter are the cold, its rarefaction and slackening, the warm."[262] This view, he too, supported with an observation from experience. When we breathe out from puckered lips, the breath is cold, but when the lips are open the breath is warm.[263] Moreover, this infinite substance air was in its rarefaction and condensation the explanation of all process and change in the universe. "Just as our *psyche,* which is air, controls us, so air and vapor compass all the universe." To the ambiguities inherent in the Greek word *psyche* we shall recur. In this passage it would be a great mistake to translate it as "soul" in the Pythagorean sense. It is that which distinguishes a living body from a corpse—the "breath," they said, has gone out of it. So that it is air which is the source of life, movement, change in our bodies. In this sense it is "divine," and in this sense, in the Ionian school, "all things are full of gods"; i.e. they are in fact subject to change, development, motion.

This point has been so much obscured by the piety of later commentators that it is worth dwelling on a moment or two longer. Cicero[264] says that

> Anaximenes held that air was god, and that it came into being and existed, that it was boundless and immeasurable and *always in motion.*

Cicero goes on to complain that Anaximenes should call by the name god anything so formless and lacking in beauty. St. Augustine,[265] too, laments that Anaximenes

> assigned all causes to infinite air, and did not deny the gods or pass them over in silence; but he did not hold that air was made by the gods, but believed that they arose from air.

Now, both these writers were, of course, discussing the question at a much later stage in the history of philosophy, when the opposition between soul and body, god and the universe, had become firmly embedded in philosophical thought. At this stage such an opposition had not yet developed or, to put the matter more precisely, was being developed by the conservative and idealistic school of the Pythagoreans. We must keep firmly in mind the two quite separate ways in which the Orphic religious notion of the strife of opposites was developing. With the Pythagoreans, it develops into the opposition of soul—body, good—evil, the limiting—chaos, with the consequent need for harmony and subordination of one member of the pair to the other.

In the Ionian school, the opposition becomes the clash of physical forces developing out of the primal unity. And if we ask whether this unity in opposition is material or ideal, matter or spirit, the question is at this stage meaningless. God or *psyche* is what can cause motion, all things are full of motion and, therefore, all things are full of gods.

This point may be made somewhat clearer if we consider the first impact of Ionian thinking on the Pythagorean and idealistic philosophy of Sicily and the West. Xenophanes of Colophon (Colophon was a city in Asia Minor, south of Smyrna) had manifest affinities in his thinking with the earlier Ionians. He was particularly interested in the study of natural phenomena. He put forward an explanation for the saltiness of the sea and confirmed Anaximander's account of the origin of living creatures by an acute observation of fossils:

> On dry land far from the sea and even on mountains shells are found; in Syracuse in the stone quarries, im-

> pressions of fish and fucoids[266] may be seen, while in Paros they have found the imprint of an anchovy inside a stone; in Malta all types of sea creatures. This, he said, occurred because all these living things were in ancient times stuck in mud, and their imprint in the mud dried [and was turned into stone].[267]

He held, too, like his great predecessor that the rainbow was a natural phenomenon and gave a naturalistic explanation for it:

> She that they call Iris [in the traditional mythology Iris was a subordinate deity] is a cloud likewise, purple, scarlet, and green to behold.[268]

He gave a purely naturalistic explanation of human beings, animals, and plants:

> Everything that is born and grows is [made] of earth and water.[269]

and

> for all of us come to be born from earth and water.[270]
> All things come from earth and end in earth.[271]

Most strikingly he rejected the nostalgic conservatism of those who looked backward for a divine revelation.

> God did not reveal all things to mortals from the beginning (*arché*), but by investigation; as time proceeds, men make more adequate discoveries.[272]

Seldom has the case for the gradual process of science been more epigrammatically put.

Sometime in middle life Xenophanes migrated to Elea and must have come into contact with the idealistic school. (He also spent some time at Catana.) And although there are elements in his thinking (or at least in the accounts which have been preserved from later commentators) which seem to compromise with Pythagorean idealism, most of his actual fragments are marked by a sharply polemical or satirical tone when he deals with the views of the idealists. His views on the subject of transmigration of the soul may easily be gleaned from the following:

> And once he was present when a puppy was beaten. And, so they say, he pitied the animal, and spoke, "Stop, don't beat him; this is the *soul* (psyche) of a dear friend, and I recognized his voice as the creature yelped."[273]

This is, of course, good clean fun. Elsewhere, when Xenophanes uses the word *psyche* he means "breath," as did his Ionian predecessors.[274]

But for the idealistic views on the gods Xenophanes reserved his most pointed barbs. It will be enough to quote a number of fragments.

> Homer and Hesiod have attributed to the gods everything that would be a shame and reproach to men: theft, adultery, and mutual deceit.[275]

and

> Mortals think that the gods are begotten as they are, and have their clothing, voice, and shape.[276]

and

> If oxen or lions had hands and could draw with their hands as men can, horses would make their gods in the shape of horses, and lions like lions—each making the gods in their own image.[277]

Pursuing the same idea, he said:

> The Ethiopians made their gods black and snub-nosed; the Thracians say their gods have blue eyes and red hair.[278]

As opposed to these simple notions of deity, he put his own view:

> One god, the greatest among gods and mortals, like to mortals neither in form nor thought.[279]

and

> It is the whole [i.e. the whole sky] that sees, the whole that thinks, the whole that hears.[280]

This "whole," then, neither matter nor spirit because the distinction was not yet present to the men of Ionia, is the universe, the real, the one.

That the interpretation here adopted is the right one, that the world or god was conceived neither as matter or spirit, neither as limited or unlimited, is conclusively proved by a passage from Aristotle, where that great thinker is discussing the philosophers of "the one." He says that

> Parmenides seems to have regarded the one as ideal, Melissus [a later Ionian, said to have been an associate of Heraclitus[281]] as material. Therefore the one regarded the world as limited, the other as unlimited. Xenophanes, who was the first partisan of the one [Parmenides is said to have been his pupil], *did not make clear his views* [on these points] and does not seem to have touched either of these concepts of the *nature of unity,* but looking up into the heaven, he says that the one is god.[282]

Xenophanes' attitude to life reflects the gay worldliness of the Ionian mercantile civilization, with its emphasis on physical joys and present well-being, on movement and travel—a sharp contrast with the love of a settled life and the rather puritanical otherworldliness that marked the Pythagoreans. (Perhaps this point deserves further elucidation. The Orphics, representing the poorer peasantry, had tended to otherworldliness as a means of escape from a wretched situation. The Pythagoreans, who speak for landed conservatism, used this same tendency to deprecate the body and its strivings, to show that the material needs of so many people were, after all, no important consideration by comparison with the life of reason or "soul." This is, of course, their position in the period of the decline of the landed aristocracy. In their prime they had not been ascetic. The rising mercantilists, however, like the men of the Italian Renaissance, were worldly, vigorous, and lusty.)

> Now is the floor made clean, and the hands and cups of us all. One sets woven garlands on our heads, another passes around fragrant ointment in a broad, flat bowl.

> The mixing bowl stands in the midst, full of well-being. And there is more wine ready, that promises never to let us down, sweet in the jars and smelling of flowers. In the midst incense sends up its pure smoke. There is cold water, sweet and clean. Brown loaves lie before us and a splendid table, burdened with cheese and rich honey. The altar in the middle of the hall is covered on all sides with flowers. Song and merriment fill the halls. And first men of good will should hymn the god with holy tales and pure words.* And after pouring a libation and praying that we may be able to do what is just [the just things]—for in this one pursues that better way—then there is no insolence [*hybris*] to drink as much as one will and come home without an attendant—that is, if one is not too old. And of men we should praise him who after drinking acquits himself well as memory and voice prove excellent.[283]

Or, with even more charm:

> As in the season of winter, one reclines by the fire on a soft cushion, after a good meal, drinking sweet wine and crunching chestnuts [literally, chick peas], this is the kind of thing one should say. "From what country do you come, and how old are you, good sir? How old were you when the Persian made his invasion?"[284]

In Xenophanes, we might almost say, Ionian materialism is for the first time unified into a world picture, a monism. He was, as Aristotle observed, the first partisan of the "One."

All the tendencies of the early materialism found their climax and consummation in the philosophy of Heraclitus of Ephesus. The social development of Ionia, it should be remembered, was somewhat different from that of Attica. The geographical position of the Ionian cities, clinging, as it were, to the coastal fringe of Asia Minor, forced their peoples into the position of middlemen. There was less land to be had. The possession of landed estates

* This little genuflection in the direction of the traditional gods does not invalidate the interpretation. Nowadays many good materialists still sing carols on Christmas Eve.

was relatively unimportant. The men of Ionia were caught in historical times between the great empires of the interior, Lydia first and then Persia, and the world of the Aegean. Moreover, founded as they originally must have been as agricultural extensions of the mainland, the tribal structure was relatively weak in the islands. There was, therefore, no social bulwark behind which landed proprietors could have defended their pre-eminence and developed a landed aristocracy. They were forced to develop into another, i.e., a mercantile; development—with an interesting consequence: in several Ionian cities, and particularly, we may conjecture, in Miletus and Ephesus, the mercantile oligarchy had only one opponent, the lower classes. They were not forced, as were the Pericleans at Athens, to fight on two fronts, i.e., against aristocrats and left-wing democrats. This is the fundamental reason why they were able to face directly *their* problem, that of trade expansion, with its philosophical counterpart—motion, directly without finding a final static equilibrium lurking in the universe. And so, the break-up of the tribal structure in Ionia fostered a class of wealthy merchants. In Attica, the same social movements gave power at first to the great landholders. The struggle, therefore, between the wealthy landholders and the merchant and financial classes, a struggle which was so conspicuous a feature of Athenian history in the fifth century B.C., took quite different forms in a city like Miletus or Ephesus. This difference helps to explain why philosophy developed first in Ionia and why a theory of dialectics—although in a most primitive form—should develop in a thinker like Heraclitus. "There is not a sentence of Heraclitus," said Hegel, "which I have not taken up in my logic." Nor, in view of the peculiar social development of Ionia, is it surprising that a thinker like Heraclitus should combine two qualities of thought which at first sight, and to a modern, may seem clearly incompatible—an aloof, scornful, even patronizing attitude toward the "people"[285] with a profound interest in the laws of change and process.

The system of Heraclitus must be described in a few words. In the first place, he put forward the view that change is the eternal law of things, that everything is in flux and that nothing is static.[286] Heraclitus held that one could not step into the same river twice, for in the interval it had changed.[287] He believed that change and process was a result of strife and the conflict of oppositions within the unity of the whole.

> War [strife] is father of all things, king of all things; it has revealed some as gods and some as men; it has made some slaves, others free.[288]

One aphorism of Heraclitus clearly points to the connection of this thinking with Anaximander and serves to recall the social genesis of this line of thought:

> One must know that war is common [to all things] and *justice is strife;* and all things come into being in accordance with strife and necessity.[289]

These strivings were held together in a sublime, if unseen, harmony.

The invisible harmony is greater than the visible.[290] The unseen all-pervading law—the unity of striving oppositions—is greater and more significant than any apparent and temporary equilibrium. This law of the unity and strife of opposites is the common element in all process and change, though men fail to recognize it.[291] Not by an acquaintance with isolated and atomic facts is the mind nurtured and insight developed, but rather by recognition of the law of process.[292] The life of one substance is the death of another.

> The life of fire is the death of earth, and the life of air is the death of fire. The life of water is the death of air, and the life of earth is the death of water.[293]

The distinction between mind and spirit is not present to Heraclitus, just as it did not appear for his predecessors.

The content which he is able to give to his account of the laws of physical process is still of a very primitive kind. He is dominated by the relatively simple cosmic entities, the traditional four elements of the cosmogonists: earth, air, fire, and water. But it will be many centuries before philosophy will reach again a position so profound and illuminating as that of Heraclitus.

Before that day can come, the age-pervading dualisms must develop, and an infinitude of factual information about process must be collected; it will be necessary to observe the process and development of human society as embodied in history, and the process of change and development as studied in the natural sciences. Our task is to continue to analyze the way in which these necessary dichotomies were developed among the Greeks. Nor will it surprise us to find that, to men engaged in wrestling with these seductive dualisms, the position of Heraclitus who transcended them appeared murky and dark; that his dialectic seemed to later philosophers a mere collection of aphorisms, and the philosopher himself the supreme peddler of paradoxes. Until rescued by Hegel, for centuries Heraclitus has remained "the dark."

Once this analysis has been appreciated, it will be possible to recognize how difficult has been the problem of re-creating the philosophies of these early Ionian physicists. The Platonic dualisms have not yet arisen for these early thinkers. They are still working, however naïvely, with a monistic concept of the universe. To ask, therefore, whether this monism is ideal or material is grossly to misapprehend the historical problem. There could be for a man like Thales no contradiction between the statements "all things are water" and "all things are full of gods." Their "one" is like the Zeus of the Orphics.

> Zeus, lord of thunder the first and the last.
> Zeus the head, Zeus the middle, all things come from Zeus.
> Zeus the male, Zeus the immortal bride.
> Zeus the foundation of earth and of starry heaven.
> Zeus the king, Zeus himself begetter of all things.
> One might, one lord, the great ruler of all things,
> One kingly form, in which are all things enfolded,
> Fire and water and earth and air, night and day,
> And Thought, the first begetter, and Love, the much delighting.[294]

But once the dualisms developed, all the king's horses and all the king's men of the philosophical schools were not able to put them together again. Plato, in dismay at the discords that he has produced or developed within the seamless unity of life and thought, exclaims in distress, as children say in their games, "Give us both." (Which hand will you have? Give us both.) The one and the many, body and matter, change and permanence—we must have both.[295] But there can be no such facile reconciliation. Just to say "Give us both" is not synthesis but mechanical juxtaposition. The Stoics carried the gallant attempt further and endeavored to bridge the rift by imagining a universe which is monistic and *both* material and spiritual (fire and reason). It was an attempt that failed. Later Stoicism more and more dropped the material aspect of its system, and the *logos* became increasingly personalized as god, fate, and providence.

Now, the Stoics claimed Heraclitus as the founder of their school and read back their notions of the *logos* into Heraclitus. Most of the ancient commentators on Heraclitus are strongly influenced by the Stoic school. As a consequence, the effort of historical imagination required to appreciate this primitive dialectic is singularly great. As with the Eleatics, there is an endless scholarly argument between the theological and materialistic schools of interpretation. In the case of the Ionian school, the answer to any such question, once these thinkers are seen in their social and historical setting, must be "neither and both." To put the matter a little differently, in this period the opposition of material forces was turned around by the idealists. The clash of material opposites became the struggle of moral good and moral bad—the struggle of mind against matter, rule against anarchy, limit against chaos, god against the universe. And in such a conflict faith must believe that bad must somehow be subordinated to good and the oppositions reconciled.

When the ideas of the Ionian school migrated to Athens, they were enthusiastically caught up by the leaders of the democracy. Anaxagoras of Clazomenae became an intimate of Pericles and exercised a great influence on such diverse minds as Socrates and Euripides. It is a profoundly illuminating study to examine the changes and development of Greek thought in the mind of

Anaxagoras, and to notice the relation between his system and the ambiguous political position of the Periclean democrats. In *Who was Socrates?* we have already analyzed the relations of the thought of Anaxagoras with his position as spokesman of the moderate or Periclean wing of the democratic movement of Athens, with their Janus-like position and the necessity to battle on two fronts. Perhaps it will be permissible to repeat a part of that analysis:

"Corresponding exactly," we suggested, "to the ambiguous position of Pericles in the struggles of Athenian politics in the last two decades before the Peloponnesian War was the theoretical system of Anaxagoras, the philosopher of the Periclean age. Only by seeing the relation of the thinking of Socrates to that of Anaxagoras can the mind of Socrates be understood.

"The political world at Athens convinced Anaxagoras that change was ruthlessly real and that the security of any institution or class, perhaps even the Periclean democracy, was only relative to the tides of human progress and might be swept away in the inevitable process of things. The democracy had vanquished the oligarchy, but how long could the democracy of Pericles itself endure? It was just as frail and temporary as any other institution, and institutions, like plants and animals, were part of the great cycle of creation and destruction. Had man's social life no other security than an endless series of transformations? As Anaxagoras contemplated the political world of democratic Athens, he must have been struck by an arresting phenomenon: how the cool, aloof, Olympian mind of Pericles dominated the chaos and the confusion, just as the city of the maiden Athena—Athena, type of the divine wisdom, born in full panoply and complete maturity from the very mind of Zeus—could order the chaos of Aegean politics. And just as the political position of Pericles was ambiguous and paradoxical, a blend of the progressive and the static, so two opposite movements manifest themselves in the thinking of his friend Anaxagoras. On the one hand, there is the consciousness of change and process, of mixture and separation.[296]

"One side of Anaxagoras, therefore, expressed the most vigorous radical skepticism. It embodied the scientific curiosity of the materialists, who carried into philosophy the enquiring spirit of the new democracy. Unhesitatingly it sought for rational explanations of all physical phenomena in terms of structure and causality. As far as science was concerned, Anaxagoras carried on the tradition of the Ionic school, whose researches and speculations dealt largely with tangible reality and natural causes.

"The other side of his thinking, however, presents a sharp contrast to the materialistic cosmology and, in fact, clearly represents a retreat from materialism and science. A world composed of bodily existence and process was not, for the reason we have indicated, enough to satisfy Anaxagoras. At this point he departed completely from previous physical philosophies by introducing the agency of *NOUS*, or mind, as the center of integration and order in the universe and as one stable principle which is unaffected by the law of change."

But now it is necessary for the understanding of the background of Plato to carry the analysis a step further and to exhibit and explain the changes that Anaxagoras introduced into the development of the philosophy of change. Anaxagoras, as we have said, represents a transition from the dialectical interpretation of Heraclitus, the culmination of Ionian physical philosophy, to the atomistic materialism of Democritus. There are important elements of Heraclitean dialectic still to be found in Anaxagoras. There is still the strife of opposites, but with a profound difference. The oppositions in Heraclitus are interactive forces, dynamic and creative of a universe. The interaction of forces in the earlier thinker is the very essence and explanation of the whole cosmic process. But with Anaxagoras the concept is beginning to lose vitality. The concept of oppositions is transformed and altered. Instead of an active interplay of forces, we now get an abstract counterposition of qualities, oppositions to be sure, but mere qualitative principles that can in no sense serve as keys to the explanation of change.

> "One must know," Heraclitus had said, "that war is common [to all things] and that justice is strife; and

> all things come into being in accordance with strife and necessity."[297]

Here we have a clear formulation of the dynamic power of the strife of opposites. But in Anaxagoras these oppositions have become simply qualitative differentiations. He says, for example:

> The things that are in one world are not separated from one another nor sundered with an ax—*neither the warm from the cold nor the cold from the warm.*[298]

He speaks of other pairs of qualities: rare and dense, light and dark, moist and dry. This is very different from the position of Heraclitus, which stresses an active opposition of forces—a constant interaction, even of the qualities:

> Cold things *become warm,* and what is warm *cools;* what is wet *dries,* and the parched is *made moist.*[299]

With Anaxagoras these qualitative oppositions are separated off, i.e. are mechanically opposed.[300]

From this point we are led directly to the problem of motion, its place and function in the cosmos, as well as its source. Anaxagoras has emptied the dialectic of its content, has taken away the strife of forces which for Heraclitus served as the immanent, self-explanatory ground of change. As we have seen, in the Heraclitean dialectic motion is inseparable from the immanent process. With Anaxagoras, the dialectic is deprived of its internal motive power and he is forced, therefore, to reconsider the whole problem of motion. Motion is no longer self-explanatory; he feels compelled to postulate a source of movement *external* to the process of physical change.

This will serve to explain the introduction of *NOUS* as the agency, responsible for change.

> And *NOUS* controlled the whole revolution, so that it began to revolve in the beginning . . . And this revolution made them to be separated off, and the rare is separated from the dense and the warm from the cold and the light from the dark and the dry from the moist.[301]

It is interesting to see physical philosophy for the first time beginning to compromise with the Eleatic assertion of unity and singleness of Being. Anaxagoras in philosophy has his counterpart in politics—the wealthy democrats who are forced, as it were, to fight on two fronts.

> All other things partake in a portion of everything, while *NOUS* is infinite and *self-ruled,* and is mixed with nothing, but is alone, itself by itself. For if it were not by itself, but were mixed with anything else, it would partake in all things if it were mixed with any; for in everything there is a portion of everything, as has been said by me in what has gone before, and the things mixed with it would hinder it, so that it would have power over nothing in the same way, that it has now, being alone by itself. For it is the thinnest of all things and the purest, and it has all knowledge about everything and the greatest strength; and *NOUS* has power over all things, both greater and smaller, that have life.[302]

Two or three things are worth noticing. *NOUS* must, he thought, be kept separate from the universe of particulars lest it be hindered in its function and contaminated in its purity. But there is not yet the opposition of Mind as spiritual to Body as material. Though in a sense *NOUS* is a creator, it is still conceived in material terms; it is matter but of a different consistency. And yet, there is here in germ the later theory of the Creator and first mover of a created universe.

Leaving *NOUS*, we turn again to the universe of movement. In Anaxagoras' conception *NOUS* seems to have been responsible for the first "revolution" which set the whole process going and caused the separation of opposite qualities. This separation may be thought of as a kind of polarization, but a polarization which was never complete—black always contains a share of white and white of black.[303] In other words, pure and complete whiteness is never opposed to total blackness. A thing is white or black because quantitatively one particular characteristic, such as whiteness or blackness, predominates in one place. This is the explanation that Anaxagoras gives of the process by which a "primary undifferentiated homogeneity" becomes the world of differentiation and complexity and things.

> Before they were separated off, when all things were together, not even any color was distinguishable; for the mixture of all things prevented it.[304]

It is as though within the primary mass separate elements were undistinguishable because they cancel each other out, as colors mixed on a palette blend into a colorless grey. The old Ionian notion of a universal homogeneous material element is here revived, as the dialectical explanation of Heraclitus fades. In passing, we may note a new direction in the history of physical philosophy. Thales and Anaximenes seem never to have regarded as a difficulty the change from original homogeneity—their universal "substratum"—to a world of things and particular objects. But to Anaxagoras the problem presents a real difficulty, particularly in view of the criticism which the rival Eleatics were making by propounding the question of how anything can become what it is not, or in other words, change. Anaxagoras asks himself much the same question:

> How can hair come from what is not hair, or flesh from what is not flesh?[305]

The answer, he thought, must be sufficient to explain the plurality of material objects. Merely asserting with Anaximenes that some such substance as air lay behind all diversity left a gap between the simple, primary matter and the complex variety of phenomena. Evidently, he felt, there must be some more satisfactory way of explaining plurality. Therefore, he felt that the immeasurable qualities of each developed thing must exist somehow in an unformed way in the seeds. Here we can perceive a kind of crude adumbration of the later and subtler Aristotelian doctrine of potentiality. It will clarify our own understanding, however, to realize that this is *not yet* the doctrine of potentiality, which posits an abstract *capacity* for becoming. It is almost as though, in Anaxagoras' thought, all the factors for the full development of a thing exist in a preformed state in the seeds. Here we have the primary polarization carried one step further. Just as in the first revolution which *NOUS* sets in motion particles of the opposites cohere at one pole, so in the seeds, particles or factors of all the qualities cohere (again, in an unformed state), and the seed partakes of all qualities.

> And since these things are so, we must suppose that there are contained many things and of all sorts in the things that are uniting, seeds of all things, with all sorts of shapes and colors and savors, and the men have been formed in them and the other animals that have life. And that these men have inhabited cities and cultivated fields as with us: and that they have a sun and a moon and the rest as with us; and that their earth brings forth for them many things of many kinds. . . .[306]

This interpretation seems to be substantiated by the exposition of Aristotle, and later of Lucretius. Aristotle says of the *homœomeria*:

> Anaxagoras of Clazomenae—prior to Empedocles in point of age, but posterior in his activities—says that the first principles are infinite in number. For he says that as a general rule all things which are, like fire and water, *homœomerous*, are generated and destroyed in this sense only, by combination and differentiation; otherwise they are neither generated nor destroyed, but persist eternally.[307]

And in Lucretius:

> Let us now also examine the *homœomeria* of Anaxagoras, as the Greeks term it, which the poverty of our native speech does not allow us to name in our own tongue; though it is easy enough to set forth in words the thing itself. First of all, then, when he speaks of the *homœomeria* of things, you must know he supposes bones to be formed out of very small and minute bones and flesh of very small and minute fleshes and blood by the coming together of many drops of blood, and gold he thinks can be composed of grains of gold and earth be a concretion of small earths and fire can come from

> fires and water from waters, and everything else he fancies and supposes to be produced on a like principle. And yet at the same time he does not allow that void exists anywhere in things or that there is a limit to the division of things.
>
> . . . here some slight opening is left for evasion, which Anaxagoras avails himself of, choosing to suppose that all things, though latent, are mixed up in things, and that is alone visible of which there are the largest number of bodies in the mixture and these more ready to hand and stationed in the first rank.[308]

For the purpose of exposition we might even sharpen the distinctness of these various levels, the primitive polarization, the seeds of all living things, and the particles which go to make up the seeds. But there would be danger as well as gain in so representing the situation to our imagination. It does not seem likely that Anaxagoras made any clear distinction between the "behavior" of matter, subject to the mechanical laws of the movement of particles, and biological law, which explains the growth of seeds. Both are present confusedly and, it seems, mixed as a cause of explanation. It is enough to notice that here again the movement of philosophy will proceed by a process of bifurcation—the materialists are to develop the notion of particles into the atomic theory, the idealists will catch up and expand the notion of levels, but subordinate everything to ideal and teleological causes.

It has already been suggested that the inconsistencies of Anaxagoras' position reflect in thought the ambiguities of his social status. And if from the standpoint of intellectual consistency this is manifest weakness, it is from the standpoint of intellectual influence a clear gain. Anaxagoras and his system stand at the parting of many ways. From his concept of *NOUS*, which Socrates was to find so unsatisfactory, developed the idealistic monism of Plato. From his physics, which (presumably) Archelaus was to find unsatisfactory because it compromised with idealism, is to develop the more mature physical philosophy of the atomic school. As the transformation of the primitive material dialectic proceeds further in the direction of mechanical and atomistic materialism, certain aspects of the problem of nature are inevitably neglected and in fact are developed only by the idealists: the problem, in other words, of "levels" of reality and behavior. This is, as we shall see, one of the really important positive aspects of the Platonic philosophy. Plato was very much conscious of the need for a hierarchical arrangement of thought corresponding to the increasing complexity of the phenomena studied. It is no accident, therefore, that there lurk in the philosophy of Anaxagoras the atomic particles of Democritus. But also, in the distinction between *NOUS* and the primitive homogeneous stuff, in the differentiation of the primary stuff into qualitative opposites, and in the discovery within these opposites of "seeds," we have a faint foreshadowing of the degrees and levels of truth and reality as finally developed by Plato. If we add that here there is present in germ the Aristotelian problem of actuality and potentiality, and that Aristotle catches up again (though on a higher level) the Anaxagorean notion of *NOUS* as the source of motion, the ground and explanation of change, we shall appreciate, perhaps, how extremely influential and suggestive was the philosophical system of the great theoretical spokesman of the Periclean democracy, the man whom contemporaries venerated and mocked as though he were "Mind" itself.

Closely bound up in a social sense with the philosophical position of Anaxagoras was, in its first stages, a movement that has since been called the sophistic movement. The Sophists can be described in a word as the educators of democratic Athens. They were itinerant and professional teachers, who frequently excited the wrath of patrician thinkers because they took pay for their services.[309]

While we notice that the Sophists attracted for the most part wealthy young men and charged some extravagant fees (Protagoras is said to have charged 100 minas[310]), it is a mistake to think that for that reason they aligned themselves "with the classes rather than the masses." This misconception, which is only too often repeated, stems from a misconception about the political and social issues in fifth-century Greece. The struggle between oligarchs and democrats was *not* wholly a struggle between rich and poor, but between two ways of gaining wealth, between landed aristocracy on the one hand, and the rising mercantilism on the other. Many leaders of the democracy from the middle to the end of the fifth century were personally wealthy men. Just how one tendency within sophism evolved in an antidemocratic direction we shall shortly see.

In teaching rhetoric or political and domestic management it was almost inevitable that they should touch on problems of philosophy, and at least two of the early Sophists, Protagoras and Prodicus, made important philosophical contributions.

Of the social relations of Protagoras there can be not the slightest doubt. He was born in Abdera early in the fifth century (around 480 B.C.). His origin was lowly, and he is said to have begun his career as a porter; even in this lowly occupation he showed signs of inventive talent, for Aristotle attributed to him the invention of the porter's pad. Giving up this calling, he became an itinerant teacher and was attracted to Athens like so much of the talent of his time by the fame of the imperial city and perhaps by the enlightened policy of Pericles. That his affinities continued to be democratic and that he did not, like Socrates, change with increasing recognition as a section of the democratic party moved to the right is indicated by the fact that he became a lawgiver for the colony of Thurii at the request of Pericles, and also that he was attacked at the end of a long life by a prominent member of the Four Hundred[311] on the charge of atheism, condemned, and his books publicly burned.[312]

There is some evidence, moreover, that he was suspected of "Medism," a stock charge levelled against the democratic leaders since the time of Marathon. We need only remember that, according to one account,[313] the same charge was levelled against Anaxagoras. Nor should it surprise us when we remember that an important part of this early sophistic teaching dealt with the relativity of institutions. We can understand why to argue that the Persian institutions had the same kind of validity as the Athenian must have seemed like treason to the super-patriots of the opposite political party. (To praise Spartan institutions, however, seemed to these same critics, strangely enough, both intelligent and just.)

The known facts of his social relations are confirmed by what we know of his philosophy. This has been much misunderstood, and two writers are mainly responsible. Plato was, as we shall see more clearly later, moved by a profound social and philosophical aversion to relativism in all its forms. Sextus Empiricus* gives us an interesting account of Protagoras' teaching, but it is to some extent perverted by the desire which is manifested all through his book to make of every previous thinker a skeptic and pure relativist. A careful examination of the crucial passage in Sextus[314] will make this clear.

> And Protagoras wants man to be the measure of all things: those that are, how [or that] they are, those that are not, how [or that] they are not.

The fact that Sextus in another passage quotes exactly the same words makes it seem likely that we have here reproduced the very language of Protagoras. A great deal will depend on the translation of the Greek word which may mean either *that* ("that they are") or *how* ("how they are"). Scholars influenced by Plato and one interpretation of Sextus have tended to translate as *that* and so make Protagoras into a pure relativist. Man becomes the standard for the existence of things and the *esse* of things is *percipi*. We can, perhaps, translate it by *how*, making man the standard not of the existence of things but of their *manner* of existence. There is, as we shall see, definite justification for this view in the passage of Sextus.

> To continue, by measure he means criterion, and by thing he means affair, so that he says that potentially man is the criterion of all affairs, those that are, how (or that) they are, those that are not, how they are not. So he

* SEXTUS EMPIRICUS (second and third centuries A.D.)

Sextus Empiricus, who lived in Alexandria and Athens, was a physician of the Asklepiadean school and greatest of the later Greek Skeptics. He developed the doctrines of the old Skeptics and handed down a complete account of members of the school. He wrote *Pyrrhonian Hypotyposes* and *Against the Mathematici*.

> postulates what appears to each man, and so introduces the principle of relativism.

This last sentence seems to point to an interpretation in terms of pure relativism. But a little while later[315] Sextus makes it quite clear that Protagoras believed in the real and independent existence of matter; what is relative is simply the individual man's perceptions of matter.

> The man says that matter is in flux and as it flows additions are made continuously in place of the things given off and perceptions are changed and altered in accordance with age and other bodily conditions. And he says that the explanation of all phenomena lies in matter; matter can be in itself all that it can seem to be to all men. But men grasp now one side of it and now another in accordance with their differing predispositions. The man who is natural [or normal] by disposition can grasp that which can appear to the natural [or normal] disposition, the unnatural [or abnormal] can grasp only that which can appear to the unnatural [or abnormal], and the same account holds true of conditions like age, sleeping, waking, and other forms of predisposition. And so according to him man is the standard of existence.

It need hardly be emphasized that this is quite a different interpretation than that of *esse est percipi*. In noticing that one's perceptions are conditioned by all sorts of antecedent and contemporary experiences, that two men with different training, in different moods or different physical conditions, will actually *see* things differently, while a profound and interesting observation for this stage in the development of science and thought, is by no means the same thing as to say that the existence of external matter depends on its being perceived. In fact he says just the opposite. He maintains the reality of matter—"matter in flux and and matter differently perceived."

Just what was Protagoras' theory of matter, whether it was nearer to the "dialectics" of Heraclitus or to the atomism of Democritus, it is impossible with our scant evidence to determine. In spite of the constant tendency in our tradition to link Protagoras with Democritus, it seems probable that the use by Sextus of the word *rheousēs* points to an affinity with the older materialism of Heraclitus rather than the new and emerging atomism of Democritus.

After giving this clear and inescapable account of Protagoras' views, Sextus slips once again into his own skeptical relativism.

> For everything that appears to a man also exists, whereas things that do not appear to any of mankind do not exist.

But in his summary he is unable to escape the conclusion that there is an "objective" element in the philosophy of Protagoras (which he calls *dogmatism*), and he connects this with the real existence of matter and its flux, as well as with the view that ultimate explanations lie in material things—not, as the idealists argued, in a spiritual reality which alone can explain the unreal and the material.

> We see, therefore, that in his views about the flux of matter, and [in the view] that the explanations of phenomena are to be found in matter, he dogmatizes; these things are not clear and we [i.e. the Skeptics] should withhold judgment.

After clearing away these misconceptions about the philosophy of Protagoras (there is no need any longer for us to toy with the absurdly unreal problem whether he meant by man, man generically or individual man), we can give a brief account of this first of the Sophists. He was, first and most important, a materialist. Seeing no need to defend any particular social vested interest, he also saw no need to postulate, as the Pythagoreans did, an ideal ruling principle as a sanction for conduct and a bulwark against change. Institutions, customs, and ideas were for him relative to a given historical situation, as they were for so many progressive Greeks in this epoch. This is perhaps best represented by Herodotus; his whole history is in one sense a demonstration of the same theme: the infinite variety of human customs, and yet because of old associations each prefers his own.

> For if one should propose to all men a choice, bidding them choose the best customs from all the customs that there are, each race of men, after examining them all, would select those of his own people; thus all think that their own customs are by far the best . . . Now of the fact that all men are thus wont to think about their own customs we may judge by many other proofs and more especially by this which follows:—Darius in the course of his reign summoned those of the Hellenes who were present in his land, and asked them for what price they would consent to eat up their fathers when they died; and they answered that no price would induce them to do so. After this Darius summoned those Indians who are called Callatians, who eat their parents, and asked them in the presence of the Hellenes, who understood what was said by the help of an interpreter, for what payment they would consent to consume with fire the bodies of their fathers when they died; and they cried aloud and bade him keep silence from such words. Thus, then, these things are established by usage, and I think that Pindar spoke rightly in his verse, when he said that "of all things law is king."[316]

This in philosophical form is the most important intuition of Protagoras. And one can see how important is this doctrine for a *progressive* social position.

In rejecting the idea of any fixed and unalterable principles of absolute validity in human affairs, he also expresses skepticism about the divine.

> As regards the gods I am not able to know whether they exist or do not exist and what they are like in form. There are many things that hinder knowledge—the obscurity of the subject and the shortness of human life.[317]

We recall just how important the divine was to the Pythagoreans as establishing a sanction for the ruling principle both within the state and within the individual. We cannot wonder that the more democratic thinkers should reject any such principle as tending to a defense of institutions that they regarded as indefensible; even though all the gods were not as conservative and oligarchical in their teaching as the Delphic Apollo. This part of the sophistic position and its social implication is nicely reflected in a fragment from Euripides:

> To do good to the living; for every man when he is dead is earth and shadow.[318]

The relativism of Protagoras was developed into the famous distinction between *nomos* (law or custom) and *physis* (nature). The Sophists held in general that laws and institutions were a thing of custom and convention and had nothing to do with the eternal nature of things. Idealists, however, regarded human institutions as having their sanction in the nature of the eternal and refused to admit the distinction between "convention" and "nature." Some later writers take the distinction back as far as Heraclitus. But while this is, in a sense, the spirit of his teaching, it is probable that this particular formula of exposition is a later construction. For example, Hippocrates[319] says of Heraclitus:

> He does not admit that law and custom agree with one another. For men have created custom by themselves with no real knowledge of the things concerning which they established it, but the gods created the "nature" of all things.

In the fifth century the opposition becomes fairly sharp; the Pythagorean Philolaus[320] uses the phrase "by nature or not by custom" (though he applies it to a mathematical theorem). The materialist Archelaus[321] uses the phrase "by custom and not by nature" and argues that what is just and what is depraved is so because of convention and not because of anything in the nature of things. Incidentally the coincidence of sophistic relativism and materialistic thinking is never clearer than in this more radical disciple of Anaxagoras. A good example of this kind of argument is put by Plato (whether historically or not we need not here discuss) into the mouth of the sophist Hippias.

> "Gentlemen of my audience," he said, "I regard you as relatives, neighbors, and fellow citizens by nature and not by convention. For the like is by nature related to the

> like, whereas custom—the tyrant—brings compulsion to many human affairs in contravention of nature."[322]

The argument which Plato put into the mouth of the sophist Thrasymachus (again whether historically or not is not to our purpose here), when he argues that justice is the interest of the ruling class, is another form of the same argument: nature—convention. And in a sense the whole task of Plato in the *Republic* is to demonstrate that justice is firmly grounded in nature and human nature. Thrasymachus' argument is, of course, the reflection in ethics and politics of the old doctrine of Heraclitus that justice is to be found in the process of material and social change and not something which stands above and apart from process. This will, perhaps, enable us to understand not only why Plato attacks Thrasymachus with so much vigor and so little scruple, but also why he cherishes a quite unphilosophical resentment against those who (like, for example, Cratylus) hold that all reality is in a constant process of change.

It is moreover vital to notice that the argument of the early Sophists and Thrasymachus is in a sense ethically neutral. And it can evolve in one of two directions. It may develop in a thoroughly democratic direction, to a defense of equality, fostering an ethic that calls for the greatest good of the greatest number. But this evolution was difficult, almost impossible, for the democrats of the fifth and early fourth centuries. Too many of mankind were left out of the range of their ethical sympathy. There were, in particular, the slaves, and to expect that even a democrat among the classical Greeks would extend the cloak of his sympathy and his theory to the slaves would be to expect too much.

Astonishingly enough, there are indications that some enlightened writers of the late fifth and early fourth centuries did actually question the eternal validity of the institution of slavery. Aristotle tells us that some thought that slavery was a "conventional" and not a "natural" institution.

> To some it seems "unnatural" to be masters of slaves. For by "convention" one man is a slave and another man is free, but in "nature" there is no difference.[323]

The thoroughly democratic perception of Lycophron that

> there is no *real* difference between lowly and nobly born[324]

was by Antiphon, the Sophist, extended to non-Greek peoples:

> By nature we are all alike, Greeks and barbarians—for we all breathe the same air;[325]

and by such thinkers as Alcidamas (a pupil of the famous Gorgias) and Philemon the essential equality of mankind was conceived to embrace even slaves:

> God has sent forth all men as free, nature has not made any man a slave.[326]

Philemon says:

> By nature no one was ever born a slave.[327]

But this was a tendency that did not and could not develop. And so the progressive philosophy of the ancient world ended in the bogs of skepticism and futility or else in the labored tranquillity of the Epicurean ivory tower.[328]

But from this ethically neutral observation another position might evolve, and historically did so: to say that justice is the interest of the stronger might be used as a defense of force, of cynicism, of brutal repression and strong-arm methods. And so it need not surprise us that from the sophistic school emerged men who, like Critias,* used the sophistic method of argument from sophistic premises and were equally irreligious and materialistic in their outlook, but drew the conclusion in a different direction—political terrorism and cynical brutality. This process

* CRITIAS (died 403 B.C.)

Critias, son of Callaeschrus, a youth educated by Gorgias and Socrates, was imprisoned in 415 for implication in the mutilation of the Hermae. In 411 he aided in recalling Alcibiades who had been banished for instigation of the above crime. He was banished by the democracy in 407 for antidemocratic activity, and fled the country. In 404, however, he was made ephor by the oligarchical party, and was one of the cruelest and most unscrupulous of the Thirty tyrants appointed by the Lacedaemonians in 404. He was slain in battle against the returning democrats and Thrasybulus.

should not surprise us, seeing that in our own generation the pure anthropological relativism of a decade or so ago has gone—in the case of several representatives of the school—in a similarly reactionary direction.

We have seen that in its first stages the progressive philosophy, reflecting as it did the first sharp social encounter consequent upon the breakup of the tribal order, developed in primitive fashion the outline of a material dialectic. It remains, in order to complete this outline sketch, to notice that the maturity of the mercantile development nurtured and fostered the spirit of sheer individualism and that this spirit of individualism was in turn reflected in the development of material atomism. This development can best be seen in the person of Democritus and to him we must briefly turn.

Democritus

We may, for convenience, link Democritus with the progressive tradition in Greek philosophy, although as we examine his ethical notions, we shall notice a real difference, corresponding to the change that had come over the social and political scene since the days of Heraclitus. We have observed that the social forces which were released by the decay of tribal society, the bitter oppositions of landowners or wealthy merchants to the landless and the dispossessed, suggested to thinkers like Anaximander or Heraclitus the notion of the strife of opposites as the explanation of process within the universe. We have observed, too, how this same social movement led to the increasingly felt opposition between body and soul, the material universe and the "mind," its ground of explanation and being; between the world of change and formlessness and unreality, and the ideal, the changeless, and the "limiting." We have noticed that the Pythagoreans and Eleatics, in their desire to defend the privileges of an aristocratic caste, were led to put their emphasis on the soul, the ideal, the changeless, and the "limiting," all principles of "law and order," whether within the universe, the state, or the individual human being.

By the end of the fifth century new social factors had entered to create new intellectual movements. We have in the first place —the rise of individualism. The development of Greek mercantilism, like its sixteenth- and seventeenth-century counterpart, had encouraged in the individual democrat the sense of self-sufficiency and individual independence. The relation between producer and consumer had become increasingly an abstract relationship. Less and less did the individual feel the need for group or national associations. And particularly in those cities which had lost their political independence, which had succumbed to the onrush of Athenian imperialism, a wealthy merchant class tended to put in the forefront of its ethical thinking—not justice, but individual self-satisfaction, happiness, tranquillity, or some such ideal as these.

This change is extremely important to appreciate, not only for the understanding of Plato; he, as we shall see later, in the *Republic* so far succumbs to the spirit of the time (and perhaps to the influence of Democritus) that he begins with the atomic, isolated individual in building up his imaginative state and endeavors to find some principle of mutual dependence.* But even more it reveals with great clarity the profound weakness of ancient materialism, and to dwell on this point (though it may seem at first sight more germane to the later history of ancient philosophy) will help us to explain to ourselves the relative helplessness of the materialistic schools in the face of Plato's opposition. Ancient materialism, which up to the late fifth century had developed in opposition to aristocratic idealism and had proved an effective weapon in the hands of democratic protagonists, now tends to become the point of view of the depoliticalized and comfortable classes in a wider, cosmopolitan world. As the small, neat, ordered polity of the city-states breaks down, to be merged in larger political units, culminating in the "world-wide" empire of Rome, many men who in the fifth century would have played an active part in the political life of a sovereign state leave politics now to "specialists" in the imperial capital and devote themselves to the things of the body, comfort, luxuries, and refinements. Or, in reaction against this tendency, more sensitive individuals pro-

* See below, Chap. 8.

claim that the pleasures of the intellect are more enduring than those of the body. They preach simplicity of life and the tranquillity of the spirit, detachment from the disturbing influences of ambition or avarice and the like. As philosophy, and in particular materialistic philosophy, became detached from the immediate political struggles of the city-state, it tended to become individualistic (and universalistic—the two tendencies march side by side). This is reflected in ethics in the doctrine that pleasure, individual ego-satisfaction, is the only goal of striving; in physics, the tendency finds expression in the "atomism" of Democritus and his successors, the school of Epicurus.

Democritus seems to have been born of a wealthy family in Abdera—a city on the Thracian mainland opposite Thasos. It is interesting to notice in the light of what we have just said that before the Persian invasions Abdera had been subject to Persia, that in the defeat of Persia she became part of the Athenian empire and revolted in the disastrous period after the failure of the Sicilian expedition. Abdera had not known political independence all through the fifth century when democratic Athens was at the height of its renown. This will explain why in some respects Democritus was ahead of his time.

His father Damasippus, according to one account,[330] entertained Xerxes on his way through Abdera, in the ill-fated expedition against Greece. From this we can conjecture that the family was from the Persian point of view politically "reliable." The son was probably born around 460 B.C. and was educated by the Magi in Persian and Babylonian "science." In his youth he seems to have come under Pythagorean influence, and he probably wrote his early works under this influence—a life of Pythagoras and a book on the Tritogeneia (thrice-born) in which he expounded the view that Athena, the goddess of wisdom, was called "thrice-born" because wisdom gives birth to three excellencies: to think well, to speak well, and to do well.[331]

His father left him a very considerable fortune, and this he quite characteristically spent in travel, so that he was reduced to great penury.[332] Travel was a favorite aid to education in the Greek age of "enlightenment." Herodotus gained from travel a skeptical relativism; Democritus, the germs of a cosmopolitan ethic.

On his return, penniless, his brother came to his rescue and gave him a tiny house to live in. Many anecdotes are preserved to give us a vivid picture of the man, his devotion to study, to science, and to something like the experimental method. One will suffice as a characterization. We are told that an event happened in Abdera which seemed, to many of the superstitious, miraculous and of profound portent. A respected and bald-headed citizen was walking outside the town when a tortoise fell from the sky and killed him. The eagle, the bird of Zeus, was seen in the sky. Democritus gave the event a thoroughly naturalistic explanation, resolutely dismissing talk of the supernatural or of fate. Eagles like the meat of tortoises, but sometimes find it difficult to get from the shell. They have, therefore, learned to drop the creatures from a great height on shining rocks, which shatter the shell and make available the meat. The eagle had simply mistaken the man's bald head for the splendor of a rock.[333] Democritus remarked that he preferred to find the explanation for one natural phenomenon rather than to become king of the Persians.[334] Such a devotion to science and scientific investigation strikes a refreshing note in classical antiquity. Incidentally, it is something to notice that his prose style and his oratory called forth warm praise from the pious and critical Cicero, who even mentions him in the same breath with Plato.[335]

When we deal with Democritus, we find ourselves faced with one of the perennial and insoluble questions of scholarship—that of his relations with Leucippus. It is a problem like that of Socrates-Plato or Pythagoras-Philolaus, and equally difficult to unravel; as a consequence it has given rise to one of the great controversies of nineteenth-century scholarship.[336] Was Leucippus the inventor of the atomic theory, or did Democritus use Leucippus as a mouthpiece just as Plato had used Socrates? Into this argument we shall not enter. But approaching the problem, as we do, from the examination of a philosopher's political and social convictions, we are content to notice that somewhere within the firm of Leucippus-Democritus, Inc. there is a transition, even a contradiction. "Democritus" stands out as a staunch and outspoken defender of democracy on the one hand.

> Poverty in democracy is as much preferable to well-being—so-called—under monarchs, as the lot of a free man is to that of a slave.[337]

Or again,

> A fine thing is equality in all things. Excess and deficiency do not commend themselves to me.[338]

Let us recall from the last chapter the importance of "equality" in democratic thinking.

But he is at the same time the forerunner, one might almost say, the founder of cosmopolitan individualism. His theory of pleasure or ego-satisfaction is the herald of a new day. He is said to have remarked that all human affairs are worthy only of laughter.

> He mocked everything, on the ground that all human affairs are worthy only of laughter.[339]

It is not for nothing that a later commentator called him the "laughing philosopher." There is no need to dismiss or to tone down such a paradox, nor need it necessarily point to two thinkers. Democritus was the philosopher of a great transition, and it is no uncommon phenomenon to find a man who expresses the mood of the old era as well as foreshadows the new.

We can only glance in a very cursory way at his philosophy in order to round out our conception of the intellectual atmosphere that Plato breathed. Democritus set himself energetically in opposition to the Eleatic denial of change and the many. But change and plurality depend on space, void. Being he defined as the full, not-being the empty, the void.[340] The atoms are eternal, invisible, and very small. They are homogeneous and differ only in shape, position, and arrangement.[341] Things are, he argues, hot or cold, sweet or bitter, hard or soft by *convention*; in *reality* there exist only atoms and void.[342] This is a very sensible disposition of the "nature-convention" argument and seems very much like a development of the position of Protagoras as we have noticed it earlier in this chapter. It admits the relativity of sense impressions (and we should, perhaps add, human institutions) without denying the objective existence of a material world.

In his account of the forces that cause atoms to "dispart and combine" he is not so happy. We have noticed how the primitive notion of oppositions in Anaximander and Heraclitus gradually breaks down as men like Anaxagoras compromise with the Eleatic criticism and try to find something permanent in the universe and some principle of reconcilation. With Democritus, this breakdown goes even further. His account of the "source of motion" is based on observation of the facts of gravitation. His observation that bodies fall downward he, rather naively, transferred to nature as a whole and assumed that heavier bodies fall faster than lighter ones. (This is, of course, founded on observation, but it is a misconstruction of the observed facts.) As a result, he thought that an eddy or vortex was set up.[343] In this way atoms of similar sizes and shapes came together to cohere and we have the passage from the homogeneous world of atoms to the heterogeneous world of things. In this way he is able to preserve the "vortex" of his predecessors, but at the cost of a mistaken interpretation of gravitation. A little more observation and his successor, Epicurus, will have to introduce chance, the "swerve" which causes atoms to jangle together and cohere. But this is, of course, unsatisfactory, and leaves materialism open to idealistic criticism. The cause of motion cannot be satisfactorily explained as a kind of endless gravitation with an uncaused swerve moving the atoms from the perpendicular. To avoid such perplexities materialism must recall the primitive insights of its first proponents—the unity and strife of oppositions—as an adequate explanation of the immanent cause of motion in the world.

Nonetheless, the system of Democritus is amazingly mature. He dealt with an almost infinite range of subject matter and always in naturalistic terms—anatomy, perception, human evolution, and the way to achieve happiness. In some ways his system is as advanced as that of the eighteenth-century mechanical materialists in France, or the deists in England. He was on intimate terms with the great anatomists and physicians of fifth-century Greece, particularly Hippocrates.[344] And the mention of Hippocrates will remind us of another aspect of thought among the more progressive Greeks.

One extremely important social function of philosophy is to protect science against the kind of idealistic criticism which would make research in (what we call today) the social, historical, or natural sciences impossible. We have already seen that the idealistic position as carried to its logical conclusion in the position of Zeno would have had just that effect. If motion, change, process are all illusion, what sense is there in studying them? But finding the laws of *process* is exactly what we mean by science. We have observed that Democritus, faced with the Eleatic position, found it necessary to establish an opposing principle that would make scientific investigation possible.

There seems to be plenty of ground for suspecting that Greek scientists were very conscious of the need to protest against the idealistic domination of philosophy if their investigations were to make progress. One of the earliest of Greek medical investigators takes a forthright stand in opposition to the Pythagoreans. It is interesting to notice, too, that medicine is one of the few sciences to make great advances in the Greek world. We may connect this with the rising price of slaves and with the fact that even aristocrats are sometimes ill.

Alcmaeon of Croton (Croton, we remember, was the center of Pythagorean influence) is perhaps the first individual whom we can describe as a medical *scientist* (although up to that time there had been a flourishing traditional medical *practice* connected with the cult of the healing god Aesculapius.) Alcmaeon is credited with the discovery of the optic nerve,[345] with the importance of the brain for thinking,[346] with theories about the canals of the ear.[347] Theophrastus (a good authority, a pupil of Aristotle, a botanist and thoroughgoing scientist) says that he related the perceptions of all senses in some fashion to the brain.[348] He is also said to have been the first to attempt to remove the eye by means of an operation.[349] He also remarked that man differs from the animal kingdom in his power of thought; animals have sensation but not thought, man has both.[350] Scholars and writers on the history of medicine, repeating each other rather uncritically, have often spoken of Alcmaeon as a Pythagorean.[351] This is most unlikely. It is true that a late writer speaks of him as a pupil of Pythagoras; (but students do not always follow throughout their lifetimes the philosophical opinions of their teachers). He is said to have dedicated his book to three Pythagoreans, but when we examine the fragment, we do not find much support for this assertion.

> Alcmaeon of Croton, the son of Perithoös, says this to Brontinos, Leon, and Bathyllus,[352] "The gods have clear insight into things unseen, as well as about mortal things; we as mortals can only infer the following."

Apart from the very debatable question whether these gentlemen were really Pythagoreans, it is a little surprising to find this introduction described as a dedication. It may just as well be controversy, an ironical willingness to leave transcendental matters to the gods and Pythagoreans, while he (Alcmaeon) confines himself to things which are verifiable by the means that he has at hand. This interpretation is made infinitely probable by a consideration of the most famous of his fragments.

> Alcmaeon held that the preservation of health was a matter of the *equal balance** of forces, moist and dry, cold and hot, bitter and sweet, and the rest; the sole rule of any of these brings sickness. For uncontrolled rule tends to the elimination of the opposite principle . . .[353]

Some very interesting points emerge from a consideration of this fragment. It is clear that the thinking of Alcmaeon starts from the traditional pattern of thought—the oppositions and their balance, strife and opposition. He vigorously rejects the Pythagorean ideal of the reconciliation of opposites through the subordination of one term to the other. He argues that health is their balance or harmony. The subordination of the one to the other he calls "monarchy," and this is destructive of health. The lan-

* The word he uses is *isonomia,* a word which we have examined in the fourth chapter in its political context, translating it there as "equality," or "equal distribution." We saw reason to think that in the fifth century it was a kind of democratic watchword against the oligarchs.

guage he uses is strongly political in its flavor. The rejection of the notion of the subordination of one opposite to another as tending to the destruction of the one sounds like the kind of criticism that a good democrat would make of the Pythagorean program of subordination for the sake of "law and order." Perhaps we ought to recall that systematic cosmological thinking in Anaximander was profoundly stimulated by the very same political and social controversy.

Nor does the view that Alcmaeon was a Pythagorean get any support from the passage from Aristotle which is most often adduced to support that view. Aristotle described the views of "certain Pythagoreans" who set up ten pairs of opposite principles or contrarieties—the limited and the unlimited, the odd and the even, one and plurality, right and left, male and female, resting and moving, straight and curved, light and darkness, good and bad, square and oblong. He then continues:

> In this way Alcmaeon of Croton seems also to have conceived the matter, and either he got this view from them or they got it from him; for he expressed himself similarly to them. For he says most human affairs go in pairs, meaning not definite contrarieties such as Pythagoreans speak of, but any chance contrarieties, e.g., white and black, sweet and bitter, good and bad, great and small. He threw out indefinite suggestions about the other contrarieties, but the Pythagoreans declared both how many and which their contrarieties are.[354]

Aristotle does not equate Alcmaeon with the Pythagoreans; he definitely separated him from the Pythagoreans, and the attitude to contrarieties which he attributes to Alcmaeon is manifestly compatible with either of the two attitudes to oppositions within society and nature which we have heretofore traced—the aristocratic theory of harmony and reconciliation, the democratic theory of their "balance." The fragment quoted just above makes it overwhelmingly certain that his theory was the latter.

All this is entirely consonant with his scientific attitude, his passion for observation, his naturalistic attitude to the brain and its functioning, his realistic relating of man to the animal kingdom, and his concomitant differentiation of man from the animal kingdom—in short, with a scientific and almost positivistic outlook which is sharply different from that of the Pythagoreans.

There has come down to us from the fifth century B.C. an extraordinary series of documents, some seventy in number, that are associated with Hippocrates and the great medical school centered in the island of Cos. Whether or not Hippocrates actually wrote these works is unimportant. There can be little question that many of them represent the outlook and scientific temper of a leading medical school of the fifth century B.C. For this reason it is of tremendous interest to compare the concept of knowledge found in these works with the writings of Plato. The difference is startling. While Plato's thinking is pervaded through and through with an *a priori* idealism, the thinking of these medical men was empirical, naturalistic, and materialistic. The Roman writer Celsus credits Hippocrates with divorcing medicine from philosophy.[355]

> Certain physicians and philosophers assert that nobody can know medicine who is ignorant of what man is; he who would treat patients properly must, they say, learn this. But the question they raise is one for philosophy: it is the province of those who, like Empedocles, have written on "nature" [physics], what man is from the beginning, how he came into being at the first, and from what elements he was originally constructed. But my view is, first, that all that philosophers or physicians have said or written on natural science no more pertains to medicine than to painting. I also hold that clear knowledge about "nature" [physics] can be acquired from medicine and from no other source, and that one can attain this knowledge when medicine itself has been properly comprehended, but till then it is quite impossible—I mean to possess this information, what man is, by what cause he is made, and similar points accurately.[356]

The writer of this treatise makes a very sharp distinction between those who practice medicine as an empirical science and those who bring to it some *a priori* idea derived from general "philosophy." In one sense we might say that he is carrying on the work of Alcmaeon; in one passage in the introduction to the treatise *On Ancient Medicine* we seem to have exact verbal reminiscences of the introduction to Alcmaeon's work:

> All who, on attempting to speak or to write on medicine, have assumed for themselves a postulate as a basis for their discussion—heat, cold, moisture, dryness, or anything else that they may fancy—who narrow down the causal principles of diseases and death among men, and make it the same in all cases, postulating one thing or two, all these obviously blunder in many points in their statements, but they are most open to censure because they blunder in what is an art and one which all men use on the most important occasions, and give the greatest honors to the good craftsmen (*demiourgous*) and practitioners in it. Of craftsmen some are poor and some are very good; this would not be the case if an art of medicine did not exist at all, and had not been the subject of any research and discovery, but all would be equally inexperienced and unlearned therein, and the treatment of the sick would be in all respects haphazard. But it is not so; just as in all other arts the workers vary much in skill and in knowledge, so also is it in the case of medicine. Wherefore I have deemed that it has no need of an empty postulate, as do insoluble mysteries [lit. "unseen and insoluble things." "Unseen" is the word that Alcmaeon had used in the fragment we have just discussed to describe the province of which the gods might have knowledge, but men could not.] about which any exponent must use a postulate, for example, things in the sky or below the earth. If a man were to learn and declare the state of these, neither to the speaker himself nor to his audience would it be clear whether his statement were true or not. For there is no test, the application of which would give certainty.[357]

There are several points of great interest in this passage. There is the insistence on observation and experiment, the rejection of any ideas which cannot be empirically verified. There is (and this is the most significant point) a deep respect for "craftsmen"—the class that Plato and his aristocratic friends treat with such profound contempt, and an insistence that a good doctor is a good craftsman, whose skill is comparable with the skill of any other artisan. There is the same ironical dismissal of the "unseen things" that we find in Alcmaeon (we might compare Herbert Spencer's "Unknowable"), the same insistence that the province of science is the tangible and the material. The work is a most exciting exposition of the "positivistic" and empirical leanings of the most advanced of the sciences in fifth-century Greece. We can infer from this how resolutely the scientific mind in Greek antiquity found it necessary to reject idealistic presuppositions if its science was to progress.

And yet the introduction of this treatise which we have just examined is not an unqualified reaffirmation of the point of view of Alcmaeon. The writer is at one with his predecessor in his emphasis on observation and practice. But Alcmaeon had developed his theory in reaction to the Pythagorean view of the harmony and subordination of opposites. He had not at all rejected the notion (by that time almost traditional in Greek thought) of the opposites and their strife. He had argued that health was an *isonomia*, an equality of oppositions, that the *monarchia*, sole rule, of any of them produced the elimination of its opposite and led to disease. But he had not in the sense of the Hippocratic writer abandoned "hypotheses," broad generalizations about the nature of process which gave unity and coherence to observed facts. In their opposition to idealistic and *a priori* generalizations, the scientists of the late fifth century tended to go to the extreme of rejecting all generalizations. They took refuge in a bare empiricism and wrote as though observation of the particular phenomena were sufficient for science. But as a recent writer has well observed, this is not the method of science:

> The monographic literature of the natural sciences, here [i.e., by institutional economists] held up as a model for economics, proceeds on the basis of at least a minimum core of agreement. Medical monographs, for instance,

> usually take some established concepts of anatomy, while economic monographs of the new school tend to start afresh each time, with each worker assuming what he finds convenient, and failing to agree even on such basic concepts as capital or income.[358]

The value, in other words, for science of the broader hypothesis has been well attested in practice in its history over the last two centuries.

It was precisely this basis of agreement which ancient science might have found in the insight of the Ionians if the structure of ancient society had been different. The parallel with the breakdown of Heraclitus' dialectic into the atomism of Democritus is exact. Democritus, in his repudiation of the position of Zeno, rejects all concepts of organism, all levels of thought, reality, and experience. The practical scientists, while they rejected the *a priori* approach of Greek idealism, rejected also all hypothesis, all general *formulae*, all theory, and reduced science to the bleakest, barest, most unfruitful kind of empiricism.

Though medicine was the best developed of the Greek sciences, practice cannot run very far ahead of theory, and practice along many technical lines was in Greek antiquity well advanced. We read in a recent writer of the "scattered stones from the great edifice of ancient chemistry."[359] Greek handicrafts, dyeing, vase making, and the rest, must have used fairly complicated chemical formulae. The subtle lines of the Parthenon must convince us that the science of optics was well advanced. The perfection of Greek statuary points to a thorough knowledge of anatomy, both human and animal. Biology, and particularly marine biology, in Aristotle reached an astonishing pitch of development. All this was overwhelmed and swept away in the mighty tide of idealism and undermined by the labors of Plato. That Greek science should now be only an antiquarian curiosity and the playground of specialists is a tribute to Plato's success and a reflection of the weakness of a slave-owning society. Yet it is well for the student to remember that there was a strong materialistic and scientific tradition in the Greek world and that this, too, was part of the background of Plato's thinking.

The stage is now set for the mighty labors of Plato: To attack and refute, if he could, the sophistic relativism and its material counterpart, the doctrine of the flux; to defend the principles of order, the changeless and the divine in nature, the inherent right of some in the state to rule, the *natural* pre-eminence of reason within the individual soul to check and harmonize the chaos of appetite; to prove that justice is eternal, firmly rooted and grounded in the nature of things; and in so doing to build the towering temple of the eternal ideas, as a monument to his master, the martyred philosopher. By examining his political career and his literary masterpiece, the *Republic*, in the remainder of this book we shall be able to see how successfully he executed it.

CHAPTER SIX

The Life of Plato

PLATO WAS BORN of a highly aristocratic family in the year 428 B.C. His father, Ariston, traced his proud lineage back to the old kings of Attica.[360] The precise details of the family tree on his father's side are not known, but he was certainly a eupatrid, a member of one of the most prominent of the Attic clans.

Plato's mother, Perictione, boasted an equally illustrious descent, and in her case more seems to be known about the family. She was a sister of Charmides, one of the ardent young patricians who fell under grave suspicion in connection with the mutilation of the Hermae and in whose house the sacred Eleusinian mysteries were said to have been subjected to a profane burlesque.[361] (Both these deeds of sacrilege were regarded by the democracy as hostile acts.) The lady was also a cousin of Critias*—a "favorite son" of aristocratic reaction and a leader of the "Thirty." The "Thirty," we may recall, were responsible for the uprising of a terroristic right-wing aristocratic conspiracy which led to a brief period of bloody dictatorship. The grandfather of this Critias was a gentleman of the same name, and his great-grandfather, Dropides, is said to have been acquainted with Solon, the last evidence of any liberal association in the family. Liberalism was apparently a Mendelian recessive. (This Dropides claimed relationship to the first Athenian archon—644 B.C.)

Plato had two brothers, Adimantus and Glaucon, whom we shall meet in the *Republic*.

His uncle, Charmides, was also a member of the oligarchic "Thirty"; he was, in fact, one of the ten archons (or magistrates) appointed by the "Thirty" at the Piraeus. He was killed at the battle between oligarchs and democrats which took place at Munychia. (May, 403 B.C.).[362]

* See below, p. 167.

Of Plato's childhood and early youth we know very little. His father, Ariston, seems to have died when Plato was a child[363] and his mother, Perictione, married again, this time her uncle, Pyrilampes. This gentleman seems to have been a picturesque character. In his youth he had been brought to trial on a charge of murder, accused, according to our account, by Pericles himself. He was defended by the great aristocratic factional leader—Thucydides, the son of Melesias. Since these two prominent political leaders were involved in the prosecution and the defense it seems safe to conclude that the murder (or at least the trial) had important political implications.[364] Pyrilampes was acquitted of the charge. Later in life some of the ancient sources indicate that he was reconciled to Pericles and the two became friendly.[365] It is altogether possible that we should relate this friendly association to the fact that Pericles, towards the end of his life, grew increasingly conservative, tended more and more to temper the program of democratic expansion and, in practical political affairs, to draw closer to, and even coalesce with, the party of the "right." From the flamboyant exuberance of his political youth the old gentleman (he must have been at least fifty when he married his niece) turned to more peaceful pursuits. His chief claim to distinction was as a breeder of peacocks.[366]

It is a pity that we know so very little of the formative years of Plato's younger life and of the purely personal influences that were brought to bear. The proper evaluation of a thinker would take into account not only social influences on his development but the psychological and personal influences as well. In Plato's case this is virtually impossible. We can only speculate on Plato's relations with his great-uncle and stepfather. Did he listen with youthful admiration to tales of the man's swashbuckling youth? Or did he revolt against the tranquillity of his hobby-ridden maturity? And what of the young stepbrother, Demos, who was so beautiful that almost every man of fashion fell in love with him and so stupid that he was deemed fit for horsemanship rather than philosophy?[367] And what was the influence of the career of his brilliant and unscrupulous cousin, Critias, a career just coming to its climax in Plato's youth? All these speculations we must dismiss for lack of evidence. The reconstruction of an ancient philosopher cannot, in the present state of knowledge, be made with as much confidence as in the case of a recent modern. One thing we can affirm, though not perhaps a matter of personality and psychological growth. Every member of Plato's family was a thoroughgoing aristocrat with the strong social pride of a great family. And every connection the family had was with the ultraconservatives and oligarchical politics. They succeeded in keeping themselves quite unspotted from the world of democracy and liberal thought.

So much for the prevailing atmosphere of Plato's younger days. It is only fair to Plato to add that if every affiliation throughout his life seems so markedly aristocratic and conservative, that this is in a sense perfectly understandable. He grew to manhood in the twilight of a democratic experiment, at a time when even democracy's own adherents were falling away and finding ever less hope in the system. Democracy was no longer advancing, progressive, creative, as it had been in the middle of the fifth century. Its inevitable expansion had invited the inevitable cataclysm, and Plato lived in the pause that preceded a great new advance.

In a period like this, the alternative to aristocratic attitudes and predispositions, no longer represented by a challenging and vigorous democracy, could not have been attractive to a well-endowed intellectual.

Before we abandon the question of Plato's early development, we must take some brief account of his relationship with Socrates. As we argued in another book,[368] the older man was a perfect symbol of the breakdown of Athenian democracy, typical of the intellectual disillusionment that many keen minds must have felt at its failure. Failing to appreciate the fundamental economic contradictions that paralyzed a democracy in a slave-owning state, such men as Socrates sighed wistfully for expert rule. It is significant that throughout his life Plato was quite conscious of the influence that Socrates represented. The older man remained to the end, in Plato's eyes, a teacher and a guide. And yet Plato could have known Socrates only for a very few years and known him at a time when the great intellectual and social changes in Socrates' outlook had been fully consummated. The experience of his conviction and execution must have contributed very markedly to Plato's brooding resentment against the democracy.

If we know little of Plato as a person in the important formative years of his life, we know a great deal about the almost incredible melee of political intrigue in which his political circle was engaged. When Plato was seventeen, in the year 411 B.C., the aristocratic forces, which had for years been in a state of relative helplessness, forced to take refuge in futile intrigues, finally found their opportunity (as a result of the great defeat in Sicily) to attack the democratic constitution openly. Popular feeling ran high against the democratic orators,[369] and the hopes of reaction were immeasurably increased by the prospect of help from Persia.[370] A committee of public safety (*probouloi*) was formed to launch the revolution.[371] Under the watchword of the "ancestral constitution" democratic political forms were cast aside. Pay for public offices (the greatest buttress of democratic political power) was abolished except for the archons and prytanes; and citizenship was restricted to a group of about *five thousand*.[372] (We need hardly dwell on the oligarchical lengths to which this constitution went.) The aristocratic "clubs" worked busily to subvert the democracy assembly to vote its own downfall.[373] Without going into wearisome details we may say in summary that the party of the so-called moderates under Theramenes was elbowed aside by the more ruthless reactionaries who clustered around the aristocratic "clubs." But such a regime could not endure without a foreign army. The centrist group, led by Theramenes, went over to the side of the democracy, the coalition regained power, and the rule of the oligarchy was terminated after four months. The effect of these exciting events (in which, let us remember, Plato's whole circle of friends and relatives was engaged) on the susceptible mind of an adolescent can easily be imagined.

Nor did the political ferment die down after the defeat of the oligarchic conspirators. For the next five years (the seventeenth to twenty-second of Plato's life) the "right" was busy reforming its ranks, digesting the political lessons drawn from its defeat, and considering new tactics to use against the democracy. Events in the last years of the fifth century show that the oligarchs must have drawn at least two important conclusions from the experience of their short-lived triumph of 411. First, that their own party was not strong enough to maintain itself in power without outside support—namely, assistance from the Spartan army. Second, that the great reserve of democratic power in Athens lay in the fleet and its sailors; that this power must be undermined before an oligarchic *coup d'état* could have a hope of success. The history of the years 406-405 represents the systematic pursuit of the second of these aims. The war with Sparta provided the oligarchs with a double opportunity. They could both intrigue with Lysander,* the Spartan general, and at the same time endeavor to betray the Athenian fleet. In the battle of Arginusae (406) it seems very probable that this latter aim was being served when the Athenian generals, urging the pretext of a storm, abandoned thousands of Athenian sailors trapped on sinking ships.

> Twenty-five Athenian triremes lay heeled over or disabled with their oars destroyed, no masts, nor any means of moving, and gradually sinking. The original crew of each was two hundred men. The field of battle was strewed with these wrecks; the men on board being helpless and unable to get away—for the ancient trireme carried no boat nor any aids for escape. No step being taken to preserve them, the surviving portions of these crews, wounded as well as unwounded, were left to be gradually drowned as each disabled ship went down.[374]

If Arginusae provided only a suspicion of treachery, the battle

* LYSANDER (?-395 B.C.)
Lysander was a Spartan admiral and commander of the Spartan navy in 407 B.C. After winning a great victory at Aegospotami he was sent to Athens with an army to assist the Athenian oligarchs against the democracy. His failure at Athens to establish a permanent Spartan hegemony in alliance with Athenian conservatives was partly due to political discord as it developed in Sparta itself.

of Aegospotami in the following year gave certain evidence. This battle resulted in a crushing defeat for the Athenian navy, and the democrats were quite convinced that some of the commanders had acted in concert with Sparta to bring about a betrayal.[375] (Those who are inclined to think too simply of the Periclean "democracy" should note that one of the accused generals was Pericles' own son.)

When the generals were brought to trial, the coalition between moderate oligarchs and democrats still functioned. Theramenes came forward as the accuser in conjunction with Thrasybulus. At the trial, philosophy found its opportunity to play a direct political role. Plato's own friend and teacher stood out alone against the outcry of the *demos*, demanding justice against its betrayers.

> Callixenus brought in a decree that the generals should be condemned by the assembly and put to death by a vote of the legislative body. It was this proposal that Socrates opposed, appealing to the *psephism* of Canonus, which provided a separate trial before the *dicasteria* (law courts) in such cases. This incident is usually quoted as a proof of Socrates' high-mindedness and courage in opposing the irrational frenzy of the democratic mob. It can perhaps be better interpreted as a move in the incredibly complicated political game that was being played by both sides in this hectic period. It was clearly to the interest of the democracy to have the generals tried before a wider and more representative body. It was equally to the interest of the oligarchy to bring them before a smaller jury which would less definitely reflect the conscious democratic policy to arraign the generals in one block and fix them with a collective responsibility. The oligarchs would naturally oppose this on the sound political principle that it would be far less serious and incriminating for individuals to be condemned than for a group to be judged guilty of antidemocratic procedure, for a decision handed down against a clique had unpleasant implications as far as the aristocratic *hetairiai* or conspiratorial clubs were concerned. The precedent to them might

> be highly dangerous. Viewed in this light it seems distinctly probable that Socrates was serving an essential oligarchic interest when he attempted to block the path of the democratic proposals. There is, perhaps, less a devotion to law and order or constitutionality in his action than a loyal piece of factional work.[376]

The idealistic philosophy insisting that the "wisest" and "best" should rule, as it did so universally in Greece, turned at this juncture in the person of Socrates to the task of showing its adherents the way. (This is not to argue, as some have thought, that Socrates was insincere in his belief. He was probably as sincerely convinced that the "wisest" and "best" should rule as he was that his own friends and associates were the "wisest" and "best.")

The year after the dreadful betrayal at the battle of Aegospotami, reaction, internal and intercivic bound together in alliance, had its opportunity. The city surrendered to Lysander, and under his protection the oligarchical clubs seized uncontested control. They named a committee of five "ephors" (the name, of course, was imitated from the Spartan magistracies) to direct the tactics of the rampant Right.[377] Critias, the cousin of Plato, was on this committee. After the most resolute of the democratic leaders had been arrested, a Board of Thirty (they were usually called "the tyrants" but the student should distinguish them very sharply from the sixth-century tyrants or leaders of nascent democracy) was established as the supreme governing power. Critias and Theramenes were both included on this board; it is clear, therefore, that a coalition of the Center and the Right was included in the plans of some, at least, of the leaders. It was Theramenes, incidentally, who negotiated the surrender to Sparta. But Theramenes again paid the penalty for the moderation of his own ambiguous position. When the terror was directed only against the democrats, Theramenes was willing to lend his support. But when it went further to include such moderate oligarchs as Niceratus, son of Nicias,[378] and wealthy metics, like Leon of Salamis, then Theramenes drew back in virtuous horror. (Socrates, too, let us recall, would not play a part in the arrest of

Leon of Salamis and so to a degree disassociated himself from friends like Critias.[379])

> "He agreed," he said, "with Critias when it was a question of condemning the "known and obnoxious democratic leaders"; but when Critias and his friends began to seize men of station and dignity it was then that he began to oppose them.[380]

It is important to appreciate the position of Theramenes on this point, because it agrees almost exactly with the feelings of Plato and Socrates. Their political program, we can suspect, was closer to that of Critias than Theramenes. But when the terror began to involve as its victims the Center and the moderate Right, both these men drew back in alarm, apprehension, and virtuous indignation.

Very many years afterwards, in the calm afterglow of old age when emotion could be recollected in relative tranquillity Plato evidently felt it important to describe his relations with the "Thirty"—his hopes and his disillusion.

> Once upon a time in my youth I cherished like many another, the hope, directly I came of age, of entering upon a political career. It fell out, moreover, that political events took the following course. There were many who heaped abuse on the form of government then prevailing, and a revolution occurred. In this revolution fifty-one men set themselves up as a government, eleven in the city, ten in the Piraeus (both these groups were to administer the market and the usual civic affairs), and thirty came into power as supreme rulers of the whole state.
>
> Some of these happened to be relatives and acquaintances of mine, who accordingly invited me forth to join them, assuming my fitness for the task. No wonder that, young as I was, I cherished the belief that they would lead the city from an unjust life, as it were, to habits of justice and really administer it; so that I was intensely interested to see what would come of it.
>
> Of course I saw in a short time that these men made the

> former government look in comparison like an age of gold. Among other things they sent an elderly man, Socrates, a friend of mine, who I should be ashamed to say was the justest man of his time [in what sense just?], in company with others, against one of the citizens to fetch him forcibly to be executed. Their purpose was to connect Socrates with their government whether he wished or not. He refused and risked any consequence rather than become their partner in wicked deeds. When I observed all this—and some other similar matters of importance—I withdraw in disgust from the abuses of those days. Not long after came the fall of the Thirty and of their whole system of government.[381]

There is no reason to think that this almost elaborately casual and highly idealized account of his adolescent enthusiasms does not represent the substantial fact: that he, in common with all his circle of friends and relations, was bitterly opposed to the democracy; that he was drawn into active political life as a subordinate of the Thirty; that he, like Theramenes, was disgusted with a terror that included among its victims relatively respectable and conservative men. If we read the seventh letter carefully, we can hardly escape the conclusion that Plato was interested, in the beginning, in the political program of Critias. But he scarcely understood why this program, in its practical development, led to violence against respectable citizens. The separation of Theramenes and Plato from Critias was not based upon an objection of principle to the extreme of oligarchy, which Critias represented. (The letter makes this clear.) Rather, as political idealists, they had never faced the concrete implication necessary to the execution of that theoretical program—political terror. Without giving up his opposition to democracy, he found it expedient to withdraw for a time from active life. Post[382] suggests that he may at this juncture have withdrawn to Thebes, where, as we know, Pythagoreanism was strong.

We need not pursue in detail the further development of the rule of the Thirty. Theramenes they put violently to death (in his last moments he playfully poured a libation from the hemlock cup to the "noble Critias"[383]). Every Athenian citizen not a member of the upper three thousand was expelled from the city![384] The number of those put to death is said to have reached the enormous (for those times and for the size of Athens) total of fifteen hundred.[385] Sophistic thought was suppressed and censored and (we are almost tempted to use a modern phrase) the books burned.[386] Xenophon's considered naïveté on this point is, as we have pointed out elsewhere, amusing.

"He presents the decree passed by the Thirty against the Sophists as a direct personal insult to Socrates himself. This is distinctly improbable, and it is a view which Xenophon himself refutes when he discloses the fact that in spite of the decree Socrates continued to teach the technique of interlocution[387]—the Thirty were not the kind of people to pass such a measure without intending its enforcement."[388]

This black terror lasted some eight months. The democrats in exile rallied their forces, and in spite of a lack of technical equipment—by sheer weight of numbers, moral strength, and the dispirit which arose among the oligarchs—were able to regain control. Their success was immeasurably aided by political opposition to Lysander within Sparta itself.

The returned democracy, Plato himself informs us, conducted itself with the greatest moderation.[389] Rightly or wrongly, it regarded Socrates as principally responsible for the excesses of his friends, pupils, and associates. The democrats seem to have felt that to eliminate Socrates would be to cut the heart out of the antidemocratic movement. The actual trial of Socrates we have discussed in another place.[390] Many years later Plato wrote the extremely brilliant, but faintly disingenuous speech which he put into the mouth of Socrates—the *Apologia,* which was probably intended for the edification of the disciples rather than for general circulation.

Plato may have taken a prominent part in the trial. He was certainly present. He was, however, absent from the execution because of ill-health.[391] A later writer says that during the course of the trial Plato himself mounted the platform to speak in Socrates' defense, that he began by apologizing for his youth, but was thereupon interrupted by the judges with shouts of "Get down, get down."[392] If true, this incident must have been very wounding to Plato's *amour propre*.

It is interesting to note that Plato represents himself in the *Apology* as one of the group of Socratic disciples who urged the master to abandon his insolent proposal to name a fine of one mina for his offense, and suggested a fine of thirty minae—a more tactful offer under the circumstances. At the same time Plato offered his own fortune as security.[393] If Socrates was resigned to his fate, Plato and his friends apparently were not inclined to give him up without a fight.

The bearing of this early experience with politics, its influence on the growth and development of the young philosopher, is not something for which we can give "chapter and verse." But we can hardly fail to be aware of how strong a factor this whole experience was in embittering the young Plato against the democracy and the "rule of the mob."

There is another side of the youthful Plato which appears to us only obscurely, but certainly in definite psychological relationship to the total process of his growth. Plato is not only a philosopher; he is also, and supremely, a literary artist and a poet. Of this, even the most casual reading of the dialogues will make one aware; and it does not, therefore, come as a surprise to the student to find that Plato had in antiquity something of a reputation for poetry.[394] In the dialogues one can hardly miss the union of artistry and argument; it forms so refreshing a contrast with labored treatises on metaphysics as seen, for example, in Kant. The blend of poetic artistry and logical discipline is an integral part of Plato's personality. Much of Plato's insight is due to the artist in him rather than the logician. It is the artist which gives him a sense of the artistic whole, of unity, harmony, and proportion. In short, an appreciation of the aesthetic side of Plato is vital to a grasp both of him and his work.

In literature, we may remark, he felt a warm admiration for the great comic dramatist, Aristophanes, in whom conservative politics and lyrical skill were so well combined. Much of the poetry attributed to Plato reads like the romantic endeavor of a young man. Love for him was an absorbing theme, particularly the love of man for boy. One of his erotic poems was addressed to Phaedrus,[395] several to a youth called Aster (one of his pupils),[396] and one to Dion of Syracuse.[397] (We shall discuss Plato and Dion very soon.)

After the trial and condemnation of Socrates, Plato with a group of his friends withdrew from Athens to Megara, where they were received under the friendly protection of the Pythagorean (or Eleatic) settlement headed by one Euclid.[398] This withdrawal was, of course, not unconnected with the unfavorable outcome of the trial. Athens was not at the moment the safest place in the world for friends and adherents of Socrates.

In the years that followed the departure from Athens, Plato seems to have gone in for extensive travelling. We know that he visited the mathematician Theodorus at Cyrene,[399] the Pythagoreans in Southern Italy and Sicily, as well as Egypt. For Egypt and its hierarchy of priests he expresses indirectly profound admiration, remarking on their marvellous sense of the antiquity of their own culture.[400] All the rest of the places mentioned have a manifest association with the conservative tradition in philosophy and politics.

While in Sicily he made a trip to Syracuse and there first became acquainted with Dion, the son-in-law of Dionysius I, the latter at that time ruler of the city. This is one of the great turning points in Plato's life, and it will be well to give an account of it in his own words. The account is found in a long letter addressed to Dion, which seems to be intended as an *apologia* for Plato's intervention in Syracusan politics. It puts his conduct in Syracuse, therefore, in the most favorable possible light.

> Upon my arrival—I found myself utterly at odds with the sort of life that is there termed a happy one, a life taken up with Italian and Syracusan banquets, an existence that consists in filling oneself up twice a day, never sleeping alone at night, and indulging in all the practices attendant on that way of living. In such an environment no man under heaven, brought up in self-indulgence, could ever grow to be wise. So marvellous a tempera-

ment as that is not in nature. That a man should grow up sober-minded would also be quite out of the question; and one might make the same statement about the other qualities that go to make up excellence of character. Neither can a city be free from unrest under any laws, be those laws what they may, while its citizens think fit to spend everything on excesses, meanwhile making it a rule, however, to avoid all industry except such as is devoted to banquets and drinking-bouts and painstaking attention to the gratification of lust. It is inevitable that in such cities there should be an unending succession of governments—tyranny, oligarchy, democracy—one after another, while the very name of just and equal government is anathema to those in control.

Now beholding this conviction in addition to the former, I travelled on to Syracuse. Perhaps it was chance, but certainly it looks as if a higher power was at that time contriving to lay a foundation for the recent events in which Dion and the city of Syracuse were concerned, for more too, I fear, unless you now follow the advice I am giving you the second time. But what can I mean when I say that my visit to Syracuse at that time was the beginning of everything? In my intercourse at that time with the young Dion, as I set before him in theory my ideals for mankind and advised him to make them effective in practice, I seem to have been unaware that I was in any way contriving, all unknown to myself, a future downfall of tyranny. At any rate, Dion, who was very quick of apprehension and especially so in regard to my instruction on this occasion, responded to it more keenly and more enthusiastically than any other young men I met, and resolved to live for the remainder of his life differently from most of the Greeks in Italy and Sicily, holding virtue dearer than pleasure or than luxury. On that account the life he led until the death of Dionysius vexed somewhat those who passed their time in accordance with tyrannic wont.[401]

Syracuse was at that time an expanding commercial empire, a successful competitor of Athens, and governed (as we shall see) by a leader of the popular faction whom Plato calls a tyrant. This accounts without doubt for the highly unflattering account that Plato gives of the kind of life that its citizens led. It will also help us to understand his enthusiasm for Dion's abstemiousness.

Under Plato's guidance Dion developed his political philosophy. "He believed in liberty for the Syracusans under the guidance of the best system of laws."[402]

Plato's stay at Syracuse on this first visit was short, and his departure was not happy. Dionysius I seems to have understood perfectly well the implications of Platonic doctrines as they bore on the political situation in Sicily. The "tyrant" was so antagonized that he had Plato sold into slavery. There are two accounts of this, both going back to fourth-century sources, i.e., to men who were living at the time the event took place. The actual manner of the kidnapping is described differently in our two authorities. One account[403] relates that Dionysius I had him apprehended in Syracuse and put on sale as a slave; the other that the "tyrant" arranged for his capture at sea.[404] According to the second story Dionysius gave strict instructions to kill Plato if necessary, but at all events to have him captured. He may have been taken to Aegina.[405] Two stories are told of how he was ransomed—one that his Syracusan friends from Cyrene released him. At all events he returned safely to Athens and very shortly afterwards (probably in the same year) founded the Academy.[406]

This exciting adventure seems so much at variance with the traditional picture of the aloof philosopher and teacher that commentators have been only too willing to reject it.*

* We may regard as typical of this skepticism A. E. Taylor's treatment of the incident. "I have said nothing of the story related, e.g., in D. L. *Vit. Plat.* 18-21, that Dionysius I had Plato kidnapped and handed over to a Spartan admiral who exposed him for sale at Aegina, where he was ransomed by an acquaintance from Cyrene. The story, though barely possible, is very improbable, and looks to be no more than anecdote intended to blacken the character of Dionysius . . ." (*Plato, The Man and His Work,* p. 5, n. I.) The story is, however, reproduced not only by Diogenes Laërtius, who was a late writer. To reject *his* testimony has seemed to many scholars reasonable. It is reported also by Diodorus Siculus, probably reproducing Ephorus; and Plutarch, who seems to have drawn from Theopompus. Both Ephorus and Theopompus are reliable historians, who were actually alive at the time the episode is said to have occurred. Diogenes,

It will help us to recall Plato's own words on the subject in the seventh letter. After all, this letter is in a very real sense a frank statement of what Plato felt had been a tactical mistake, namely to have permitted his philosophical doctrine to be drawn into practical application in a hostile political environment. The seventh letter is an *apologia* in face of the well-known fact that the philosopher *had* been engaged in practical politics. At all events he returned safely to Athens and founded his school—the Academy.

The founding of the Academy is an important turning point, not only in Plato's career, but in the history of Platonic thought. His doctrines now become systematized in the teachings of a school, a school which offers the opportunity for collective study and scholarship and will carry on the tradition of Platonism for many centuries.

Plato made three trips to Syracuse during the course of his lifetime—the second about twenty years after founding of the Academy, as a man of about sixty. An invitation to return was extended to him shortly after the death of his old adversary Dionysius I and, as we might suspect, Dion was largely instrumental in arranging the invitation. The death of Dionysius and the problems which immediately arose about the succession threw Syracusan politics into a very considerable turmoil. To understand why Dion felt it particularly appropriate to avail himself of Plato's influence we must digress momentarily and examine the recent development of Syracusan politics.

Dionysius I had been a great ruler, and under his direction Syracuse had emerged as the principal state in Sicily. His reign is in some sense comparable with the great days of the Athenian democracy; or perhaps even more comparable with the period of

---

furthermore, mentions Favorinus twice, and in the details of his story differs from both Plutarch and Diodorus, i.e., he is influenced by yet a third tradition. He also speaks of "some other writers." The evidence definitely indicates that the story was current in Plato's lifetime. If we were to accept the canons of historical criticism implied in Taylor's treatment, we should have to abandon much of our knowledge of Sicilian fourth-century history (which comes very largely from Ephorus, secondly Theopompus), and much besides.

the sixth-century "tyrants" in Athens and Corinth when those two cities were leading the movement towards commercial expansion and greatness.

In the successful fight against the Athenian invaders (415-413) Syracuse had become a great power. The war had done for Syracuse something comparable to what the defeat of Persia had done for Athens. The Sicilian city had built up her fleet, successfully withstood the greatest power of that age, and acquired an imperial consciousness. New horizons opened up for Syracuse. There was the larger stage of the Western Mediterranean, now removed from Athenian threats, on which she might play a more imperious part.

This turn in affairs was reflected in Syracusan internal politics. Let us remember that Syracusan success in the war against Athens had been based very largely on the threat, both potential and actual, that the Spartan land force had presented to Athens on the Greek mainland. From the time of the Athenian invasion of Sicily in 415, Sparta and Syracuse had been bound in close alliance. A Spartan general Gylippus had directed the actual defense of Syracuse; and to give further aid to her ally, Sparta fortified Decelea on the northern boundary of Attica. (Both these tactics were conceived by Alcibiades and expounded to the Spartans, after his desertion of the Athenian cause.) By constant forays into Attica the Spartan army prevented Athens from ever throwing her full power against Syracuse.

After the victory in war, these new possibilities for Syracusan expansion still depended on keeping Athens and Sparta, the two great powers of Eastern Greece, permanently at odds. This end was achieved by a continuous alliance between Syracuse and Sparta. That situation explains the peculiar paradox that Syracuse—a progressive, commercial, democratic state—was forced to keep up at least some form of formal engagement with the most backward and conservative of all Greek states. Under war conditions, it is easy to see that Spartan influence gained undue weight in Syracuse in proportion to the strength of the native pro-Spartan aristocracy. But when the war was over, the democracy was in a position to redress the balance.

In 409 the democrats under Diocles were strong enough to banish by a vote of the popular assembly the great and distinguished pro-Spartan general Hermocrates. He was killed, we may add, in 407 while endeavoring to restore himself by force.

Thereafter there was a pronounced flowering of Syracusan democratic institutions, many borrowed, interestingly enough, from her great enemy, Athens. Of this, the age of flowering for Syracusan democracy, Dionysius I, who came to power in 405, was the head and the symbol, much as Pericles had been in Athens. Though called a tyrant by Greek conservatives, he was a constitutional magistrate of the commonwealth, elected by the popular assembly as general with supreme power. The fleet was even more considerably built up and the city refortified; Ortygia was made into a fortified harbor like the Piraeus. Many slaves were enfranchised and made free citizens in order to build up a stronger class of artisans. In a long and bitter struggle with Carthage, Syracuse more than held her own. By 385 Syracuse reached the height of her power; she had control over nearly all *Magna Graecia* and even made an alliance with the powerful cisalpine Gauls. Her influence was felt strongly in Eastern Greece, where she continued to ally herself with Sparta against Athens.

We can now appreciate the turmoil into which Syracusan internal politics were thrown when Dionysius I died. Everything, as both aristocratic and democratic factions realized, turned on the succession.

Dionysius I had died in 367. The story runs that Dion, his daughter's husband, endeavored to visit the dying man and influence him in his choice of a successor. The candidates Dion suggested were Hipparinus and Nysaeus, two young boys, Dionysius' sons by Aristomache. Had they been chosen, Dion would have been practically a regent. The court physicians, however, refused to allow him into the death chamber—an interesting-sounding episode. They are also said to have made assurance sure by giving the aged ruler a sleeping potion to guarantee him against Dion's influence.[407] As a result the succession passed to Dionysius II. The only opposition to the young man came from his own household and those who clustered about Dion. Thus it was in order to influence the young Dionysius II, who was still at an impressionable age, that Dion took the liberty of inviting Plato to return to Syracuse as a guide and teacher for the new ruler. Plato's own words will explain Dion's intention:

> After that [the death of Dionysius I] he felt in his heart that he would not always be alone in holding this belief [in the downfall of tyranny and the introduction of "Right" political rule], which he arrived at under the guidance of right reasoning. In fact he saw it growing in others too, *not many,* but at any rate in some, and took note. He thought that Dionysius might perhaps become one of these through the co-operation of the gods —furthermore, he felt it to be absolutely necessary that I come to Syracuse as soon as possible to lend a hand in the work.[408]

When we have discussed Plato's philosophy more fully, we shall understand much better the "work" that Dion had in mind for Plato to do. It will suffice now to suggest that he (Plato), like Socrates, was urging his concept of the rule of the "wisest and best." Plato was, accordingly, summoned and arrived on the scene.

One further point will help us to understand this visit and its motivation in Plato's mind. For well over a century, as we have seen, Greek conservatives had looked to Sparta as the major bulwark of their political power. But, at the battle of Leuctra (371 B.C., i.e. just four years before the death of Dionysius I) the fundamental weakness of Sparta had been dramatically exposed by Epaminondas and his Thebans. Sparta, in other words, was now manifestly helpless to play the role in universal Greek politics that she had played for so long. The conservatives were forced to look elsewhere, and Dion of Syracuse must have seemed an almost God-given answer to their problem.

It need not surprise us that Plato's ambitious program encountered practical difficulties almost from the start. He was able to launch Dionysius successfully into his curriculum of theoretical studies, particularly mathematics.

> In conformity with the regular Academic course the pupil was started on the study of mathematics, and geometry became the fashion at court. To this no one could object; but Plato's ethical and political teaching was not so harmless. We hear that on one occasion when sacrifice was being offered in the domestic chapel and the customary prayer for the safe continuance of the tyranny was recited, the tyrant, to the great consternation of his ministers, exclaimed, "Stop cursing us."* Philosophy then, it seemed, meant the end of the tyranny and the abasement of all who throve thereon.[409]

We can read between the lines and infer the same thing from Plato's own account of his experience as an educator.

> So Dion and I gave Dionysius this advice. Since he had been treated by his father as he had, and had had no experience of education or of suitable instruction, he must in the first place [regulate his daily life]; then when he had made a start, he must win to friendship with himself and to *moral harmony* others from among his kinsmen and companions.[410]

Moreover, Plato himself explains the difficulties which he encountered.

> When I arrived, for I must be brief, I found the whole environment of Dionysius seething with cabals and with malicious reports to the government about Dion.[411]

Those who were struggling against Dion, fearing that Dionysius might have a change of sympathy, persuaded him to recall Philistus from exile; he was a man well educated "in words," thoroughly experienced in the ways of tyranny. They expected that he would be an antidote to Plato and philosophy.[412]

Philistus was a historian, much admired in antiquity, and above all an active and militant supporter of the regime of Dionysius I (he had, however, been exiled by the elder statesman for a mistake in his private life).[413] Historical science, we may observe, is

* The prayer was apparently an oblique sermon, even a political harangue.

counterposed to moral philosophy in the intellectual and political contest for the mind and allegiance of the ruler.

On this occasion historical science won. Dion was sent into exile. "I," says Plato in the letter of explanation that we have already quoted,

> took his part as best I could, but I could do little; and in about the fourth month on the ground that Dion was plotting against the government, Dionysius put him aboard a small boat and expelled him dishonorably. Thereupon all of us who were friends of Dion were in terror lest Dionysius should accuse and punish someone else for complicity in Dion's plot. As for me, a rumor actually got abroad in Syracuse to the effect that I had been executed by Dionysius because I was responsible for the whole course of events.[414]

Plutarch gives us the political account of Dion's banishment. Negotiations were proceeding between Carthage and the Syracusan government for terms of peace. A letter was intercepted addressed by Dion to the Carthaginian magistrates, instructing them to insist on his (Dion's) presence at the final negotiations "on the grounds that they would be able to negotiate a more durable settlement with his help."[415] When the sentence of exile was pronounced Dion was dispatched in a rowboat to Italy.

From this point events became spectacular. Plato, as he himself explains, remained in Syracuse with the hope of detaching Dionysius from his democratic following and effecting a reconciliation between Dion and Dionysius. Plutarch gives us a hint that this was not an entirely visionary project.[416] As a result of the wild intrigues that we have just sketched, the democracy did not entirely trust Dionysius. Plato, as we have said, remained in Syracuse. He himself describes the impossible position in which he found himself.[417] In a letter addressed to Dionysius he writes:

> After this, whether it was the work of man or of god or of chance, with your help Dion was exiled and you were left alone. Do you suppose that under those circumstances I could have any partnership with you in the govern-

ment? For I had lost the intelligent partner; and the foolish one I saw abandoned to the company of a multitude of base men, not governing but supposing he governed, being in fact under the sway of men such as I have mentioned. What was I to do in this situation? Was I not forced to do as I did, that is, as a precaution against envious calumnies to give no further heed to political affairs; and to attempt by all means to bring about a renewal of the greatest possible friendship between you and Dion, in spite of your separation and disagreement? You are yourself a witness to the fact that I never relaxed my efforts to bring this about. And at last, though with difficulty, we did reach an agreement to the effect that I should take ship for home since you were involved in war; but that, when peace was made, Dion and I were to return to Syracuse; and you on your side were to invite us.

Relations with Dionysius II became strained to a degree that promised actual danger to the person of the philosopher. Plato found himself a virtual prisoner at Syracuse, and it was only with the greatest difficulty that Plato was able to persuade Dionysius to send him back to Athens.

Dion, in the meantime, had not fared so badly. The demands of his friends in Syracuse had compelled Dionysius II to permit him the enjoyment of his private fortune.

Dion dwelt in the upper city of Athens,* with Callippus, one of his acquaintances, but for diversion he bought a country place, and afterwards, when he sailed to Sicily, he gave this to Speusippus, who was his most intimate friend at Athens. For Plato desired that Dion's disposition should be tempered and sweetened by association with men of charming presence who indulged seasonably in graceful pleasantries. And such a man was Speusippus; wherefore Timon, in his *Silli,* spoke of him as "good at a jest." And when Plato himself was called upon to furnish a chorus of boys, Dion had the chorus

* The "upper city," as distinguished from the Piraeus.

> trained and defrayed all the expenses of its maintenance, and Plato encouraged in him such an ambition to please the Athenians, on the ground that it would procure good will for Dion rather than fame for himself.
>
> Dion used to visit the other cities also, where he shared the leisure and festal enjoyments of the noblest and most statesmanlike men, manifesting in his conduct with them nothing that was rude or arrogant or effeminate, but rather great moderation, virtue, and manliness, and a becoming devotion to letters and philosophy. This procured him the emulous good will of all men, and decrees of public honors from the cities. The Lacedaemonians even made him a citizen of Sparta, without any regard for the anger of Dionysius, although at that time the tyrant was their zealous ally against the Thebans.[418]

And so we can reconstruct fairly accurately the kind of life that Dion was leading in these years of exile—between 366 and 357. He made Athens his headquarters and lived in close association with the members of Plato's Academy, and in particular with Plato's nephew, Speusippus. He lived on a palatial estate (which when he returned again to Sicily he gave to Speusippus). He spent a considerable portion of his time travelling about to various Greek cities, establishing contact with the "best and most politically minded." He showed himself pre-eminent in the aristocratic and Platonic virtues (Plutarch mentions three of the four qualities that Plato idealizes in the *Republic*—"temperance, courage, virtue"; only wisdom was omitted from the list). He also exhibited the peculiarly Platonic excellence of "good form."* He was made an honorary Spartiate, an almost unheard-of distinction for that city to bestow on any foreigner.

In 361 Plato, in accordance with the agreement mentioned in the third letter, made a last visit to Syracuse, accompanied by Speusippus and other members of the Academy. He found the court as uncongenial as he had expected. Aristippus, the Cyrenaic, was now something like a court philosopher, teaching that pleasure

* See below, p. 219.

or individual self-satisfaction was the only legitimate motive for human action.*

> Plato was unable even to raise the question of Dion's recall, and his repeated attempts to do so soon began to annoy Dionysius. The increasing estrangement was hailed with delight by Aristippus and other rival philosophers at the court; it is recorded that, when an eclipse of the sun had been predicted by Helicon of Cyzicus, Aristippus remarked that he too had a prediction to make; and that, on being asked what this was, he replied "I predict that there will soon be a breach between Dionysius and Plato."[419]

There was. On this third occasion it took the strongest influence from his friends, and especially the Pythagoreans, to rescue Plato and procure his safe return home. In a letter, supposedly addressed to Dionysius II, Archytas, the Pythagorean—at that time ruler of Tarentum—writes:

> All of us who are friends of Plato have sent to you, Samiscus, and Photidas, to claim of you this philosopher in accordance with the agreement which you made with us. And it is right that you should recollect the eagerness which you had to see him, when you pressed us to secure Plato's visit to you, promising to provide for him and to treat him hospitably in every respect, and to ensure his safety—both while he remained with you, and when he departed. Remember this, too, that you were very delighted indeed at his arrival, and that you expressed great pleasure at the time, such as you never did on any other occasion. And if any unpleasantness has arisen between you, you ought to behave with humanity, and restore the man unhurt; for by so doing you will act justly and do us a favor.[420]

With the last visit to Syracuse we get our final glimpse of Plato's active political career. It is interesting to notice that Plato is credited with no political activity in his native Athens. He seems to have regarded Athenian politics as much too closely

* See above, p. 149.

tied up with the Athenian democratic constitution. The situation was beyond hope and beyond redemption.

> And in his own country he did not meddle with state affairs, although he was a politician as far as his writings went. And the reason was, that the people were accustomed to a form of government and constitution different from what he approved of.[421]

After his lifetime of practical experience Plato now and for his remaining years gave all his energy to teaching and writing.

His nephew, Speusippus, took on the burden of active political duty. When Dion, about the year 360, began to sense new possibilities for an aristocratic restoration in Sicily, Speusippus actively co-operated in raising mercenary troops for an armed expedition. After three years of preparation they were able to collect a force of only three thousand men.[422] Their followers were evidently more devoted than numerous. Plato did not accompany the expedition in 357, feeling perhaps, the *Cambridge Ancient History* explains, "that a private quarrel did not justify the spilling of Syracusan blood." This may have been the reason, but on the other hand, seventy-one is a rather advanced age for active campaigning.

The fate of the expedition and the succeeding turmoil of political intrigue in Syracuse, though a fascinating subject, is beyond the scope of this book. One observation is rather revealing. Just as, after the battle of Leuctra with its disclosure of Spartan weakness, Plato turned to Dion of Syracuse, so, after the failure of Speusippus' attempt to restore Dion, Speusippus addressed himself in a famous letter[423] (which almost all scholars now accept as genuine) to Philip of Macedon, endeavoring to bring him more completely within the orbit of Greek politics and, we may suppose, to have him play the role that Sparta had formerly assumed and that they had envisaged for Dion.

Ten years after the expedition of Dion and Speusippus set out, the aged philosopher died (347), and on his deathbed named Speusippus his successor as head of the Academy. Professorial readers will notice with interest that Speusippus was preferred to Aristotle, the greatest intellect of antiquity, apparently on the ground that from a political point of view he was a safer man.

PART TWO

THE REPUBLIC OF PLATO

CHAPTER SEVEN

The Argument with Thrasymachus—What Is Justice?

THE STAGE has now been set for the entrance of Plato the philosopher, and that powerful thinker makes an entrance worthy of the setting. His great literary and philosophical masterpiece, the *Republic*, has exercised an incomparable influence over the minds and imaginations of Western man; hardly a century has escaped this influence, direct or indirect. And yet the influence has not always been entirely a healthy one. So much is this true that one or two modern writers, impatient at the direction which Plato has given to modern thought, have described him as the "father of unreason" and have incontinently murmured that it would have been better for science and thought if Plato had never lived. Such partisanship, whether of praise or blame, is profoundly unhistorical. It is a result of viewing Plato's ideas, in abstraction from their specific historical context, as concerned mainly with "value judgments" of the true and the good, judgments which are abstractly and universally valid, altogether without reference to the social and intellectual context which produced them. Part of this serious misvaluation of Plato arises from what we might describe as "the metaphysical prejudice"—the tendency to think of Plato primarily as the exponent of a system of thought and reality. In working out this system of truth, critics seem to suggest, Plato made stray sallies into the realm of practical politics, but these are an aberration, pardonable perhaps, because not too serious, in an intelligence otherwise detached and profound. It is the same metaphysical prejudice, in fact, which causes the tradition to think of Thales as the first "philosopher" because he was the first to put into formal and sober prose a traditional cosmological notion. They neglect too much the slow process of informal, poetical speculation about man and society, and particularly the growth of intuitions and profound prophetic utterances about the nature and meaning of justice.

And yet the very title of Plato's greatest work should save us from this misconception. He does not proclaim his dialogue as a treatise on truth or reality, but as a treatise "On the state, or about justice." Plato is in some ways wiser than his critics. He knew that the essential problem of Greek philosophy before his time was the problem of justice and its relation to the structure of the actual as well as the "ideal" or conceptual state.

The *Republic* begins with a charming *mise en scène*, laid in the house of Polemarchus, brother of the orator Lysias, (probably) in the year 411-410.[424] These were troubled years in the history of Athenian democracy; 411 was the year of the counterrevolutionary *putsch* of the Four Hundred, and there can be little doubt that many of Plato's protagonists were actively engaged on the side of the counterrevolution.[425]

Once this point is kept firmly in mind, one or two factors in the *mise en scène* become peculiarly significant. We have elsewhere described[426] how the "moderate" democratic following of Pericles, in the period of crisis for the Athenian empire, began to break up and to evolve in contradictory directions, and how the "liberal patricians" and wealthy members of the mercantile or "industrial" class began to coalesce with the "few" in opposition to the extreme democracy of Cleon, Hyperbolus, and other such leaders. Of this tendency, Cephalus, who owned a shield factory employing one hundred and twenty slaves in the Piraeus, provides a good example. Of the more extreme right-wing element Socrates can be regarded as a spokesman,—putting forward, not the brutal "right-wing" cynicism of an Antiphon or a Critias, but the somewhat idealized position of the conservative Pythagoreans and Eleatics and their heretical disciples. It should be sufficiently apparent, by now, that Thrasymachus represents the position of the "left-wing" democratic imperialists, men who proclaimed that the state was simply the reflection of class forces and that there was no transcendent principle of justice to which one could appeal.[427]

Thus in the introduction to the first book, the three main political positions of the last decade of the fifth century are very well represented. In the crisis of the Athenian democracy, there was a strong tendency for the "centrist" democrats like Cephalus to coalesce with the more ruthless and realistic "right-wing." And so in the opening pages of the *Republic* Cephalus is cajoled and admonished by Socrates, but there is no attempt at refutation. Serious argument is reserved for Thrasymachus, against whom Socrates directed all his fire, supported, no doubt, by the sympathetic silence of Polemarchus, Cephalus'[428] "heir to the argument."

It is interesting to notice, too, that Socrates treats the old age of Cephalus with extraordinary deference. We know from other sources that Socrates was freely accused of setting sons against their fathers, in an age when many "centrists" of the older generation through loyalty or indolence clung to the tradition of Pericles, while their sons, more brutally clear-sighted, toyed with the ideas of an Antiphon, a Theramenes, or a Critias. It is, perhaps, to dispel the unpleasant impression of this accusation and this fact, that Socrates' deference to Cephalus is emphasized. It is not old age that he objects to, but inflexible old age that will not yield to the logic of the new movement of reaction.

Cephalus' discussion of wealth is not without interest in this connection. He explains that his grandfather had made much money; that his father had lost heavily. He himself would be content if he could hand down to his sons what he had himself inherited or a little more.[429] If we reckon roughly thirty years to the generation, his father had presumably operated during the Periclean ascendancy; his grandfather during the more conservative regime of Cimon. Here again is represented a gentle, subtle wooing of the wealthy "centrists," suggesting that Pericles might, perhaps, not have represented their interests so well as they had supposed.

In the argument of Socrates with Cephalus the word "justice," the supreme theme of the book, is introduced, though with a quite inadequate definition—"to tell the truth and pay one's debts." Once the central theme is introduced, Cephalus is characteristically and ironically bowed away to his religious duties. When the real argument begins, there is little need for this wraith from the past; the younger generation represented by Polemarchus falls heir to the argument.[430]

But Polemarchus is vague and confused. He puts forward, in a quotation from Simonides, a quite inadequate formula, true enough, however, as far as it goes, "It is just to pay back what one owes." Socrates brings out of the armory a favorite weapon (to this we shall recur in a moment)—the analogy of the arts to enunciate a high-sounding ethical principle—that it is not just to injure any one at all, whether friend or enemy. The saying of Simonides is worthy only of "tyrants" and democratic leaders—Periander, or Perdiccas, Xerxes, or Ismenias of Thebes. (The introduction of a leader like Xerxes is perhaps intended to confuse the real issue, the attack on wealthy leaders of the *demos*.)

But all this is trifling byplay. The real argument is provided by Thrasymachus of Chalcedon who is depicted in a characteristically unflattering fashion. He gathers himself together like a wild beast for the spring. In coarse and violent language he exhorts Socrates to be done with such trifling and clearly define what justice is. In mock dismay and with an elaborate irony Socrates turns to this new opponent (fortunately he had looked at the wolf before the wolf had looked on him, and so avoided the unpleasant fate of being struck speechless).[431] After some elaborate persiflage, in which is satirized the greed of the sophistic teachers, who will not teach unless they first draw pay, Thrasymachus is made to lay down *his* definition of justice—it is the interest of the stronger in the sense that a ruling class legislates in its own interest.[432] "Some cities are governed by tyrants, in others democracy rules, in others aristocracy." And each form of government enacts the laws with a view to its own advantage, a democracy, democratic laws; a tyranny, tyrannical laws, and the others likewise.[433] This statement of the case, based presumably on observed facts in the actual government of its city-states, is the culminating point of generations of thought about the meaning of law, the state, and justice. It corresponds with the judgment of cosmology that all things are in flux. And both formulations, whether in the ethical or cosmological form, move Plato to furies of dissent. His spokesman, Socrates, moves ponderously to the attack. His first shaft should have been easily parried. He remarks that ruling groups frequently make mistakes about their own self-interest. (He might have added, if Cephalus had still been present to receive the barb, that mistakes about their own self-interest have peculiar fascination for those who hold the "centrist" position.) But this does not in itself provide sufficient reason for taking refuge in an abstract principle of justice, which is somehow more universal and more valid than any particular individual or class self-interest. But that is precisely the trap into which Thrasymachus falls. Instead of basing himself on observed facts about actual states, he takes refuge in a conceptual ruler, who *in so far as he rules* cannot make mistakes. This excursion into the idealistic realm of the pure concept unsullied by any contact with the tactable realities of actual government is precisely to the liking of the conceptualist Socrates. But we must remember that Plato was writing the dialogue; it is hard to believe that any actual flesh-and-blood Sophist could have been so stupid. (And yet, although Plato is clearly exaggerating the intellectual helplessness of the Sophists, it is important to notice that there were real historical reasons for this very helplessness. The argument of Chapter Five has doubtless made clear to the reader the social cause for the philosophical failure of the Sophists. They were putting forward democracy as an abstract concept in defense of a social order that was, after all, a mercantile slave-owning society.) And a conceptualist cannot be answered merely with a display of bad temper such as Plato attributes to Thrasymachus. For by falling into the trap, the Sophist enables Socrates to proceed with his merrily conceptual analogy between government and the arts. The function of an art is to be as complete and "scientific" as possible. The art of healing exists only to heal and to advance the boundaries of its science to the uttermost. "Horsemanship" considers only the well-being (or the better breeding) of the horse. The art of government, therefore, considers only the interest of "the weaker and the ruled." Now, in a conceptual society in which there were no clashes of economic interest, in which a physician was free to consider not profit but science only, and in a state where government did not represent a class hegemony, where there was no difference of economic interest between the governing and the governed, this description might have validity and merit. Faced with the actualities of Greek politics it must have seemed a ridiculous caricature. It is no wonder that Thrasymachus lost his temper (any alert reader might do the same). He calls Socrates a "snivelling innocent" and proceeds in a long harangue to return to the plane of the actual; but on a different level. He now no longer argues as he had previously that actual governments actually rule in the interests of a class; he launches into a praise of brute force and praises (very much like the Athenians in the Melian dialogue) the rule of the strong. We have already observed that the ethically neutral position of sophistic objective relativism can proceed in either of two directions—in hope and imagination to a society where the conflict of classes is eliminated and government can really operate on the principle of the greatest good of the greatest number; or it can result in a defense of strong-arm methods and a defense of brute force. Thrasymachus under the skilful prompting of Plato, takes, as the argument proceeds, the second position, and his first quite able perception has become historically confounded with a worship of brute force; and to "agree with Thrasymachus" has come to mean (again with Plato's assistance) wilfully to side against the angels. The violence and brutality of Thrasymachus is cleverly contrasted by Plato with Socrates' humility and ingratiating irony. A predisposition is cunningly created to accept the idealistic argument and to dwell with Socrates in the empyrean of pure concept.

For Socrates now proceeds to make a distinction between the "art" of money-making and art as such—a distinction that is abstract in the light of the highly competitive, power-seeking Greek life. If all physicians could neglect fees, if all governors could be really disinterested! But in default of a society which could produce such a state of things, the position here taken by Socrates is at best an attempt at reform by individual ethical "conversion"; and, historically, this may have been successful in the case of individuals but never in the case of a class. At worst it draws a veil of pastel-colored camouflage over the brutal realities, the subjugation of one class to another.

Pursuing his analysis in the same conceptual terms, Socrates equates justice with wisdom and "virtue," injustice with ignorance and vice.[434] But there is unhappily an ambiguity involved in the Greek word *arete* which vitiates his argument. The word may mean either functional excellence or moral virtue. It is the "function" of a knife to cut. Its *arete* or excellence is to cut well. We sometimes use the word in a transitional way when we say of a man that he is a "good-for-nothing." As Socrates develops his argument, the ambiguity becomes even more startling. A horse has a function; it has also an excellence. Eyes have a function to see; they have also an excellence, keen eyesight. The "soul" has a function—to manage, to rule, to deliberate, and so on. But if a function, then an excellence. What is the excellence of "soul"?[435] Justice. To live well, then, means to be just. But to live well is to be happy. And so the just man is happy.

A more completely dyslogistic argument could scarcely be imagined. Here we have a supreme example of the use or misuse of teleology. As we watch Socrates' practical use of the weapon which teleological analysis gives him, we find illumination shed on his dissatisfaction with Anaxagoras' failure to apply teleology as an all-embracing cosmic principle.[436] The surface plausibility of the argument turns, of course, on the ambiguity inherent in the Greek word *psyche*. We have already traced something of its development.* *Psyche* means first and foremost "life" (not as a universal principle, but individually, concretely), what distinguishes a living body from a corpse; it means, secondly, "reason" as opposed to the body; and, as we have seen, the Pythagoreans had developed the theory of soul as a unifying and governing principle, set in opposition to, and (ideally) in control of, the "chaos" of bodily appetites. And thirdly, Socrates seems to be smuggling in a third meaning—soul as "moral consciousness." Now only by a conscious confusion of these three meanings of the same Greek word is there given even a superficial plausibility to the judgment that the "excellence" of "soul" is justice and that

* See pp. 52 and 86.

the just life is a happy life. The ambiguity inherent in the Greek word for "soul" is reinforced by the ambiguity inherent in *arete* or excellence. Excellence of functioning is not really the same as moral virtue and could only be applied to the word "soul," *psyche* in the third and narrowest of its meanings—moral consciousness.

This then is the somewhat windy fare on which Socrates must feast at the festival of the goddess Bendis. It is no wonder that the confused and unhappy Thrasymachus relapses into the silence of utter disgust. To do him justice, "Plato-Socrates" is hardly satisfied with his "demonstration." What he had thought was an argument turns out to be merely a prelude. A longer road and a more toilsome discussion is needed to make even faintly convincing the idealistic concept of justice.

CHAPTER EIGHT

The Social Contract Theory of the Origin of the State

Two ingenuous and starry-eyed young men now take up the burden of the argument. In spite of the skill with which these two gentlemen are depicted as individuals, they still represent a type—a type of hereditary wealth and privilege which, because it has for so long existed unchallenged, has come to look on life with quiet eyes, and to view human affairs with a serenity which it mistakes for objectivity. Here we have another nuance in the meaning of the word justice. The two who now take up the struggle seem to regard justice rather uncritically as *what is*, the actual, the organization of society which has proved for them so comfortable and rewarding. Justice is used once again in something like its original meaning—the folkways, the actualities of an existent society, but viewed, of course, as meaning the folkways of a possessing class.

Now these young men are profoundly troubled. The secure fortress of their complacency and material well-being is increasingly buffeted by the waves of a new and swelling tide. To put it concretely, they are disturbed by the onslaught of mercantilism and democracy, which threatens to undermine for them all that they hold dear. And this seems to them like (as we should put it) a crime wave, a surge of lawlessness, of irrationality, and sheer abandon, the rule of brute force and the worship of equality. (They lack, of course, the historical equipment and the historical objectivity to realize that the movement which had thrown into eminence their forebears, or at least their class analogues, had seemed generations before, to the men of that time, equally lawlessness, the ruthless and brutal tyranny of "gift-devouring kings," whose appetites and aggressions trampled under foot all justice and all right.*)

And so now the challenge comes to Socrates from his own camp. These young men have heard rumors of the sophistic arguments. They want a thoroughgoing and "philosophical" defense of their position. They do not want to listen to platitudes, like "honesty is the best policy." They do not want to hear that justice is an evil necessity, that it is an unspoken compact "neither to commit nor to suffer injustice," a compact which has a kind of pragmatic validity because no one can satisfy all his desires and the attempt to do so would produce social chaos. And so gallantly they play the part of devil's advocate. We paraphrase: "Let us give to both types the power to do what he wills. . . . We should find the just man, urged on by covetous aggression (which every creature by *nature* pursues as a good, but by *convention and compulsion* he is compelled to a respect for equality), going to just the same place as the unjust man. As proof we have the famous fable of the ring of the ancestor of Gyges which conferred invisibility. Finding the ring, he entered upon a successful career of outrage, plunder, pillage, and political advancement.

"In order to clarify the issue let us set up in imagination two types—one, the unjust and lawless man who must be competent, strong, and clever, able to evade detection by his skill or to defy it because of his strength, shrewd to measure means and ends, and able to cloak his misdeeds in the mantle of fair morality. On the other side, let us place the good man, whose morals are no seeming, who has none of the rewards of justice, but only the tortures which the world inflicts on a misunderstood innocence; let him go to torture and death secure in nothing but the consciousness of his own rectitude. For now justice seems too much equated with earthly rewards and the power that wealth gives to bribe even the gods. But strip from each rewards and reputation. Which life is the better?"

"Yes," said his brother, Adimantus, "and there is more beside. The gods, too, are on the side of the just man and give him many rewards, in this life and the next. But for the unjust man they

* See p. 42.

reserve many vindictive punishments. And then there is the account of the poets. Justice is a noble thing, but painful and difficult; excess and injustice are pleasant and easily acquired, but frowned on by conventional esteem. It is the appearance of virtue that all men value. The thing to do, therefore, is to put on a front of virtue and then plan to commit injustice on a big scale and with impunity. This we can do by forming political 'clubs,'* or there are teachers of rhetoric who will help us in law court or assembly. As for the gods: well, perhaps, there aren't any gods, or they do not concern themselves with human affairs. If there *are* gods, all we know of them is from the poets, and the poets are unanimous in holding that every god has his price. Then, too, there are plenty of professional religionists who are ready and eager to help us pay the price. Why, then, Socrates, should a man who is powerful or wealthy or clever practice justice? So, come, show us what justice is in itself and what it does to the soul of its possessor; and injustice, too. Only then can we know which is the better. Do not praise rewards or seeming. Show us what each is in its inmost essence."

The two young men (who were probably Plato's brothers)[437] thus put to Socrates the challenge. How does Socrates meet it? After a little literary byplay he plunges with ardor into his analysis. And first he postulates a principle which is of great importance, we might say central, for the theme of the *Republic*—the analogy between the individual and the state. (Later in the book the parallelism is extended to the sciences and to reality in general.†) Man is the state in epitome; the state is the individual writ large. If we can find the origin of justice in the state, we shall know something about it in the individual "soul." What is the origin of justice in the state? Or, more generally, what is the origin

* The part played by the aristocratic clubs in the decade of counterrevolution had been very considerable. And the Pythagorean "clubs" were the traditional defenders of aristocratic interest. Note the air of impartiality which is here created—the conservative clubs, the democratic sophists. Remember the dramatic date of the *Republic*, before sophism had broken down into cynicism.

† The parallel is, of course, not a discovery but is implicit in Pythagorean teachings. See above, p. 83.

of the state? The origin of the state is to be found in the fact that no one of us is sufficient unto himself. We have all of us need of others. Our needs of food, clothing, and shelter. And so the first unit or association will be a farmer, a builder, a weaver; perhaps we should add a cobbler and one or two other craftsmen. This would be the "most rudimentary polity"—the simplest and most essential form of human association. In such a grouping we shall discover that one man has one set of *natural* aptitudes, another man another.[438] So specialization means the multiplication of crafts and craftsmen—carpenters and smiths, neatherds and shepherds. And with specialization we shall have exchange. We must import, and in order to import we must have produce for the market. Hence we shall have traders, and we shall have to establish a market place. A market place involves people who specialize in trade; but in properly organized cities, these are people who are weak in body and useless for any other task.[439] So we have shopkeepers; and finally we must have people who sell their strength—men whose mental power makes them unworthy to associate with us, but whose strength of body fits them for toil. So wageworkers are needed in our state. In such a state men will live in idyllic simplicity, living on barley and wheaten cakes kneaded on rushes or clean leaves; they will sleep on rustic beds strewn with smilax or myrtle; and so they will feast, drinking their own wine, "with garlands on their heads, they will sing hymns to the gods and pleasantly consort together, not begetting children beyond their means, guarding against poverty and war."

"A city of pigs," said Glaucon. One must let them have the conventional luxuries of food, furniture, and attire. And so, Socrates makes a distinction between the "healthy" city of Arcadian simplicity and the "fevered" city of luxurious living. Somewhere in the transition we shall discover justice and injustice. For the luxurious city will need swarms of attendants, servants, and tutors. Men and women will devote much care to their appearance and will learn to eat pork. And a territory which was once sufficient will no longer be so. So with luxury comes war, and in luxury (great and important discovery) we have found the origin of war. And with war arises the need for a professional army and men who specialize in this particular work. These will be the "guards"[440] for our city and we shall have to pay great attention to their education. This leads to a long discussion of the education of the "guards," which we shall reserve for a later consideration.

At this point we may make an observation. Pride of craftsmanship, based on skill and specialization, was, as we have seen, a democratic ideal. It represented the contribution of the fifth-century artisans to the intellectual atmosphere of that century. It was most consciously propounded by Hippocrates and his medical school. Plato, in accepting specialization and by making of government a specialized art, succeeded in giving the notion a quite different and highly aristocratic content. In so doing he neatly turned the democratic weapon against the democracy.

In this account of the origin of the state there is much that is quite startlingly naïve as well as something that is, for the period, profound. We should notice in the first place that, even though Plato never mentions Democritus, the intellectual problem is in a sense set for him by the Democritean position. Or, to put the matter more exactly, social forces had proceeded to the point in their evolution by the time of Plato and Democritus where the theory of the isolated individual seemed natural to both progressive and conservative thinkers. In attempting to ground his theory of justice firmly in "human nature," Plato must somehow bring individuals, originally isolated, together and find some "natural" bond of cohesion.[441] Otherwise there can be no "justification" for the form of human association that we call the state. It was perhaps the realization of the dangers and pitfalls into which this theory of the origin of society led him which induced Plato to give a quite different account of the genesis of society in the *Laws*.[442] Moreover, Plato shows very great insight when he maintains that the state is based on an increasing specialization and an increasing interdependence of craftsmen and crafts. If we may recall our discussion earlier in the book, we may note the sharp difference between Homeric life and fifth-century society in this regard. Plato, however, very cleverly interprets this mutual dependence of increasing specialization as a "natural" inequality.

Plato, like so many modern thinkers since the Renaissance, endeavored to base his theory of the state on a theory of human nature: we are by nature interdependent, each one of us is fitted by nature to do one particular task. This is the central fact in the secret of the origin of society and the justification of justice. Incidentally, as we shall observe later on, this "natural unlikeness" leads readily to the notion of "natural inequality" and the theory of some men who are nature's rulers, and others nature's ruled. The affinities of this view with later attempts to found the defense of a particular form of social organization on a theory of an original "human nature" are very striking.

> The noble savage of Rousseau, the "economic man" of the classical economists, the "economic subject" of Boehm-Bawerk, the "farmer isolated from all the world," or the "inhabitant of the forest primaeval" who forms the starting point of other marginal utilitarian economists; each of these and one other [the Freudian "id"] is an isolated man. It is from the characteristics of some such individual that we are to deduce the nature of society. Social institutions are to be accounted for by reference to the desires and impulses of "natural man."[443]

From this concept of an isolated man endowed with an inherent need for others Plato then developed his notion of the evolution of society. Greek literature is full of nostalgic references to a golden age in the past, and there can be little doubt that all are due to traditional reminiscences of the older tribal order. As we have seen in our previous discussion, the process of technical advance and reorganization which broke up the Greek gentile society worked untold hardship for the great majority of mankind, although it favored many individuals in society and as a process and as a whole was progressive, necessary, and good. And now in the period of the mercantile democracy it was relatively easy to paint the process which brought war and "injustice" into the world as originating in trade, and particularly the increasing incidence of luxury or, as we should say, a rising standard of living. We have already, in previous chapters, given an account of this social development of the Greek world. In view of this development Plato's account seems a most extraordinary mixture of naïvete and insight. He has much more sense than most idealistic thinkers of the primary economic motivations of things. The "city" or, as we should say, the state originates in men's needs for food, clothing, and shelter. A teleological view of the state is established for Plato as for Aristotle by making a distinction between origin and validity. The state *comes into being* for the sake of life, it *exists* for the sake of the good life.[444]

At the same time, the concession that Plato here makes to economic realism is relatively a slight concession. His account of social evolution bears little relation to history or to fact. There was, of course, never a time when isolated individuals wandered around loose in the forests and suddenly came to feel a need for mutual support. The isolated individual is an abstraction, a fiction, and no valid philosophical structure can be built on so tenuous a foundation. At every stage of social evolution man is moulded from infancy by a whole nexus of relations, in the family, the tribe, the clan, or the state. Moreover, the economic "independence" of a unit, say the family, is a very relative thing. It is obviously much higher in a stage of self-sufficient agriculture than it is in a world-wide industrial society. And finally the account which Plato gives of the growth of the state is almost absurdly abstract. He does not show in any specific way how the rise of commerce, production for the market, breaks down the older tribal relations, creates or at least fosters the institution of slavery, creates the institution of private property with its manifold inequalities, makes necessary the state as an instrument of coercion for the possessing class, and fosters both internal friction and external warlike aggression. All these important aspects of the historical development of the post-Homeric period Plato passes over in almost complete silence. And yet, unless he examines the specific historical evolution of the Greek state, his attempt to justify the state as the organ of "justice" must remain to the last degree bald and unconvincing.

Plato's account of the education of the "guards," with its prescription for a mixture of physical and literary training in order to make the "soul" at once high-spirited and gentle, is so well known that we can at this time pass it by with little comment except to observe that in the light of specific Pythagorean practice it was not so novel or so "enlightened" as it might seem when viewed in abstraction from its historical context. We have already noticed the account given of Pythagorean education and have noted that in actuality the aim of the Pythagoreans was the self-development of a ruling and possessing class. But to the education of the "guards" we shall have to recur when we have examined Plato's description of them and of their social function.

Nor is there need to make many observations about Plato's strictures on arts and the poets except to notice the consciousness in Plato that all art has a social function and involves an element of what we should call propaganda. Nothing could be further from Plato's mind than the modern theory of "art for art's sake." From Plato's point of view, the demand for censorship of the artists is a perfectly logical demand and is perfectly consistent with his whole authoritarian position.

Nor need we spend much time, in the light of our previous analysis, with his specific criticisms of the poets. In essence Plato's criticism is a reaction against an earlier and non-moralized stage of Greek religion. We have already seen what exactly the process of moralization meant. In the passage from a mere tribal father (with remnants in his make-up of his earlier function as a nature god) to the lord of the universe, the fountainhead of justice, the sanction of a particular social order, and the heavenly analogue to earthly rule, it was inevitable that Zeus should still retain many traces of his more unsavory past, particularly when that past had been enshrined in poetry of a quite singularly compulsive charm, and poetry which was still the chief medium for literary education in the Greek world. To Plato the defense of the divine as a cosmic ruling principle, the sanction for earthly rule and for a justice which was the direct antithesis of equality, was so important that he could hardly bear with equanimity the cloying traces of Zeus' quite amoral and premoral past.

CHAPTER NINE

The Sociology and Psychology of the Platonic Virtues

THE AFFINITY of the thinking of Plato with Pythagoreanism, and also, as a consequence, Plato's relation to the actualities of contemporary Greek society, begin to be most apparent in the fourth book. After the long essay on the education of the "guards," Adimantus breaks in with a question:

> What will be your defense, Socrates, if anyone objects that you are not making these men very happy and that through their own fault? For the city really belongs to them and yet they get no enjoyment out of it as ordinary men do by owning lands and building fine big houses and providing them with suitable furniture and winning the favor of the gods by private sacrifices and entertaining guests and enjoying too those possessions which you just now spoke of, gold, silver, and all that is customary for those who are expecting to be happy? But they seem, one might say, to be established in idleness in the city, exactly like hired mercenaries, with nothing to do but keep guard.[445]

The question of the economic remuneration of the "guards" will be raised later when we come to consider Platonic "communism." For the moment we must concentrate on Plato's reply. It is not our function, he argued, to foster the well-being of any part of the state but of the whole. If our "guards" were wealthy, they would no longer be "guards," just as farmers dressed in fine robes and decked with gold would no longer be farmers, nor potters, if they were allowed to feast and tend the wheel when they pleased, would any longer be potters. (The assumption of Plato that comfort and an economic abundance destroy craftsmanship will seem quaint to many readers. It has this justification in the fifth-century democracy which Plato was criticizing—that, in a society of sharp class distinctions and yet relative social fluidity, an artisan who prospered frequently rose from his own class and took to new and more "gentlemanly" (in Plato's sense) work. Thus, to quote only two very obvious examples, Socrates began life as a stonecutter, Protagoras as a porter. Increasing wealth and recognition in both cases destroyed them *qua* stonecutter or porter. But to generalize from this about the nature of all workers in all types of society is manifestly absurd.)

By an adroit transition Plato goes on to discuss the question of the ideal city's efficiency in war. His point boils down to this. Whereas other cities are in no sense unified, containing (each within one framework) two cities, the rich and the poor, the city of fancy which he is building in imagination will be a unity, and a unity based on economic simplicity. In such a conflict the unified city will always be able to find allies within the framework of its rivals "by offering to the one faction, the property, the power, the very persons of the other."[446]

All of this has a very familiar ring. It bears a startling similarity to actual Spartan practice. On a basis of relative economic simplicity and a landed aristocracy that acted in effect as an occupying garrison, Sparta was able to keep great influence in Hellenic politics (though rarely sending an army outside the Peloponnesus) by supporting oligarchic and reactionary factions in the other Greek states. This is a fact so well known to students of Greek history that it hardly needs specific documentation. We need only remember that, when the actual showdown came in Athens, the oligarchs could hold power in Athens only so long as Lysander was actually on the spot with a Spartan garrison.

Nor will the modern reader be without his suspicions when the "guards" are represented as poor men whose merits and power are not to be rewarded with individual wealth. We are so used to dictatorship of great wealth which goes to any lengths to pose as something different—the independent revolutionary action of the lower middle classes, for example as in Hitler's Germany—that we are inclined immediately to suspect that Plato's "guards" would, in practice, represent the actual economic interests of a class, and in all probability of a landed class and no mere ideal utopian governors. The historical conduct of the Pythagoreans and of Socrates, of Plato himself and his nephew Speusippus, will serve to heighten this suspicion, and suspicion will become very much like certainty as Plato develops his argument further.

There is only one salvation, he goes on to argue, for the state. The "guards" must be constantly vigilant against any kind of "innovation" in the regime of education—music and gymnastics—that Plato has prescribed for them.

> For a change to a new type of music is something to to beware of as a hazard to the whole structure. The modes of music are never disturbed without unsettling the most fundamental political and social conventions, as Damon affirms and as I am convinced.[447]

Plato's recognition of the class affinity between art and music on the one hand, and politics on the other, is distinctly refreshing—and only seems startling to us because we have in our upbringing so much idle chatter (going back ultimately to the neo-Platonists) about abstract artistic forms and rhythms. This passage again strikes a modern reader as curiously "idealistic." Plato suggests that a change in literary modes will produce social and political change rather than, as we should argue, result *from* social and political change.[448] We are irresistibly reminded of Parmenides, who compelled the citizens to take an oath not to change his laws; and the discussion we then put forward of the social significance of this reluctant attitude to change will apply equally well to Plato.*

Plato's aversion to the mercantile democracy† is equally apparent in his opposition to the litigation which commercialism inevitably meant. The litigious tastes of the Athenian democracy were almost a stock theme of the comic poets, particularly the conservative Aristophanes; and the endless lawsuits conducted

* See above, p. 99.

† In the *Laws* he would place the good state so far from the sea that merchants could not get to it. Cf. Pythagoras.

in Athens were one of the main burdens of complaint from the "allied" (or subject) states of the Athenian Empire. Now comes Plato to take up the attack. It is a sign of ill-health when a city abounds in lawyers and doctors. In the earlier society of the tribe and under the Arcadian oppression of the landed aristocracy there had been no such need. There were probably few members of either profession in contemporary Sparta. Once we have established aright our educational system (and incidentally reverted to an earlier stage of social evolution—the rule of a landed aristocracy) then there will be no need to regulate by legislation all the infinite details of

> contracts with workmen, and actions for foul language and assault, the filing of declarations, the impaneling of juries, the payment and exaction of any dues that may be needful in markets or harbors, and in general market, police, or harbor regulations and the like.[449]

It would not be fitting to dictate to good and honorable men (the Greek phrase is *kaloi kagathoi*).* It is not simply to "good and noble" "guards" in general that Plato would entrust the care of his state, but to good and noble men of aristocratic birth as opposed to the democracy, men marked by a set of aristocratic virtues, with the pride and privilege of caste, and endowed with a supreme contempt for mercantile life and trade. It is no wonder that such men would solve the details of commercial intercourse. They would solve them presumably by a major operation involving the expeditious extermination of the patient.

The busy, teeming political life of democratic society, always "multiplying such petty laws and amending them in the expectation of attaining what is best," is like the life of men who are sick, yet from "intemperance are unwilling to abandon their unwholesome regimen."[450] The only cure is a complete change of life. Otherwise it is like trying to "behead the Hydra."

This is all that we need in the way of legislation. The rest we must leave to the Delphic Apollo,† who will give the sanctions

* For the significance of this phrase see the addendum at the end of this chapter.

† For the role of Apollo in Greek social life see above, p. 53ff.

of religion to the prescription of the lawgiver. Apollo is, in matters like this, the traditional interpreter; he interprets "the religion of their fathers"[451] for all mankind.

"Then, O son of Ariston, your city is built." The ancestral customs, we might paraphrase, are recalled, Apollo is exalted to his proper place, and every trace of mercantile domination is expunged. Where now is justice to be found? For our city is good in the full sense of the word.

As, then, our city of imagination is wise, brave, temperate, and just, if we can find the other three, what is left will be justice.* If we can find wisdom in the state, and bravery and "temperance," then justice will be isolated and must stand revealed. Plato, let us notice, assumes the traditional four virtues as an exhaustive list and then proceeds by what critics have dignified as the method of residues, to isolate the fourth by ticking off the first three.

Where then is wisdom to be found? A city is not called wise because of the skill of its craftsmen, its carpenters, or makers of wooden pots or brass utensils, nor again because its farmers are skillful. Where *does* wisdom reside? Clearly in the rulers, the "guards." And the craftsmen are many, the guardians, few. A city is wise then because of the virtue of the few, and wisdom is the prerogative of the "guards."

Now courage? Where does that reside? In those who are to defend the city, the military "assistants" of the "guards." What is courage? It is the indelible conviction that "things to be feared" are precisely those which the lawgiver has designated in their education. It is a "right opinion," fostered by law through education, about what is to be feared and what is not. Such a conviction, implanted by the lawgiver and by tradition, must be like a fast dye, not to be washed out by pleasure or pain or fear—emotions more potent than any lye or soap to wash away the dye of steadfastness. This then resides in the military "assistants," and is their peculiar prerogative.

* The logic here is distinctly shady. Shorey remarks, "He," in the infancy of philosophy, "is quite as well aware as his censors can be in the senility of criticism that he is not proving anything by this method, but merely setting forth what he has assumed for other reasons." It is not often that unanimity can be so easily attained. But just what are the *other reasons*?

Plato's emphasis on courage is both interesting and significant. Let us recall that in the following century the materialist Epicurus put forward the idea of "hide and live" (*lathe biōsas*). The difference is, of course, that for Plato philosophy is still directed at practical and political ends, it is still a philosophy for action. Plato, living as he did in a democratic environment, felt the need for change to aristocratic government, and hence stressed courage as an essential quality in men who wish to effect change. The preference for the purely contemplative life does not become dominant until the time of Aristotle. The Epicureans, of course, with their emphasis on personal enjoyment, exhorted their followers to shrink from every kind of political activity. Yet there are premonitions of this attitude in Plato. If the philosopher does not happen to be born in the "city that suits his nature," he will keep aloof from politics, he will cower, as it were, behind a wall, taking cover from the storms of dust and sleet until the tempest has passed by.

Now how about "temperance"? Where can that be found? "Temperance" is a kind of order and a mastery over certain pleasures and lusts. The "temperate" man is master of himself. But what is the meaning of such a phrase as this? That the soul of man has a better part and a worse part,* and self-mastery means the control of the *naturally* worse by the *naturally* better. If, because of bad breeding or evil associations, the better part, which is the smaller, is dominated by the many and the bad, then we call such a man "intemperate" and say that he is not master of himself.†

> Just as in man, then, the smaller ruling part governs the "mob" of motley appetites and pleasures and pains one would find chiefly in children and women and slaves

* This is a refinement of the Pythagorean antithesis; The desires are not now assigned to the body but to the "lower" part of the "soul." However, it was not convenient for Socrates to make this distinction when he was proving to the discomfiture of Thrasymachus that justice is the "excellence" (or smooth functioning) of "soul." See above, p. 193.

† We do not have an English equivalent for the phrase "weaker than himself," the opposite of "master of himself."

> and in the many and the bad of those who are called freemen.[452]

So in the ideal state one finds the domination of the desires that reside in the many and the bad by the wisdom and desires that reside in the few and self-restrained. This, then, is the temperate city, and temperance does not, like courage and virtue, reside only in one class; it resides both in the rulers and the ruled. It is an agreement *based on nature*, between the ruler and the ruled, between the few and the many, that the former ought to govern, the latter submit to government.[453] This, then, is the meaning of "temperance": it is harmony, unity, concord; it is agreement between *natural* rulers and *natural* inferiors as to who should govern and who should submit.

Only one or two comments are needed for this breathtaking assumption. The meaning of nature and human nature on which Plato is striving to base his philosophical defense of aristocracy has suffered a perceptible extension. He began by postulating a "natural" need that men have one of the other; he now comes to postulate a "natural" inequality by which some men are fitted to rule and some to be ruled. The "law of nature" which the more generous-minded Sophists rejected in the case of slaves is now extended by Plato to include the democracy. The apparent inequalities which depend, in any such society as the Greek (or our own), on a thousand accidents of birth and upbringing, are thus by Plato carried right back to the nature of things and made the justification for the aristocratic state. Here is, in another form, the Pythagorean doctrine of "geometrical equality" and the rejection of bare or arithmetical equality as a principle of justice. This, too, is the meaning of harmony and concord in the state; it is an agreement between "natural" governors and "natural" governed (we can surmise that the "agreement" is in practice a little easier for the former); it is a willing submission of the "lower orders" to the dictates of men whom they must accept as their "natural" masters. It is the willingness of the "lower orders" to "do their duty in that state of life to which it has pleased God to call them." "Temperance" is equivalent to "my station and its duties," and the station and its duties are based on an inexorable natural inequality, let "sophists" and democrats rage as they will. Justice, as Plato develops the concept, is the philosophical defense of the aristocratic state, which in a period of reaction, after the glorious and creative age of democracy, was forced in practice to become the authoritarian state (as it seemed ready to do at any moment in theory).

Where, in all this, is justice? There follows a pretty piece of literary byplay. The huntsmen surround the thick and tangled covert, lest the quarry escape. The leading huntsman, Socrates, makes his way in, with comments about the tangles and the shadows. He catches sight of his game and gives the view-halloa.

> "I believe we have found the trail, Glaucon, and I don't think it will get away." "Goodness," said he. "What numbskulls we were," said I. "Like people who hunt high and low for something they hold in their hands. We have been talking about this all the time. We have said that each one man should confine himself to one pursuit in the city, the pursuit for which his *nature* is most *naturally* adapted. And to do one's task and not to meddle in many is justice which can then be defined as one man, one task for which he is *naturally* fitted."[454] [One man, one task—in accordance with nature.]

So then justice has been triumphantly based on the bedrock of natural law. It is the recognition that of the three classes in the state, the one should rule and give out decrees and utter judgments; the other should assist with armed might and (if we may quote again Solon's phrase) bring force to the dictates of justice. The third, ordinary people, the many, the democracy, should toil and believe, submit and obey. This is, in a sense, the culminating point for us, too, in our long pursuit of the "Greek concept of justice." The word has proved an elusive quarry and has, Proteuslike, taken on many shapes. And, as we recall, at one point it seemed in danger of becoming equated with equality (*to ison*) or, at least, the moderate form of the same idea, "equality before the law" (*isonomia*).* Here is the final rejection of any such

* "The law, in its majestic equality, forbids both rich and poor alike to sleep under bridges, to beg in the streets, and to steal bread." ("La majes-

view. The ghost was successfully laid; for the rest of antiquity and well into the modern world there was little notion (except among slaves, proletarians, and Christians, nor firmly among them) that justice might be equality. This was a passing dream of liberal thinkers in the great creative days of the Athenian democracy, not to be revived until the modern democratic movement, and then with richer content and a more concrete reality in a society no longer based on slavery.

And yet Plato is basing his theories on an interesting and important observation. As we have already observed, it was the increasing specialization of crafts that had made the rise of trade and the democratic movement possible. It is, to say the least, distinctly interesting that Plato is, so far as we can judge, infinitely more aware of the necessary prerequisites of the commercial democracy than are the democratic thinkers themselves. At the same time, and characteristically, he transforms the specialization of *classes,* assumes that one class is naturally fitted to rule, and in so doing turns an important perception about the social base of the commercial democracy and the meaning of social and economic progress into a powerful weapon of antidemocratic argument.

The process by which the meaning of *diké* is transformed is now complete. To summarize an argument—the *way* in Homer became the *protest* of the dispossessed in Hesiod. In Solon it became the reconciliation of classes in the prescriptions of a lawgiver. Radical thinkers of the fifth-century democracy maintained that it was equality or equality before the law, while the Pythagoreans argued that it was a subtler and more recondite kind of equality, that would permit of the eminence of the "best." Socrates, expressing doubt about the possibility of ever finding an eternal justice, was only sure that it was not what democratic

---

tueuse égalité des lois, qui interdit au riche comme au pauvre de coucher sous les ponts, de mendier dans les rues et de voler du pain."—Anatole France, *Le Lys Rouge,* p. 118.) It is interesting to notice that the slogan of the French Revolution, "Liberty, Equality, Fraternity," tended to be modified by the triumphant "haute bourgeoisie" into an abstract "equality before the law" with "equal" opportunity to engage in commerce and industry.

statesmen, artisans, and thinkers, thought it might be. Now in Plato it has found, as it were, a resting-place: it is a specialization of functions as between classes, based on a *natural* inequality.

Is, then, our demonstration complete? "Not quite," said Plato. "We must refer our definition back to the individual, and if it is confirmed there all will be well."[455] The state was thought to be just because three "natural" kinds of nature (classes) existing in it each performed its own function. And are there these three forms in the individual too? Basing himself on a concept of contradictions—that the same faculty cannot give rise to opposite actions—Plato concludes that the human soul has three "faculties" and that each of these faculties has a different function. The three parts or faculties of the soul are reason at one extreme, desire at the other, and midway what he calls *thumos* or *to thumoeides*, the high-spirited. This last is a very elusive category and it would almost seem to be included to make the tripartite schematization complete. The tripartite plan he propounds in the state may derive indirectly from his actual experience with Athenian politics; for in Athens the middle-of-the-road democrats of the Periclean circle represented an ambiguous class that could, in different circumstances, be drawn either toward democracy or toward reaction (we recall the nickname of Theramenes: "the buskin," as fitting either foot). Whether this is the actual derivation of this schematic plan or not, *thumos* is a "faculty" that can be drawn in either direction. When it is drawn toward reason, it lends a kind of emotional urge to the dictates of "thought," and we can almost translate it as emotion, in so far as it is good emotion, as opposed to the passions which are very plural and bad. (It is now becoming apparent that to Plato, plurality has a democratic flavor; it is reminiscent of "the many" and, therefore, *evil.*) At all events, the moral problem for Plato takes the simple form of a conflict between reason and desire, a conflict which he illustrates by the story of a man who had a morbid impulse to look upon some corpses outside the Long Walls. And for a time his reason resisted, but

> overpowered in spite of all by his desire, holding his eyelids wide, he rushed up to the corpses and said,

> "There, you poor fools, feast your fill on the lovely sight."[456]

A man may be compelled by his desires against his reason; he is then angry with himself; high spirit or anger, in such a circumstance, becomes an ally of reason and the man is in a position to subdue and eradicate the desires. As Plato puts the matter elsewhere in the *Republic*, beneath the mask of human person there are present a lion, a man, and a many-headed beast. If reason, typified by the man, makes alliance with the lion of *thumos*, then they can keep in order the many-headed beast. In other words, the ethical task, for Plato, is to unify or integrate the personality. When this process of integration is accomplished, the individual can be said to be both happy and good.[457]

Exactly, then, as the good state is the unified state, so the just man is the unified and integrated man, one who estimates every one of his multiple and chaotic impulses and desires in the light of the well-being of the whole personality. Or, in other words, it is the task of training to develop *purpose* in the human individual so that he shall not be tossed hither and yon by every wind of impulse but rather make each impulse find its place in and contribute to the unity of the whole. And the validity of "justice" in this sense, that is, harmony or integration in the individual and the state, can no more, Plato argued, be questioned than the value of physical health itself, which is also in a sense a harmony of differing parts. (Let us recall Alcmaeon of Croton and his teaching about the meaning of health.)

This doctrine is so important for ethical theory and so attractive as a guide to conduct that there is a very natural tendency for philosophers and commentators to forget its origin in Plato's mind. And yet the scheme of parallels which he constructs between the individual and the state gives so manifest a clue to Plato's thinking that it is but an ill service to misunderstand his meaning, to see the strength but not the weakness of his teaching on this point.

Let us return to the question of the state. Plato, standing as he did in the middle of a period of bitter class struggle, longed for unity within the state, for a polity which should not be two cities within one framework—the city of the rich and the city of the poor. It is a desire with which we can sympathize if unity is to be attained by removing the deep-seated antagonism between the possessors and the dispossessed; this can only be done, of course, by removing the economic reasons for antagonism as, e.g., in modern socialist theory. Plato was in no position to envisage such a solution. He was a member of the ruling and landed class in a slave-owning society; his passion for unity, therefore, (we remember the memories that still lingered in the Greek world of the Arcadian simplicity of primitive tribal society) took the reactionary form of a demand for subordination, the willing submission of the "natural subordinates" to their "natural superiors." And instead of using the great technical advances that mercantilism had brought in its train for the general good, Plato can see nothing but the "evils" of democracy in a class-riven society. He calls, therefore, for an abandonment of most of the progress that the world had made up to his day, for a return to more primitive economic forms, for a reduction in the standard of living of everyone, because wealth coming to the few had brought such manifold abuses.

The parallel with the individual is exact. However desirable integration may be as an ethical ideal, the unified and disciplined service, for example, of a great social purpose, yet this integration cannot be achieved by neglecting, thwarting, repressing the body and denying the validity of its functioning. Let us remember, again, the Pythagorean source of this distinction between soul and body, the passion to prove the validity and justice of a ruling power in the state. Plato's attempt to achieve integration by subordination and repression in the human individual is precisely parallel to his attempt to achieve a unified state by the subordination of those who toil. In other words the logical (and historical) outcome of Platonic theory was asceticism, and an asceticism which became increasingly stern and harsh. But let us remember that Plato's asceticism is founded on the actualities of Spartan practice, that it envisaged as rewards for the best warriors unrestricted intercourse with either sex, and that it had little in common with modern Puritan asceticism. But it is clear that there is a limit beyond which asceticism cannot go in denying to the body the validity of its functioning. If the most elementary desires for food and drink are not satisfied, the individual will perish; without reproduction, the species becomes extinct. No ancient theorist went so far as to advocate this, but ancient literature teems with exhortations to limit one's desires—exhortations to the rich to avoid provoking envy, to the poor to avoid discontent and rebellion. Here again antiquity was to a degree conditioned by its economic situation. Living as they did, always in an economy of scarcity, the *distribution* of economic goods was their most vital and insoluble problem. Abundance or luxury for one man meant quite literally starvation for another. Living, as we do, in an economy of potential abundance, the achievement of unity in the state will for us necessarily take a quite different form. So that it will be easier for us to appreciate the passion of ancient idealists for unity, harmony, and concord within the state than to approve the specific proposals that they put forward to attain that end. Yet to appreciate fully and clearly the origin of this impulse in the Pythagoreans and Plato and to be in a position to see the strong and weak points in their contentions will be the best possible basis for understanding the more "philosophical" aspects of Plato's work.

Addendum I

We have already mentioned the almost technical significance of the term *kaloi kagathoi,* the noble and good—the gentlemen—the phrase that aristocrats applied to themselves as opposed to the vile, *ponēroi,* and the many, *to plēthos*. Perhaps it will assist in establishing the central point if we look back at the history of the phrase and concept. In building the ideal state, Plato has in mind turning back the clock of social evolution and entrusting the control of the state to the landed proprietors (and this in spite of his fine language about divorcing his "guards" from economic rewards). The first definite political associations of the phrase *kaloi kagathoi* are to be found in the plays of Aristophanes, whose dislike for the democracy is clear in almost every play. In the *Knights*, for example, a definite contrast is made between the *ponēroi*, or base-born, and the *kaloi kagathoi*. *Demos* has rejected the latter in favor of lamp dealers, cobblers and leather sellers (735). In the *Frogs* (718-37), a comparison is made between two kinds of coin: the old kind, the noble and good, well-born, temperate, and just—those who are reared in palaestra, chorus, and "music"; the new coinage is the brazen, foreign, ruddy, base-born, and sprung from base-born. (The whole passage is worth reading for its use of aristocratic words as praise and their reverse as terms of biting contempt.)

In Thucydides (VIII, 48) the people called *kaloi kagathoi* are contrasted with the *dēmos*. In Xenophon's *Memorabilia* (I, 6, 13) Socrates makes an interesting remark—it is prostitution to offer one's beauty to all comers for money, but he who willingly associates with someone he knows to be *euphuēs* is doing what befits a *kalos kagathos*. Xenophon comments that Socrates is trying to lead his hearers to *kalokagathia*. The sophist offers his wisdom for money to all comers, but the man who associates only with the "well-born" and teaches him all he can does what befits the *kalos kagathos*. The evidence might be multiplied, and the point will be reinforced when we consider Plato's attitude to "temperance." In general it can hardly be gainsaid that *kalokagathia* is equivalent to noble birth, that it implies an aversion to mercantile life and the crafts (the only two approved "crafts" for *kaloi kagathoi* are farming and war—Xen. *Oecon.* 4, 4)—its characteristic virtues are *eleutheria* (liberal education—Xen. *Memor.* 1. 2. 29; 3. 10. 5; Cf. *Symp.* 8. 23), justice, and temperance. The elusive significance of the word "justice" has been already indicated. *To the word "temperance" we shall have reason to recur.*

Addendum II

The Greek word *sōphrōn*, which we translate "temperate," is a difficult one to convey in English. It clearly has little to do with "temperance" in the modern sense, particularly after generations of warfare against Bacchus and his modern counterpart John Barleycorn. There are many connotations to the word which will become clear if we examine its use by Plato's predecessors. We have observed already, in discussing the religion of Apollo, the development of an aristocratic ethic of "nothing too much." He who succeeds in this ideal is the *sōphrōn* or "temperate" man. The verb *sōphronizein* means "to repress excess" and so to chastize or punish—particularly one's social inferiors. In Xenophon (*Mem.* I. 16) masters chasten the lusts of their slaves by means of hunger. In Persia an official each year went the rounds of the provinces with an army to repress *hybris* or rebellion. This task was called *sophronizein* (Xen. *Cyr.* VIII. 6. 16). In the same work, Tigranes tells how his father learned discretion by being outwitted and made to feel inferior to Cyrus. Cyrus asks, "Is it enough to make men temperate—to learn that other men are better than they are?" Tigranes admits that chastisement is also necessary (*Cyr.* III. I. 16). Thucydides uses the word in the same way (VI. 78) for the chastisement of the Syracusans and for the regime of severe economy and retrenchment instituted in 413 (VIII. I. 3). In Thucydides the words have asociations and overtones that are distinctly aristocratic. It is associated with the virtue of reverence (*aidōs*), and in the very interesting reflections which the historian makes on the evils of civil war and revolution—the watchword of the democracy, "political equality" (equality before the law), is specifically counterposed to the aristocratic slogan of "temperate" aristocracy—*aristokratia sōphrōn* (III. 82). So in the negotiations that led to the counter-revolution of the Four Hundred a more "temperate" constitution is made the condition of the king's intervention. The following clause in the passage, lest we should be in doubt, explains the meaning of a more "temperate" constitution, namely, to restrict office to the few (VIII. 53). (Thucydides comments that the *demos* took badly the suggestion of oligarchy.) To the "temperate," the characteristic praise-word for aristocracy, was frequently contrasted the "intemperate" (*akolastos*—the word is derived from *a*-privative and *kolazein*, to punish) a state of being unpunished. This is applied to the democracy and particularly the sailors, as in Euripides' phrase—the "intemperate mob, naval anarchy" (*Hecuba* 607). Perhaps this will be sufficient to suggest that "temperance" has connotations in Plato's mind of a peculiar sort—connotations that the ordinary English translation of Plato hardly brings out.

CHAPTER TEN

The Education of the "Guards"

PLATO'S THEORY of the right kind of education for the "guards" of his ideal state is presented in the metaphor of harmony and proportion which he (like the Pythagoreans) has developed to express his notion of justice. We have already seen what importance the Pythagoreans attached to musical "harmony" and mathematical proportion as providing a kind of intellectual justification for their concept of the "unified" harmonious state, based on a view of justice which is not equality, but a balance to be attained through a mathematical ratio of inequality. We have seen in the last chapter how Plato endeavored to base his theory of the state and of justice on a similar concept of "natural" inequality.

The parallelism there suggested extends to his views on education. This can be best demonstrated by considering Plato's views side by side with those attributed to Pythagoras. Plato held that early education should be based on "music" (what we should call the "arts"—as in our phrase Bachelor of Arts) and gymnastics. Both these aspects are intended to mold the "soul" rather than the body, although the importance of the body is not entirely overlooked. Asceticism had not yet progressed so far that anyone might suppose that the body could be neglected or even abused in order to nurture the soul. As we have seen, the Pythagorean-Platonic theory represents the first movement towards asceticism and gives it a basis in theory. But before asceticism can develop as a world view, centuries of development will be necessary and the decay of ancient society will have to make men turn in revulsion from a hopeless world.

The two types of education are in a sense to be regarded as complementary: the literary education is intended to make the "soul" sensitive (*malthakos*); the education in gymnastics is intended to make the "soul" high-spirited and brave. Plato here makes a rather sharp criticism of the conventional education of professional athletes: it does not, he thought, produce the kind of physical equipment that a soldier needs; it produces a drowsy disposition, which is aroused on occasion for a short period to great and abnormal activity; and it unfits the soldier to stand changes of climate or of diet. But with modifications in the direction of simplicity, the conventional training of athletes will serve for the "guards."

So much for the training of the body. But this matter of the sensitive "soul" must be examined a little further. Plato seems to have a little more in mind than is apparent on the surface to the modern reader. He is most concerned with the inculcation of a certain sensitivity to rhythm, harmony, and proportion.

> And is it not for this reason that education in music (i.e. literature, music, and the arts) is most sovereign, because more than anything else rhythm and harmony find their way to the inmost soul and take strongest hold upon it, bringing with them and imparting grace (*euschemosune*) [The word is a difficult one to translate and "grace" does not convey its suggestions. It means literally of good figure, form, or shape, and elegant in figure, mien, or bearing, graceful;[458] one is almost tempted to use the catch phrase of the British governing class, "good form."], if one is rightly trained, and otherwise the contrary.[459] And further, because omissions and the failure of beauty in things badly made or grown would be most quickly perceived by one who was properly educated in music, and so, feeling distaste rightly, he would praise beautiful things and take delight in them and receive them into his soul to foster its growth and become himself beautiful and good. The ugly he would disapprove of and hate while still young and yet unable to apprehend the reason, but when reason came, the man thus nurtured would be the first to give her welcome, for by this affinity he would know her.[460]

Underlying this account of the values of a liberal, or literary, or humanistic education, there is the thoroughly Pythagorean assumption that beauty was based on harmony and certain simple mathematical proportions. The child who is thus reared by an association with these harmonies will come later in life to recognize the mathematical proportions involved and will be well started towards the unconscious appreciation of the necessity for harmony (in Plato's sense) within the man and the state. Let us recall again that Pythagoras advised his followers to build a shrine to the Muses as the patrons and protectors of "harmony."

It is no accident that Greek art of the fifth century, and particularly Greek architecture, did exhibit these simple mathematical relations. We have suggested, elsewhere, an analogy between the thought of Anaxagoras and the architecture of the Parthenon. Critics have replied that this is no more than a kind of literary analogy without basis in logic or fact. To argue this is to fail to appreciate the peculiar importance of "harmony" as a political principle of an authoritarian state as it was developed by Pythagoras and Plato. It was obviously a point of the greatest importance to Greek conservatives and to such middle-of-the-road democrats as the circle of Pericles, Phidias, Socrates (in middle life), and Anaxagoras. And so firmly entrenched is this concept of mathematical harmony and proportion as an artistic principle in the unconscious and the tastes of the tradition of the Western world, that many cultivated people to this very day feel, as though by a kind of instinct, an appreciation for an art which bases itself on Greek mathematical harmony.

Once the importance of harmony is firmly grasped in Pythagorean-Platonic thinking, it will give us a clue to the understanding of Plato's aesthetic and also his program of education. His plea that children should be, from earliest infancy, surrounded with "beautiful things" is couched in such luminous prose and strikes so responsive a chord in the feelings of cultivated men and women, that it may seem to some ungracious to look at his views in their specific social context. Nonetheless, we cannot escape the conviction that Plato is using "beautiful things" in no general or universal sense. Much that we should regard as supremely beautiful is scornfully dismissed. The poets of the Greek tradition are criticized because, as we previously suggested, they wrote in a stage of society before religion became "moralized" and before Greek religion was transformed into a sanction for a particular view of "justice." And, also, we might add, because too many poets like Euripides, as Aristophanes had already cleverly and dramatically argued, made their plays a vehicle for democratic ideas. There can, however, be little doubt that Plato's real "canon" (or standard) of the beautiful was political and social. In his authoritarian state there would be no room for poets unless they conformed to the social and aesthetic rules which he and his aristocratic confreres laid down. His discussion of the various "modes" of music is governed by the same principle. It is fortunate for Plato's reputation that he lived in a period (unlike our own) in which the authoritarian state could make provision for the more creative kinds of culture.

But there was a great deal in contemporary and recent Greek art which could not escape the eagle eye of Plato's political censorship. In the third book as well as in the tenth he makes a sharp, even a savage, attack on the dramatic poets. Plato charges dramatic writers, first, with depending mainly upon illusion for success, and second, with weakening character by overstimulating the emotions.[461] Underlying this criticism are two assumptions which we have already noticed in their development: 1) the changeless and immovable is good; the changing and transitory, baffling and evil; 2) only the rational soul of man can achieve this good, and the body with its passions and emotions is bad. Tragic drama, because it deals with the transitory and quickens and excites our feelings, Plato dismissed as unworthy the attention of that fully rational "guard" who was to oversee and govern his ideal state. The conclusion is, of course, shocking to the modern reader, who very naturally objects to a moral censorship of his reading and his thoughts. Infinite ingenuity of commentators has been spent in softening or explaining away Plato's views. But too few are willing to criticize the assumptions which led Plato's ruthlessly logical mind to such strange conclusions. And yet a sentence in his discussion of the arts would bring us up short and make us examine once again the validity of these assumptions. "Never," argued Plato, "are the fashions in music changed without changes in the most fundamental laws in the state."[462] This is startling both in its truth and its falsity. Plato perceives in full clarity the important interconnection between thought, literature, music, and the arts on the one hand, and social institutions on the other. But the modern thinker will feel that Plato has with almost loving exactitude put the cart before the horse. To take a modern analogy: almost anyone might admit an interconnection between the mode of music known as jazz and the social turmoil of the postwar world. But few, nowadays, would be so bold as to argue that "jazz" was the "cause" of the gaudy decade which succeeded the last war, so much as a symptom and a reflex of its social movements. As against those modern thinkers who wish to isolate every phenomenon and divide life up into a series of watertight compartments, Plato is clearly right in insisting on the seamless unity of life, society, and knowledge. But in arguing for the primacy of the "idea" as the creative principle, rather than seeing the idea as an outgrowth of economic forces and productive relations, he had been led by his social conservatism, his Pythagorean associations, and his preference for the changeless and static, into serious error.

The education in music and gymnastics will take the young man in hand up to the time when he enters for the first time into public life. Now Plato faces the problem of the selection of those who are to be the ruling class and their differentiation by training from those who are ruled. This selection must take place in full accord with the principle which has already been laid down, the principle of "natural inequality." When the "soul" of the young neophyte of the ruling class enters upon public life, he will have to recognize from the beginning, as a principle, subordination to authority. In every state, Plato holds, like the Pythagoreans before him, there must be a natural superior who imposes "convictions" (*dogmata*) upon those who are "naturally" subordinate. Those are to be chosen for promotion to the functions of ruling who prove themselves after rigorous examination best qualified to cling, through thick and thin, in evil times and in good, in the face of witchery or force, to the *dogmata* laid down for them by their elders and those in authority, that the "interests of the state are identical with his own interests"[463] as a ruler. And so our recruits have to be tested at all times to see if they will prove themselves hard to bewitch, clinging to "good form," good guardians of themselves in all things subject to rhythm and harmony.

Plato's political program is now beginning to emerge into the clear light of day. We shall have to examine later his view that the interests of the governing class and the state as a whole are fundamentally one; we shall have to face the problem of whether Plato has really succeeded in unifying his state or whether his high-sounding principle is not really a rationalization for the subordination of the interests of the ruled to the interests of the governing.

He is, at all events, very conscious of the difficulty of getting his assumptions accepted, and, like all authoritarians, he is very sensible of the political value of the lie, of *mythopoesis*, (myth-making) in order to win the assent of the governed.

> "How then," said I, "might we contrive one of those opportune falsehoods of which we were just now speaking, so as by one noble lie to persuade if possible the rulers themselves, but failing that the rest of the city?"[464]

This noble lie, Plato was careful to explain, would not be an innovation but an old Phoenician tale. Even Plato finds it a story that would require no little power of persuasion to make it plausible and accepted; he indulges in an elaborate literary byplay before Socrates launches into the falsehood,

> that in reality all our training and educating of the rulers and soldiers and the rest of the city were as it were dreams; in reality they were under the earth being moulded and fostered and their weapons and the rest of their equipment being formed. But when they were completely fashioned, then the land which is their mother brought them forth to birth, all bound by the tie of blood relationship and all owing to their land the obligation of patriotism; but God in fashioning those of you who are fitted to hold rule mingled gold in their generation, for which reason they are the most precious—but

> in the helpers silver, and iron and brass in the farmers and other craftsmen. And as you are all akin, though for the most part you will breed after your kinds, it may sometime happen that a golden father would beget a silver son and that a golden offspring would come from a silver sire and that the rest in like manner would be born from one another.[465]

And so it would be the primary function of guardianship to demote the unworthy, any child of golden parents who was found to have in him a trace of silver; and conversely to promote the really worthy—any child of silver parents who proved himself all golden.

This old Phoenician tale has been a large mouthful to swallow even for those with real talent for discipleship. Shorey[466] dismisses Plato's critics scornfully and briefly as "Rousseau-minded readers." Professor Taylor argues hotly that the various levels are not to be regarded as "castes"; that in reality Plato made room for the democratic principle of the "open career" for ability and character; the provision that the "guards" must promote the worthy is "absolutely destructive of caste."[467] We may be permitted, perhaps, a moment's skepticism about whether, in practice, artisans and farmers could in reality find opportunities for promotion in view of the rigorous system of education which Plato prescribed. One can suspect that Plato's concession to democratic instincts of justice and equity is, in reality, a more or less verbal concession. As Nettleship points out,

> The system as later developed in Book V (where Plato relies on attention to breeding to keep up the standard of the ruling class) would apparently not admit of promotion from the lower class, but only of degradation to it. He is evidently apprehensive of the tendency of aristocracies to degenerate.[468]

This, however, is not the important point. It is not the degree to which the "guards" will or will not become a "caste," but the very fact that Plato so calmly postulates a "natural inequality" in human beings and builds the whole structure of his society on this assumption that impresses us.

He is assuming, in other words, that the observed facts of apparent inequality due to the accidents of birth and the nature of social conditioning are based on an inequality grounded firmly in the nature of things. He could not, of course, know the extent to which the apparent inequality was a result of economic and social development, nor could he realize what concrete historical forces had produced this inequality of economic condition. He simply makes the aristocratic assumption that the "inequality" which resulted from social and economic conditioning corresponded exactly (more or less) to an inequality based on nature. He is, in other words, arguing as Pythagoras had done before him and as Aristotle was to argue after him, that "nature" had fitted some men to rule, and some to be ruled, some men to follow, others to lead, some men to be slaves, some to be free. He is doing simply the same thing, though in a less subtle way, that some modern "intelligence tests" are striving to do: viewing inequality as innate, and intelligence as a kind of fixed and static possession. All this strikingly confirms our view that the central preoccupation of the idealistic thinkers of classical antiquity was to refute the notion that justice has anything to do with equality.

At the end of the third book, with the help of a "noble lie" and with the necessary defiance of democratic convictions, our "guards" have been selected. In the fourth book, Plato has explained that these "guards" will be the repositories of wisdom in the state, as their assistants will embody courage. In the fifth book, Plato goes on to discuss their mode of life. It has been well said that the tone of the next three books is markedly different from that of the rest of the *Republic*. There is less self-confident urbanity.

> Socrates is represented as feeling at every step that he is in direct antagonism to public opinion, as almost afraid to say what he has to say, and yet as convinced and prepared to face the skepticism and ridicule with which he knows he will be met.[469]

Our discussion must help us to understand the reason for this tone of defiance.

Plato feels that he has now established his case for a "unified" state. Starting with the notion of the isolated individual units as explained above, he has passed to the "natural" mutual dependence, which turns out on examination to imply a "natural" inequality. The state is, therefore, something quite different from a mere collection of individuals. It is a true organic unity, a unity in difference. Just as in the individual the ethical ideal is "to become one out of many," so in the state that organization is best in which there is no mention of "mine and thine," but all work together for the common good. The analogy of the human body is irresistible, and Plato does not neglect to draw the analogy.

> [The best ordered state is that] which most nearly approaches the condition of the individual—as in the body, when but a finger of one of us is hurt, the whole frame, drawn toward the soul as a center and forming one kingdom under the ruling power therein, feels the hurt and sympathizes all together with the part affected, and we say that the man has a pain in his finger; and the same expression is used about any other part of the body, which has a sensation of pain at suffering or of pleasure at the alleviation of the suffering.[470]

Just as a healthy body is one which functions harmoniously, so the healthy state is one in which each individual contributes according to his capacity to the well-being of the whole. And just as no one can question the validity and usefulness of health in the body, so harmony in the state is something axiomatic; no one can question its desirability.

The notion is, of course, profoundly attractive. One is reminded of the teaching of St. Paul[471] and St. John[472] about the Church as the "Body of Christ"—the true vine of which each member is a branch. In such a community, Paul argued, each member could make his own specific contribution.

> Now there are diversities of gifts, but the same Spirit.
>
> And there are diversities of administrations, but the same Lord.

> And there are diversities of operations, but it is the same God which worketh all in all.

But important as it is to compare the doctrine of Plato with that of the early Christian Church, it is equally important to notice one specific and vital difference. The doctrine of the early Church represented in a social sense the protest of the poor and lowly and outcast against the upper-class Pharisees first, and the wealth and might of the Roman Empire second. And economically, the earliest Christian congregation was organized on the basis of a primitive communism, each member selling his goods and paying the proceeds into a common treasury.[473] In so far as this primitive ideal proved unworkable in practice, to that degree the ideal of St. Paul also experienced a practical breakdown. When, as for example in the recent civil war in Spain, we find large numbers of the hierarchy of the Church taking one side in a bitter civil war and large numbers of the humbler clergy and the laity taking the other, we ought to reflect that important economic differences (or, to put the matter more exactly, different relations to the modes of production) have intervened to make nonsense of St. Paul's vision of the perfect organic community. The one side was economically associated with the semifeudal landowners and aristocrats; the other with the men and women who work for wages. And perhaps the ideal that Plato, St. Paul, and St. John hold up before us can only be realized in practice when these profound differences in relation to the productive mechanism are eliminated.

This point is so important for an understanding of Plato's teaching that we may put it in another way. Plato, looking back upon a hundred years of Athenian democracy, which represented, as we have seen, an unstable equilibrium of forces—landed aristocrat, merchant, wage worker, and slave—looked back and sighed for the old unity of the tribe which did represent an organic society; and he even toyed with the notion that he could recall the past by banishing commerce from the state, or at least ignoring it. But neither Plato nor anyone else can so ignore the actualities of history. And in practice his theory, as we have seen, leaned heavily towards the landed aristocracy. It is impossible to avoid the well-grounded suspicion that the Platonic "guards," like the young men "who alone as it chanced had leisure to devote themselves to philosophy,"[474] in practice (if such a scheme could have been put into practice) would have been, and could have been, recruited only from the aristocratic class. Such a state as Plato conceived is not unity in difference; it is unity achieved (as in a modern fascistic state) by ignoring or suppressing all dissident elements.

And so Plato appears to some as a kind of idealistic fascist. The phrase is dangerous because it ignores the important differences between modern fascism, as a dictatorship of a section of monopoly capitalism, and landowning reaction in a slave-owning city-state. Let us ignore this problem and for purposes of our argument describe Plato as an idealistic, authoritarian reactionary. The question then remains: what relative weight shall we attach to the idealistic aspects and the more realistic and authoritarian aspects of Plato's thinking? If we had to settle this question by the pure light of reason, the debate would be endless and perhaps, a solution could never be reached. But fortunately we have a definite, historical touchstone. The Platonic philosophy, as we have already noticed and as Aristotle long since observed, was very closely related to the Pythagorean; there is the same defense of landed conservatism, the same aversion to commerce, the same passion for harmony, the same idealization of a ruling class, and the same insistence on the necessity of benevolence toward the ruled. But we know, in the case of the Pythagoreans, that political necessity frequently caused them to mitigate their mildness against the unregenerate rebels of the democratic faction. We know that in practice the rule of the Pythagoreans was the rule of one faction in the Italic states over another, and that this rule was sometimes bitterly resented. We know, too, that the political opponents of the Pythagoreans were not always deceived by their ardent preachments of harmony and regarded it, doubtless, as a rather diaphanous garment with which to conceal the naked realities involved in the absolute rule of one class over another. The sad experience of Plato himself in Syracuse points in the same direction. It is very difficult to avoid the conclusion that if the Platonic *kallipolis* had ever come down from the clouds and found earthly realization, it, too, would in practice have been forced to neglect the idealizing aspects of Plato's thinking; it would have necessarily favored the landed aristocracy and equally have incurred the suspicion of the mercantile democrats. Its "harmony" would have been forced harmony, its health would have been the disturbing quiescence of coma.

The education in music and gymnastics combined will take our neophyte up to his twentieth year; and at one point Plato seems almost to hint that this is enough.[475] But in the latter half of the *Republic* he makes apparent his real conviction that the education in music and gymnastics is to be regarded as subordinate and preliminary, leading up to a more thorough-going training.[476] The education in "music" has conferred certain positive advantages. It has made the young man or woman who is to be trained for political responsibility sensitive to certain fundamental laws of harmony, it has conferred what Plato calls *euharmostia*, an almost instinctive response to artistic and musical harmony. But it has quite failed to make him understand the mathematical principles which underlie this harmony, and the place of all particular harmonies in the totality which is the ordered universe. The complete education for political leadership will unveil these secrets, too, and make it possible for the "guard" to contemplate "all time and all essence." To explain this requires a long circumnavigation. We must first follow Plato as he unfolds his concept of logic; and this is a task for a later chapter. At this point it will be convenient for completeness' sake to summarize Plato's convictions on the inadequacy of the training in "music" and the outlines of a further progress.

Although the education in music has created a subconscious predisposition to welcome the harmonies which Plato feels are vital, it does not teach the youth to apprehend these harmonies as part of a scientific whole:

> they are apprehended, not in the systematic form of science in which each part is seen to be connected with each other, but as a multitude of isolated instances, each com-

> plete in itself and containing its own justification . . .[477] the education in music . . . showed examples of courage, temperance, and justice, but it did not show "wherein they are good,"[478] what is the end to which they all converge, and which gives unity and meaning to their variety; and without some such perception how can we be said to "know" justice, or even to possess it? We may know it in one form, but we might mistake it in another; we may think we have got hold of it at one moment, in one place, under one set of circumstances, but it may escape us when we have changed our point of view. This is why the results of the first education are "sketchy" and "inexact" and require "filling up" and completing by a further education.[479]

What is this "higher" education to be? First we must notice what it is not. Most emphatically it is not education in crafts (arts, sciences), all of which are vulgar and degrading.[480]* Since it is not to be the "crafts," what then? Arithmetic and calculation, in which, in a sense, all arts partake. But arithmetic has another value besides its usefulness for commerce and the crafts—it is a powerful force which draws men toward reality; it challenges the mind to examine the confusions of sense and to make exact definitions. If one knows arithmetic "in the spirit of a philosopher and not of a shopkeeper," it compels the soul to reason about abstract number and rebels against the introduction of visible or tangible objects into the argument.[481] It enables the "soul" to seize hold of the real, to rise above the changing.[482] Arithmetic, then, must be part of the higher education of the philosophical "guard."

Geometry, too, leads its devotees to turn their eyes away from this transitory and perishing world if it is properly learned and abstracted from the necessities of everyday life (it is incidentally very valuable for a soldier, and that is one craft which Plato did not despise).[483] So the rulers of *kallipolis* will be trained in geometry, for "geometry is knowledge of the ever-existent and not of that which comes into being and passes away." After geometry, astronomy—not for the awe and reverence excited by a contem-

* For the word *banausic* or vulgar see Note at the end of this chapter.

plation of the starry heavens, but because of the value of the abstract principles that they embody.

> What astronomy is to the eye, harmony is to the ear; the two are sister sciences as the Pythagoreans say and we, Glaucon, agree.[484]

This, too, must not be studied as the vulgar teachers of music have studied, with a mere empirical emphasis on strings and chords; even the Pythagoreans have fallen short. They investigate the mathematical relations involved in harmony; they enquire why some numbers are harmonious and some are not; they never attain to the underlying principle of harmony which gives meaning and intelligibility to the mathematical harmonies which the Pythagoreans have striven to discover.

The years between twenty and thirty in the education of the philosophical "guards" seem to be devoted to these mathematical pursuits. It should now be apparent that Plato's prescriptions are by no means motivated by any passion for abstract science as such. Mathematical studies are valuable because they tend to turn the attention away from the things of the senses to the realm of pure reason; because they divert attention from the changing to the static and the fixed; and finally, because they lead to a search for the "principle" of "harmony" which as Plato believed, *did* underlie everything in the universe and *should* be present in the man and the state. The social motivation of all this, after our discussion of the Pythagoreans, should now be clear, but it has been too often obscured by commentators who speak as though this ten years' training in mathematics were equivalent to what we should call "science." It is evident that much of what we should call "science," natural or social—medicine and biology, as developed by the Hippocratic school, sociological history as exemplified so magnificently by Thucydides, embryonic chemistry as developed by the needs of craftsmanship and commerce—all these sciences Plato would eliminate because they were bound up too much with change, movement, and historical process, because they were disciplines too ineradicably bound up with the interests of mercantilism and the mercantile democracy.

The years from twenty to thirty are not to be devoted only to science. The neophyte must also serve his apprenticeship in military service and at the same time test the strength of his moral convictions in the face of pleasure and pain, fear and persuasion, which meet him in the course of his public duties.[485]

The culmination and coping stone of the educational structure Plato calls "dialectics." This pursuit takes all of a man's time from the age of thirty to thirty-five. However, Plato's use of the word "dialectic" raises so many questions connected with his general philosophical outlook that we must postpone consideration of it until a subsequent chapter.

We may now sum up Plato's plan for the complete education of his ruling class. Nettleship's summary will make the whole scheme clear in its gradations and their interrelation.

> Those who are to go through the advanced course of study that has now been proposed must begin their training young, and even their first studies are to be as little compulsory as possible. Up to the age of about seventeen or eighteen the education of *mousikē* (i.e. literature and the arts) described in the earlier books will go on; and in addition the elements of the sciences (i.e. mathematical studies) will be learned, but without system. After this will come a course of exclusively "gymnastic" training, lasting till the age of twenty. This means a systematic bodily training, including military exercises and directed toward preparing the young men for the service of the state in keeping order at home and in fighting against foreign enemies. It serves the further purpose of giving them a good foundation of bodily health for their future work, and of training them in courage and self-control. It will be so hard that they cannot at this period do any intellectual work; but, says Plato, what a man shows himself to be at his gymnastics will be a very good test of his general character. At the age of twenty, a further selection will be made of those who have distinguished themselves most, and these will be advanced to the next stage of education. This will consist of two parts. There will be a systematic scientific course continuing to the

> age of thirty; and, while they are occupied in this, the great point to be attended to will be whether they show the faculty for dialectic, the power of "seeing things together." But alongside of this a training in the public service, chiefly military, will be going on; and here the chief test to be applied to a man is whether he is steadfast and shows constancy to the principles he has been taught. At the age of thirty a further selection will be made. Those who are now approved will enter upon the study of dialectic proper, which will continue for five years, unaccompanied by any other work. (Probably this is meant to include a study of the principles of morality and human life; for it is in this connection that Plato describes the dangers of dialectic for those who are not fitted for it by the tenacity with which they hold fast to the principles of right that they have been taught.) At thirty-five begins the really serious work of the public service, and it lasts for fifteen years. During these years the Guardians will be acquiring the experience necessary for rulers by actual contact with forms of good and evil about which they have been taught; and all the while they will be continually tested to see if they stand being "pulled about in all directions" by the circumstances with which they have to contend. From fifty onwards, those who are still approved are alternately to study the good itself and in the light of it to govern and organize the state. They will be the supreme council in the state, dividing their time between theoretical study of the good, and practical government. Finally, when they die, they will be buried with public honors, and worshiped, if the Delphic oracle allows, as divine beings, or at any rate as blessed and favored by the gods.[486]

As we are endeavoring to see Plato "in the light of history" rather than of "pure reason," it may be well at this point to compare his educational plan with that of the Pythagoreans. Again Aristoxenus will come to our assistance.[487]

> In general they thought that there was no greater evil than anarchy. For the nature of mankind is such that a man cannot be saved unless he has an overseer. As re-

> gards rulers and ruled they held this opinion: they said that rulers should be not only wise but also benevolent; and that subjects should be not only obedient but devoted to their superiors. And they thought it well to pay heed to each stage of human life—that children should be trained in letters and other studies, that young men should be instructed in the customs and laws of the city, that men should devote themselves to action and the service of the state, that old men should concern themselves with thought, standards, and advice with full knowledge. This would insure that children would not be silly, young men childish, mature men adolescent, nor old men foolish. And they said that even from childhood nurture should be systematically applied to convince them that order and symmetry was a fine and useful thing, but lack of order and of symmetry was disgraceful and disadvantageous.

The passage sounds like a first draft of Plato's educational system—there is the same division of life into four periods—childhood, up to the age of twenty, youth from twenty to forty, maturity from forty to sixty on. There is the same prescription of a kind of education proper to each time of life; there is the same underlying motive in each case to make the child, the youth, and the man receptive of harmony and symmetry as well as understanding the principles which underlie that harmony and symmetry. We recall the history of the Pythagorean school in actual practical politics; it is difficult to escape the conclusion that Plato is thinking of education in similar terms—as a ruling class and an intellectual occupying garrison with which to control the people of his state.

One other point we must make before adjourning our consideration of Plato's educational plans. Our philosopher was convinced that education was more than a process of mere intellectual development. He insisted that it was equally a process of moral and aesthetic training—a matter of bringing the feelings and the "will" into harmony with the convictions of the intellect. We have already noticed some of Plato's convictions about the need for aesthetic training—the pursuit of beauty at least in the form of harmony. And although it was apparent that the specific form in which this insight presented itself was limited and narrow, that it arose in Plato's mind as a defense for an interest which to some may seem circumscribed and even sinister, it is nonetheless a valuable insight. For generations and centuries education has tended to focus attention only on the training of the intellect, so that Plato's insistence on the roundedness of human nature and the consequent need for a many-sided plan of education may even now seem to some "progressive."

A similar judgment might be passed on his remarks about the moral aspect of education. The *genesis* of these ideas is limited, and the interests which they seek to defend are the interests of a class. He constantly insists that education should be the prerogative of the few, those of "right-nature"; these few must be not "bastards," but "legitimate" children of philosophy,[488] "sound in limb and sound in mind"—not one-sided cripples.[489] They must be quick to learn, steadfast, retentive. "They must be indelibly dyed with the dye of law and order, so that they may combine what is hard to find in combination: constancy and steadiness of character with speculative activity and aspiration." Otherwise, Nettleship goes on to say,

> the study of dialectic will continue to bring upon philosophy the charge which is so often made against it, that it unsettles the mind and undermines morality.[490] For as we have already heard, philosophy is a double-edged instrument; the speculative spirit, which demands to have its beliefs justified and its experience accounted for, may by a turn of the hand become the spirit of revolution, denying the validity of all beliefs and the nobleness of any experience.

Here Nettleship describes exactly the anxiety of Plato that philosophical students should be chosen from the "right class" and that both morally and intellectually philosophy should be a bulwark against change and revolution. And yet Plato as a moral teacher frequently transcends the bias which prompts his ideas. Nowhere is this more true than in his description of the moral qualities of the "philosophic" nature. Consider, for example, one passage in which Plato describes the moral and physical courage that intellectual understanding brings.

> "The intelligence, then, that is endowed with a magnificence of breadth and the power of contemplating all time and all existence, would it be able, do you think, to regard human life as a great thing?"
>
> "Impossible," he said.
>
> "And such a man will regard death as no dreadful thing?"
>
> "No."
>
> "True philosophy would have nothing to do with a cowardly and illiberal nature."
>
> "I don't think so."[491]

Now the particular cast which Plato gives to his observation is highly aristocratic, a code of *noblesse oblige*. And the philosophical implication, as we shall see more fully in a subsequent chapter, is that knowledge culminates in the contemplation of a static, unchanging real, which has little to do with change, process, or the world of social actualities. Nonetheless, Plato's position, in spite of the anomalies of its setting, enshrines a valuable positive insight. "To comprehend the historical process as a whole" is not only in itself an intellectual ideal. It is also, as all the great of the earth from Solon to Alexander, Spartacus to Caesar, Galileo to Napoleon will testify, as well as all the unknown heroes of humanity who in the present age contend for a fairer and juster world order, a means of steeling the will and bracing the endurance. It is part of the positive content of many of the great traditional religions—the self-abnegation of Christianity—to gain life one must lose it; as well as the endurance of the Stoics. Here, as so often, a Platonic truth is revealed on examination to be a magnificent half-truth.

Addendum

In nothing is Plato's aristocratic prejudice more notable than in his attitude to *banausia*—the characteristic which he assigns to manual workers. It may be of interest, therefore, to examine a little the history of the word and its adjectival form *banausos*.

The word is usually derived from *baunos*, a furnace, and *auo*, to light, and in its original meaning it was applied to a workman who uses fire in his labors.[492] It distinguishes the craftsman from agriculture, the military life, and the other pursuits more proper to an aristocratic way of life. Herodotus, describing the warrior castes in Egypt, remarks that none of them was allowed to busy himself with the labor of an artisan.[493] Sophocles describes the "art" of archery as no vulgar (*banauson*) one.[494] Xenophon makes a sharp antithesis between any vulgar (*banausikē*) craft and *kalokagathia*, a word which, as we have seen, sums up all the "gentlemanly" virtues.[495] In the *Oeconomica* Xenophon gives us the most explicit rationalization for this particular prejudice:

> The occupations called menial (*banausikai*) are despised, as it is quite right that they should be frowned upon in our states. For they mutilate the bodies of those who work at them, compelling them to indoor, sedentary occupations, and sometimes to spend the whole day by the fire. And when bodies are made effeminate, then souls, too, are greatly enervated. And the crafts called menial give a man no opportunity to devote himself to his friends or to the city; so that men of this sort seem incompetent to benefit friends and defend their country. So that in some states, and particularly those that seem to be the best governed, no citizen may engage in menial tasks.

This prejudice Plato fully shared. In the *Symposium* the characteristic antithesis is drawn between the "wisdom" of an artisan and the divine knowledge of love that mediates between gods and men.

> The man who is wise in the latter is a semi-divine being; the man who is wise in arts and handicrafts is vulgar (*banausos*).

A similar contempt for crafts and tradesmen is evidenced in the *Gorgias*. In the *Republic* Socrates speaks with profound scorn of those

> little men (*anthropisboi*) who seeing this land open to them—take a leap out of their own crafts into philosophy.

> In the exercise of their own contemptible little craft they are not devoid of skill; but they are attracted by the magnificent repute which attaches to philosophy, but pursue it imperfectly. Just as their bodies are crippled by their arts and crafts, so are their souls maimed and disfigured by the vulgarities (*banausiai*) of these former pursuits.

Such people, in one of Plato's most brilliant pieces of imagery, are "like a bald little tinker, who has just got out of durance and come into a fortune: he takes a bath and puts on a new coat, and is decked out as a bridegroom going to marry his master's daughter."[496] Such a notion will give rise to evil and bastard offspring; so men of this kind will spawn sophistries instead of true philosophy. The whole thing is a savage and brilliant attack on the Sophists.

The wisdom of the Sophists is like that of a wild-beast tamer. By long association he has come to know the impulses and moods of the monster, when one should approach it, when one should stroke it, when it is savage, when it is gentle, and the noises it makes to express these various emotions. Knowledge of these moods and emotions the Sophists called wisdom.[497] The beast is, of course, the mob, the Athenian people in their democratic assemblies, and Plato's criticism of the Sophists is that they express in their thinking the needs and wishes of the multitude. To more democratic thinkers it might be a matter for praise rather than reproach that their thinking expressed the needs of the nameless and hardly articulate many. Not to Plato, but by this time we are beginning to see something of the motivation for such attacks.

In the passage which has given rise to this note,[498] the "crafts" are all dismissed quite categorically as *banausai*—vulgar, menial. A sharp distinction is made between such studies as "music," gymnastics, mathematics, astronomy, and dialectics and the knowledge which pertains to practical skill. It is important for us to remember that in dismissing the "crafts," Plato dismisses most of what we should call science, whether pure or applied.

Later in the work Plato asks why *banausia* and handicraft are a reproach. The reply is that they represent a revolt of the lower side of a man's nature against the best within him:

> A man is unable to control the creatures within him, but has to court them, and his great study is how to flatter them.[499]

The social analogy is inescapable; just as democracy represents the upsurge of merchants and artisans, so vulgarity and *banausia* represent the revolt of a man's lower nature.

One other reference from the middle dialogues will add something to the picture. In the *Theaetetus* Socrates says:[500]

> To know this, that god is perfectly just and whoever is justest is most like god, is wisdom and true excellence; but the other little skills and those things which in political affairs seems to be wisdom are vulgar and in the crafts are *banausic*.

Nor does Plato ever outgrow this prejudice. In his last work the *Laws* the same theme recurs; he dismisses all education which aims at the possession of money or bodily strength or wisdom without "thought" and "justice" as banausic and ungentlemanly—not worthy to be called education at all.[501] He dismisses some forms of gain as "ungentlemanly."

> No man ought, or indeed will be allowed, to exercise any ungentlemanly occupation, in pursuit of which *banausia,* which is spoken of as a most disgraceful thing, destroys the freeman's character.[502]

A little further on, the reason for the prejudice is made even more apparent:

> We shall have no excessive money-making out of *banausia,* or vile money-breeding or money-feeding either.[503]

This passage is most interesting in that we have the explicit association of the *"banausia"* of trade with usury; and they both excite a patrician contempt. Any readers of this book who have lived in England and have heard a sneering reference by old-fashioned aristocrats and professional people to those who are "in trade" will have no difficulty in estimating the depth of this prejudice in Plato and evaluating it for what it is worth.

CHAPTER ELEVEN

How the "Guards" Were to Live

PERHAPS the most startling aspect of Plato's thinking is the demand that his governing class should live a communal life, eschew family life in the ordinary sense, and be deprived of personal property. Critics who have viewed Plato under the pure light of reason and the impure light of prejudice have used this prescription of his to defend the most opposite social institutions. To some his plan has seemed to be almost prophetic of the monastic organization of the church government in the Middle Ages, with the Pope corresponding to the "philosopher king," the hierarchy to the "guards," and the "regular" (or monastic) clergy to the auxiliaries. To others it has provided a kind of philosophical aura of sanctity for Lord Macaulay's reforms of the civil service, the creation of a skilled administrative class to serve the needs of the rising English bourgeoisie and the expanding British Empire.

In the modern period when socialistic and communistic theories have evoked violent partisanship, Plato's views have seemed like an ancient analogue to the theories of Karl Marx. In the burst of violent patrioteering which accompanied America's entrance into the first World War, Plato's *Republic* was even suppressed as subversive literature. At this last supreme historical paradox, Plato's ghost must have laughed very sardonically. Here, too, the light of history will provide a clearer illumination.

The fifth book of the *Republic* begins with a pleasant bit of byplay. The fourth book, it will be recalled, provided the "refutation," such as it is, of Thrasymachus' position in the first book. Thrasymachus, we may remember, had argued that justice was the interest of the class in power. Socrates set to work to demonstrate that it is something quite different—it is harmony in the state and in the individual soul. And then, using a metaphor from medicine, since health was harmony, justice was health, beauty, and good condition within the soul.[504] Justice, then, was *according to nature* and not, as the Sophists argued, a mere *convention*. And by an extraordinary confusion Socrates (i.e. Plato) made it appear that this *justice* was the same thing as *law-abiding*. It had nothing in common with such "unjust acts" as pillaging temples, thefts, and betrayals—either in private, of one's comrades, or in public life, of the city.[505] (The reader will not need to be reminded that Thrasymachus had not at all meant *law-abiding* when he talked of justice. He had in mind rather the kind of property relations which express themselves in various codes of law and constitutional arrangement.) During the whole of this extraordinary *tour de force* of "refutation," Thrasymachus had been bludgeoned into silence. But now, after accomplishing his task, Plato, in the fifth book, has a moment of chivalrous feeling toward a beaten opponent. He allows Thrasymachus to make a point. Socrates had mentioned the communal life of the guards as regards the possession of women and children. But now he seems to be passing the subject by without any further treatment. Glaucon and Adimantus discuss in whispers whether they shall let him get away with it. But Socrates explains that he had deliberately neglected the discussion because it was long and toilsome. In the first book, however, Socrates had urged that the pursuit of knowledge was so much more important than the search for gold. If they were searching for gold, no trouble would be too much; they would not because of politeness let the quarry escape.[506] When Socrates shows reluctance to pursue the argument, Thrasymachus breaks in, "Do you think, Socrates, that we have come here to *smelt gold* and not to listen to arguments?" After this tiny Pyrrhic victory, Thrasymachus' usefulness in the dialogue is ended. He is not heard from again.

Socrates launches into a discussion of sex and childbearing in the ideal state. We are rearing our men to be guards over the flock.[507] Can there be women guards too? Or are they incapacitated by childbearing from taking part in this task? (The comparison in Socrates' mind is undeniably with sheep dogs. The female dog can perform the tasks of shepherding as well as the male.) No, they can both share in the tasks of guarding, except that women are naturally weaker. So then we must give them the same education, music and gymnastics. (And if, because of our habits and conventions, it seems ridiculous for women to exercise naked in the gymnasium, we should remember that not so many generations ago it seemed ridiculous to the Greeks for *men* to exercise, as it still does to many barbarians. We must not be disturbed by the sneers of the wits.) Since we have agreed that justice means one man, one task in *accordance with nature*, what has nature to tell us of men and women? Their natures are different. But is the difference generic and essential, or is it as trivial as the difference between bald and long-haired men? After a little discussion it is agreed that for the central task of "guarding" the difference is not essential or relevant.

> Men and women have the same *nature* when it is a matter of guarding the city, except that one is stronger, the other weaker.[508]

And so we must give them the same tasks, selecting them by the same rules, giving them the same education and letting them live with the male rulers and share with them the tasks of guardianship. But the tasks given to the women should be lighter.[509]

This is the "first wave." Women (in the "guard" class) should (like sheep dogs) share in the task of guarding the flock and should be trained for it just as their mates are trained. To many this has seemed like a revolutionary proposal, and Plato has appeared as a great and enlightened feminist. Two points are worth making. In the late fifth and early fourth centuries a great deal of discussion was obviously going on in enlightened circles in some Greek cities about the position and place of women in society. The first effect of the breakup of the tribe had been to reduce women to economic subordination. But the rise of mercantilism and the consequent development of individualism had tended to create a greater freedom in sex relations and, in particular, had raised the problem in some enlightened quarters that women (like slaves) were human beings and had, as a consequence, rights.* This thoroughly humane and admirable tendency is best represented by the poet Euripides, whose sympathy for human problems is manifest in almost every play. But the conservatives were quick to take up this interest and this tendency and use it for their interest. Aristophanes, for example, who gave expression to the point of view of the conservative and anti-imperialistic peasantry in their opposition to the war, burlesqued the interests of the progressives in the problem of women in several plays, extravagantly suggesting that if women ran the state there would be no more war. Feminism is for Aristophanes a weapon in his antidemocratic, antiexpansionist peace campaign. What does it mean for Plato? If we were to group all three writers (Euripides, Aristophanes, Plato) under the one conceptual tent-word "feminist," we should fail to see some important specific differences. For Plato, women's sharing with men the task of guarding or ruling is intended to strengthen the hold of his ruling class; moreover, it is intended possibly as a partial concession to democratic prejudice against the aristocratic cult of male homosexuality. We should reflect that homosexual relations were an important part of the military preparations of several Greek states, particularly Sparta and Thebes. Before the battle the Spartans sacrificed to Eros,[510] and we are told it was because

> they are convinced that in the comradeship of a pair of friends fighting side by side lay safety and victory.

There is no need to pursue the subject. For the Spartan male squire, Plato would substitute women, mounting them on horseback and allowing them to follow the battle.† It is an important concession to Athenian feeling. And yet it is clear that Plato himself shared in the aristocratic preference for homosexual relations.[511] And even in the ideal state he will permit distinguished warriors to gratify themselves with lovers of either sex.[512]

* It is interesting to notice that one charge that Plato always makes against the tyrant is sexual irregularity. This reflects the feeling of Greek conservatives about the newer tendencies.

† Homosexuality seems to be bound up with the transmission of property in a landholding society. It was, therefore, particularly characteristic of aristocratic states and groups.

The "second wave" which Plato has to face is even more overwhelming. He will enjoin the common possession of women for the "guards," but under the strictest sort of control. His purpose is twofold. First, eugenic, to ensure that "the best" shall breed and the worse shall not. Second, to ensure that among the ruling class all distinctions of "mine and thine" shall be broken down and that the *private family* shall be destroyed along with personal possessions. (To put the matter a little more concretely, Plato does not want to go back so far in history as to resurrect the competitive rivalry of the old local families [*genē*]; their differences ought to be transcended and subordinated to a unified, political oligarchy, to the state. In Aristotle's language the first of these two kinds of oligarchy is based on dynastic choice, the second is more political.)[513]

To deal with the first point. The analogy is consciously made between the eugenic breeding of dogs and the eugenic breeding of human beings. The "guards" will use all the resources of mythology, religion, and the "medical lie" to ensure that only the "best" shall consort with the "best,"[514] that the number of marriages shall be regulated by social utility, and that the population (in the "guard" class) shall be controlled with a view to war and disease.[515] The best warriors will be given greater sexual freedom so that more children will be born of their stock.[516] The children of the best stock are to be reared in a public *crèche*; offspring of inferior stock, and even inferior specimens from "good" parents, are to be hidden in a dark unmentionable place, a euphemism for infanticide.[517] (In Sparta, unwanted children were thrown into the *apothetai*; a word which we might almost translate "refuse heap.")[518] The rearing of the children will be the task of professional nurses,[519] so that their mothers will be freed for warlike and political work. Women shall be allowed to breed from their twentieth to their fortieth year; men from their thirtieth to their fiftieth year.[520] Against breeding children outside these limitations Plato would bring every taboo of custom, sanction, and traditional religion. But when his men and women had passed the age limits, he would permit free intercourse (with a few restrictions to prevent incest), but recommending abortion or infanticide to prevent their offspring from being reared.[521] What does Plato expect to achieve by this radical departure from Athenian practice? He explains for us:

"Shall we try to find a common basis by asking of ourselves what ought to be the chief aim of the legislator in making laws and in the organization of a State—what is the greatest good, and what is the greatest evil, and then consider whether our previous description has the stamp of good or of evil?"

"By all means."

"Can there be any greater evil than discord and distraction and plurality where unity ought to reign? Or any greater good than the bond of unity?"

"There can not."

"And there is unity where there is community of pleasures and pains—where all the citizens are glad or grieved on the same occasions of joy and sorrow?"

"No doubt."

"Yes; and where there is common but only private feeling a State is disorganized—when you have one half of the world triumphing and the other plunged in grief at the same events to the city or the citizens?"

"Certainly."

"Such differences commonly originate in a disagreement about the use of the terms 'mine' and 'not mine,' 'his' and 'not his.' "

"Exactly so."

"And is not that the best-ordered State in which the greatest number of persons apply the terms 'mine' and 'not mine' in the same way to the same thing?"

"Quite true."

"Or that again which most nearly approaches to the condition of the individual—as in the body, when but a finger of one of us is hurt, the whole frame, drawn toward the soul as a center and forming one kingdom under the ruling power therein, feels the hurt and sympathizes all together with the part affected and we say that the man has a pain in his finger; and the same expression is used about any other part of the body, which has a sensation of pain at suffering."

"Very true," he replied, "and I agree with you that in the best-ordered State there is the nearest approach to this common feeling which you describe."

"Then when any one of the citizens experiences any good or evil, the whole State will make his case their own, and will either rejoice or sorrow with him?"

"Yes," he said, "that is what will happen in a well-ordered State."

"It will now be time," I said, "for us to return to our State and see whether this or some other form is most in accordance with these fundamental principles."

"Very good."

"Our State, like every other, has rulers and subjects?"

"True."

"All of whom will call one another citizens?"

"Of course."

"But is there not another name people give to their rulers in other States?"

"Generally they call them their masters, but in democratic States they simply call them rulers."

"And in our State what other names besides that of citizens do the people give the rulers?"

"They are called saviors and helpers," he replied.

"And what do the rulers call the people?"

"Their maintainers and foster-fathers."

"And what do they call them in other States?"

"Slaves."

"And what do the rulers call one another in other States?"

"Fellow-rulers."

"And what in ours?"

"Fellow-guardians ['guards']."

"Did you ever know an example in any other State of a ruler who would speak of one of his colleagues as his friend and of another as not being his friend?"

"Yes, very often."

"And the friend he regards and describes as one in

whom he has an interest, and the other as a stranger in whom he has no interest?"

"Exactly."

"But would any of your guardians think or speak of any other guardian as a stranger?"

"Certainly he would not; for every one whom they meet will be regarded by them as either a brother or sister, or father or mother, or son or daughter, or as the child or parent of those who are thus connected with him."

"Capital," I said. "But let me ask you once more: Shall they be a family in name only; or shall they in all their actions be true to the name? For example, in the use of the word 'father,' would the care of a father be implied and the filial reverence and duty and obedience to him which the law commands; and is the violator of these duties to be regarded as an impious and unrighteous person who is not likely to receive much good either at the hands of God or of man? Are these to be or not to be the strains which the children will hear repeated in their ears by all the citizens about those who are intimated to them to be their parents and the rest of their kinsfolk?"

"These," he said, "and none other; for what can be more ridiculous than for them to utter the names of family ties with the lips only and not to act in the spirit of them?"

"Then in our city the language of harmony and concord will be more often heard than in any other. As I was describing before, when any one is well or ill, the universal word will be 'with me it is well' or 'it is ill.'"

"Most true." [522]

By abolishing personal property and by breaking up the self-contained autonomous family, Plato expected that he would attain to a unified state. And yet, if one examines his proposals it is obvious that he has not done what he promises. Only the "guards" feel this sense of unity and common purpose. The rest of the state—artisans, merchants, or peasants—does not share in the vision or in the crusade, but simply basks in the afterglow. If the lower orders will accept without question the "natural" right of the "guards" to rule, the state might achieve unity of a kind. Otherwise, we can suspect, the old Pythagorean formula already cited might have to be invoked.

> One must fight [i.e., against unregenerate rebels] not with words but with deeds, and war is a lawful and holy thing if one fights as man to man.*

The political views and conduct, as well as the intellectual outlook of the Academy, resemble so strikingly those of the Pythagoreans that it will be fruitful to explore a little further. Both the Academy and the Pythagorean school systematically took part in politics on the conservative or oligarchical side. Both of them acted as the theoretical spokesmen of landed conservatism; both of them intervened actively in politics, framing constitutions where their own faction was dominant and acting as a kind of political club where the balance of parties was very even. Both of them put forward an intellectual position stressing the inherent and natural right of the "fittest" to rule; and arguing that it was the function of others to obey. Both groups show a very considerable prejudice against the mercantile democracy, and both would eliminate commerce or at least visit it with the strictest supervision and (in Plato's case) confine it to the physically and mentally unfit. The intellectual and philosophical structures they put forward were very similar—great stress was laid on harmony and mathematical proportion as the clue to the meaning of justice. The great difference is that the Pythagoreans in our accounts of them are a little more naïve in expressing their outlook, a little more articulate about their social conservatism, a little less subtle in concealing a social outlook under philosophical forms. This is, of course, partly a matter of tradition and experience.

The historical similarities between the Academy and the Pythagorean clubs are worth stressing, because to those who read the *Republic* as a masterpiece of abstract thought it reads like a powerful plea for the rule of the wise and the good. And, put thus abstractly, this is a position with which no one could quarrel.

* See page 85.

But there is no reason to suppose that in practice Plato's pupils and followers would be any less biased in favor of social conservatism than were the Pythagoreans, or any more gentle and tolerant in carrying their views into effect.

No discussion of Plato's longings for an upper-class communism can fail to take some account of his attitude to Sparta and the Cretan cities, where this system was in actual operation. It is significant that in the *Laws*—a product of old age and political frustration—he makes his protagonists an Athenian aristocrat, a Spartan, and a Cretan. We must, therefore, discuss briefly the actual institutions of the latter two states. For these are, after all, the sources in practice of Plato's theory, just as the Pythagorean doctrines constitute his *starting point* in theory.

For a number of historical reasons Sparta evolved quite differently from the progressive and mercantile Greek states, the group which Athens typifies. In order to understand this point, which rests, after all, on the peculiar economic and social organization of pre-Homeric Greece, we must crave the reader's indulgence for going back a considerable historical way. For institutions native to Sparta probably had their genesis in the great period of migrations which ushered in the historical period in Greece.

The primitive agricultural life based on irrigation in the river valleys of the Nile and the Tigris and Euphrates developed, as a concomitant, nomadic tribes centering in the oases and extensions of the productive system in smaller river valleys, for instance in the Danube. The lack of suitable areas for extensions characterized by a high degree of similarity in their natural structure did not, however, decrease the pressure emanating from the river valleys; thus the migrations continued and the people were forced not only to settle in regions with different geographic and geological conditions, but also to change their methods of production gradually in conformity with changed settings. But as these migrations arose in a period when slavery was not yet economically profitable, the tendency was for each migration to set in motion the tribes with which it came in contact. Sparta's geographical position, however, made this impossible, and as a consequence the invaders had to settle down as a conquering class and an occupying garrison.[523] For a short time Sparta was in the vanguard of a historical movement; but it was, interestingly enough, one of those historical leaps which, later on, when Athens and other states were developing in a mercantile direction, made it inevitable that Sparta should lag behind and develop peculiarly conservative tendencies. This early pattern of Spartan development was reinforced by two great events—the Messenian Wars which increased the subservient population, and a great earthquake (in 464 B.C.) in which many of the ruling class perished. The Spartan aristocracy, from this time on, and even earlier, had to develop thoroughly repressive institutions. Though trade was permitted, it was allowed only to non-Spartans, forbidden to citizens. Though for a time industry flourished (as evidenced by the development of Spartan pottery), in the second half of the sixth century it died away. And Sparta in the fifth century had become a peculiar polity—the polity of a landholding aristocracy ruling with the utmost repression over slaves or Helots. Romantic conservatives like Plato (and realistic conservatives, too), failing to understand the historical process involved, based their criticisms of democratic institutions on the fact of Sparta, and as a consequence idealized the slaveholding state. Almost to the end of the sixth century B.C. the evolution of Sparta was comparable with the development of other Greek States. In particular, Spartan pottery shows a continuous and steady development, both in richness of design and skill of execution. Spartan ware was an object of export and was found as far away as Cyrene.[524] In addition, Sparta played a creditable role in the Olympic games.*

From a well-known poem of Alcman which makes mention of a plowshare, it has been conjectured that in early times in Sparta the Spartiates themselves took part in agricultural tasks.[526]

But towards the end of the seventh century (probably) a great reorganization was effected in Spartan life. This change completely altered the direction in which Sparta was to develop. The

* From 615 to 580 the names of forty Spartans appear on the lists of Olympic victors (excluding winners in the chariot races); in vivid contrast we may note that from 580 to 516, only two names appear.[525]

transformation is associated in tradition with the name of a famous lawgiver, Lycurgus. Lycurgus is said to have travelled to Crete, studied the laws of the Cretans, and been much impressed by the manner in which the dominant Dorian caste in Crete maintained its supremacy.

> Moreover, in the times before this they had the worst laws of almost all the Hellenes, both in matters which concerned themselves alone and also in that they had no dealings with strangers. And they made their change to a good constitution of laws thus:—Lycurgus, a man of the Spartans, who was held in high repute, came to the oracle at Delphi, and as he entered the sanctuary of the temple, straightaway the Pythian prophetess said as follows:
>
> Lo, thou art come, O Lycurgus, to this rich shrine of my temple,
> Loved thou by Zeus, and by all who possess the abodes of Olympus.
> Whether to call thee a god, I doubt, in my voices prophetic,
> God or a man, but rather a god I think,
> O Lycurgus.
>
> Some say in addition to this that the Pythian prophetess also set forth to him the order of things which is now established for the Spartans; but the Lacedaemonians themselves say that Lycurgus, having become guardian of Leobotes, his brother's son, who was king of the Spartans, brought in these things from Crete. For as soon as he became guardian, he changed all the prevailing laws, and took measures that they should not transgress his institutions.[527]

This twofold attribution of the sources of the Lycurgan laws is highly revealing. Constitutions and laws are, of course, a response to a developing situation, and are not purchased as ready-made copies from other states. Nonetheless, the link with Apollo is an interesting religious affiliation, in view of what we know of Delphi's politics;* the connection indicated between the Spartan and Cretan polities reveals, as we shall show, an appreciation of important historical similarities.

The situation in Sparta at the end of the seventh century seems to have been very critical. The Messenians, the non-Dorian native population living to the south of Sparta revolted against the conquerors and succeeded in defying Sparta for many years. At the end of the second Messenian war (circa 631 B.C.) Sparta had successfully subjugated the natives. But the net result of Sparta's success was greatly to increase the numbers and the proportion of the subject people. We have no accurate figure as to what the proportion of Spartiates to natives may have been—estimates range from one to seven to one to fifteen. At the same time the Spartiates (or full Spartan citizens) were not themselves fully united and were, therefore, in no position to consolidate the rule of their own small minority over the conquered population. This was because of the fact that a natural process of development was going on in Sparta, which tended to concentrate the land in the hands of a few of the Spartiate families. The situation among the Spartiates was somewhat comparable with that which faced Solon in Attica some years later. But there were important differences. The geographical position of Sparta had made trade difficult and colonization across the seas as an outlet for a relative surplus population impossible. The seizure of the Messenian land, though partly motivated by pressure of population, had at the same time increased the ratio of subject peoples and made the increasing stratification of Spartan society inevitable. Thus while the reforms of Solon laid the foundation for the developing Athenian "democracy," the work of Lycurgus led only to a revivification of oligarchy.

Lycurgus, therefore, reconstructed and reinforced the rule of the Spartiate class in a way that would meet both the problem of Spartan disunity and the necessity for keeping in subjection the immensely more numerous Helot population.

In the first place, he redistributed the available land into separate shares, assigning nine thousand shares to the Spartiate class,

* See page 53ff.

and thirty thousand shares to the *perioikoi.* This latter group, composed apparently of some Spartans, some non-Spartiate Dorians, and some natives (Thucydides,[528] however, twice mentions similarities in dialect between their speech and the Spartan, thus indicating the possibility of common racial origin), seems to have evolved partly by attending to the trading requirements of the early Spartan colonization in the Peloponnese. The lots of land assigned to the Spartiates must have been considerably larger than those given to the *perioikoi,* since the whole Helot population was absorbed in cultivating the land of the Spartiates. The ruling Spartans, however, were expressly forbidden by the Lycurgan legislation to engage in *any* economic activity. Agricultural labor was the province of the Helots, and commerce (to the extent that it existed) was carried on by the *perioikoi.* The social function of the Spartiates was from this time forward to act as an occupying garrison and a military caste, exercising police surveillance over Sparta's conquered territories and peoples. It is a remarkable historical fact that so small a minority were able to hold power in these circumstances so long. It is no wonder that their accomplishment excited the wonder and respect of landed conservatives throughout the Greek world.

How was this amazing achievement made possible? In the first place, an absolute solidarity and unity was established among the ruling Spartiate group. We have already mentioned the reallocation of land, which provided economic equality within the governing class. Furthermore, all Spartiates were given an equal voice in the "popular" assembly. The ephors or chief magistrates were elected *by lot* from among the Spartiates. And to ensure the feeling of communal interest, common meals were established for the Spartan men.

In order to ensure the continued repression of the Helot population, a permanent and sufficient military organization was a basic requirement. Sparta characteristically always relied on its heavy armed land force. The famous Spartan discipline was aimed at achieving this. Babies who seemed physically unfit were murdered by exposure. From boyhood Spartan men were trained to the severest kind of regimen. Self-denial and hardihood were made ideals. We may recall the famous story of the Spartan boy, who being trained to steal for the good of his class, stole a fox and concealed it under his tunic, stoically making no outcry though it gnawed at his very vitals. In Sparta, the asceticism which we have noted as developing in Pythagorean philosophy became savage reality.

The *perioikoi* were to act as an auxiliary army on constant call at the discretion of the Spartan king. The Spartiates themselves were organized into special military establishments, a kind of secret police was organized, made up of Spartan youths who spied on the Helots, prevented any kind of opposition or protest from developing, and even perpetrated acts of violence against the submerged groups. Each year the ephors were required to make a formal declaration of war against the Helots, in order to "keep them in their place." When such normal measures proved inadequate, abnormal devices could be called into play. The great Greek historian Thucydides, describing the Athenian occupation of Spartan territory at Pylos, took the opportunity to comment on the Spartan treatment of the Helots and to relate a characteristic incident.

> They (i.e. the Spartans) were also glad of a pretext for sending out of the way some of the Helots, fearing that they would take the opportunity of rising afforded by the occupation of Pylos. *Most of the Lacedaemonian institutions were specially intended to secure them against this source of danger.** Once, when they were afraid of the number and vigor [or, in an alternate reading of the text, obstinacy] of the Helot youth, this was what they did: they proclaimed that a selection would be made of those Helots who claimed to have rendered the best service to the Lacedaemonians in war, and promised them liberty. The announcement was intended to test them; it was thought that those among them who were foremost in asserting their freedom would be the most high-spirited and most likely to rise against their masters. So they selected about two thousand who were crowned with garlands and went in procession round the temples; they

* Emphasis ours.

> were supposed to have received their liberty; but not long afterwards the Spartans put all out of the way, and no man knew how any one of them came to his end.[529]

A sharp change in this period was effected in Spartan foreign policy. They eschewed all foreign adventure and strictly limited themselves to the territory already possessed, aiming to secure their pre-eminence in this sphere of influence by a system of pacts and alliances. They cut off all relations with the outside world as far as humanly possible, particularly with democratic and commercial states. Traders they admitted, but only under strict supervision. A characteristic of Spartan policy was the distrust of strangers, and their systematic expulsion was a common phenomenon of Spartan political life.

Perhaps the most conservative of all Spartan institutions was their provision that only after a man had completed his full military service and attained the age of sixty years, was he admitted into the *gerousia* or senate of old men. Some aspects of the rearrangement attributed to Lycurgus were very short-lived. Within fifty years significant signs of inequality were again developing within the Spartiate class.[530]

> It has come about that some of the Spartans own too much property and some extremely little; owing to which the land has fallen into few hands.

Land again began to be concentrated into fewer and fewer hands; political democracy, consequently, among the Spartiates grew less, and divisions of opinion even about foreign politics began to develop. Nonetheless the reorganization had sufficient elements of stability to enable Sparta to play her peculiar role throughout the sixth and fifth centuries—herself the great conservative land power of Greece proper, she remained for conservatives elsewhere a beacon of hope and a fortress of stability. Nonetheless there was much of difference between the *reality* of Sparta as she actually was, and Sparta as she was philosophically idealized.

Crete, too, we must briefly examine. Aristotle compares the constitutions of Crete and Sparta as examples of oligarchy and concludes that they are closely similar.

> The Cretan policy is closely parallel to the Lacedaemonian; but although in some small respects it is rather superior, its general character is one of less finish. One might suspect, even if history did not relate, that the Lacedaemonian polity has been in most of its features modeled upon the Cretan; and as a general rule ancient institutions are not so finely elaborated as more modern ones.[531]

For our purposes it will be sufficient simply to mention the main outlines of the economic and political organization of Crete—to show, on the one hand, its close affinities with the Spartan state and, on the other, a few outstanding differences that made it a peculiarly interesting example for Plato's consideration.[532]

In Crete, as at Sparta, the great problem of the ruling class was to maintain supremacy over a large subject population. In Crete, as at Sparta, the conquering Dorian group kept itself distinct and aloof from the native peoples and was confronted with the task of perpetually securing its hold over them and guaranteeing a full degree of stability within the ranks of the ruling group.

The Cretan cities achieved the first part of this careful separation of the subject population into two classes: one composed of slaves who were actually *owned* by their Dorian masters, and the other of serfs who were inalienably bound to the land and constituted the chief class of economic producers. The Cretan serfs are particularly interesting, for they represent the closest approach in ancient times to the medieval institution of legal serfdom. This class was permitted to own property (and perhaps their own homes) and had access to the law courts for protection of their legal rights. At the same time they were not permitted to leave the land and were forced to contribute part of their produce to the Dorian citizens. This system of legal serfdom marks the greatest difference between Crete and Sparta, and in a sense might be called an advance. For the admission of the serfs into legal status and the recognition of their right to hold property and enjoy some measure of personal independence made rule over them considerably easier. We may contrast this with the Spartan view, which regarded the Helots as an enemy population, and even went to the length of formal declaration of war against them.

The position of the ruling Dorian caste at Crete illustrates to perfection the achievement of in-group unity and political stability. As we have suggested, this was the central task confronting a minority ruling group, which in states like Sparta and Crete would inevitably consist of a very small class in relation to the numbers of the subject and conquered peoples. And it would not be stretching the argument too far to remark that Plato faced a very similar problem in the need to unify his class of "guards" for their task of ruling the state. Hence the establishment of political unity and harmony among the Spartan and Cretan rulers provided a model for the Platonic ideal of collective and democratic life among the "guards."

The oligarchical clubs at Crete were organized as the foundation for social and political life. Every Dorian, i.e., citizen, was a member of a political club and every member of a club was a citizen. Noncitizens were called non-clubmen (*apetairoi*). This system represents the most efficient organization of a dominant class to be found anywhere in the Greek world. It was efficient both in its inclusion and its exclusion.

The *agora*, or general assembly of all free citizens, was the instrument of political expression for all free citizens. The ten Cretan *cosmoi* corresponded roughly to the Spartan ephors. They were chief magistrates with wide legal and political powers.

For the rest Cretan institutions closely resembled Sparta. There was a similar systematic training of young men for their role of political pre-eminence. From his sixteenth to his eighteenth year the young Cretan neophyte served a kind of apprenticeship in an organization for those of his own age. After these two years of preliminary training he was formally presented for membership in the citizen body and in a club for adult men. To foster the communal sentiment of in-group solidarity, a regular system of men's messes was instituted as at Sparta and among the Pythagoreans. The richer citizens were expected to contribute more toward the common meals than their less prosperous fellows. The actual production of this surplus was, of course, the function of the serf.

Crete, however, shows us an interesting variation of the usual oligarchical pattern in the way it handled the problem of its commercial needs. While at Sparta the attempt was constantly made to outlaw foreigners and traders, or at least remove their influence as far as possible, at Crete aliens were permitted to practice their trades and contribute to the general well-being of the Cretan citizens. This is perhaps the reason why, whenever they contemplated Cretan institutions, Greek conservatives tended to "look at each other with a wild surmise." For there commerce was permitted but had not developed a commercial class to challenge the pre-eminence of old families. The reason for this happy consummation in Crete was, however, quite simple. Trade was for the most part in the hands of foreigners who lived in a kind of ghetto, or more euphemistically, a separate quarter of the town, in barracks under state supervision, and under the watchful eye of a special magistrate (one of the *cosmoi*), whose particular duty it was to keep these useful but dangerous people in order.

As at Sparta women enjoyed important privileges, prerogatives which were actually codified into a definite system of law. Their marital rights were protected, as well as their rights against violation or adultery. When a woman was the only heir to landed property, she was required by law to marry a member of her own family, and, failing this, any member of her own tribe could claim her. But goods that a woman produced herself, by weaving or other feminine tasks, she might in part herself own. These and other Spartan institutions, which to many Greeks seemed like a mere feminine license, form an interesting background for Plato's "feminism." Aristotle, we may observe, was critical on the ground that such institutions gave too much freedom and privilege to women.[533] At Crete, just as in Plato's speculations about the ideal state, a systematic attempt was made to keep a constant proportion between the number of citizen families and the number of available "lots" of land.

It is no wonder that institutions such as those typified by Crete and Sparta should evoke enthusiastic praise from Plato, should lead him to observe that they were widely admired, and stimulate him to proposals so widely at variance with accepted Athenian custom. In these institutions we can trace the source of most of Plato's political doctrine.

Viewed in its historical context, there can be little mystery about the much debated Platonic communism. It represents part of the constant debate among Greek conservatives as to how their power could best be maintained. Sparta had shown a magnificent capacity for building a relatively stable government and a relatively static set of institutions. But Sparta, Plato could hardly help noticing, had produced no school of philosophy, and in the period of her oligarchical success, no art. Such a system could hardly, in its oligarchical nakedness, prove effective at Athens, where art and discussion were popular passions. The Cretans had shown a splendid capacity to organize oligarchy and had even been able to admit some commerce into their state without disrupting its aristocratic stability. But Crete, too, had in recent centuries exercised little influence on the general intellectual development of the Greek world. The Pythagoreans, on the other hand, had for a century or so shown marked success in solving their political problems. They had in so doing developed an appealing philosophical propaganda, created an important philosophical system, fostered great advances in mathematics, and enunciated principles of harmony and proportion which had tremendous implications for the evolution of Greek art. And yet, the Pythagorean hegemony was coming to its close. Except in occasional cities like Tarentum, where Archytas, the Pythagorean, still ruled and studied mathematics, the hegemony of idealistic philosophers in the cities of Sicily and Southern Italy was almost at an end. And they had never played a successful or dominant role in Greece proper. Perhaps the Pythagorean regime had not proved itself sufficiently ruthless in crucial moments. Or perhaps the sum of objective conditions made it impossible for conservativism to do in the West what it had in the Peloponnese. At all events the problem as it presented itself to Plato was, broadly speaking, to work out a new technique for the organization of oligarchy which should combine Spartan and Cretan political success with Pythagorean intellectual and artistic achievement. The proposals of the *Republic* represent a manifesto directed to these ends. The philosophical implication of the state, the harmony of the orders, the education of a ruling class—all are directly in the Pythagorean tradition. Many of the institutions of Platonic communism were directly borrowed from Sparta or from Crete.

It remains to notice that neither the Pythagoreans, nor Spartans, nor Cretans, not even the genius Plato himself, could succeed in the aim that they set out for themselves: to unify the state without removing the profound economic reasons for division, to build up a static and unchanging constitution giving power in perpetuity to a minority, to develop for evermore such resources of persuasion and repression that the minority could induce or intimidate the great majority in the state to accept a regime so entirely opposed to their own immediate and obvious interests. The unity and harmony of the state on which Plato dwells so much could only have been in practice what it was in Sparta or Crete: the unity of the ruling class. And the happiness of the whole state, which he postulates as an ideal, could hardly have overflowed from the rulers in sufficient quantities to give to the thirsty commoners more than an occasional tantalizing drop.

Nevertheless, when we have apprehended Plato's communism as the romantic nostalgia of a conservative for the untroubled security of tribal society, when we appreciate its connection with Sparta, Crete, and the Pythagoreans, we have by no means exhausted the problem. Plato did not solve in actual practice the problems of the Greek city-state. And the landed conservatism of the Greek world was so manifestly inadequate to the new day that was dawning in the fourth century that, as we can now recognize, Plato's age was the twilight of the landholding oligarchy throughout the Greek World. In the last analysis the forces maturing in the Eastern Mediterranean must sweep into the historical discard the pre-eminence of landed estates and old families. The more mature form of economy based on trade, exchange, and handicrafts must inevitably triumph, particularly when it found in Macedon its secular arm. Plato did not find the solution by creating a fresh stereotype for decaying reaction. But, and this it is important to emphasize, Plato's radical opponents could advance no solution either. We have seen that ancient democratic "imperialism," as exemplified by Athens, was self-defeating; the necessary expansion of its political control produced an answering opposition. The control of a merchant class in a slave-owning economy produced an economy that was only a little less repressive, a little more "democratic" and responsible to the popular will, than oligarchy itself. And if Plato could not ensure a solution by abolishing mercantilism and making secure the rule of the landed families, there was equally no solution in the "radical" demand for the redistribution of land and the abolition of debts. Could such a "solution" *per impossibile* ever have been put into effect, it would have cancelled the tremendous advance in productive skill and human control over nature which had resulted from the breakup of the tribe and the evolution of the institution of slavery. It would have meant reducing the economy of the ancient world once again to the barest kind of self-sufficient agriculture. The economy of the ancient world, let us always remember, was an economy of scarcity. And whereas today it is feasible to solve our basic economic problem by taking advantage of rational distribution of our actual and potential abundance, in antiquity no such alternative was possible. Neither radical nor conservative "economic" thinkers could solve in any rational terms the problem that this particular historical stage presented. And, as we shall see in the next chapter, the social dilemma was reflected in philosophy.

Granting, then, that Plato had no real solution for the social and economic problems of Greece in the fourth century B.C., we must nonetheless recognize it as a great historical moment when a thinker formulates certain things with such tremendous clarity. It is a great historical moment when a philosopher realizes that the things which divide mankind are largely based on economics, on possessions. And even though his prescriptions were to be applied only to the governing class, it is of tremendous importance that a thinker should have realized that harmony in society depends upon an agreement about what is "mine" and what is "not mine."* It is tremendously significant that for the first time an analyst of society should see clearly and express firmly the idea that social divisions are a result of private and individual property. And even though in actuality Plato's abolition of private property was directed only to the class of "guards" and intended only for the perpetuation of oligarchy, it has nonetheless remained throughout history an important stimulus to thought about society and an important challenge to remove those economic differences on which the strife between classes rests. It is, moreover, of great interest to observe that it was just this aspect of Platonism which drew the heaviest fire of criticism from Aristotle and others.

Even if Plato did not have, and could not have, any clear prescriptions for realizing in practice his ideal of society as an organism, it still remains true that it is a potent ideal and has historically remained as a ringing challenge. Let us remember Plato's formula and reflect that it is, in some respects, one of the great historical moments, when a philosopher contemplating the historical experience of his tribe and state could perceive that the things which divided men all resulted from a failure to agree upon what is "mine" and "not mine."

The third wave which our swimmer has to surmount is one that at first sight seems (Plato is conscious of this) the most paradoxical of all—the philosopher must rule. The thinker must be king. Plato's doctrine we can reproduce in Plato's own words:

> Until philosophers are kings, or the kings and princes of this world have the spirit and power of philosophy, and political greatness and wisdom meet in one, and those commoner natures who pursue either to the exclusion of the other are compelled to stand aside, cities never will have rest from their evils—no, nor the human race, as I

* It is the comparative neglect of the economic aspect of communal living in early Christianity which has made it impossible for the historical Church ever to live up to the ethical ideal of its founder. The common property of the early Church applied only to consumption goods, all it could be at that historical stage.

> believe—and then only will this our State have a possibility of life, and behold the light of day.[534]

In the light of our discussion of the historical relations of Plato's thought, it is hardly necessary to labor the obvious affinities of this conviction. If we were to look for a historical model for Plato's philosopher-king, we might perhaps look to Tarentum, where Archytas still ruled in the interests of conservatism and at the same time advanced the science of mathematics;* and incidentally assisted Plato when the aspirant to philosopher-kingship was in trouble with his political enemies. There is hardly need to look for a political precedent. The Republic is the triumph of hope over experience, the wish to bring together political power and philosophical theory as the Pythagoreans in their great days had once done. And yet, this again is in itself no bad idea. To harness exact science to human welfare, to bring knowledge of forces both natural and social to bear on the problem of government means in effect a tremendously hopeful perspective for human welfare and individual happiness. The state of both science and society in Plato's day made the hope merely utopian. But the ideal remains as an effective challenge.

Moreover, within the realm of theory itself, we find in yet another form that Protean "strife of opposites" which, as we have seen, is one of the key notions of developing Greek philosophy. Conservative and idealistic thinkers, shrinking in horror from the dogma of Heraclitus that process is strife, and justice is nothing to be found beyond strife, invariably try to reconcile their oppositions. Here is the last of the oppositions to be reconciled—the opposition between the theoretical and the practical life—and Plato desperately strives to bring them together in the ideal of the philosopher-king. For Aristotle the cleft will be wider, the attempt to bridge them hopeless; for the first time the preeminence of the speculative life over the practical life, of the professional life over the strife of politics, the professorial over the practical, the labor of intellect over the labor of the hands, will be explicitly stated and the two left unreconciled.

* For Archytas see above, p. 75.

Plato expends much of his great art in defending this seeming paradox, explaining why philosophy has fallen into disrepute and why, therefore, it should seem strange to his hearers to suggest the union of political power and philosophy. The very qualities of mind and spirit that make the philosopher pre-eminent may turn him aside from the pursuit of philosophy to the worship of wealth and power. Philosophy is then like a maiden deserted and hard pressed by unworthy suitors.

> For though philosophy be in this evil case, still there remains a dignity about her which is not to be found in the arts. And many are thus attracted by her whose natures are imperfect and whose souls are maimed and disfigured by their meannesses, as their bodies by their trades and crafts.[535]

The supreme difficulty, in other words, is that philosophy will fall into the hands of traders and craftsmen, who

> take a leap out of their trades into philosophy, those who do so being probably the cleverest hands at their particular craft.[536]

"Are they not exactly like a bald little tinker who has just got out of durance and come into a fortune: he takes a bath and puts on a new coat, and is decked out as a bridegroom going to marry his master's daughter who is left poor and desolate."[537] From such a marriage what could result except vile and bastard sophisms, pleasant enough to the ear but devoid of true wisdom?

The actual situation of philosophy in the Greek states is comparable to a ship:

> "If I am to plead their cause, I must have recourse to fiction, and put together a figure made up of many things, like the fabulous unions of goats and stags which are found in pictures. Imagine then a fleet or a ship in which there is a captain who is taller and stronger than any of the crew, but he is a little deaf and has a similar infirmity in sight, and his knowledge of navigation is not much better. The sailors are quarrelling with one another about the steering—every one is of the opinion that he

has a right to steer, though he has never learned the art of navigation and can not tell who taught him or when he learned, and will further assert that it can not be taught, and they are ready to cut in pieces any one who says the contrary. They throng about the captain, begging and praying him to commit the helm to them; and if at at any time they do not prevail, but others are preferred to them, they kill the others or throw them overboard, and having first chained up the noble captain's senses with drink or some narcotic drug, they mutiny and take possession of the ship and make free with the stores; thus, eating and drinking, they proceed on their voyage in such manner as might be expected of them. Him who is their partisan and cleverly aids them in their plot for getting the ship out of the captain's hands into their own whether by force or persuasion, they compliment with the name of sailor, pilot, able seaman, and abuse the other sort of man, whom they call a good-for-nothing; but that the true pilot must pay attention to the year and seasons and sky and stars and winds, and whatever else belongs to his art, if he intends to be really qualified for the command of a ship, and that he must and will be the steerer, whether other people like it or not—the possibility of this union of authority with the steerer's art has never seriously entered into their thoughts or been made part of their calling. Now in vessels which are in a state of mutiny and by sailors who are mutineers, how will the true pilot be regarded? Will he not be called by them a prater, a stargazer, a good-for-nothing?"

"Of course," said Adimantus.

"Then you will hardly need," I said, "to hear the interpretation of the figure, which describes the true philosopher in his relations to the State; for you understand already."[538]

But if the truly philosophical nature—which will be harmonious and marked by "good form," endowed with a good memory, quick to learn, a friend (even a relation) of truth, justice, courage, and temperance;[539] a temperament, too, which because it is a "spectator of all time and all essence," will be magnificent in scope and will regard human life as a small thing; he will be prepared, therefore, to lose his life in order to save it—if such a nature and temperament should get control of the state, then human nature might be saved. The philosopher will drive into the fields everyone over the age of ten years, train children in his own likeness and ways, and so establish the *kallipolis* or ideal Platonic Utopia.[540] Failing this, the concept remains a "model set up in the heavens," a constant standard of comparison by reference to which we can evaluate every other form of state. This complete failure in Plato to make any provision for a gradual evolution toward his ideal state has usually shocked critics in the modern world who have been influenced by the evolutionary philosophy of Darwin. It is very interesting to note that the materialistic philosophers, insisting as they rightly did, that everything must have an adequate cause, made no provision in their theory for leaps in nature and history. And yet this aspect of process is in some ways as useful a concept as that of gradual change. While the materialists were abandoning it, the idealists clung to it. It was historically to be enshrined in the religious concept of miracle, i.e., an event both uncaused and cataclysmic.

In the actual world of affairs declensions from the ideal will be manifold and will fall into four main types. To each type of state there will correspond an individual; and both polity and man are described with great psychological insight and sociological (as opposed to historical) skill. The implications of the method are highly interesting. Plato suggests that the essence of an institution is the psychological make-up of its individual component.

> For we cannot suppose that states are made of "oak and rock," and not out of human natures which are in them and which, in a figure, turn the scale and draw other things after them.[541]

This, at least, is implied in his parallelism between the types of individual and the types of state. Here is an epitome of the idealistic method as applied to politics. Hegel will, centuries later, work out the implications of this method, though with infinitely more sense of historical process and greater metaphysical skill. For Hegel, history is a continuous unfolding of its subjective essence; for Plato, the problem is simply to grasp and exhibit this same subjective essence. Moreover, a consideration of these sketches of decadent forms of polity will almost inevitably induce this reflection. The problem that Plato faced of putting forward a program in purely political terms was not a simple one. The *Republic*, we ought by now to be convinced, was not a monument of abstract thinking, but in a very real sense a "tract for the times." And yet the blunt advocacy of a political program is something he hardly ventures. It is only in the *Laws*, when old age brings weariness with philosophical subtleties, that Plato's political program is more bluntly expressed. At the stage of the *Republic* he introverts the argument, as it were, and, in default of a political manifesto, takes refuge in psychological analysis and sociological typology. In so doing he created a type of thinking which has proved something of a *damnosa haereditas*, a horrid legacy, a constant encouragement to minds which shrink from the concrete and specific characteristics of an institution and content themselves with examining its external forms.

> What are the types of individual and polity, that question, I said, is easily answered; the four governments of which I spoke, so far, as they have distinct names, are, first, those of Crete and Sparta, *which are generally applauded;** what is termed oligarchy comes next; this is not equally approved, and is a form of government which teems with evils; thirdly democracy, which naturally follows oligarchy, although very different; and lastly comes tyranny, great and famous, which differs from them all and is the fourth and worst disorder of the state.[542]

* Italics ours. Is it necessary now to emphasize that this applause comes entirely from ultraconservative circles? Even Aristotle does not share this loyal enthusiasm. A more literal translation would be "applauded by the many"; but we can hardly accept the adroit and most disingenuous suggestion that "the many," i.e., "the democracy," applauded these constitutions. There is plenty of evidence that the fifth-century Athenian democracy bitterly opposed them.

We can only urge the student to reread for himself, and very carefully, these brilliant sketches which trace the declension of individuals and politics from Plato's aristocratic ideal to their final perversion in "tyranny." He should keep in mind the actual affinities with Crete, Sparta, and Pythagoreanism that we have here traced, and notice in particular the way that Plato, in good Pythagorean fashion, endeavors to give a mathematical justification to his political ideas, culminating in the astonishing dictum that the "tyrant" is just seven hundred and twenty-nine times removed from happiness.[543] (Seven hundred and twenty-nine is a beautifully cubed number.) The student will then be in a position to estimate for himself the extent to which the Platonic Utopia is an idealization of actual conservative practice and institutions among the Greeks.

CHAPTER TWELVE

The Philosophy of Plato

So FAR we have discussed many aspects of Plato's thinking, all bound up with what might loosely be called his social philosophy, his general views of such problems as individual morals and social relations, the meaning of justice, and the nature and function of the state. We must now consider Plato's philosophy in the narrower sense of the term, Plato's views on the universe, God, and nature and the human soul. This is the aspect of Plato's thinking which has proved most influential through the ages; it is the aspect of Plato which even today holds the most compelling appeal for the metaphysically minded. And because the thinking of Plato has too often been seen in the abstract, quite unrelated to the practical problems with which the thinker was dealing, it has seemed to many to have a timeless significance.

The argument of the book so far may have convinced the reader that no one of the early Greek philosophers was thinking about these problems in the abstract; that in the back of their minds and usually quite well to the fore in their consciousness were always important practical problems about the nature of justice, the function of the state, the possession of material goods, and the legal justification therefor.

This is particularly true of Plato. We have seen that Plato was intensely interested in the practical life of his times—that he made frequent trips to Syracuse in the endeavor to exercise an influence, even a control, over the course of political events. We have noticed that Plato and his Academy were eager to write constitutions and codes for the Greek city states (e.g., Cyrene). And throughout the *Republic* we have noticed as the dominant social leitmotif a view of justice as rooted in the nature of things, as based in "natural" inequality, as postulating, therefore, a "harmony" in conflict, a subordination within the state of the "naturally" inferior to the "naturally" superior.

As we pursue this set of ideas into the realm of more formal philosophy, we may notice some interesting, even startling, parallels. The analogy between individual and society as microcosm and macrocosm we have already noted. Now we must pursue the analogy a little further:—just as the individual is a chaos of discordant impulses and desires which must be brought into unity and harmony, just as the state is a conflict of contending interests and classes which must be brought into the harmony of subordination to "natural" governors if the state is to be well governed and happy, so each particular aspect of reality which science strives to know, and reality as a whole which "philosophy" must strive to grasp, presents itself to the mind of the aspirant for knowledge as a chaotic, discordant conflict of particular "things," shapeless and unintelligible. It is the function of mind to bring order out of the chaos, to see beneath each set of "facts" the principle which gives it unity, meaning, intelligibility, yes, even reality and being. And mind, then, must be trained to "turn away" from the chaos or flux of particulars, and must learn to focus on the unity and harmony of the principle that somewhere underlies them.

In explaining how this can be, Plato succeeded in drawing together all the main threads of the conservative philosophy as they had so far developed. He carried forward the Pythagorean passion for the harmony of discords and opposites as a principle of explanation. He carried even further the notion that the ground of explanation for the appearances of phenomena must be thought of as mathematical. He picked up the Socratic conceptualism: the notion that a "universal" or principle was the only real thing and only genuine object of knowledge—all else nothingness and unreality; lack of knowledge of such things the grossest ignorance. He caught up and developed the Eleatic passion for the changeless and static and the unalterable. His problem was to give some content to this abstract Eleatic "Being" and explain its relation to the world of change. He thus took over a notion which was implicit in Pythagorean thinking, and which (as we saw above*) seems to have become explicit with the Eleatics: the idea of the two realms—the realm of knowledge and the shadowy realm of change and mere appearance—approached respectively by the "way of truth and the way of opinion." And finally, he accepted the Pythagorean doctrine of the antithesis between soul and body, was passionately convinced of the primary importance of soul, the relative and secondary importance of body, and at times he even argued that the body with its passions is a hindrance to the unsullied and blissful life of the soul. And in so doing he was faced with the problem of knowledge—how the immaterial and spiritual soul can come to know the gross corporeal inert mass that he called "matter." The task of harmonizing and synthesizing these various strains of development and uniting them into a coherent philosophy of idealism is Plato's central task and the major preoccupation of his Academy. His perennial influence is a tribute not only to his success, but also to the indefatigable capacity of comfortable and well-bred philosophers in almost every subsequent generation to believe (particularly if belief tends to justify the pre-eminence of themselves and their class), to give support to the human prejudices of the dominant classes in society—their conviction that nature has created men unfree and unequal and that harmony consists of the rule of the "best" over willing subjects. That Plato did not entirely succeed, however, in weaving all these various strands into a completely harmonious pattern, that in one dialogue one aspect of his desire and search should predominate, in another some other, is attested by the perpetual controversy to which the works of Plato are constantly subjected by the countless generations of loving if quarrelsome disciples. The spectacle of academic dispute will disturb us a little less, perhaps, if we once grasp the central affirmations of Platonism, which, as we have seen, deal with the nature of man, justice, and the state; and if we realize that the various philosophical weapons which he employs are in a sense complementary means for demonstrating his central point. We shall be then less

* See page 98ff.

disturbed to find shifts and differences of emphasis in the various dialogues and even within the same dialogue.

Equally it is important to notice a certain consistency in the polemics which he directs against those who disbelieve that justice is an eternal principle, who believe that justice and other elements of a code of living are relative to a historical development, who believe in the reality of change, who refuse to deny that change is baffling and ununderstandable, who believe even that change is the only reality; and, last but by no means least as a clue to the understanding of Plato, all those who called themselves democrats, all who believed in equality of rights before the law. All such dangerous groups Plato embraced in a systematic and scathing condemnation, called them Sophists and other abusive terms and, to top the heap of reprimand, *rheontes,* believers in the flux, in change, in movement, process, and progress.

Though the specific modes of expression differ, the conviction of Plato is constant. It is a social conviction which takes philosophical forms. It will be convenient to begin with the "two ways"—the "way of opinion" and the "way of truth." We have already observed this distinction present in germ in the thinking of the Pythagoreans and Eleatics. To Socrates, however, turning as he did almost violently away from physical investigation to a contemplation of what he conceived to be "spiritual" essence, the "opinion" of men about the external world and the life of society had little or no value. To Socrates, it was necessary to "know" the principle, the universal, the essence, or one was completely ignorant. One must know "what justice is in itself" or one could not be said to know anything about it. And so the opinions of the many, all the half-formulated convictions by which ordinary men lived, were, from a philosophical point of view, entirely valueless. For Socrates, there was no middle way between knowledge and abject ignorance. All that distinguished Socrates from the vulgar herd was the recognition of his own ignorance. The mission to make men recognize their own ignorance and strive for knowledge of absolute principles was, toward the end of his life, Socrates' supreme task.

When, therefore, Plato began his life work, there were two

attitudes within the idealistic tradition to the ordinary workaday "principles" by which the ordinary man lived. There was the tendency to think of them as the "thought of mortals in which there is no true way at all," to make an abrupt unmediated distinction between knowledge and ignorance, to treat with contempt the views of ordinary men, as "ignorance" parading as knowledge, to insist that any view which is not based on the universal principle and a definition which is always applicable to particular circumstances has no value whatsoever. The other tendency is to think of the "way of opinion" as having a claim to truth in a secondary or derivative sense. Opinion is *not* knowledge, but it in some way partakes of knowledge. It is the task of education to lead the soul out of the realm of shadows and half-truths into the clarity of organized thought and the unity of a principle behind the particular that we call "science."*

Socrates' convictions, were, as we have seen, highly aristocratic. They were in a sense based on prejudice, and prejudice of a highly aristocratic kind, the profound belief that only the expert, the specialist, could govern aright, that government demanded wisdom and insight, qualities that a democracy could never attain. Nor, of course, was this an entirely absurd idea in the late fifth century in democratic Athens. We have already observed that Athenian democracy, and particularly the extreme democracy, led to the most predatory overseas expansion and destroyed itself by yielding to every vaulting intoxication and dream of plunder. The demand for the rule of the "moral expert" was a not altogether irrational reaction to this extreme democratic imperialism. But Socrates' (and Plato's) affirmation of the need of "wisdom," his rejection of the opinion of the many, is at times so violent that it begins to verge on the merest prejudice. In one of the earlier dialogues his contempt for the kind of morality that is based on mere habit and unsystematic reflection is revealed as so deep and profound that he is driven to a position of unqualified hedonism: the "wisdom" and "knowledge" on which virtue is to be founded are simply the maximum of pleasure and the minimum of pain.[544] (This is a position which Plato repudiates with

* See page 101.

an almost comical emphasis in the *Republic*.[545]) Protagoras is holding the opposite view: that political and private morality is something that concerns Everyman; that it is not the subject of any special science, but the product of a common instinct of humanity; and that, therefore, there are no special experts from whom it must be learnt, but that, in a sense, everybody teaches it to everybody.[546] For Zeus had sent Hermes* to bring "reverence and justice," the gift that made possible man's survival.

There is no need to press too far the suggestion that at any point Socrates seriously believed that pleasure was the hidden principle of wisdom for which men were searching. Plato's idealistic principles reject any such blasphemous suggestion with righteous horror. For our purposes the important thing is this: Here we have very sharply posed the two views of morality, two ways of life—the democratic exemplified by the Sophist Protagoras, the aristocratic represented by the idealist Socrates. And in rejecting the democratic view of morality, Socrates also rejects "opinion" and reaffirms his central conviction that "virtue is knowledge" and knowledge is knowledge of an eternal, changeless principle.

The keynote of Plato's thinking on this subject can be found in the *Republic*.

> We have discovered, as it seems, that the conventional views of the many about nobility and other subjects, toss about as it were between "not being" and "being" in any pure sense.[547]

With this we compare the sentence from Aristoxenus which purports to give the views of the early Pythagorean school on the matter of opinion.[548]

> They hold that they spoke as follows about opinion. It is foolish, they said, to take heed of every opinion of everyone, and especially to those of *the many*; for to form correct opinions and to understand belongs to a few only. It is clear that this means "those who know," and these are few in number. Thus manifestly such a

* For the significance of Hermes see p. 56ff.

> power would not belong to the many. On the other hand it is also foolish to disregard every conception and opinion; for some will be untaught and uncorrected.

The implication is unavoidable. In rejecting or modifying Socrates' abrupt and ummediated distinction between knowledge (which is virtue) and ignorance (which is vice), Plato goes back to an earlier strain in the conservative tradition of thought, develops it farther and gives it infinitely more content. We now have a threefold schematization: there is knowledge, opinion, ignorance. But more: corresponding to knowledge, there is a whole realm of existence: namely, being. Corresponding to ignorance, there is (we can hardly call it a realm) not-being. What of opinion? It is "clearer than ignorance, murkier than knowledge."[549] It is in one sense the indispensable prerequisite to knowledge, the starting point for the activity of mind, which by finding the common element in the flux of changing things, peeling away the irrelevant and combining the relevant, is able to "turn from" opinion and the sphere of opinion, the world of change—that rolls uneasily between being and not-being—to the clear light of truth and pure reality. A great deal of Plato's language deals with this theme—the *ascent* of the soul from appearance to reality, the turning of the soul from murky twilight and the shadows of the realm of change to the pure light of reality clearly apprehended. At the end of Book Six he uses the figure of the "divided line" to express with a specious parade of mathematical accuracy the relation between the two realms, and the activities proper to both. At the beginning of Book Seven he uses the famous parable of the "cave," to express the same relation. As long as we have not yet learned to rise above the realm of change and opinion, we are like prisoners who sit enchained, with heads held rigid watching the flickering shadows of the passing show cast by the fire. But if we are released from our bonds and go to the world above, we are at first blinded by the glare and can see only dimly. But as our eyes get accustomed to the strange light, we gain a clarity of perception and a precision of knowledge that we had never known before, until at last we can even look at the sun, the source of all light, and come to comprehend things as they are.

At this stage of Plato's thought it is the negative aspect of "opinion" that is uppermost in Plato's mind. The *Symposium* and the *Phaedo*, in particular, seem to be counterparts and complements of each other, the former dwelling upon the *positive* relation of the particular and the universal, the latter upon their *negative* relations:

> the former giving us a view of the education of man in which sense and opinion are treated as stepping stones on which he may rise to the truth, while the latter regards sense and opinion mainly as hindrances to his progress, and insists on the necessity of a complete emancipation from them.[550]

And in the *Republic* the unsatisfactory nature of opinion as inchoate, changing, and unintelligible is very much in his mind.

> Of all the many noble things there is none which may not appear to be base, of the many just acts, none which may not appear unjust, of the many holy things, none which would not appear unholy.[551]

Plato is thus brought face to face with the relativism of the sophistic philosophers. None of our codes, our institutions, our ideas, and our taboos can be said to represent a reality and a truth that is eternally and unalterably the same. What seems just and noble to one man will to another seem unjust and base. How can we resolve this discord? Only by dismissing *both* as "appearance" and inviting the soul to the upward ascent where principles and truth are to be found. A man must awaken from his dream, press onward and upward, and find the reality which is changeless and of universal validity.

> He who recognizes the existence of beautiful objects but not of beauty itself, and is not capable of perceiving it even if it be pointed out to him, does he not seem to live in a perpetual dream rather than in waking reality?[552]

There is a great deal of language that suggests the religious conversion and the sacred quest in Plato's account of this turning from shadows and dreams to light and truth. There is a strong strain of the mystic in Plato, and he belongs in the tradition of all those who, like Pythagoras, Plotinus, and the Christian teachers, have preached renunciation of the goods of "this" world as meaningless shadows or even a positive hindrance to the true life of the soul. And yet even in the clear cold light of science, avoiding the shadows and half-lights of mystical ecstasy, we need not dismiss the distinction developed by Greek idealism as absurd and useless. It is, on the contrary, a distinction that we use all the time. Suppose, to take a simple example, we want to know why America entered the last war. We shall immediately begin to make a distinction between the *apparent* causes—say, waves of moral indignation that swept the country, the effect of atrocity stories, the appearance of German warships off the American coast, the moral revulsion against unrestricted submarine warfare —on the one hand, and the *real* cause or causes on the other, however we envisage them. Yet here one should notice an important distinction. The historian who feels a sense of obligation to truth does not have a passion to learn so much *what was* as *what happened*. He does not seek to delineate a set of static institutions but to grasp the dynamics of a developing situation. It is true that for this purpose he makes the distinction between appearance and reality, but he uses the *more* static, the *more* abstract, the *more* universal, as instruments with which to understand the *more* changing, the *more* particular, and the *more* concrete. This is the profound difference between Platonic idealism and the modern philosophy of science. And yet, here, too, there is an aspect of the truth in Plato's treatment of the matter which ancient materialists necessarily overlooked.

We can, perhaps, understand this phase of Plato's personality a little better if we catch up another strand which is woven into the total pattern of his thinking. Plato tends to identify the *body* and its sensations with the perception of the world of change, with opinion; and to identify the thought of *intellect* or *soul* with knowledge and the contemplation of true reality. Here we notice the development of two interrelated tendencies—the religious or mystical tendency with its ascetic overtones: the depreciation of the body and its needs, praise of the "soul" and its activities. The other tendency is closely related—to undervalue the senses: sight, touch, hearing, smell, and so on as sources of exact knowledge, to value much more highly "thought," as not only nobler but firmer in its apprehension of truth. We can think of these two phases of thinking—the mystical and the "rational"—as closely interrelated. The second arises to give content to the notion of the first, and the bond of union between the two is the common opposition to sensation, matter, a world which is apprehended as constantly in process, change, or flux.

We have observed how, among the Pythagoreans, the opposition between soul and body first began to take conscious shape, evolving from Orphic notions of the "kernel of immortality" imbedded in the grain of wheat. We have seen that the Orphic notion that the body was wretched was transformed into the Pythagorean belief that the body was evil. We have noticed the content that they gave to this view: the notion that the body was chaotic, anarchic, subject to *hybris*, going beyond "due measure"; that there had to be a ruling principle in the human individual, just as there had to be a ruler or a ruling class in the state, if anarchy was to be avoided.[553] This "soul" in the early Pythagorean school was regarded as immortal and associated with the "vital principle" of the universe. It was subject to the circle of rebirth and might reappear in animal as well as human form.[554]

But for the Pythagoreans, as later for Plato, the notion of the ruling soul must be given a better, a more articulate, explanation. This, in a sense, is the function of their researches into number. But it is also, and this is here our immediate point, the kernel of their convictions about the immortality and transmigration of the soul.

The belief in transmigration seems to go back to a very early stage in the development of thought. Plato, in a famous passage, attributes to the Orphics the belief that the body (*sōma*) is the tomb (*sēma*) of the soul and goes through some extraordinary semantic agilities to demonstrate the point.[555] The Pythagoreans, as we have already suggested, refined Orphic beliefs by interpreting them in an aristocratic direction. At all events, the contrast between soul and body, the pre-eminence of soul and the importance of transmigration, can be dimly discerned in our tradition about the Pythagoreans, probably going back to Pythagoras himself. It is this view which Xenophanes satirized in the famous fragment which we have mentioned earlier.

> They say that he was present when a puppy was being beaten. That he pitied him and spoke as follows, "Stop, do not beat him, for it is the soul of a dear friend, and I recognized it when I heard it speak."[556]

This doctrine must have always been present in the Pythagorean school. Philolaus (a fifth-century Pythagorean) speaks as follows:

> And both the ancients who discourse about the gods and the seers bear witness that because of certain punishments the soul has been yoked to the body and buried in it as a tomb.[557]

The escape of the body from the tomb, its reincarnation in successive bodies, its gradual growth in knowledge until it arrives at something like a final grasp of the essential harmony of things, all these are views in the early Pythagorean school which seem to be well attested. There seems to be some evidence that "memory" was important in the tradition of the school in its earliest days.[558] At all events, as we shall see in a few moments, the importance of "memory" or recollection of previous births is an important part of Plato's teaching and one that he—almost unquestionably—derived from the Pythagoreans.

The clue to the relation between soul and body the Pythagoreans probably found in the notion of *harmonia*, which, we have already observed, is one of the most important Pythagorean discoveries. The social roots of this dogma seem inescapable; it was an attempt to give philosophical, mathematical, and mystical "justification" to the rule of a powerful though declining class. In the human individual as in the state and the universe harmony was an ideal, a principle of order which brought attunement to the strife of opposites. Toward the end of the fifth century the school seems to have realized that to think of the soul as a "harmony" meant to hold a materialistic view of its nature and function; it implied that when the parts of the body dissolved in death, soul, too, was dissolved in the dissolution. In Plato's dialogue, the *Phaedo*, Echecrates is made to say:

> This doctrine that the soul is a kind of attunement (*harmonia*) of us has always had and still has a strong hold on me, and you reminded me, as it were, in enunciating it that I too once believed it.[559]

But the notion of the soul as *harmonia* did not do what was required of it: demonstrate the immortality of the soul. It led in other words to a materialistic or at least a semi-materialistic notion of the soul. From this conclusion Echecrates recoils and calls for another more convincing demonstration of the soul's immortality.

> Just as though I were starting from the beginning I am in dreadful need of another demonstration to persuade me that when a man dies his soul does not die with him.[560]

The central affirmation was one of faith; when one discursive or mathematical demonstration proved a weak weapon, it was necessary to find another. This will only surprise us if we expect philosophy to be coldly rational; but we have noticed so many social wellsprings of thinking in the development of pre-Platonic philosophy that we should by now be prepared for the view that the emotional and sociological conviction is primary, the form which the thinker gives to it is secondary.

The discovery that the Pythagorean concept of harmony does not prove the immortality of the soul is, of course, a heartbreaking one. It is a poignant moment for Greek idealistic thought when its leading thinkers suddenly awaken to the realization that to describe the soul as a "harmony" of the bodily parts does not lead to a belief in its deathlessness. Rather the reverse—when the body decays and its parts scatter, the *harmony*, too, must have disappeared. The spokesmen of idealism are, as Echechrates says, in "dreadful need" of another demonstration. There can be little doubt that it is in the light of this passage in the *Phaedo* that we must read Plato's attempt in the *Republic* to provide just such a rational demonstration. With again an elaborate air of casualness Plato launches into his proof:

> "And yet no mention has been made of the greatest prizes and rewards which await virtue."
> "What, are there any greater still? If there are, they must be of an inconceivable greatness."
> "Why," I said, "what was ever great in a short time? The whole period of threescore years and ten is surely but a little thing in comparison with eternity?"
> "Say rather 'nothing,'" he said.
> "And should an immortal being think seriously of this little space rather than of the whole?"
> "Of the whole certainly. But why do you ask?"
> "Are you not aware," I said, "that the soul of man is immortal and imperishable?"
> He looked at me in astonishment, and said: "No, by heaven: Are you really prepared to maintain this?"
> "Yes," I said, "I ought to be, and you too—there is no difficulty in proving it."[561]

This is the "simple proof" which Socrates then brings forward to fill the breach in the idealistic position which has resulted from the painful discovery of Echechrates. Everything that exists has its own peculiar good and its own peculiar evil. The evil corrupts and destroys, and each thing, therefore, is destroyed by its own peculiar evil, iron, for example, by rust, corn by mildew, timber by rot, and so on. Now the peculiar evil of soul is injustice. But injustice does not destroy the soul. Therefore, the soul is immortal. This is, of course, the final triumph of faith over reason, and a student who has even faintly tasted of the modern temper will wonder that such arguments could have been taken very seriously for over twenty centuries of intellectual history. Another attempt is equally unconvincing.

> The soul through all her being is immortal, for that which is ever in motion is immortal; but that which moves

> another and is moved by another, in ceasing to move ceases also to live. Only the self-moving, never-leaving self never ceases to move, and is the fountain and beginning of motion to all that moves besides. Now, the beginning is unbegotten, for that which is begotten has a beginning; but the beginning is begotten of nothing, for if it were begotten of something, then the begotten would not come from a beginning. But if unbegotten, it must also be indestructible; for if beginning were destroyed, there could be no beginning out of anything, nor anything out of a beginning; and all things must have a beginning. And therefore the self-moving is the beginning of motion; and this can neither be destroyed nor begotten, else the whole heavens and all creation would collapse and stand still, and never again have motion or birth. But if the self-moving is proved to be immortal, he who affirms that self-motion is the very idea and essence of the soul will not be put to confusion. For the body which is moved from without is soulless; but that which is moved from within has a soul, for such is the nature of soul. But if this be true, must not the soul be the self-moving, and therefore of necessity unbegotten and immortal?[562]

It is interesting to notice that the old notion of the materialists that soul is the "capacity for motion" inherent in things, as, for example, in the magnet, is here adroitly turned around, transformed into an independent source of motion within the human body, and so made to serve the ends of mysticism.

We are now prepared to turn to the *Meno* of Plato, in which the doctrine of recollection and the immortality of the soul makes an important contribution to the rounded picture which we call the Platonic philosophy. Discussing the nature of virtue with the young man Meno, Socrates and his interlocutor arrive at a complete *impasse.*

> "And how, Socrates," says Meno, "will you inquire into that which you know not? What will you put forth as the subject of the inquiry? And if you find what you

want, how will you ever know that this is what you did not know?"[563]

"I know, Meno, what you mean; but just see what a tiresome dispute you are introducing. You argue that a man cannot inquire either about that which he knows, or about that which he does not know; for he knows and has no need to inquire about that . . . nor about that which he does not know; for he does not know that about which he is to inquire."

The problem, as Caird points out, is central for idealistic philosophy. It is an inevitable dilemma once the separation of body and soul is accepted as a major premise of thinking.

> If science were merely an analysis of ordinary experience, and did not yield anything more than we can find in such experience, it would be useless, for it would not bring us a step farther than we were before. If, on the other hand, it does carry us beyond such experience, must it not be a kind of leap in the dark? If the premises anticipate the conclusion, what is the use of drawing it? If they do not anticipate the conclusion, how can it legitimately be drawn?[564]

A dilemma like this, one might suppose, would lead Plato to re-examine the postulates and the chain of reasoning which had led him to this *impasse*. But unhappily the Pythagorean dualisms of soul and body, mind and matter, subject and object, consciousness and external world were by that time so firmly embedded in the tradition of idealistic philosophy that retreat seemed impossible. Socrates went boldly forward to new heights of mysticism, drawing on the old convictions about the immortality of the soul.

> SOCRATES. I have heard from certain wise men and women who spoke of things divine that—
> MENO. What did they say?
> SOCRATES. They spoke of a glorious truth as I conceive.
> MENO. What was that? And who were they?
> SOCRATES. Some of them were priests and priestesses, who have studied how they might be able to give a reason for their profession; there have been poets also,

> such as the poet Pindar and other inspired men. And what they say is—mark, now, and see whether their words are true—they say that the soul of man is immortal, and at one time has an end, which is termed dying, and at another time is born again, but is never destroyed. And the moral is, that a man ought to live always in perfect holiness.
>
> For in the ninth year Persephone sends the souls of those from whom she has received the penalty of ancient crime back again into the light of this world; and these are they who become noble kings and mighty men and great in wisdom and are called saintly heroes in after ages. The soul then, as being immortal, and having been born again many times, and having seen all things that there are, whether in this world or in the world below, has knowledge of them all; and it is no wonder that she should be able to call to remembrance all that she ever knew about virtue, and about everything; for all nature is akin, and the soul has learned all things; there is no difficulty in her eliciting, or as men say learning, all out of a single recollection, if a man is strenuous and does not faint; for all inquiry and all learning is but recollection. And therefore we ought not to listen to this sophistical argument about the impossibility of inquiry; that is a saying which will make us idle, and is sweet only to the sluggard; but the other saying will make us active and enterprising. In that confiding, I will gladly inquire with you into the nature of virtue.

Two points come out clearly. Knowledge depends on the immortality and transmigration of the soul and its power of "remembering" the experiences of a past existence. This is the famous Platonic (and, we must add, Pythagorean) doctrine of reminiscence or recollection which has made so profound an impression on mystics since Plato's day. It is impossible to do as Caird does—dismiss the mystical form in which this doctrine is expressed and regard it as a

> convenient way of bringing before us the idea that the acquisition of knowledge is not the process of putting

> something into the mind *ab extra*, but the evolution of something involved in its own nature—the doctrine that the mind is potentially all that it can know.[565]

The mystical form in which the doctrine is presented must be taken seriously, literally, and not sublimated into a Kantian doctrine of "a priori categories of understanding." Socrates illustrates his point by a very lively demonstration (which the student should by all means read):[566] a slave boy who knows no geometry is made to arrive at a correct apprehension of a geometrical proposition. This is regarded by Socrates as a triumphant demonstration that the slave boy "remembered" the theorem as a result of the experience of his soul in a previous bodily existence, as a proof that learning is the process of recollection.

From these various strains of thinking we can observe an attitude developing, an attitude which by Plato is fostered into the most mature statement of Greek idealism. Before we plunge into the problem of the Platonic "idea," it may be well to pause, summarize, and so describe this developing attitude to the meaning of reality. It is founded on the conviction that most of our institutions, our beliefs, and our perceptions are at best only partially true and perhaps wholly untrue. It is the function of the thinker, therefore, to penetrate behind the veil and find the truly true and the really real. This can be done only by a ruthless criticism of the "opinions" of "the many," and this process of search and criticism needs a long and painful training. The "real," when it is found, will be found to consist in a "harmony" or "reconciliation" of oppositions, without negating the fundamental inequalities inherent in things. This harmony will be comparable to a mathematical principle and will be discoverable only by mathematical search. Each "thing" that "appears" to our senses will somehow represent its inner principle of harmony, and it is the function of mind to find this numerical or mathematical ground of explanation. This real, when discovered, will be changeless, static, unalterable, and (because these idealistic thinkers gave names of high compliment and warm emotional compulsion to their "real") will be called "eternal," "ineffable," and "blessed." And finally this real, this principle, this eternal, this "idea," as we must now begin to call it, must be apprehended by the mind or spirit; it involves turning away from the carnal experience of sensation and devoting oneself to pure, abstract, intellectual endeavor. This involves the severe disciplining of the body; it is necessary that the body with its impulses should be kept in check by the "soul." We have here the first draft of a theory and a practice which has been profoundly influential in the European and American tradition, *asceticism*. It is important to notice that the theory and practice of these Greek aristocrats is not yet asceticism, but that it is its historical forerunner. The Greek conservatives allowed themselves many indulgences of the body which later morality has frowned upon, and in particular they made something of a cult of *paiderastia*, opposing it to ordinary, "commonplace" relations between the sexes involved in family life. Family life and normal sexual behavior they, perhaps, despised as too usual, too normal, we might almost say too democratic, and opposed to it the aristocratic cult of homosexuality. We have noticed in another place that this opposition in their minds was symbolized in the idealization of Socrates; his sharp and brutal treatment of Xantippe, made into a symbol (as we suspect quite unhistorically) of Socrates' democratic and normal past, contrasts vividly with his passion for transcendental notions and his tender caresses for the lovely locks of Phaedo.[567] Most commentators who come to Plato from the later, more specifically religious and Christian, tradition of idealism find themselves somewhat embarrassed to explain or explain away Plato's frank cult of homosexuality.

Certain bodily indulgences were thus allowed. The emphasis in this first draft of historic asceticism was directed rather to self-restraint in the use and enjoyment of material goods—let us remember the advice of the Delphic oracle again—and a severe and Spartan self-discipline and training of the body for military needs. When we recall the political position of the Pythagoreans as the spokesmen of a small, but wealthy and powerful, landed minority, when we recall the position of the Spartiates, a tiny occupying garrison in the midst of a slave (or Helot) population, we can begin to understand the emphasis that they put on the military, or quasi-military, self-discipline that was to lead later to a thorough-going asceticism.

To sum all this up in the technical language of philosophers, we may see in it a powerful impulse towards "dualism," the theory of an unalterable opposition and consequent strife between soul and body, the one and the many, permanence and change, spirit and matter (creative mind and the created universe), particular and universal, knowledge and experience. The problem of the relation between these complementary abstractions will now become the supreme perplexity of philosophers; henceforward they will be involved in an inextricable dilemma and will be faced with an impossible task—the attempt to heal the cleft which they have themselves created, and which, once created, makes it impossible to view the seamless web of nature "steadily and whole."

Plato, drawing on the experience of the past, developed the main lines of approach as adumbrated by Pythagoreans and Eleatics. For him, as for his predecessors, the "idea" or "universal" is known only by mind or "soul"; it is static and unchanging, and has little to do with the "opinion of the many" about the just and the noble. It, too, in a sense, is a harmony, an organic unity of seemingly disparate elements, and a harmony which (Plato thought) could be explained in mathematical terms. It is, perhaps, in the notion of an idea as an organic principle of unity, under which a mass of particulars can be subsumed, that Plato makes his greatest "metaphysical" contribution. And this we ought to pursue a little farther.

As our starting point we may take the passage in the *Meno* which we have already quoted.

> As all nature is akin, and the soul has learned all things, there is no difficulty in eliciting, or as men say learning, out of a single recollection all the rest, if one is strenuous and does not faint.

We must also recall the parallelism (implicit in Pythagorean thinking, explicit in Plato), to which we have already referred, between the individual man, the state, and a branch of science. Each of them is a chaos. In the individual, there is a chaos of desires, which must be brought into unity, or as we should say today, must be integrated and harmonized by the sovereign "reason." In the case of the state, there is the risk of "anarchy," the rise of the uncoordinated desires of the lower classes, of the governed. In a science "or a branch of knowledge," there is a chaos of particulars, of unordered and chaotic facts which the mind must bring into unity and subsume under one explaining "idea." (We use the word "science" because Plato's views, properly modified, present an interesting picture of how knowledge is in fact organized in the sciences. At the same time, it is well to remember that most of what we should call "science" Plato scornfully despised and rejected; for science (in the modern sense) is after all bound up with progressive techniques, and this in general and as a historical phenomenon is a function of the rise of a middle class. Insofar as "science" developed in antiquity it was bound up with all the things that Plato liked least—the democracy and the mercantile life—and it found its philosophical expression in the philosophers of matter and the flux. Plato is interested primarily in ethics, politics and aesthetics, and it is from these disciplines that he draws examples of how the mind functions.) It is the task, then, of mind to discover the principle of unity that lies behind the flowing pageant of appearance and change.

> He who recognizes the existence of beautiful objects but not of *beauty itself*, and is not capable of perceiving it even if it be pointed out to him, does he not seem to live in a perpetual dream rather than in a waking reality?[568]

In this search for the principle of order, unity, the changeless, "opinion" is the necessary starting point. Opinion is in a sense ambiguous, it is the necessary *datum* which the mind must systematize and bring into order; but if it is mistaken for knowledge, it becomes a hindrance, and sense and sense experience hamper the pure activity of "soul."

> When in its perception of things it uses the body as an instrument apprehending through sight or hearing or any other sense, then it is dragged down by the body into the region of things that never maintain their identity; it wanders and is confused, and loses control of itself, and is, as it were, intoxicated, because it is dealing with things that have no permanence in themselves. But when it returns into itself and reflects, it passes into another region, the region of that which is pure and everlasting, immortal and unchangeable; and feeling its kindred thereto, it dwells there under its own control and has rest from its wandering, and is constant and one with itself, as are the objects with which it deals.[569]

In this passage the difficulties into which Plato is led by his preference for the static and the changeless come out very clearly. The quest of the soul comes to be a semi-mystical ascent, a turning aside from the things of senses, a search for a "one" that negates the "many," or that is at least beyond the many and (as Aristotle complains) separate from the many. The great philosophical discovery of the universal was infected with the taint of its origin and could not escape the prejudices of its discoverers. And yet the notion of a principle or a law by which we apprehend and control the changing world is not an absurd notion. The chemist in his laboratory performs a number of experiments, mixing, say, an acid and a salt. As a result of a number of such experiments he is able to express his results in a formula, an equation. There is a sense in which we might speak of the formula as the unchanging thing, the particular grams of salt and acid which he uses and washes away down the sink as the changing. Nor is it absurd to think of the ground or principle of explanation as mathematical. It is true in many, if not all the sciences, that the more nearly we can reduce our facts to mathematical formulae, the more completely can we be said to understand them. And yet, as we have previously argued, we use the *more* universal to explain the *more* particular, the *more* abstract to explain the *more* concrete, the *more* static to explain the *more* changing and so on. For the modern scientist, in other words, the mathematical formula is a device which he discovers to enable him to predict and control the changing world of material and social relations. For Plato it was, for the reasons which we have previously suggested, a device for turning away in horror from the flux of matter and the torrent of history.

Thus Plato goes astray in making the antithesis between the law or universal and the changing facts which it strives to explain. In the ecstasy of his quest Plato carries very far forward the tendency to think of the function of thought as "contemplation" instead of "manipulation" of the world, of society, of material reality. This impulse is already so strong that in Plato's great successor, Aristotle, a sharp distinction will become explicit between the "practical" life and the contemplative life; the latter, the life of pure thought, of contemplation, will be infinitely preferred. And there can be little doubt that the development of this wholly unfortunate tendency is to a degree due to the Greek aristocratic prejudice against any work with the hands, any knowledge, therefore, that came from manipulation, with the consequent preference for "pure" thought and "pure" (mathematical) science.*

Another perverse tendency develops in Plato's thought as a result of his prejudice against the changing, of his predilection for the static. For the scientist (as we today easily recognize), the law is an attempt to explain (and therefore to control) the *relations* between things. But for Plato there was a law not so much of relations as a "universal" which gave the ground of intelligibility and even existence to *things*. Thus the particular horse, infected as he is by the taint of mortality, changing as he is every particle of his material being, is an object of "opinion" and to a degree "unreal." The reality is the conceptual horse, horseness, the horse in itself—so much so that in the *Republic*, Plato goes so far as to argue that the artist who paints a bed is "three degrees removed" from reality, is painting an imitation of an imitation.[570] The really real is the conceptual bed, i.e., bedness;

* It should be observed that in Plato this tendency is not entirely mature. Plato and his pupils still think of philosophy as an instrument of social change but in a reactionary direction.

the actual bed (in which one sleeps) an "imitation" of this concept, the bed that the artist depicts an imitation of that imitation.

To sum up this point rapidly; for Plato, *law* is the essence of science just as it is for the modern scientist. But with one clear difference; while, for Plato, law must be eternal and even forcibly divorced from material, tangible things, for the modern scientist, law is only valid as a working hypothesis, a generalization or a prediction which gains meaning only when re-applied to the judgment and control of the facts which it sets out to explain. For Plato, the final justification for law is that it should be self-explanatory and self-sufficient. Trends in physics over the last few decades have increasingly emphasized the mathematical aspects of that science. It is, however, extremely important to point out that mathematics is used by modern physicists to describe dynamic processes as well as relatively static relationships. This, mathematicians in Greek antiquitity never appreciated. Greek mathematics, like Greek idealism, was too much an aristocratic cult-science to serve as a ground of explanation for the changing.

But, at the same time, part of Plato's greatness consisted in this. There was for him an element of discovery in his attitude to law. The universal is not simply a mental manipulative formula applied by the thinking mind to a set of facts. By raising facts to the level of intelligibility, as law, it raises the facts themselves to the level of meaning and intelligibility.

At the same time Plato sees clearly that "facts" do not explain themselves. In other words "facts" can never articulate a law *for us*. (In modern empirical thinking there is far too much language which suggests that the only task of the scientific mind is to collect all the relevant facts and then they will virtually combine themselves into a ready explanation, into truth.)

> Plato does not, like most moderns, begin with the subjective consciousness, and ask for an object corresponding to it; he begins with the object and goes on to realize that it is essentially an "object thought," an intelligible object.[571]

To most students who read the dialogues of Plato there seems an inescapable contradiction between the law as eternal and self-abiding, and the law which is "one" with facts. To this question we shall return shortly.

We have already observed the fatal discord which comes into the classical philosophy: on the one hand, the materialists like Democritus, fully conscious though they are of the material roots of things, are unable to develop any theory which will sufficiently explain the levels of multiplicity; in consequence, they are thrown back on a theory which reduces all things to some overly simple substance. On the other hand the idealists—culminating with Plato—are able to keep a sense of the levels of conscious thought but only at the expense of tearing everything loose from the world of things, and concrete material reality.*

We cannot pass by without dealing a little more positively with this point, and it may become clearer if we examine a modern parallel. This we can do while recognizing that in modern science there is infinitely more solid scientific content on both sides of the argument. A very cursory sketch of modern psychological theory will perhaps illustrate how painfully science, after so many centuries, is at last beginning to bring together again the two necessary aspects of thought which were held in antiquity only in the opposite camps of idealists and materialists.

† The problems of psychology were "solved" by McDougall to an extensive degree by the simple expedient of the postulation of "instincts." These alleged "instincts" were thought to be absolutes, intrinsic to the nature of human beings, unlearned, and universal in the population. They are easily seen to be relatively modern counterparts of the ancient notion of entelechy. The most articulate, and almost the last, of their defenders, William McDougall, described himself as a "vitalist."

"Vitalism" in general, and the instinct hypotheses in particular,

* To this we might add that in Aristotle even the many-sided variety of things is appreciated explicitly. In Plato such an appreciation is only implicit.

† Fearing to venture too gaily into the sphere of psychological specialists, I have asked my colleague, Dr. Lynn Baker of the University of Wisconsin, Milwaukee Extension, to prepare a short account of this movement. He kindly consented and the following page has been contributed by him.

were vigorously attacked in the United States on the grounds that:

(a) many of the alleged instincts are not really universal. Here the importation of ethnological data immediately convinces one that acquisitive behavior, for instance, varies so markedly among cultures that it is impossible to suppose any "basic" and "universal" instinctive drive to such activity.

(b) many of the alleged instincts are learned patterns. The experimental work of numerous investigators has demonstrated this point.

(c) the postulation of instincts is a tautological device and, as such, nonexplanatory. Thus, a high frequency of occurrences of combative behavior was the primary datum from which the "combative instinct" was inferred. Following this, combative behavior was then "explained" to be the result of the alleged instinct. "Why do people fight?—Combative instinct." "How do you know there is a combative instinct?—People fight."

In place of instinct was then substituted the materialistic concept of the reflex arc. Most notable use of the latter concept was made by such "behaviorists" as J. B. Watson, who wished to explain all behavior in terms of "concatenations of reflexes."

Now observe that the "vitalists" have based their explanation on attributes intrinsic to the nonmaterial psyche. The "materialists," on the other hand, have based their description on processes thought of as intrinsic to the material structure of the body. In both cases, however, the individual is thought of as a separate unit and the attributes as intrinsic attributes. The superiority of behaviorism (and scientific psychology in general) is that it at least directs its attention to an experimental attack on a substantial person.

The results of such a direct experimental attack are most enlightening. Conscious processes, for instance, were thought of in terms of reflex arcs involving the larynx. Thought and verbalization were made synonymous. But most bodily processes which are responses are themselves stimuli for further responses. This means that we must substitute the notion, *reflex circle,* for our notion of *arcs*. But a very important part of the reflex circle that is speech is wholly outside the body of the individual and consists in a *relation* between him and some other individual—is, in short, in a social context.

Hence, from the crude materialism of the early behaviorists, we reach a position in which the old dilemma proves no longer to have horns. It is not necessary to choose in psychology between mind and matter, since these are not a dichotomy. Psychology remains a materialistic science, but its primary datum consists in a relationship which emerges from a context which is, among other things, social. Mind is neither stuff nor soul, but a level of description of process, and the solution of the Platonic body-mind paradox is essentially identical with the solution of Zeno's paradoxes in mathematics.

We have already observed how important a part the notion of the clash and reconciliation of opposites played in the development of early Greek philosophy; reaching a high point, as it were, as clash in Heraclitus, as reconciliation in the Pythagorean school. We have noticed, too, the close affinity between the materialistic school and early sophistic thinking. The clash of oppositions was remodelled by the early Sophists into an elaborate technique of political and moral controversy. Socrates in his early life had learned from the Sophists and during that period was attacked by the conservative Aristophanes as an eristic quibbler. Later, as we have seen (perhaps because the criticism took effect), Socrates transformed this technique into a dialectic of words and ideas. For the later Socrates, dialectics (which to the Greeks meant simply conversation) were used as a technique for criticizing democratic institutions.[572] With Plato the dialectical method was immensely widened to include the whole range of interplaying ideas; ideas which in their mutual opposition are the stepping stones by which the thinker reasons his way to a real and nonmaterial supersensuous universe. For Plato, the education of the guards in dialectics is the final stage of an education which brings them ever closer to this "real" world.

"Then you will make a law that they (the guards) shall have such an education as will enable them to

> attain the greatest skill in asking and answering questions?"
>
> "Yes," he said, "you and I together will make it."
>
> "Dialectics, then, as you will agree, is the coping stone of the sciences, and is set over them; no other science can be placed higher—the nature of knowledge can no further go?"[573]

It is this education that enables them, after a prolonged training in the unconscious (music) and the conscious (mathematics), to grasp harmony and mathematical concords, to reach the essential of a real and supersensuous world.

> "And so, Glaucon," I said, "we have at last arrived at the hymn of dialectic. This is that strain which is of the intellect only, but which the faculty of sight will never the less be found to imitate; for sight, as you may remember, was imagined by us after a while to behold the real animals and stars and last of all the sun himself. And so with dialectic. When a person starts on the discovery of the absolute by the light of reason only, and without any assistance of sense, and perseveres until by pure intelligence he arrives at the perception of the absolute good, he at last finds himself at the end of the intellectual world as in the case of sight at the end of the visible."
>
> "Exactly," he said. "Then is this the progress which you call dialectic?"
>
> "True!"[574]

Plato, thus, transforms the notion of dialectic. The earlier materialistic as well as the eristic, controversial dialectic he carefully and wholeheartedly repudiates, as something quite different from the dialectic of pure reason. The former varieties lead to "lawlessness" (i.e. political and moral criticism, skepticism or, as an aristocrat would say, "anarchy").

> "And here, my friend, great caution is required."
>
> "Why great caution?"
>
> "Do you not remark," I said, "how great is the evil which dialectic has introduced?"

"What evil?" he said.

"The students of the art *are filled with lawlessness.*"[575]

In opposition to the dialectic of mere controversy Plato sets up his notion of a pure intellectual discipline. No one of the particular sciences, he suggests, is based on principles free of all contradiction; no one of them, therefore, is sufficient in itself, and each must find its place in the whole scheme of final rationality as its own inherent contradictions are resolved. This process of resolution, as the postulates of each science are found to be in conflict with each other, is the task, as Plato conceives it, of dialectic. It is the supreme unifier of separate and different sciences; it puts each science in its place in the whole. The man, then, who is capable of this kind of supreme synthesis is alone worthy of the name of dialectician. He is, in Plato's phrase, the "synoptic dialectician"—capable of a complete and unified *Weltanschauung*.[576] He alone is the philosopher, he alone should be king, he alone is capable of governing the state.

Let us recall that in the transition from Anaxagoras to Democritus the materialistic school of philosophy was busily abandoning the fruitful notion from which philosophy had sprung. It is just in so far as the materialists abandon a dialectic conception that their outlook becomes narrowed into an inadequate atomism; while Socrates and Plato in contrast take up this discarded method, divorce it completely from concrete relationships and, instead of using it to explain material changes and process, make it an intellectual symbolism, a description of the upward ascent of the "soul" to a world of "pure ideas."

In the process of changing sides, what materialism lost idealism gained. Throughout history the compelling appeal of the Platonic influence has been its insistence on the total picture, the world view. From Heraclitus on, materialism, as it develops into pluralism, tends to become less and less coherent, less capable of grasping the problems of life and thought as a whole. By contrast, Platonic idealism has loomed as gigantic in its dimensional completeness, capable, even though only abstractly, of doing justice to all the rich complexity of things. Even to this day, schools which begin with a pluralistic and fragmentary assumption fail to explain and expound even the limited problems which they pose for themselves. By isolating an event, by failing to see it as part of an historical, unfolding pattern, they distort the very nature of the event with which they are dealing.* To this tendency the Platonic ideal of the "synoptic" is a necessary and salutary corrective.

In all this, just as in his discussion of integration and harmony, Plato sees clearly at least one true side of the real, a side that, more and more, ancient materialists were coming to neglect. As his opponents in their zeal for a materialistic explanation emphasized increasingly the atomic independence of each thing, Plato manfully argued for their organic interconnectedness. It is important to note, however, that for Plato organic interconnectedness as a metaphysical argument was not enough. Why not? We have seen that between Plato's formulation of the universal which is one with "things," and shared in by "things," and the universal which exists alone as a final truth in itself there was a major contradiction. It has often been suggested that in the realm of metaphysical "philosophy" this contradiction is inescapable. In short, for all Plato's eloquent language, the problem still remains of how to pass from the particular thing to the universal. What other argument could he use to demonstrate that somehow everything shared in this final truth? In this context Socrates' account of the great change which came over his life and thinking as told in the *Phaedo* becomes peculiarly significant.[577]

> Socrates expected from Anaxagoras a theory of the universe as an order based not merely upon law but upon *design*, not upon efficient, but upon final causes. He had expected that Anaxagoras would reduce the order of the universe to a system arranged in view of an *absolute good.*[578]

It is not merely law that in Plato's view is all important, but design that is shaped in the image of an absolute good. This appeal to ethical ends, Plato feels, is necessary to buttress the

* The writer has in mind such modern schools as philosophical empiricism and institutional economics.

whole argument and accomplish the transition. And so it is necessary that the idea should be not only final and all-embracing but also "good." But the good must be the good for someone or something. And it does not take much acuteness to see that this someone or something is "Man"; i.e., that the whole world process must be subordinated to *our* wishes, desires, and ends. This is the easier for Plato because of the ambiguities (which we have already pointed out) in the Greek word *aretē* (virtue—excellence). Each thing in the universe, he thought, had a function. It was good, it possessed *aretē* (virtue—excellence) when it performed that function well. The function, e.g. of a carving knife, is to carve meat; the function of a pruning hook is to prune the vine. We should notice in each case that the reference is to the desires and needs of human beings. Now, Plato thought, as each thing has a function for which it is designed and for which, if it performs its function well, we can describe it as well-adapted, so each organic and organizing principle in a science, and ultimately the organic principle in the universe as a whole, must be described as good.

> From this point of view the *Republic* exhibits to us a series of stages in the process of defining the idea of the the good. In the first book, it is represented (as Socrates had represented it) as the goal of the individual life, which each man has to discover for himself by a consideration of his nature as a man and of the work for which it fits him. Then, at the next stage of Plato's argument, man is shown to be essentially social, essentially a member of a State, so that he can find his good, only as he discovers his proper place in the social organism, i. e. the place for which his special tendencies and capacities fit him. But even here Plato cannot stop; for the social organism itself has to be regarded *sub specie aeternitatis;* and, so viewed, it is found to be a *microcosm*, a little world in itself, but one which can attain the perfection of which it is capable only when it is molded after the similitude of the *macrocosm*. Hence it is the philosopher—who lives in the contemplation of the universe and apprehends the principle of order that

is manifested in it—and he alone, who can give to the State its true or ideal constitution. He alone can make all things "after the patterns hewed him in the Mount." Thus ethics and politics find their ultimate basis in a theology which contemplates the world as a teleological system, and of this system the Idea of Good is the end and principle.

The next step is taken by means of an analogy, which is really more than an analogy, since the object used as an image is declared to be the "offspring" or product of that which it is taken to illustrate. In other words, the material world, from which the image is drawn, is not for Plato an arbitrary symbol of the ideal reality; it is its manifestation or phenomenal expression; and, therefore, the principle of unity in the one is essentially akin to the principle of unity in the other. Now, what is the principle of unity in the material world? It is, Plato suggests, the sun; for the sun, as the source of the heat which is essential to growth, may be regarded as the cause of the existence of the objects we see; while at the same time, as the source of the light, it reveals the forms and colors of those objects, and enables us to see them. In like manner, Plato bids us regard the Idea of Good as at once the cause of existence to all things that exist, and of knowledge to all minds that know them. It is thus "beyond existence" and "above knowledge"; as it is that from which they both originate, and by which they are united to each other as elements in one whole. By the aid of this analogy, therefore, Plato carries us beyond the conception of a principle of unity in the objective world, and suggests to us the thought that, if the Idea of Good is the ultimate cause or reason of the universe, it must be also the principle of unity in the consciousness of man, the principle that constitutes his intelligence and makes knowledge possible to him.

The third and last point in Plato's exposition of the Idea of the Good is derived from its relation to the other ideas. In the *Phaedo,* as we saw in the last lecture, he had already spoken of a regressive method that goes back from one idea to another till it reaches a principle

> which is ultimate and self-sufficient. Here he speaks of a similar method by which the intelligence advances from the special sciences to philosophy. Each of the special sciences is shown to have some organizing idea which gives order, self-consistency, and systematic connexion to our view of a special sphere of reality, and thus lifts us above the empirical coexistence and sequences of phenomena within that sphere. But, as the world is one world, and all special spheres of reality are parts of one great all-inclusive sphere, it is impossible for the intelligence to be satisfied with the results of the special sciences. The principles of these sciences are hypothetical, in the sense that they are not ultimate but find their basis in something deeper and more comprehensive than themselves. The true dialectician is "one who sees things in their unity," who is unable to rest in any fragmentary and incomplete view of things, but must feel insecure till he has found one all-embracing principle, which enables him to view the universe as a systematic or organic whole. Having found such a principle of principles he will be able to give their proper place to all the investigations of the special sciences.[579]

The Idea of the Good, then, is the teleological principle of Socrates as applied not to the individual life but to the universe.

But in Plato's hands this Protean contradiction takes yet another shape. So far the idea has been exhibited as a principle of unity in a sense, *within* phenomena or things, as giving meaning, intelligibility, and even existence *to* things. But the universal or idea in another sense goes beyond things; it is lone and self-abiding. It is "over and beyond existence and surpasses it in dignity and power."[580] Now as Plato's philosophy, in his hands and in those of his successors, comes to take on more and more of a theological tinge, as the "Idea of the Good" is more and more persistently identified with God, this contradiction becomes increasingly a perplexity. Is God to be conceived as (in the language of theologians) immanent in the universe, a principle of unity within things; "in Him we live and move and have our being"? Or is God to be thought of as apart from the universe (in theological language transcendent), the source of its existence but separate, alone and apart, supremely disinterested in the mere temporal and material events of this world? Plato never gives any final answer, and the student who has followed the argument so far, will recognize that no answer can be given and that within the patterns of idealism, once the dichotomy of mind and matter is admitted, no answer is possible. The question will plague idealistic and religious thought through the centuries—except those for whom a solution is possible, by juxtaposition and through faith, in the doctrine of the Trinity.

Plato, to do him justice, realizes the insoluble problems that he and his idealistic predecessors have introduced into philosophy. In the later metaphysical dialogues the problems which his method introduces are exhaustively discussed. In the *Parmenides* various accounts of the relation between the idea and material existence are raised, to be dismissed as all unsatisfactory. In a well-known passage in the *Phaedrus* he seems to recognize that "up to the one" is not enough; there is also "down to the many."[581]

> SOCRATES. First, the comprehension of scattered particulars in one idea . . . the speaker defines his several notions in order that he may make his meaning clear, as in our definition of love, which whether true or false certainly gave clearness and consistency to the discourse.
>
> PHAEDRUS. What is the principle, Socrates?
>
> SOCRATES. Secondly, there is the faculty of division according to the natural ideas of members, not breaking any part as a bad carver might. But, as the body may be divided into a left side and a right side, having parts right and left, so in the two discourses there was assumed, first of all, the general idea of unreason, and then one of the two proceeded to divide the parts of the left side and did not desist until he found in them an evil or left-handed love which the speaker justly reviled; and the other leading us to the right portion in which madness lay, found another love, having the same name,

> but yet divine, which he held up before us and applauded as the author of the greatest benefits.
>
> PHAEDRUS. That is most true.
>
> SOCRATES. I am a great lover of these processes of division and generalization; they help me to speak and think. And if I find any man who is able to see unity and plurality in nature, him I follow, and walk in his step as if he were a god. And those who have this art, I have hitherto been in the habit of calling dialecticians.

But to recognize the cleft in nature and reality is not enough. Plato would strive to heal it. In a well-known passage in the *Sophist* he speaks of the great oppositions—the one and the many, the permanent and the changing; *and he wants both.*[582] But no such facile solution is possible. Once the great dualisms of idealistic tradition have been introduced into thought, once the great rift has developed in society, there can be no easy reconciliation, no mechanical juxtaposition. The philosopher may exclaim "give us both," but the rift is none the less there. Between thought and its object, between mind and matter, between the creator and the created universe, the one and the many, the permanent and the changing, there is a great gulf fixed. With all his brilliance and subtle insight, Plato, the architect of the eternal ideas, builds what is after all a magnificent palace of half truths. This even he came to realize in part. As the whole theme of this book must have made clear—the rift in thought reflects the rift in society. Until that conflict is resolved in actuality, or at least in hope, the troubling doubt that haunted Plato must continue to perplex his philosophical successors.

AMICUS PLATO, AMICIOR VERITAS.

CHAPTER THIRTEEN

The Academy and the Later Dialogues

THE ACADEMY of Plato, its role and functioning, has been misunderstood by scholars. The very word Academy and its adjectival form, academic, have, in almost all modern languages, come to be associated with education at one of its levels or in one of its branches.

> "It is not wonderful, therefore," writes Professor Cherniss[1] "that by a more or less conscious retrojection modern scholars have attached the particular significance which 'Academy' has in their milieu to that garden of Plato which was situated in the suburb North West of Athens called 'Academia' after a mythical hero. So to the German philologists of the last century Plato was the first organizer of scientific research and his Academy was a kind of German university with a regular program of lectures by the professor and seminars in which the more mature students were apportioned plots of scientific ground to cultivate under the watchful eyes of the master. A French Platonist describes the Academy in terms of a French University with 'Conferenciers' and professors of various faculties; and an Englishman says that 'it resembled a modern college—' college in the English sense, of course, with its Master, Fellows and Scholars."

The retrojection, as Cherniss remarks is natural. Scholars who usually toil in a college or university are likely to imagine the school of Plato rather in terms of their own personal experience.

With this misconception of the Academy as 'the first University' has gone another, closely linked with it and perhaps equally natural—the tendency to deny any consistent political role to its members. Gomperz[2] vigorously denies that the Academy played any coherent or consistent part in the political life of the times. He lists members of the Academy who seemed to take a different, even a contradictory position in relation to institutions, personalities and events. Unhappily Gomperz' argument carries less conviction than it might because of the neglect of any serious attempt to establish a chronology, which might assist us to find a pattern. And secondly an absorption with the abstract forms of political analysis often tends to obscure the real and consistent interests which a statesman or philosopher is striving to defend or protect. It is quite conceivable that different weapons would be used at different periods to protect the same interest—at one time oligarchy at another monarchy—just as to-day it may be at one moment 'isolationism' and, at another when circumstances have changed, 'interventionism.'

Wilamowitz-Mollendorf admits the political role of the Academy but denies that it was exercised in Athens.[3]

More recent writers, particularly in France have modified or even reversed these judgements. Pierre Maxime Schul writing in the *Revue des Etudes Greques* remarks as follows:

> Reading now a list of the disciples of Plato and underlining the names of those whose political activity was notorious, we shall be astonished to see that the pure theoreticians are much less numerous among them than one had believed and that the men of the Academy did not fail to exercise on occasion a political activity.

After citing a number of examples of such activity he concludes:

> These brief indications are perhaps enough to underline the role of the Academy in matters political. They indicate to us that people turned naturally to the Academy to ask for law givers and legislators, counsellors and experts. They demonstrate that many of its pupils did not hesitate to translate into the realm of deeds more or less faithfully the ideas of the Master.[4]

In a recent study which is both learned and penetrating Magalhaes-Vilhena remarks:

> We must not forget that the ideological struggles represented not only oppositions of a purely doctrinal kind—arguments

> purely philosophical; they also represented social conflicts having the deepest repercussions. Men were discussing the life of Athens and its destiny. It is the very foundation of policy which is at stake. The polemics of Socratics and anti-Socratics (Plato against the democrats and demagogues, the rhetoricians and the sophists; Plato and Xenophon and Isocrates against Polycrates, Polycrates against Plato) all this is the expression on the intellectual plane of the antagonisms, which in the bosom of the dominant slave-owning class, set in opposition the democrats to the anti-democrats, the slave owners of non-aristocratic origin (traders, merchants, usurers, ship owners) to the elite of the slave-owning aristocrats who felt themselves menaced by an economic growth founded not on the possession of landed property but on the possession of movable wealth.[5]

A few pages later he remarks:

> But for Plato, as for Xenophon, the movement which was tied to the name of Socrates and which had its expression in the 'Socratic discussions' is more than a strictly philosophical movement. It is a movement both political and social. It is one of the forms, in short, intó which the dominant class at Athens —the slave owning class—reflected and translated everything. Everyone who possessed the means to acquire political rights in Athens was enrolled either as a partizan or an enemy of the democratic movement in the state; a movement which developed and strengthened with the increase of commerce and industry and moveable wealth, to the detriment of the interests of the land owners—the men of aristocratic origin; (among this number Plato counted himself) these men hoped to reconquer their lost privileges and to take into their own hands the government of the state.[5a]

All this is well and ably said. But if it is accepted, as I think it should be, it would project something of a revolution in the methods of Platonic studies. Scholars in the past have tried to find an intellectual consistency in the thought of Plato. They have tried to bring one metaphysical doctrine into harmony with others. Or if they have admitted an evolution of doctrine they have placed it upon the purely abstract and intellectual plane—that empyrean of abstract thought where disembodied ideas meet, jostle, clash and modify each other for no apparent reason. Intellectual consistency in Plato has been notoriously difficult to find. As a consequence Platonic studies are after these years and centuries still in a state of confusion and it is hard to find two scholars who will agree about the simplest proposition in the realm of logic and metaphysics.

On the other hand, if we assume, (as I think we should) that the Academy was first of all a political organization, that its primary function and purpose was the defense of international conservatism, a number of important points suggest themselves. The attached chart gives the main structure of the Republic. In this dialogue was propounded with a wealth of elaboration and with infinite suggestiveness in many fields of enquiry Plato's program for the last years of the fifth century B.C. in Athens. His program can be summed up in a phrase. Plato believed as did Cicero in the *concordia ordinum* the harmony of the slave-owning, governing class, now at variance and torn asunder by dissension. He wanted land-owning aristocrats and wealthy merchants to combine; by combining they could check the democratic movement and make life again secure for those who possessed great wealth—whether wealth in land or wealth in moveable property. This hope and this program Plato expressed in a parable: The man (symbolizing *reason*) should combine with the lion (*wholesome emotion*) to keep in order the many-headed beast (*desire*).

To put into practice the spirit of this parable was perhaps the meaning of Plato's first experience with practical politics. At the time of the crisis of Athenian democracy that followed on severe reverses in the Peloponnesian war Plato threw himself heart and soul into the counter-revolutionary movement of the 'Thirty.' As he tells us (many years later) in the Seventh Letter, he had expected great things from this political movement. In the same letter he tells us, too, how disillusion came to him. His patron and mentor Socrates was sent by the 'Thirty' to arrest Leon of Salamis, a wealthy metic.[6] Now such an action meant the destruction of any plan of *concordia ordinum*—the unity of the two severed wings of the governing group. It meant rather the unabashed dictatorship of the land—owning aristocracy. Plato's political instinct even at that early age told him that the basis of popular support for such a dictatorship was too narrow. Events proved that he was right.

The period that followed from 399 B.C. was marked for a number of years by the ascendency of Sparta. In place of imperial Athens the Greeks cities found, not the seductive dreams of autonomy promised them by Sparta, when Sparta was engaged in the death struggle with Athens. Rather they found themselves subjected to the yet more imperious, yet more oppressive rule of the Spartan conqueror. Xenophon, himself a convinced philo-Laconian, gives a disturbing picture of the ascendency exercised through all the Grecian cities, not merely by the ephors and the public officers but even by the private citizens of Sparta. "The Lacedaemonians," says he in addressing the Cyreian army, "are now the presidents of Greece and even any single Lacedaemonian citizen can accomplish anything he pleases." "All the cities," he remarks in another place, "then obeyed whatever order they might receive from a Lacedaemonian citizen."

Not merely was the general ascendency, remarks Grote, thus omnipresent and irresistible, but it was enforced with a stringency of detail, and darkened by a thousand accompaniments of tyranny and individual abuse such as had never been known before under the much decried empire of the Athenians."[7]

There can be little doubt that the empire of Sparta was oppressive in a way that the Athenian empire had never been. Sparta had won important political support throughout Hellas by posing as the champion of national liberation against the democratic and mercantile imperialism of Athens. The Greek states were soon to learn that whereas Athens had whipped them with whips, Sparta would whip them with scorpions.

> "Taking all these causes of evil together—the Dekarchies, the Harmosts and the overwhelming dictatorship of Lysander—we shall be warranted in affirming that the first years of the Spartan empire, which followed upon the victory of Aegospotami were years of all-pervading tyranny, and multifarious intenstine calamity, such as Greece had never before endured."[6a] . . . "And what made the suffering yet more intolerable was that it was a bitter disappointment and a flagrant breach of prom-

> ises proclaimed, repeatedly and explicitly, by the Lacedaemonians."[7a]

Sparta's success in the Peloponnesian war had been at least partly due to the fact that she gave expression and leadership to the Greek passion for civic autonomy. This feeling, because of geography, tradition and the historical development of Hellas, was very strong. The Athenian empire by flaunting this passion and by reducing so many of the allied states to subjection was very unpopular. Athens had become an *arche tyrannikes,* a tyrannical empire.[8] Sparta had been able to capitalize on this unpopularity and to pose as a crusader for civic autonomy. When Sparta proved herself a harsher taskmaster than Athens had ever been, the revulsion of feeling throughout the Greek world was profound.

> "For more than thirty years preceding—from times earlier than the commencement of the Peloponnesian War—the Spartans had professed to interfere only for the purpose of liberating Greece, and of putting down the usurped ascendency of Athens. All the allies of Sparta had been invited into strenuous action—all those of Athens had been urged to revolt—under the soul-stirring cry of 'Freedom to Greece.' The earliest incitements addressed by the Corinthians to Sparta in 432 B.C. immediately after the Korkyraean dispute, called upon her to stand forward in fulfillment of her recognized function as 'Liberator of Hellas' and denounced her as guilty of connivance with Athens if she held back. Athens was branded as the 'despot city,' which had already absorbed the independence of many Greeks and menaced that of all the rest. . . . And the banner of general enfranchisement which the Lacedaemonians thus held up at the outset of the war, enlisted in their cause encouraging sympathy and good wishes throughout Greece."[9]

> "The victory of Aegospotami with its consequences cruelly undeceived everyone. . . . The Dekarchies of Lysander realized that precise ascendency of a few partizans which Brasidas repudiates as an abomination worse than foreign-dominion; while the harmosts and garrisons installed in the dependent cities along with the native decemvirs, planted the second variety of mischief as well as the first."[10]

Sparta ruled her empire, not as Athens had done by encouraging the mercantile and democratic elements in each state, but by basing herself on the narrowest and most reactionary oligarchies and supporting these oligarchies with garrisons and armed force. Moreover, the new-found wealth and power was not without its effect on Spartan institutions. The older way of life that the Greeks had attributed to Lycurgus could not survive the introduction of coined money in large amounts.

> "It is from this time and from the proceedings of Lysander that various ancient authors dated the commencement of her degeneracy, which they ascribe mainly to her departure from the institutions of Lycurgus by admitting gold and silver money. . . . There can be no doubt that the introduction of a large sum of gold and silver into Sparta was in itself a striking and important phenomenon when viewed in conjunction with the peculiar customs and discipline of the state. . . . But Plutarch and others have criticized it too much as a phenomenon by itself; whereas it was one characteristic mark and portion of a new assemblage of circumstances into which Sparta had been gradually arriving during the last years of the war, and which were brought into the most effective action by the decisive success of Aegospotami. . . . Lysander, enslaved only by his appetite for dominion, and himself a remarkable instance of superiority to pecuniary corruption, was not the first to engraft that vice (i.e. avarice W.) on the minds of his countrymen. But though he found it already diffused among them, he did much to impart to it a still more decided pre-dominance, by the immense increase of opportunities and enlarged booty for peculation, which his newly-organized Spartan Empire furnished. Not only did he bring home a large residue in gold and silver but there was a much larger tribute imposed by him upon the dependent cities, combined with a number of appointments as harmosts to govern the cities. Such appointments afforded abundant illicit profits, easy to acquire, and even difficult to avoid, since the decemvirs in each city were eager thus to purchase forbearance or connivance for their own misdeeds. So many new sources of corruption were sufficient to operate most unfavourably on the Spartan character, if not

> by implanting any new vices, at least by stimulating all its inherent bad tendencies."[11]

By a neat, if unscrupulous manoeuvre Lysander was able to make his own nominee, Agesilaus, a king in Sparta. These two men between them conceived the most intoxicating dreams of empire.

> "The ambition of Agesilaus . . . was yet more unmeasured in respect to victory over the Great King (i.e. the King of Persia W.) whom he dreamed of dethroning or at least of expelling from Asia Minor and the coast. So powerful was the influence exercised by the Cyreian expedition (even the least classical of our readers will have heard of the expedition of Xenophon and his ten thousand Greeks. W.) over the schemes and ambitions of energetic Greeks; so sudden was the outburst of ambition in the mind of Agesilaus for which no one before had given him credit."[12]

It is a pity that this period is not better known to students of philosophy. It is a pity that the Spartan hegemony did not find an Aristophanes to poke fun at its dreams and its excesses. For whereas every educated man has heard or read with relish the satire of Aristophanes against Athenian democratic imperialism, only specialists are fully aware of the implications of the Spartan hegemony and the problems that it created. And yet this period and the one which succeeded the breakdown of the Spartan attempt at Empire provide the historical background for many of Plato's most important dialogues. There can be little doubt that the political and social problems of the period form the background for Platonic thinking. And the thought of Plato never wandered far from the scene political.

What were the political sympathies of Plato and his friends during this period of Spartan ascendency? There can be little doubt about the right answer to this question. Conservatives at Athens remained enthusiastically pro-Spartan. We can conjecture this on a number of grounds. Xenophon, who clearly shares and perhaps reflects the political sympathies of the Platonic circle, makes of Agesilaus almost the hero of his history. His work on that king was nothing less than a resounding panegyric. And this is true in spite of the fact that Xenophon criticizes Sparta for departing from the ideals and institutions of Lycurgus.

> Formerly, the Spartans chose to associate with each other and live a moderate life at home. They did not want appointments as harmosts and so degenerate through flattery. In old times they were afraid to be seen possessing gold. Now there are some Spartans who display their gold most ostentatiously. Formerly they drove out foreigners and forbade their own citizens to travel abroad, so that they would not become too easy-going in their ways as a result of foreign associations. But now those who have the reputation of being the leading citizens want a continuous employment as harmosts abroad. Once their aim was to be worthy to rule; now they strive to get and keep command rather than to deserve it. And so of old the Greeks used to beg them to take the lead against evil-doers; but now many states beg each other to combine and keep Sparta from renewing her empire. Nor can we wonder that the Spartans have gained this bad reputation since they have betrayed both the advice of Delphi and the institutions of Lycurgus.[13]

This criticism of Sparta by an ardent philo-Laconian is, as Grote remarks, 'instructive.' Although Xenophon admits that Sparta has fallen away sadly from his ideal of primitive agrarian and aristocratic 'simplicity' he sees nothing for it in practice but to support the power politics of his 'ideal' state. Although the tables of Sparta have come to rival the more notorious tables of Syracuse, he can see no alternative in the realm of practical politics but to support Sparta's imperial designs. The socio-psychology of Xenophon's mind at this juncture is worthy of meditation. He is forced by the logic of events to support the power politics of his ideal, while admitting to himself that his ideal has abandoned its ideals.

Is this also the position of Plato and his friends? Everything points to an affirmative answer. The thirty years, approximately, of Spartan ascendency co-incide with a period of great literary activity for Plato. It is the period of the Socratic dialogues—the period in which the Master, the only victim of the triumphant return of the victorious democrats to Athens, was being built up as a conservative saint. In this process of *hagiopoiesis* (canonization) both Plato and Xenophon shared with enthusiasm. It is also the period of the great literary dialogues, including the Republic, with its sublime choral symphony in praise of the eternally unchanging. Plato is evidently well satisfied with the course of events in the period of Spartan ascendency.

In an historical sense the empire of Sparta did not last long. Were it not for the writings of Plato we could, perhaps, dismiss its attempted hegemony as one of the least significant of all the attempts of one state to establish empire over others. As a combined empire by land and sea, Sparta's lasted only ten years. In 394 B.C. the battle of Knidos put an end to Sparta's ambition to be a great naval power the successor by sea to Athens' maritime empire. The debacle by sea did not prove too great a shock to Greek public opinion. For over a century there had prevailed the assumption that whereas Sparta was great on land, it was the Athenians who were destined to be foremost on the seas. A Spartan defeat on land—that would be different. In due course that, too, came. Some twenty years later in 371 B.C. Epaminondas and his Theban army roundly defeated the Spartan force led by Cleombrotus.

> The event came like a thunder clap upon every one in Greece, upon victor as well as vanquished, upon allies and neutrals, near and distant alike. The general expectation had been that Thebes would be speedily overthrown and dismantled; instead of which, not only had she escaped, but had inflicted a crushing blow on the military majesty of Sparta.[14]

The imagination of every student and every reader of Greek philosophy should range around this stupendous event. It is a crucial moment in the history of ancient thought. The military ascendency of Sparta which had been accepted as almost axiomatic for almost two centuries of Greek history and of Greek thought was overthrown. The event was as dramatic for the Greek world as the battle for Stalingrad and the subsequent destruction of the *Wehrmacht* was for ours. Every politician, every intellectual in all of Hellas was forced to think the problems of theory and of practical politics out again.

What was the effect of this event on the Academy? If we are right in our assumption that the Academy was the leading organizational force for Greek conservatism, we should expect to notice some perturbation. Our expectations are not to be disappointed. To put the matter shortly the men of the Academy went scurrying all over the Greek world to devise fresh bases of power for the protection of its ideals. Four years later in 367, we find Plato himself landing in Syracuse in a desperate attempt to influence the course of Syracusan politics in accordance with his ideas.

If there should in any quarters still linger the notion that this excursion into politics was the accidental or even absent-minded venture of a philosopher otherwise impartial and detached, a careful reading of the Seventh Letter should be enough to put this notion to rout. Plato in that epistle uses all the highly surcharged language of his peculiar morality to defend the 'Doric' way of life and to heap scorn on the life of wealthy merchants.

> 'Upon my arrival, moreover,' (this was on the first journey but there is no reason to think that Plato's opinions changed) 'I found myself utterly at odds with the sort of life that is there termed a happy one, a life taken up with Italian and Syracusan banquets, an existence that consists in filling oneself up twice a day, never sleeping alone at nights, and indulging in all the practices attendent on that way of living. In such an environment no man under heaven, brought up in self-indulgence could ever grow to be wise. . . . That a man should grow up to be sober-minded would also be quite impossible."[15]

But the Academy was not content, as Schul well remarks, with its grand effort in Sicily. It sets out its political stakes in many directions. Nor was it to be expected so great a power as Macedon should be entirely overlooked. We are told by Athenaeus, referring to a letter of Plato's nephew Speusippus, that Plato was always on good terms with Archelaus.[16] This worthy monarch has been well characterized by C. F. Smith:[17] 'He was as famous for the splendour and success of his reign as for the crimes by which he obtained the throne.' This is probably the Archelaus who was king of Macedon from 413 to 399. If so he must have befriended Plato when the latter was quite a young man. In the Gorgias Plato repays this kindness by relating that Archelaus was the illegitimate son of Perdiccas II and obtained the throne by the murder of his uncle Alcetas, his cousin and his half-brother.*

Coming to the times with which we are more particularly at this moment concerned, we find Plato sending a trusted pupil, Euphraeus of Oreus with a letter of introduction to Perdiccas, the reigning monarch of Macedon.[18] Plato recommended his follower as a suitable adviser, a man well-qualified to advance the interests of the king. Euphraeus apparently established an austere regime at the Macedonian court. 'He organized the circle around the king,' we are told, 'so pedantically that no one could partake of the common mess unless he knew geometry or philosophy.'[19] One can well imagine that Euphraeus set his entrance requirements too high for the semi-barbarous court. The situation has overtones even of the comical. Nonetheless for a time he reigned at the court 'like the king himself.'[20] Euphraeus seems to have taken a full, even a leading part in the intrigues which gave the better known Philip his start. Perdiccas was by him persuaded to cede a province to Philip, where he raised troops and gained his first military base. ("Having learned much about the art of war from Epaminondas," conjectures Grote.) Later the paths of the Academy and the Macedonian monarchy diverged more and more widely. Speusippus was forced to recall this earlier and important favour that the Academy had done to Philip in order to ward off Philip's slanderous language about Plato.[21] Seldom has history proved so ungrateful. Euphraeus later died in his own native land a convinced opponent of the Macedonian party and was hailed by the patriotic and anti-Macedonian groups as a martyr to Hellenic freedom.[22]

The career of Euphraeus seems to mirror what we may call the main tendency within the Academy—an earlier flirtation with Macedonia followed by growing estrangement and bitterness as the Academy pursued doggedly its pro-Syracusan alignment. (To say this is not to deny that some individuals who at one time or another had been pupils at the Academy pursued a pro-Macedonian line. At least one in Gomperz' phrase beat the recruiting drum for

* Athenaeus regards this account as an example of Plato's love of scandal.

Philip.[23] And as we shall see below the growing divergencies of political tendencies finally after Plato's death led to something like a schism in the Academy.)

It is exceedingly difficult to gauge the significance of another episode connected with the Macedonian monarchy in which pupils from the Academy played a leading part. In 359 B.C. Philip was able to make himself sole ruler of Macedon. Not long after his accession we find a neighbouring king, Cotys of Thrace, supporting the claims of a pretender to the Macedonian throne, Pausanias. The bribes of Philip caused him to abandon his attempts.[24] In the following year Cotys was assassinated by Heracleides of Ainos and his brother Python. The murderers were greeted by the Athenians as benefactors.[25] Whether this episode should be connected with the power politics of the Academy or with the growing 'national' rivalry between Macedon and Athens; or whether it is, as represented, a purely personal act of vengeance for a wrong done to the father of the two murderers is in the present state of our evidence, difficult to say. The golden crown and the title of benefactor point strongly, to say the least, towards a political rather than a purely personal motivation for the act.

While these exciting events were going on Plato, himself, was in Syracuse assisting Dion with preparations for a *coup d'etat* against Dionysius II whom Plato was vainly endeavouring to influence in the direction of 'philosophy.'

It would unduly stretch the length of this chapter to detail the many flirtations of the Academics with political power, whether as lawgivers, counsellors, political rulers, assassins or organizers of armed intervention. It is nonetheless important to emphasize the intense and far reaching political efforts of the pupils as well as the master in the decade that followed the battle of Leuctra and even beyond. After the collapse of Sparta, Greek conservatism felt itself naked and defenseless as it had not felt itself for a century and a half. Grote[26] describes 'the alteration of opinion produced everywhere in Greece with regard to Sparta, by the sudden shock of the battle of Leuctra. All the prestige and old associations connected with her long-established power vanished; while the hostility and fears, inspired both by herself and her partizans, but hitherto reluctantly held back in silence now burst forth into open manifestations.'

Nor can there be any doubt of the main direction which the thoughts of Plato and his followers took at this important turning point of Grecian history. While Syracuse seemed the ideal field for their activities, they were unwilling to renounce completely any state of greater Hellas where their political concepts seemed to have a chance of success.

The splendid historical imagination of Grote has painted for us in vivid and striking colours the situation in the Greek world following the battle of Leuctra.

> The Hellenic world was now in a state different from anything which had been seen since the repulse of Xerxes in 480–79. The defeat and degradation of Sparta had set free the inland states from the only presiding city whom they had ever learned to look up to. Her imperial ascendency, long possessed and grievously abused, had been put down by the successes of Epaminondas and the Thebans. She was no longer the head of a numerous body of subordinate allies, sending deputies to her periodic synods—submitting their external policies to her influence—placing their military contingents under command of her officers (Xenagi)—and even administering their internal governments through oligarchies devoted to her purposes, with the re-inforcement, wherever needed of a Spartan harmost and garrison. . . . But this loss of a foreign auxiliary force and dignity was not the worst which Sparta had suffered. On her northwestern frontier . . . stood the newly constituted city of Messene, representing an amputation of nearly one-half of Spartan territory and substance. The western and more fertile part of Laconia had been severed from Sparta, and was divided between Messene and various other independent cities; being tilled by those who had once been Perioikoi and Helots of Sparta.
>
> In the phase of Grecian history on which we are now about to enter—when the collective Hellenic world, for the first time since the invasion of Xerxes was about to be thrown upon its defense against a foreign enemy from Macedonia—this altered position of Sparta was a circumstance of grave moment.

The debacle in the realm of practical politics did not however undermine Plato's faith in his political ideal. As late as 453 he was still proclaiming the virtues of the 'Doric' way of life.[27]

> Nevertheless I advise you, the friends of Dion, to imitate both his loyalty to his country and the temperate way of living that he followed. . . . In case anyone cannot live in the Doric fashion that was the tradition of your fathers, but seeks instead to live like the slayers of Dion, in Sicilian fashion, do not call upon him to aid you, and do not suppose that he can ever live loyally and righteously. Call upon the rest, however, to aid in the colonization of all Sicily and in bringing about equality under the law, both from Sicily itself and from the whole Peloponnesus. Have no fear of Athens either; for there exist men there too who surpass all mankind in virtue and who loath the crimes of treacherous assassins.[28]

It is not to be thought that all these exciting events could go by without some modification in Plato's thought. In this expectation we are not disappointed.

The Phaedrus is usually regarded as a transitional document falling mid-way between the Republic and the Thaetetus. The method of analysis used in this book tends to confirm this judgement. The Republic, it will be remembered, in its tri-partite structure, carried through fairly consistently, (as the diagram printed here makes clear) seems to represent Plato's political program for the last crisis of the Athenian democracy in the last decade of the Fifth Century. In the striking image which Plato uses the lion must make alliance with the man to keep in order the many-headed beast. Reason and 'good emotion' must band together to keep in order the chaos of impulse and desire. And in politics the two upper classes—those who base their economic position on the possession of land and those who base it on the ownership of moveable wealth must combine to keep in order the common folk. In the Phaedrus

---

For the social significance of the ethical terms here used see below. On the Athenians who can be relied on Post is surely right in seeing this as a plea for members of the Academy (Note 35, p. 151.) The same writer is equally right in thinking that among the most significant passages in the letter are these which defend Dion against the charge of unnecessary bloodshed op. cit. p. 59.[29]

Fable	*Psychology*	*Fable*	*State*	*Virtues*	*Education*	*Knowing*	*The Known*	*Science*
			Philosopher King	Justice	*Dialectic*			
Gold	Reason	Man	"Guards"	Wisdom	Mathematics	Knowledge	What Is	The Idea
Silver	"Good Emotion"	Lion	Auxiliaries	Courage	Literature & Gymnastic	Opinion	The Changing	
Iron Copper	Passions	Many-headed beast	People	"Discipline"	Beautiful things	Ignorance	What is Not	The Example

it is most noticeable that the image has been changed. The 'soul' in its earthly passage is compared now to a charioteer who drives a pair of winged horses, one of which is noble, the other ignoble.

> Of the nature of soul, though her true form be ever a theme of large and more than mortal discourse, let me speak briefly and in a figure. And let the figure be composite—a pair of winged horses and a charioteer. Now the winged horses and the charioteers of the gods are all of them mortal—noble or of noble descent, but those of other races are mixed; the human charioteer drives his in a pair; and one of them is noble and of noble breed; and the driving of them of necessity gives great trouble to him.[30]

In this parable is pictured once again the three-fold nature of man—reason, unselfish devotion or 'good emotion' and the acquisitive impulses. And surely reading this parable which parallels and yet at the same time reverses the earlier parable of the Republic, it is not fanciful to see reflected the three fold structure of classes in the Athenian state. But, we are compelled to notice, the emphasis has now shifted. No longer does Socrates now talk in terms of an alliance between the two upper groups; rather his plea is now for the subordination of both (though one is noble and the other ignoble) to one. The program of the *concordia ordinum* had broken down in practice. Critias, we may remember had turned the terror against Leon of Salamis and Theramenes. The earlier ideal is succeeded by a more (from Plato's point of view) realistic program. The function of guidance must now be the monopoly of 'reason' and, we might add, patricians.

But within the structure of the Phaedrus there is even more articulate response to the new demands and the new conditions. For a philosopher who is preparing to launch himself on 'the wave of the future' and lend his thought, his insight and his organizing ability to support his faction in Syracuse, it would be impious and even absurd to argue that only the changeless is real. The problem for Plato is now, and will so remain for the rest of his creative life, the problem of how change may be controlled in the interest (it is not cynical to add) of himself and his partizans. To assist him in developing a philosophy of 'controlled' change, he found ready to hand and ingeniously used an old insight of the Ionian physicists. For the Ionians, let us remember, the mark of 'soul' was that it should be self moving and capable of transmitting motion to others. Of this power, as we have seen, the magnet was the symbol; and all things are full of gods. 'It was only,' argues Skemp,[31] 'after this had been related to the Orphic-Pythagorean ideas of the soul . . . that the full valuation of *kinesis* (motion, change, alteration), within the Platonic scheme of things could be fully realized. To follow the argument of Skemp further:

> The relating of the Pythagorean *arche* (i.e. source or principle of change W.) to the Pythagorean immortal *psyche* is revealed in a passage which rises abruptly in the second discourse of Socrates in the Phaedrus, and in its style differs markedly alike from the myth that follows it and from the rest of the dialogue. To show that the lover's madness is a gift from heaven, Socrates says, we must examine the nature of the soul, its actions and its passions. Its nature is to be immortal, and this is the proof of it: Soul is immortal in all its forms. For that which is ever in motion is immortal, while that which imparts to something else the motion it receives from elsewhere, being liable to move is therefore liable to cease to live. Thus it is only the self-moving which, being constant to its own nature, never ceases to be in motion and which moreover, is the fount and origin of everything else that moves. Now an origin is ungenerated. For all that comes into being must of necessity come into being from an origin; but the origin itself cannot come into being from anything. For if the origin came into being from something else, the coming into being would not arise from it as an origin. Further, since it is ungenerated it must also be indestructible. For once an origin is destroyed, it can never come into being from anything else; nor can anything else come into being from it—if we allow that everything must come into being from an origin. It follows then that the self moving is the origin of motion; and it can be no more destroyed than it can come into being, else the whole heaven and all that is coming-into-being within it must collapse and come to a standstill and never thereafter possess anything that causes them to move and brings them into being. Since then

> the self moving has proved to be immortal, one may say safely that precisely this is the origin and definition of soul. For body everywhere, when receiving its motion from within itself is ensouled; for this is the characteristic nature of soul. If it is really so, then, that the self moving is soul and nothing else, it must needs follow that the soul is immortal.[32]

The passage is remarkable and worthy of a few remarks. It anticipates to a marked degree the doctrine which has become in the popular mind associated first of all with Aristotle—the question *hothen he kinesis* the source of movement and the answer *to proton kinoun akineton,* the first mover, itself unmoved or Aristotle's definition of God. But for our purpose much more significant is the light it sheds on Plato's response to the changing needs of his time and his class. Here is no longer simply a stubborn clinging to the unchanging and a hymn in praise of static perfection. Here is rather the thought that the world, with all its changes, its variableness, its mutability has a kind of reality, a derivitaive reality it is true, but none the less a real significance and meaning.

But change is analysed now as two fold—the self moving i.e. spirit and that which receives its motion from outside, i.e. matter. The importance of this passage has, perhaps, been too much obscured by many centuries of an almost passionate interest in the doctrine of the immortality of the soul. To prove that soul is immortal does not seem to be Plato's primary concern. Rather he wants to argue that all soul controls or should control all soulless matter and, therefore, the soul is akin to the eternal.[33]

The new note in Platonic meditations here being given its dramatic introduction is this: Since change is real and for our purpose valid: How can change be controlled? What is the significance of 'soul' as a controlling principle vis-a-vis the controlled principle, matter? And what is the political value of this analogy for a group that is now forced to admit the reality of change but is eager that change should be controlled in its own interest?

If there is doubt in the mind of scholars as to whether the Phaedrus should be dated before or after Leuctra, there is little argument about the dating of the Theaetetus. This work was almost certainly produced in 368 or early in 367. In any case it appeared before Plato set out on his second expediton to Syracuse.

Conditions, let us repeat, in the Greek world had changed. The collapse of the short-lived maritime empire of Sparta had been followed by the exposure of her weakness as a land power. Plato and his followers were desperately looking for new bases of political influence. In a mood compounded of hope and desperation, they were preparing to launch themselves on the 'wave of the future.' In such a mood and in such circumstances it would be idle and senseless to praise the changeless as alone real. The mood of the Phaedo and the Republic had to be modified.

> The doctrine of *kinesis* (motion, change, W.), writes Skemp, may be called a later doctrine because all the important passages . . . belong to the later group of critical dialogues which begin with the Theaetetus. (Or the Phaedrus. W.) This doctrine, therefore, may be regarded as a development of Plato's thinking in the years of the established Academy when the disaster to his Sicilian expedition had driven him to look deeper than did the astronomers and mathematicians who worked with him into the source of those regular law-abiding motions which they were making the subject of constant study and detailed discussions.[34]

In these changed circumstances, the Theaetetus represents a fresh examination of the old doctrine of Heraclitus and his school that change is the all-embracing law of the universe. This is not to argue, what would be clearly false, that Plato went over to the Heraclitean doctrine. But he was forced to examine it again with increasing sympathy. In a well known passage[35] he puts forward the theory of certain 'cleverer men.' I quote from Taylor's summary. (Taylor translates *kompsoteroi* more refined persons. I have said 'cleverer men'; the reader will realize that we are referring to the same people.)[36]

> Yet . . . the case in which Socrates is one year taller than Theaetetus but the next shorter, seems to create a difficulty. In this case Theaetetus has grown, but Socrates has neither grown nor shrunk. He *is* now what he was *not* last year 'shorter,' and

yet there has been no process of 'coming to be shorter.' How are we to explain this paradox? . . . It might be explained by the theory of certain more refined persons (kompsoteroi) whose secret Socrates offers to disclose. Their theory is this. As has already been suggested, the only reality is motion. There are two types of motion, the active and the passive. The mutual friction or interference (tripsis) of an active and a passive motion, regularly gives rise to a twin product, sense plus sensible quality, and neither of these is ever to be found without its twin. And this twin process is itself, again, a pair of movements, though of movements more rapid than those which gave rise to it.

Thus to apply the theory to the case of vision, you have first two 'slower' causative 'movements' (the 'active' movement *here* is supposed to be the 'event' which is the visual apparatus, the passive is the 'event' which we call the environment); when there is an 'interference' of these two motions, in that very process there emerge two correlated 'quicker' movements, neither of which ever exists without the other, 'vision in act' and 'Colour seen.' Thus the couple 'seeing eye' and 'colour seen' are themselves a dual more 'rapid' event produced as an effect by the mutual interference of the two 'slower' causal motions. It follows that all predication is strictly relative. The 'causal' motions themselves are strictly relative to one another, each is 'active' or 'passive' only in relation to its correlate; and similarly in the 'effect' the seen colour is seen only by this 'seeing eye' and this 'seeing eye' sees only *this* colour. 'Being' is thus strictly a relative term. To speak accurately, we ought never to say 'x is' but 'x is relatively to y'. If we omit the qualification, it is only because of an inveterate linguistic bad habit. Socrates does not commit himself to this theory of 'absolute becoming' any more than to any other, but he has stated it because we cannot dispose of the assertion that 'is' equals 'appears to me' without deciding this still more fundamental question.

It seems likely that this doctrine of 'active' and 'passive' motion in the universe must have seemed to Plato most exciting and useful for his own social purposes. Later in the dialogue he returns to the classification of motion—change or alteration and locomotion. The division we reach at 181b, remarks Skemp, seems to have real validity.[37] Skemp also notices that this is a formal recognition of the movement of the sphere on its own axis as a 'kind' of motion and this will be of cardinal importance for the fusion of astronomy, psychology and metaphysics that will meet us in the Timaeus.

If we can regard the Theaetetus as Plato's attempt to get something positive for his own point of view from the Heraclitean school, the Parmenides, a dialogue which apparently comes out soon after the Theaetetus, is an application of this gain to discussion with the Eleatics. This school, it will be remembered, had argued that only the static and changeless 'One' is really real. In opposition to this position Socrates argues (and I quote Skemp's summary):[38]

> The Eleatics must be given a stronger dose of their own physic. The consequence of affirming one being must be rigorously examined. If the One, simple and absolute, be affirmed, it cannot have limits or shape or be in space or be whole, like itself, exist, or be knowable (and Parmenides had insisted on all these *semata*—characteristics W.) any more than it can become, grow, change or have parts or internal differences (which Parmenides had denied). On the other hand once posit one *Being* and you must deduce indefinite plurality, extension, shape, sameness and difference, rest and motion. . . . Thus when Parmenides asserts a sphere full of being, he has no right to deny to it motion and change. Therefore in the sense in which the sphere 'exists' motion also 'exists'; the sign *akineton* (changeless W.) is arbitrary. . . . Plato holds that certain kinds of motion are logically deducible from the hypothesis of One Being. These are coming into being and passing away, combination and separation, likeness and unlikeness, increase and diminution.

At first sight from this account we are back where we started from and Plato has reached a principle which is little more exalted than common sense. The world of change is somehow a part of the real. We are no further advanced on our task—that is Plato's task of finding out how the world of coming into being and passing away may be controlled. But there can be no question that President

Hardie is right when he maintains '. . . it is certain that Plato was, in the later dialogues, preoccupied with the philosophy of becoming and that he was dissatisfied with what Burnet calls the 'acosmism' of Euclides and the Eleatics.[39] But, on the other hand, Plato was not at all content with a notion of the changing world as uncontrolled. To quote Skemp again:

> This does not tell us anything about the *aitia* (cause W.) . . . This *aitia* in its relation to Psyche and Nous (Soul and Mind) is none the less a real and necessary element in the scheme of things, and we shall find in the Sophistes how a place equal in honour with the static forms is at last secured for it.[40]

In Plato's mind there seems to be developing the conviction that the changing world (what the ordinary man would call the world of reality) must find its ground of explanation and its principle of order and control in Mind. Therefore it is rather natural that he should next turn to the problem of the kind of mind which can understand and so control the changing universe in general; and the kind of political director who can understand and so control the movement of political affairs. These two problems so closely interrelated in Plato's thought and Plato's social passion are dealt with in two dialogues—the Sophistes and the Politicus.

The Sophistes is a kind of summary of some of the leading arguments of Greek philosophy—the argument between pluralists and monists—those who regard the universe as consisting of many independent and unrelated things and those who regard the universe as essentially one; the argument between materialists and idealists; and the argument between those who believe the universe is static and those who believe that change is the ultimate law of things. For Plato's developing theory of change the last argument is the most significant. I quote from Skemp:[41]

> *Stranger:* I see your point. You mean this. If knowing is to be regarded as a kind of acting, it follows necessarily that being known becomes in its turn a kind of being acted upon. Now Reality according to this argument is acted upon in so far as it is known and in so far, therefore, as it is moved—which is a

thing that could not happen to the motionless reality we have described.

Theaetetus: Exactly.

Stranger: But tell me in Heaven's name are we really to be so easily convinced that in actual fact the Whole of True Being has in Itself neither motion nor life nor Soul nor intelligence—that it neither lives nor thinks, but is an Awful, Holy, Unmoved and forever Established Thing, without any mind in it.

Theaetetus: Well, I must grant you, my friend, that this is a strange doctrine, if we are asked to assent to it.

Stranger: But are we to say that it has mind but no life?

Theaetetus: Impossible.

Stranger: But if we say that it has them both, can we deny that it has them resident in a soul?

Theaetetus: How else could it have them?

Stranger: But then, if it is admittedly possessed of life, mind and soul can we imagine its being, for all its vitality, completely static and immune from motion?

Theaetetus: All this seems quite unreasonable to me.

Stranger: Then that which is moved and motion itself are to be admitted real?

Theaetetus: Yes.

Stranger: We conclude, then, Theaetetus, first that if real things are motionless, there can be no mind anywhere to exercise itself on any object.

Theaetetus: Exactly.

Stranger: But, secondly, if we admit that all things pass and are moved, by this doctrine, too, we shall remove this same factor, mind, from the totality of the real.

Theaetetus: How so?

Stranger: Do you think that, if there were no freedom from motion, there could be anything that abides constant in the same condition and in the same respects?

Theaetetus: There could not.

Stranger: And can you make out mind as existing anywhere without such abiding objects?

Theaetetus: Certainly not.

Stranger: Well then with all the forces of reason we must meet the enemy who makes dogmatic assertion on any question

> while at the same time cutting away the very basis of knowledge, intelligence and mind?
> (In passing it is interesting to notice that the 'friends of motion' are still the enemy, W.)
> *Theaetetus:* Most certainly.
> *Stranger:* So it appears that the mind of the philosopher—the true philosopher who places these as valuable above all other things—is forced to a novel conclusion. He cannot accept, on the one hand, the view of the Whole of True Being as static, the view alike of those who believe in one Form and those who believe in many. Nor, on the other hand, can he listen for a moment to those who teach universal motion. He must be like the children who ask for 'both please' in dealing with everything in the universe, moving and unmoved; he must teach that the Whole of true True Being is 'both.'

The Sophistes which seems to be next in the order of Plato's developing thoughts carries forward the argument. Skemp's conclusions on the modification of Plato's thinking seems to me both just and judicious.[42]

> The Sophistes leaves us with forms on the one hand (Man, Motion, Rest, Being, Suffering) and life, mind and soul which can be called collectively *kinesis* (motion, change, W.) on the other. Both are 'truly real.' Not all *kinesis* is truly real; spatial motion is not. We reach a finding of double significance. *Kinesis* can be used of non-spatial activity as manifested by a *psyche* (soul, W.). This *kinesis* exists within the confines of 'True Being'.... It is other than the forms but as real as they, and shares their elevation above the phantasmagoria of becoming. 'True Being' is more than the Forms.
> The Sophistes also gives us an interesting passage in which the 'demiurgic' (a demiourgos was a craftsman; therefore the adjective demiurgic means 'creative' as a carpenter 'creates' a chair. W.) work of God is distinguished from the workings of *Phusis aneu dianoias* (Nature without mind. W.).... The interest (of this passage) is in its preparing us for the serious attempt in the Timaeus to give a physical and cosmological account of the working of the divine artificer and the random spirit of the world untamed. Here they are stated in opposition; in the Politicus we shall find them brought closely together.

> Only in the Timaeus are they 'causes' whose workings can be traced in detail in the *Ouranos* (sky; heaven. W).

The social meaning of all this is surely clear. Change is for Plato not now unreal. But change must be 'rational' and controlled by 'mind.' And mind for Plato is easily identifiable as the interest of one's own class.

Complementary to the Sophistes is the dialogue the Politicus. The former deals with the kind of thinker who can understand the laws of rational change. The latter deals with the kind of 'statesman' who can apply these laws.

> The Politicus, writes Skemp, (and I agree) has an importance[43] for our subject both as a whole and in its myth of the age of Chronos in particular. . . . Writing after Syracuse and in one of his critical dialogues, Plato still clings to the figure of the philosopher-king who appears as the one wise ruler, who can be above law and modify law because he is the master of the art of government and has in himself the vitality and insight to sustain the state. The conclusion to which Plato has been driven at this stage of his experience is nicely expressed in his myth of Chronos.[44]
>
> Ever to abide in the same relation and the same condition is the privilege of the divinest of all things alone; the nature of the bodily does not entitle it to this rank. Now the Heaven, or Universe, as we have chosen to call it, has received many blessed gifts from him who brought it into being, but it has also been made to partake in bodily form. Therefore, it is impossible for it to be free from change altogether, and yet so far as may be it is moved with one motion and as nearly as possible keeping the same relations. For this reason it has received its reversal of motion, for this (i.e. reversal of motion, W.) is the least possible distortion of its proper motion. But to revolve ever by his own power is possible only to the lord and leader of all things that move; for him to change from one direction of motion to another would flaunt Heaven's law. It follows from all this that we must not say of this Universe either that it revolves ever by its own power, or that it is ever and completely under God's power and yet receives two contrary revolutions from His impulse; or again, that there are

> two gods at contrary which reveal themselves in its contrary revolutions; we must assert the only remaining possibility, as we did just now, and say that at times it is assisted on its way by the transcendent divine cause, gaining life once again and an immortality renewed from its Artificer, while in the other periods when it is left to itself it revolves under its own power and when it is released, it has by that time gathered such force that it revolves in the reverse sense for tens of thousands of revolutions because its size is so great, its balance so perfect and the pivot on which it turns so small.

The active and passive movements of the Phaedrus have become the rational and irrational movements of the Politicus. And the central theme of the Politicus, let us reflect again, is the personality of the Statesman who is to exercise social control. By this time it does not need much imagination to divine which movements in the sphere of society and politics would seem to Plato to be rational, and which to be irrational and bad.

In the dialogue called the Philebus, we find two familiar concepts counterposed as definitions of the supreme end of human conduct—pleasure and thought.

> The attitude taken by Plato, remarks Taylor,[45] in the dialogue to this discussion is, to all intents and purposes, precisely that of the 'moderator' in the schools of the Middle Ages, determining a *quaestie disputata*. The arguments produced by both parties are reviewed and weighed, and the balance is struck between the disputants. It is decided that the issue shall be narrowed down to a consideration of the 'good for man' in particular. When the question has been thus delimited, it is 'determined' that neither pleasure alone nor thought alone is the 'good' or best life for men; the best life must include thought and grateful feeling; but of the two 'thought' is the 'predominant partner.'

Here, too, we seem to have a modification of earlier convictions. In the Republic, Plato had repudiated with quite comical emphasis the notion that pleasure might have anything to do with the good.[46] Now pleasure is given a positive importance, derivative and secondary it is true but still an importance all its own.

One incidental point in a consideration of the dialogue made by Skemp is of great importance. Plato seems again to be giving an increased emphasis and a positive significance to the world of change and 'Mixture.'

> The significant thing, writes Skemp,[47] is the description of these natural states and objects as *gegenomene ousia* (Being that comes and goes, W.) and of their creation as *genesis eis ousia* (a birth into being; a coming to be, W.); it is better to regard this as a new valuation of the natural order than to insist that *ousia* (being, W.) must imply that we are dealing with the Forms. (On this point, still quoting Skemp, I follow Natorp: Es ist sehr to beobachten, dass hiermit, zum ersten Mal in dieser Deutlichkeit, das Werden einen ganz positiven Sinn erlangt). (It is most important to notice that here for the first time with this clarity, the realm of becoming plays a quite positive role.)[48]

Mind, then, or soul orders the universe, which is no longer thought of as completely static and passive but as in a sense active and changing. The contrast with the position where it is the business of mind to pass from the contemplation of change to the contemplation of the real and the changeless is very striking. Quoting Taylor's summary:[49]

> What, again, about the 'intelligence,' knowledge, wisdom preferred by Socrates. Into what class does this fall? We are agreed to reject the theory that the course of the universe is 'random' (Eike 28d) and agree with the traditional belief that it is directed by a supreme wisdom (Phronesis) and intelligence (Nous) in every particular. Now when we look at our own constitution, we see that the materials of which our body is made are only small parcels of the great cosmic masses of similar materials, and that these constituents are found in a much higher degree of purity from other ingredients elsewhere in the universe than in our bodies. The 'fire' in us is small in bulk and 'impure' in substance by comparison with the fire in the sun. And again the 'fire' or 'water' is fed and kept up by that in the larger world (29c). And generally our little body is fed by the mass of body without us (29e). By analogy, we may infer that since there is a soul in us, it too

> comes from a greater and brighter soul in the universe. Also, we see in our own case that when things are amiss with the body, it is the intelligence, resident in the soul, which re-establishes order by means of the medical arts. So we may reasonably hold that in the universe at large the same holds good. The order in it is due to intelligence (Nous) and intelligence is found only in souls. So we may hold that there are superhuman souls, and that it is their intelligence which is the cause of cosmic order (30d).

Skemp[49a] writes of the glorification in the same dialogue of Nous, Basileus (Mind, the King, W.). The terms of the encomium are, as he says, interesting.

> The 'elements' in terrestrial creatures and the souls that govern them are said to be less pure than the divine mind and pure elements of the *Ouranos* (Universe, W.) here named Zeus. Yet is is one and the same *aitia* (cause, W.) manifesting itself in all and governing all. It is the fount of vigour and healing. It sets in order years, seasons, months. This appeal from microcosm to macrocosm implies that it is the function of *Nous* (intelligence, W.) in the *Ouranos* which is all-important, even in a question concerning the good for man.

The tendencies here outlined culminate in two important dialogues which by general agreement represent the maturity of Platonic thinking.

The 'theological' tendencies (for so we must inevitably begin to describe them) find their climax and their expression in the Timaeus. The political program finds its latest, and perhaps most despairing expression in the Laws.

The Timaeus, as Taylor remarks was the 'one Greek philosophical work of the best age with which the west of Europe was well acquainted before the recovery of Aristotle's metaphysical and physical writings in the thirteenth century.' The work has, therefore, achieved an influence on the development of Christian theology which transcends its intrinsic worth. Even Skemp describes it as an attempt at a 'rational theology.' As I have remarked elsewhere, tastes in rationality evidently differ. To the mind acquainted with modern science, much of the Timaeus must read like examinable nonsense.

It would be beyond the possible indulgence of any publisher to give even a summary of the Timaeus. The student should consult Taylor's brilliant condensation. For our purpose it is enough to note that the elaborate picture which Timaeus is made to give of the creation of the visible universe embodies the notion of a 'craftsman' (demiourgos) who creates by looking to the pattern of an eternal idea; that this creative craftsman or 'God':[50]

> took over the whole of the 'visible' which was in a condition of chaotic disorder and made it into an ordered system since order is *better* than chaos. For the same reason, he put *mind* (Nous) into it, and, as mind can only exist in a soul (psyche), he gave it a soul, and thus the sensible world became 'by the providence of God, a living being with soul and mind.' The model in the likeness of which he made it was, of course, a *noēton* or 'intelligible' something complete and whole (*teleion*) and something living. The sensible world, then, is the sensible embodiment of a living creature or organism (*zōon*) of which all living creatures are parts.

There is, too, an elaborate explanation of the movements within the 'world soul' of the 'Same' and the 'Other'—the one rational, the other irrational.

> The circle of the Same and Other, being circles primarily 'in the soul' of the world have an epistemological as well as an astronomical significance. Their absolutely uniform revolutions symbolize—perhaps Timaeus means that they actually embody—in the one case science of the eternal and unchanging, in the other true conviction (*doxa*) about the temporal.[51]

There is the antithesis of 'intelligence' and 'necessity'—again the one rational and the other irrational.[52]

> . . . the work done by Intelligence in the construction of the sensible world. But this world is a 'mixed' product, born of Intelligence (*Nous*) and Necessity (*anagke*) (pronounced *ananke*) and we must now describe the contribution of Necessity to the whole. The relation between Intelligence and Neces-

> sity which is also called the 'errant' or 'irrational' cause (*planomena aitia*) is that 'for the most part' Intelligence is superior (*archon;* the ruler, W.), Necessity is servant, or slave, but a willing slave; Intelligence 'persuades' (*peithei*) Necessity.

Plato's passion for social control, in other words, has given birth to a full blown theology with an elaborate and fanciful cosmology —a theology and a cosmology, which, moreover, profoundly influenced the thinking of mediaeval Europe.

The theological tendencies of Platonism are continued in the Laws as part of an elaborate blueprint of an authoritarian state. This dialogue can probably be dated after 356 B.C., and was the product of the last years of Plato's life. It was probably composed with a more directly practical motive than any other work of the philosopher.

> The men of the Academy were constantly in demand as 'lawgivers' to advise on setting up of constitutions in new states or in the revival of old ones.
>
> Plato sent Aristonymos to the Arcadians, Phormio to Elis, Menedemus to Pyrrha. Eudoxus and Aristotle wrote laws for Cnidus and Stagirus. Alexander asked Xenocrates for advice about kingship; the man who was sent to Alexander by the Greek inhabitants of Asia and did most to incite him to undertake his war on the barbarians was Delius of Ephesus, an associate of Plato.[53]

This work was evidently a draft memorandum for the instruction of those pupils who were entrusted with tasks like these.

In the Laws, Plato's political views are so clearly enunciated that there is little or no excuse for misunderstanding. In this work his prejudice against the mercantile democracy as best exemplified in the Athens of Pericles is spelled out in chapter and verse. The Utopia which Plato would have liked to build is to be built at least ten miles distant from the sea. There are excellent harbors but this is regarded as a supreme misfortune. It must have a fair proportion of hill and plain and wood. There is more rock than plain and this is an advantage.

> Then there is some hope that your citizens will be virtuous; had you been on the sea, and well provided with harbors, and an importing rather than a producing country, some mighty saviour would have been needed, and lawgivers more than mortal, if you were ever to have a chance of preserving your state from degeneracy and discordance of manners. But there is comfort in the ten miles; although the sea is too near, especially if, as you say, the harbours are so good. Still we may be content. The sea is pleasant enough as a daily companion, but has indeed also a bitter and brackish quality; filling the streets with merchants and shopkeepers, and begetting in the souls of men uncertain and unfaithful ways—making the state unfriendly and unfaithful both to her own citizens, and also to other nations. There is a consolation, therefore, in the country producing all things at home; and yet, owing to the ruggedness of its soil, not providing anything in great abundance. Had there been abundance, there might have been a great export trade, and a great return of gold and silver; which as we may safely affirm, has the most fatal results on a State whose aim is the attainment of just and noble sentiments. . . .
>
> Ath. Well, but let me ask, how is the country supplied with timber for ship building?
>
> Cle. There is no fir of any consequence, no pine, and not much cypress; and you will find very little stone-pine or plane-wood, which shipwrights always require for the interior of ships.
>
> Ath. These are also natural advantages.[54]

Mercantilism is bad for the state. Naval warfare teaches men to withdraw in cowardly fashion. It does not teach them to respect those worthy of honour but 'pilot and captain and oarsmen and all sorts of rather inferior persons.' The land battles of Marathon and Salamis were good; the naval battles of Salamis and Artemisium made the Hellenes no better.[55]

The Utopia of the Laws, then, is to be built so far from the sea that it could never be corrupted by mercantilism. It will have 5040 households—a magical number, the product of all integers up to seven. It will have an elaborately devised constitution of an authoritarian kind—the 'law guarders' a body of 37 elderly men; an assembly ingeniously chosen from the four economic grades in the state, so as to give substantial power to the higher and above all a 'Minister of Education' whose duty will be to safeguard every aristocratic prejudice in the education of the young. (Because it will be necessary to pay teachers they must be foreigners.) And worst of all there will be a 'nocturnal council' (shades of Herr Hitler.) to preserve tradition. This state apparatus would govern all aspects of life—prescribe what books might be read and oversee the marriage bed and the numbers of its offspring. Crime would be punished in this order—sacrilege, treason, parricide. Unorthodox opinions about religion must be sternly put down—the belief that the gods do not exist, that they are indifferent to human welfare, or that they can be bribed. This state apparatus will dictate and control all matters of taste and artistic creation, looking particularly to the example of Egypt where even art was apparently stereotyped. And so in an atmosphere of Arcadian, agrarian simplicity the essential patterns of political life that Plato thought all important can be preserved. To misunderstand the social implications of Platonism after a reading of the Laws seems like wilfullness or invincible ignorance. With a quite magnificent understatement Taylor writes:[56]

> What inevitably impresses a modern reader most unfavourably is the special severity with which injuries committed by a slave on free persons are treated. This is, however, a direct consequence of the recognition of the servile status, which gives these crimes something of the character of mutiny.

If the Republic represents the 'Genesis of Plato's Thought', the Laws represent its maturity.

Perhaps it would not be beyond the scope of this work to say a word or two about the 'secession' from the Academy represented by the departure of Aristotle and Xenocrates for Asia Minor. In so doing we shall add content to a sentence in the first edition which some critics have thought too cryptic. Professorial readers will notice with interest that Speusippus was preferred to Aristotle, the greatest intellect of antiquity, apparently on the ground that from a political point of view he was a safer man.[57] Let us begin with Werner Jaeger's statement of the case.

Nevertheless, Aristotle's departure from Athens was the expression of a crisis in his inner life (perhaps in his outer life, too, W.). The fact remains that he never came back to the school in which he had been educated. This was presumably connected with the question of Plato's successor, which would inevitably determine the spirit of the Academy for a long time to come, and the decision of which could not meet with Aristotle's approval in any event. The choice, whether Plato's own or that of the members, fell on Plato's nephew, Speusippius. His age made it impossible to pass him over, however obvious Aristotle's superiority might be for all who had eyes to see. The decisive consideration was perhaps certain external circumstances, such as the difficulty of conveying the Academy to a metic, although this was afterwards overcome. The choice of Speusippius continued Plato's family in the possession of the property. Whether, in addition to such reasons of external expediency, personal antipathies also played a part, it is no longer possible to say; but on general grounds it is practically certain that they must have done so.

One thing, however, is certain; it was not Aristotle's criticism of Plato's fundamental doctrines that prevented him from succeeding to the headship of Plato's Academy. Speusippius himself had declared the theory of Ideas untenable during Plato's own lifetime,* and had also abandoned the Ideal numbers suggested by Plato in his last period; he differed from him in other fundamental particulars as well. And that Aristotle was not meanly but highly thought of in the school when he left Athens is proved by the person who accompanied him, namely Xenocrates, the most conservative of all Plato's students with regard to alteration of the doctrine, but at the same time a thoroughly upright man.

The departure of Aristotle and Xenocrates was a secession. They went to Asia Minor in the conviction that Speusippius had inherited merely the office and not the spirit. The spirit had become homeless, and they were setting out to build it a new place. For the next few years the scene of their activity was Assos on the coast

* Perhaps Speusippus was changing in response to changed conditions as Plato himself was changing.

of the Troad, where they worked in common with two other Platonists, Erastus and Coriscus from Scepsis on Ida.

The importance of this period has not been recognized. Plato's Sixth Letter, the genuineness of which has been convincingly demonstrated by Brinckmann, is addressed to Erastus and Coriscus, two former students now in Asia Minor, and to their friend, Hermias, Lord Of Atarneus. The two philosophers are to put themselves under the protection of Hermias, since, while persons of excellent character, they are devoid of worldly experience; Hermias on his part is to learn to appreciate their steadfast and trustworthy friendship. This remarkable relation between the two companions of Plato and the prince of Atarneus has been illuminated by an inscription, first published by Boeckh, in which 'Hermias and his companions' (the formal phrase Hermias kai hoi hetairoi) occurs five times in the original) make an alliance with the people of the city of Erythrae. The newly discovered commentary of Didymus on Demosthenes *Philippics* leaves no doubt that the companions who here appear along with Hermias as legal parties to the contract are none other than the two philosophers from the neighbouring town of Scepsis, as was already probable from Plato's letter.

> Hermias was a man of lowly origin. That he was an eunuch is not to be denied. Even the story that in earlier years a bank had employed him as a money changer at the counter presumably rests on fact, although it is related by Theopompus, who describes him as unpleasantly as possible. He began by getting possession of some mountain villages in the neighbourhood of Ida. Later he obtained public recognition from the Persian administration and was allowed to adopt the title of prince, presumably after the payment of an adequate sum. His residence was at Atarneus. His steadily growing political influence extended the area under his control to an astonishing size. In the end he must have maintained a substantial contingent of mercenaries, for he reduced rebellious places to obedience by military raids, and he afterwards withstood a siege by the Persian satrap.
>
> When this oligarchy of wise men was established the philosophers naturally demanded that Hermias study geometry and

dialectic, just as Plato had once demanded it of Dionysius, his pupil Euphraeus of Perdiccas king of Macedon, and Aristotle of Themison of Cyprus.[58]

Hermias apparently followed the lead of the Academy, devoted himself to study and modified his political program in accordance with their instructions. What had proved impossible in Sicily became actuality on a small scale in Asia Minor and something like a branch of the Academy was established there. Hermias gave Aristotle his niece and adopted daughter Pythias as his wife. We may conjecture that it was under Aristotle's influence that Hermias entered into an intrigue with Philip, thereby betraying his Persian benefactors to give Philip a bridgehead across the Aegean at a time when the Macedonian career of expansion was just beginning. Aristotle went to Macedon in 343/2 as tutor to the young prince, Alexander. Soon afterwards, Aristotle heard that Hermias had paid with his life for his duplicity. He was tortured to make him confess his secret treaties with Philip and his last words were reported to have been 'Tell my friends and companions that I have done nothing weak or unworthy of philosophy.'

Plato had died in 347 and this last flicker of political success may have encouraged and cheered his dying days. What, however, seems more certain is that the political tendency represented by Aristotle did not commend itself fully to the orthodox succession in the Academy. For with the Macedonian monarchy a new thing was coming into the world—the attempt to unify the ruling groups in all Greek states and solve (temporarily) their problems by a program of ruthless expansion. It was Aristotle rather than the orthodox Academy who launched himself most resolutely on this particular 'Wave of the Future.' We can conjecture that the increasingly sharp criticisms which Aristotle launched against the doctrines of his master; his tendency to modify aristocratic idealism in a realistic direction was not unconnected with the new and more realistic political alignment.

From a political point of view the life of Plato must be regarded as a failure. One political disappointment followed another. And after his death the Academy which he founded drifted more and more into a backwater of Greek politics, leaving actual political influence to the more realistic Lycaeum of Aristotle. Plato would, however, have been consoled to know that he laid down firmly and well the line along which conservative and idealistic philosophy has developed ever since. If *per impossibile* the spirit of Plato could gaze down from the Elysian fields and watch the development of Western thought over the centuries, his spirit must on many occasions have been tempted to chuckle very sardonically.

APPENDIX

Suggested Reading

The bibliography for early Greek philosophy in general and for Plato in particular is, of course, enormous. In addition to works mentioned in the footnotes, the following works are recommended as additional reading in connection with the various subjects treated in the text. Wherever possible the student is referred to books in English and to works that should be easily available in the ordinary college library.

ABBOTT, EVELYN (ed). *Hellenica: Essays*. London, 1898.

BAILEY, CYRIL. *The Greek Atomists and Epicurus; A Study*. Oxford, 1928.

BONNER, R. J. "Justice in the Age of Hesiod," *Classical Philology*, III (1913).

BONNER, R. J. and SMITH, GERTRUDE. *The Administration of Justice from Homer to Aristotle*. Chicago, 1930.

BOSANQUET, B. *A Companion to Plato's Republic*. London, 1906.

BURN, A. R. *The World of Hesiod*. London, 1937.

BURNET, J. *Greek Philosophy: Thales to Plato*. London, 1914.

———. *Early Greek Philosophy*. 3rd ed. London, 1920.

BURY, J. B., COOK, S. A., and ADCOCK, F. E. *The Cambridge Ancient History*. Vols. IV, V, and VI. (Particularly Vol. IV, Chap. 15, Cornford.) London, 1927.

CAIRD, EDWARD. *The Evolution of Theology in the Greek Philosophers*. One-volume edition. Glasgow, 1923.

CAMERON, ALISTER. *The Pythagorean Background of the Theory of Recollection*. Menasha, Wis., 1938.

CHILDE, V. G. *New Light on the Most Ancient East; the Oriental Prelude to European Prehistory*. New York, 1924.

———. *Man Makes Himself*. London, 1936.

CIACERI, E. *Storia Della Magna Grecia*. Milan, 1928.

———. *Orfismo e pitagorismo nei loro rapporti politico-sociali*. Naples, 1932.

CORNFORD, F. M. *From Religion to Philosophy*. London, 1912.

———. "Mysticism and Science in the Pythagorean Tradition," *Classical Quarterly*, XVI (1922) and XVII (1923).

CORNFORD, F. M. *The Laws of Motion in Ancient Thought.* Cambridge, 1931.

———. "Parmenides' Two Ways," *Classical Quarterly,* 1933.

DE LATTE, A. *Études sur la littérature pythagoricienne.* Paris, 1915.

———. *Essai sur la politique pythagoricienne.* Liège, 1922.

ELEUTHEROPOULOS, A. *Wirtschaft und philosophie.* Vol. I, *Die Philosophie und die Lebensauffassung des Griechentums auf Grund der gesellschaftlichen Zustände.* Berlin, 1900.

ENGELS, F. *Origin of the Family, Private Property and the State.* Chicago, 1902.

FARNELL, L. R. *The Cults of the Greek States,* 5 Vols. Oxford, 1896-1909.

FIELD, G. C. *Plato and his Contemporaries: A Study in Fourth-Century Life and Thought.* London, 1930.

FITE, W. *The Platonic Legend.* New York, 1934.

FRANK, E. *Plato und die sogenannten Pythagoreer.* Halle, 1923.

FREEMAN, E. A. *History of Sicily from the Earliest Times.* 4 Vols. Oxford, 1891-94.

FREEMAN, K. *The Work and Life of Solon.* London, 1926.

FULLER, B. A. J. *History of Greek Philosophy.* 3 Vols. New York, 1923-31.

GIGON, OLOF. *Untersuchungen zu Heraclit.* Leipzig, 1935.

GLOTZ, G. *The Aegean Civilization.* London, 1925.

———. *Ancient Greece at Work.* New York, 1926.

———. *La Solidarité de la famille dans le droit criminel en Grèce.* Paris, 1904.

———. *The Greek City and its Institutions.* New York, 1930.

GROTE, G. *History of Greece.* 9 Vols. New York, 1857.

———. *History of Greece. ed. Mitchell and Caspari.* One-volume edition. London, 1908.

GUTHRIE, W. K. C. *Orpheus and Greek Religion.* London, 1935.

HALL, H. R. *The Ancient History of the Near East.* 6th ed. London, 1924.

———. *The Civilization of Greece in the Bronze Age.* London, 1923.

HARRISON, J. E. *Themis: A Study of the Social Origins of Greek Religion.* Cambridge, 1927.

HITZEL, R. *Themis, Dike und Verwandtes.* Leipzig, 1907.

JARDE, A. F. C. *The Formation of the Greek People.* New York, 1926.

JAEGER, W. *Paideia; The Ideals of Greek Culture.* Oxford, 1939.

Leaf, W. *Troy: A Study in Homeric Geography*. London, 1912.

Lee, H. D. P. *Zeno of Elea*. Cambridge, 1936.

Lutoslawski, W. *The Origin and Growth of Plato's Logic*. London, 1905.

Macchiero, V. *Eraclito*. Bari, 1922.

———. *From Orpheus to Paul: A History of Orphism*. London, 1930.

Minar, E. L. Jr. *Early Pythagorean Politics in Theory and Practice*. University of Wisconsin thesis, 1940.

———. "The Logos of Heraclitus," *Classical Philology*, XXXIV, 1939.

Moore, C. H. *Ancient Beliefs in the Immortality of the Soul*. London, 1931.

More, P. E. *Platonism*. Princeton, 1917.

———. *The Religion of Plato*. Princeton, 1921.

Myres, J. L. *Who Were the Greeks?* Berkeley, 1936.

Nettleship, R. L. *Lectures on the Republic of Plato*. London, 1920.

Nilsson, M. P. *Minoan-Mycenaean Religion*. London, 1925.

———. *The Mycenaean Origin of Greek Mythology*. Berkeley, 1932.

———. *Homer and Mycenae*. London, 1933.

Nizan, P. *Les materialistes de l'antiquité*. Paris, 1936.

Rathmann, W. *Quaestiones Pythagoreae, Orphicae, Empedocleae*. Halle, 1923.

Ridgeway, W. *The Early Age of Greece*. 2 Vols. Cambridge, 1901-1931.

Ritter, C. *The Essence of Plato's Philosophy*. New York, 1933.

Robin, L. *Greek Thought and the Origins of the Scientific Spirit*. New York, 1928.

Rohde, E. *Psyche: The Cult of Souls and Belief in Immortality Among the Greeks*. Tr. from German. New York, 1925.

Shorey, P. *The Unity of Plato's Thought*. Chicago, 1904.

———. *What Plato Said*. Chicago, 1933.

———. *The Republic of Plato* (Loeb ed.). New York, 1930-1935.

Taylor, A. E. *Varia Socratica*. Oxford, 1911.

———. *Plato, the Man and His Work*. London, 1922.

———. *Socrates*. New York, 1933.

Ure, P. N. *The Origin of Tyranny*. Cambridge, 1922.

Watmough, J. R. *Orphism*. Cambridge, 1934.

Zeller, E. *Socrates and the Socratic Schools*. London, 1877.

———. *Plato and the Older Academy*. London, 1876.

List of Abbreviations

Abhand. d. Berl. Akad. *Abhandlungen der Akadamie der Wissenschaften,* Berlin.
Aeschines. Aeschines
fals. leg. de falsa legatione.
cont. Ctesiphon. contra Ctesiphontem.
Aesch. Aeschylus
Eum. Eumenides
Prom. Prometheus.
Septem. Seven Against Thebes.
Aët. Aëtius.
A.J.P. American Journal of Philology.
Alc. Frag. Alcman, *Fragments.*
Anon. *Vita Thuc. The Anonymous Life of Thucydides.*
Anth. Graec. *The Greek Anthology.*
Apollodor. Apollodorus
Apol. Rhod. Apollonius Rhodius
Apul. Apuleius
Flor. Florida.
Arist. Aristotle
Ath. Pol. The Constitution of the Athenians.
Eth. Nic. The Nicomachaean Ethics.
Met. The Metaphysics.
Meteor. The Meteorology.
Phys. The Physics.
Rhet. Rhetoric.
Arist. (?) Aristotle (?)
Mag. Mor. The Magna Moralia.
Aristoph. Aristophanes
Equit. The Knights.
Nub. The Clouds.
Plut. Plutus.
Thesm. The Thesmophoriazusae.
Aristox. Aristoxenus
Arnob. Arnobius
adv. Gent. adversus Gentes

Athen. Athenaeus
Aug. St. Augustine
Boeth. Boethius
Inst. Arith. De Institutione Arithmetica.
Bursian. C. Bursian's *Jahresbericht über die Fortschritte der Altertumswissenschaft.*
C.A.H. Cambridge Ancient History.
Caird. Edward Caird, *The Evolution of Theology in The Greek Philosophers.*
Chalcid. Chalcidius
in Tim. in Platonis Timaeum.
C.I.A. Corpus Inscriptionum Atticarum.
Cic. Cicero
ad. Quint. frat. Ad Quintum fratrem.
de Nat. Deor. de Natura Deorum.
de Orat. de Oratore.
Tusc. Tusculan Disputations.
De Latte, *Politique*. De Latte, *Essai sur la Politique Pythagoricienne.*
Demos. Demosthenes
de Fals. Leg. De Falsa Legatione.
Diod. Sic. Diodorus Siculus, *The Library of History.*
Diog. Laërt. Diogenes Laërtius
Eupol. Eupolis fragments, in *Comicorum Atticorum Fragmenta*, ed. Koch.
Eur. Euripides
Alc. Alcestis.
Heracl. Heracleidae.
Hipp. Hippolytus.
Euseb. Eusebius
P.E. Praeparatio Evangelica.
Chron. Hier. Chronicorum Libri.
Frag. Fragments
Gell. Aulus Gellius
N. A. Attic Nights.
Herod. Herodotus, *The History.*
Hes. Hesiod.
Hesych. Onomatol. Hesychius, *Lexicon.*
Hippol. Hippolytus
Ref. Refutation of all Heresies.

Hom. Homer
Il. Iliad.
Od. Odyssey.
Iamb. Iamblichus
in Nic. in Nicomachi Arithmeticam Introductionem.
V.P. Vita Pythagorica.
Protrep. Protrepticus.
Isoc. Isocrates
ad Phil. or. ad Philippum Oratio.
Kern. Kern
Orph. Frag. Orphicorum Fragmenta.
Kirschner. Kirschner
Prosop. Att. Prosopographia Attica.
Lucr. Lucretius
de rer. nat. de rerum natura.
Lys. Lysias
cont. Alcib. contra Alcibiadem.
cont. Eratos. contra Eratosthenem.
Macr. *Macrobius*
Somn. Scip. The Dream of Scipio.
Nettleship, *Lectures.* Nettleship, *Lectures on the Republic of Plato.*
Pauly-Wissowa. Pauly-Wissowa, *Realencyclopädie der klassischen Altertumswissenschaft.*
Paus. Pausanias, *Description of Greece.*
Pind. Pindar
Ol. Olympian Odes.
Pyth. Pythian Odes.
Plato. Plato
Apol. Apology.
Crat. Cratylus.
Epis. The Letters.
Gorg. Gorgias.
Phaedr. Phaedrus.
Prot. Protagoras.
Rep. Republic.
Soph. The Sophist.
Theaetet. Theaetetus.
References to Plato without the mention of the work refer to the *Republic.*

Plut. Plutarch
adv. Col. adversus Colotem.
Dion. Life of Dion.
Lyc. Life of Lycurgus.
Peric. Life of Pericles.
Strom. (Ps.?) Plutarch, *Stromateis.*
Symp. Quaestionum Convivialium Libri.
Themist. Life of Themistocles
Porphyr. Porphyrius
de Abs. De Abstinentia.
V.P. Vita Pythagorae.
Proc. Proclus
In Remp. In Platonis Rempublicam Commentarius.
Schol. Scholiast (ancient commentator)
Sext. Sextus Empiricus
Pyrrh. Outlines of Pyrrhonism.
Simplic. Simplicius
In Arist. Phys. Commentary on Aristotle's Physics.
Soph. Sophocles
El. Electra.
Her. Heracles.
Oed. Col. Oedipus at Colonus.
Phil. Philoctetes.
Stob. Stobaeus
Ecl. Eclogae.
Flor. Florilegium.
s.v. *sub verbo.*
Theog. Theognis, *Elegies.*
Theophr. Theophrastus
de Sens. de Sensu et Sensibilibus.
Thuc. Thucydides, *History.*
Var. Soc. *Varia Socratica,* A. E. Taylor.
Vors. Diels, *Die Fragmente der Vorsokratiker,* 5th ed.
Xen. Xenophon
Hell. Hellenica.
Cyrop. Cyropaedia. The Education of Cyrus.
Memor. Memorabilia.
Oecon. Oeconomica. A Treatise on Household Management.
Symp. Symposium.
Zeller. Zeller
Ph.d.Gr. Die Philosophie der Griechen.

Footnotes

CHAPTER I

Page references without indication of author or book refer to Plato's Republic. Italic numerals that follow each footnote refer back to the page in the text.

[1] In these pages I have relied heavily on the judgment of Prof. Karl H. Niebyl. I hope that his *Economic History* will soon appear, so that those who are interested in filling out this sketch may have the material available to do so. —— *18.*

[2] *Od.* VII. 103. —— *18.*

[3] *Il.* IX. 658. —— *19.*

[4] *Il.* XXIV. 622 ff. —— *19.*

[5] *Il.* XXII. 449; for further instances of friendly relations between master and slave see *Od.* VII. 8; XV. 363; *Il.* III. 386. —— *19.*

[6] *Od.* XVI. 304; IV. 735. —— *19.*

[7] *Od.* VI. 69; XIX. 78 —— *19.*

[8] *Il.* XXIV. 734. —— *19.*

[9] *Od.* XXII. 466. —— *20.*

[10] The figures are, including compound and adjectival forms,

	Iliad	*Odyssey*
Bronze	392	95
Iron	22	25

In Gehring's *Index Homericus* steel is not mentioned in either poem. We hear of it first in Hesiod (*Works and Days* 149), fairly frequently in the fifth century, e. g. Herod. VII. 141; Pind. *Pyth.* IV, 125; Aesch. *Prom. VI.* 64; Soph. *Frag.* 604, etc. —— *20.*

[11] *Il.* XXIII. 832 ff. —— *20.*

[12] *Od.* I. 179. —— *20.*

[13] *Od.* XV. 329; XVII. 565. —— *21.*

[14] *Reallexicon der Vorgeschichte,* herausgegeben von Max Ebert, Vol. III, 61, 66; H. R. Hall, *The Ancient History of the Near East,* p. 78-79; Ugo Antonelli, in *Enciclopedia Italiana,* XV, 110-112. —— *21.*

[15] Glotz, *Ancient Greece at Work,* p. 34. —— *21.*

[16] *Il.* VI. 234 ff. —— *22.*

[17] *Il.* XVIII. 593. —— *22.*

[18] *Il.* X. 351.——*22.*

[19] *Il.* VIII. 186.——*22.*

[20] Mr. Tom Silverberg has worked out in detail the evidence for these two statements in a paper that will, I hope, be published shortly.——*22.*

[21] *Od.* XIV. 99 ff.——*23.*

[22] Glotz, *op. cit.,* p. 36.——*23.*

[23] *Od.* IX. 221 ff.——*23.*

[24] E. g. *Il.* XI. 325; XII. 41, etc.——*23.*

[25] Glotz, *op. cit.,* p. 37; e. g. *Od.* IV. 369; XII. 251.——*23.*

[26] *Il.* X. 353; *Od.* VIII. 32.——*24.*

[27] *Il.* XVIII. 542; *Od.* V. 127.——*24.*

[28] *Od.* XVII. 297 ff.——*24.*

[29] *Il.* XVIII. 551; *Od.* XVIII. 368.——*24.*

[30] Glotz, *op. cit.,* p. 41.——*24.*

[31] *Il.* XVIII. 561 ff.——*25.*

[32] *Il.* XVII. 53-56 ff.——*25.*

[33] *Il.* XVIII. 596; cf. *Od.* VII. 107.——*25.*

[34] E. g. *Od.* III. 466.——*25.*

[35] *Od.* VI. 96.——*25.*

[36] *Od.* VII. 112 ff.——*25.*

[37] *Od.* XXIV. 244 ff.——*25.*

[38] Blacksmiths—*Od.* III. 432; IX. 391; *Il.* XII. 295; XV. 309, etc. workers in hides (tanners, etc.)—VII. 221; carpenters—*Od.* XVII. 340; XIX. 56; XXI. 43, etc.; potters—*Il.* XVIII. 601; town criers—*Il.* V. 785; goldsmiths—*Od.* III. 425; physicians—*Il.* IV. 190, 194; XI, 518, 835; *Od.* XVII. 384.——*25.*

[39] *Il.* VII. 221.——*26.*

[40] *Od.* XXIV. 211, 366, 389; *Od.* XX. 383.——*26.*

[41] *Od.* II. 319; *Od.* XXIV. 300; *Od.* VII. 43.——*26.*

[42] Glotz, *op. cit.,* p. 9.——*27.*

[43] Glotz, *op. cit.,* p. 9.——*27.*

[44] *Od.* VI. 87.——*27.*

[45] Plut. *Solon* 21.——*28.*

[46] The nomenclature of politically organized bodies remains fairly fixed throughout the history of the Athenian city-state. And these terms—accurately or imaginatively—reflect their origins in the old tribal order of society.——*29.*

[47] *Od.* XV. 267.——*29.*

[48] *Il.* II. 363 ff.——*29.*

[49] *Il.* XXIII. 87.——*29.*

[50] *Il.* II. 212 ff.——*30.*

[51] *Il.* IX. 121 ff.——*30.*

[52] *Od.* VII. 84 ff.——*30.*

53 *Il.* V. 613.—— *31.*
54 *Il.* II. 705.—— *31.*
55 *Il.* X. 315.—— *31*
56 *Il.* V. 613.—— *31.*
57 *Od.* XIV. 211.—— *31.*
58 Soph. *El.* 162; Eur. *Alc.* 920; *Hipp.* 152; *Ion* 1073; *C. I. A.*, 765; etc.—— *31.*
59 *Il.* XI. 490.—— *31.*
60 *Od.* IV. 644.—— *31.*
61 *Od.* I. 392 ff.—— *32.*
62 *Od.* XI. 489 ff.—— *32.*
63 *Od.* XVIII. 357 ff.—— *33.*
64 *Il.* IX. 449-570; *Od.* XI. 27 ff.—— *35.*
65 *Il.* XXIII. 592; IV. 160.—— *35.*
66 *Il.* III. 320.—— *35.*
67 *Od.* VI. 207; XIV. 278; XVII. 475.—— *35.*
68 *Il.* XVI 386.—— *35.*
69 For a full and exceptionally interesting discussion of this process the student should consult the two articles of Wade Gery in *Classical Quarterly,* 1931.—— *36*

CHAPTER II

70 Jane Harrison, *Themis,* p. 516.—— *40.*
71 Aesch. *Seven Against Thebes* 84.—— *40.*
72 Soph. *Frag.* 598 (ed. Nauck).—— *40.*
73 Pind. *Pyth.* II. 155.—— *40.*
74 *Od.* IV. 691 ff.—— *40.*
75 *Od.* XIX. 169-71.—— *40.*
76 *Od.* XIV. 59 f.—— *40.*
77 *Od.* XI. 218-220.—— *40.*
78 *Od.* XXIV. 254 ff.—— *40.*
79 *Od.* XIV. 81-84.—— *40.*
80 *Il.* XIX. 179-80.—— *40.*
81 *Works and Days* (Loeb ed.) 110-201. trans. Evelyn White.—— *42.*
82 *Works and Days* 192.—— *42.*
83 *Works and Days* 203 ff.—— *42.*
84 *Works and Days* 257, 283.—— *43.*
85 *Works and Days* 217.—— *43.*
86 *Works and Days l. c.*—— *43.*
87 *Works and Days* 256—— *44.*
88 *Works and Days* 210-265.—— *44.*
89 Arist. *Ath. Pol.* XII. 14a—— *46.*

[90] Plut. *Solon* XIV. This is the account of Phanias, the Lesbian. —— *46.*
[91] Arist. *op. cit.* XII. —— *46.*
[92] The phrase is Mr. Winston Churchill's. —— *46.*
[93] Demos. *de fals. leg.* 254 ff. trans. Linforth. —— *47.*
[94] Kern, *Orphicorum Fragmenta,* 21; Plato *Laws* IV. 716 A. trans. Jowett; cf. Kern, *Orphicorum Fragmenta,* 105. Herm. *In Plat. Phaedr.* 248 C. —— *48.*
[95] Proc. *In Remp.* II. 144, 29; Kern, *Orph. Frag.,* 158. —— *48.*
[96] Plato *Laws* 716. trans. Jowett. —— *48.*
[97] For an admirable discussion of the "Social value of the Dionysiac Ritual" see George N. Belknap, *Univ. of Oregon Studies, Humanistic series,* 1925. —— *49.*
[98] I Cor. XV:35-44. —— *50.*
[99] *Od.* XI. 489-91; Plato *Rep.* 386. —— 50.
[100] *Rep.* 386 C ff. —— *50.*
[101] Plato *Gorg.* 493 A; *Crat.* 400 B. —— *51.*
[102] Rohde, *Psyche* (Eng. ed.), 345. —— *51.*
[103] *Il.* V. 440 ff. trans. Murray. —— *53.*
[104] *Il.* I. 9; XIV. 336; *Od.* XI. 318; *Hymn to Hermes* 500, 523; *Hymn to Apollo* 178. —— *53.*
[105] *Od.* VI. 162; *Hymn to Apollo* 27. —— *53.*
[106] *Il.* I. 37, 451. —— *54.*
[107] *Il.* V. 446; VII. 83; XVI. 515. —— *54.*
[108] *Il.* IV. 508; XV. 243 ff. 360; XVI. 715 ff.; XVII. 71 ff., etc. —— *54.*
[109] *Il.* I. 43 ff.; XXIV. 605; *Od.* III. 279; VIII. 227; XI. 318 —— *54.*
[110] *Il.* I. 64, 99, 456. —— *54.*
[111] *Hymn to Apollo* 131; *Il.* I. 602. —— *54.*
[112] *Od.* VIII. 79. —— *54.*
[113] *Il.* I. 72, 86. —— *54.*
[114] *Od.* VIII. 488. —— *54.*
[115] Mrs. Clara Smertenko, *Univ. of Oregon Studies, Humanistic Series,* 1925. —— *54.*
[116] *Herod.* VII. 10 E. trans. Macaulay. (Macaulay translates "God"; the Greek is *ho theos.*) —— *55.*
[117] E. g. *Odes* II. 10. But it is a very frequent theme in the verse of his mature years. —— *55.*
[118] *Odes* I. 35. —— *55.*
[119] This idea has been developed and the evidence for the evolution of Hermes has been collected by Mr. Norman O. Brown. To him I express my deep gratitude and venture to hope that he will publish his paper in an expanded form. —— *56.*
[120] E. g. *Od.* V. 29. —— *56.*

[121] *Od.* XXIV. 1 ff.——*56.*
[122] *Il.* XXIV. 343-4.——*56.*
[123] *Il.* XIV. 490.——*56.*
[124] *Eriounios*; *dōtōr eaōn.*——*56.*
[125] *Od.* XIV. 442. ff.——*56.*
[126] *Od.* VIII. 334 ff.——*56.*
[127] *Od.* V. 99 ff.——*56.*
[128] *Hymn to Hermes* 171.——*57.*
[129] By Mr. N. O. Brown.——*57.*
[130] *Hymn to Hermes* 515.——*57.*
[131] *Hymn to Hermes* 515.——*57.*
[132] *Hymn to Hermes* 577; Mr. N. O. Brown, *op. cit.*——*57.*
[133] Mr. N. O. Brown.——*57.*
[134] *Hymn to Hermes* 155.——*58.*
[135] Aristoph. *Plutus* 1162. trans. Rogers.——*58.*
[136] *Hipparchus* 228 D.——*58.*
[137] See Pauly Wissowa, *agoranomoi.*——*58.*
[138] Diod. Sicul. V. 75.——*58.*
[139] *Crat.* 408 a.——*59.*
[140] *Peace* 429.——*59.*
[141] *Peace* 200; *Plutus* 1170.——*59.*
[142] *Peace* 193.——*59.*
[143] *Peace* 425.——*59.*
[144] *Plut.* 1151.——*59.*
[145] Mr. N. O. Brown has worked out these suggestions in great detail in a paper soon to be published.——*59.*
[146] *Cratylus* 406 C.——*60.*
[147] *Laws* 674 A.——*60.*
[148] *Laws* 815 C.——*60.*
[149] *Laws* 653 D.——*60.*
[150] Arnob. *adv. Gent.* 3, 31; cf. Aug. *de civitate dei* 716.——*61.*
[151] E. g. *Il.* VI. 305.——*61.*
[152] *Frag.* 12. ed. Linforth.——*61.*
[153] *Theog.* 886-900. For the birth of Athena: Hom. *Hymn to Athena;* Pind. *Ol. 7,* 38; Stesichorus *ap. Schol. Apol. Rhod.* 1310——*61.*
[154] For Athena as the giver of the olive: School of Aristoph. *Nub.* 1001; Suidas *s. v. Moriai*; Schol. Soph. *Oed. Col.* 705; Apollodor. 3. 14. 1.
[155] *Il.* V. 60. *Od.* XX. 72.——*61.*
[156] Farnell, *The Cults of the Greek States,* I, 314. For Athena as patron of arts; Schol. Soph. *Oed. Col.* 56; Paus. I. 30, 2; Plato *Laws* 920 D.——*61.*
[157] Paus. I. 28. 7; Strabo 396; Herod. VIII. 5; Plut. *Themist.* C. 10;

Aristoph. *Thesmoph.* 1136; Eur. *Heracl.* 770; Aesch. *Eum.* 997. —— *62.*

158 Paus. I. 22. 4; *C. I. A.*, I, 4; *ib.*, II, 471; 678; Soph. *Phil.* 134; Eur. *Ion* 1528; Aristoph. *Equit.* 581. —— *62.*

159 Soph. *Phil.* 134. "The worship and the title express in part the peaceful character of the goddess, who has laid aside her helmet after the battle." (Farnell, *op. cit.*, 313.) —— *62.*

CHAPTER III

160 Meritt and West, *The Athenian Assessment of 425* (Univ. of Michigan, 1934) p. 90. —— *67.*

161 Thuc. V. 84 ff; III. 2 ff. —— *68.*

162 Arist. *Ath. Pol.* II. —— *68.*

163 Plut. *Solon* 22. —— *68.*

164 Tod, *Greek Historical Inscriptions,* No. 26. —— *71.*

CHAPTER IV

165 See below p. 249 f. —— *76.*

166 Diog. Laërt. VIII. 1, 3; Aristoxenus *ap.* Porphyr. *Vit.* 9. —— *78.*

167 Iamb. *V. P.* 33. —— *97.*

168 Iamb. *V. P.* 34. —— *79.*

169 Iamb. *V. P.* 248; cf. Porphyr. *V. P.* 54. —— *79.*

170 We here give the traditional account. Minar (*op. cit.*) thinks that our sources put together two episodes which were chronologically widely separated and that there is evidence for political struggle lasting nearly a century. —— *79.*

171 Hegel, *Werke,* ed. Michelet, XIII, 1, p. 218. —— *80.*

172 Dicaearchus, Aristoxenus, Timaeus. —— *80.*

173 Diog. Laërt. VIII, 46; Suidas s. v. Aristoxenus; Gell. IV, 11. —— *80.*

174 Apollonius in Iamb. *V. P.* 254 —— *81.*

175 Stobaeus *Flor.* 43, 93; De Latte, *Politique,* pp. 143 ff. —— *81.*

176 Apollonius in Iamb. *V. P.* —— *81.*

177 *V. P.* 174-176. —— *82.*

178 Iamb. *V. P.* 31. —— *83.*

179 Kern, *Orph. Frag.*, 4. —— *83.*

180 Iamb. *V. P.* 175. —— *83.*

181 *Il.* XXII. 116; *Od.* VIII, 81; *Od.* I. 188. —— *83.*

182 "It is not justifiable to attempt to tone down or explain away the remarkable sentiment that the possible inferiority of prevailing laws is no reason for changing them." (Minar, *op. cit.*, p. 10.) —— *84.*

183 For the Pythagoreans on "anarchy" see Iamb. *V. P.* 175; Stobaeus *Flor.* 43, 49; cf. Iamb. *V. P.* 183; also De Latte's discussion of Hippodamus, *Politique,* pp. 125-161, 193.——*84.*

184 Aristox. in Diog. Laërt. VIII. 16.——*84.*

185 Iamb. *V. P.* 182-183.——*84.*

186 Iamb. *V. P.* 99-101, 183; Stob. *Flor.* 43, 49; Porphyr. *V. P.* 38. ——*84.*

187 Iamb. *V. P.* 232.——*85.*

188 E. g. Plato *Phaedo* 61 E; Diog. Laërt. VIII. 46; Diog. Laërt. III. 6; Timon *Frag.* 54 D *ap.* Gell. III. 17. 4; Arist. *Met.* A 987A29-31.——*85.*

189 Stob. *Flor.* 43, 94.——*86.*

190 Minar, *op. cit.* p 43.——*86.*

191 Stob. *Flor.* 43, 49.——*87.*

192 Iamb. *V. P.* 203.——*87.*

193 Iamb. *V. P.* 175; Stob. *Flor.* 43, 49.——*87.*

194 Iamb. *V. P.* 45 ff.——*87.*

195 Iamb. *V. P.* 179; see De Latte, *op. cit.,* p. 57 n. 2.——*88.*

196 Quoted by Glotz, *Ancient Greece at Work,* p. 157.——*89.*

197 III. 82.——*89.*

198 For "temperance" see below, p. 208.——*89.*

199 Herod. V. 78.——*89.*

200 *Il.* XI. 705.——*89.*

201 *Od.* II. 203-4.——*89.*

202 *Il.* XII. 421-423.——*89.*

203 *Works and Days* 327, 752.——*89.*

204 Arist. *Ath. Pol.* XII.——*89.*

205 Stob. *Ecl.* I. 498.——*90.*

206 Aët. V. 30. 1; *Vors.* 24B4; see below, p. 153 ff.——*90.*

207 The whole of Book V of the *Nicomachaean Ethics* is of interest in this connection, especially V. 9. I.——*99.*

208 *Cyrop.* I. 3.——*90.*

209 *Vors.* 68B102.——*90.*

210 Arist. *Eth. Nic.* V. 8. 1132B21; cf. *Mag. Mor.* I. 34, 1194A28 ff. ——*91.*

211 *Mag. Mor.* I. 1, 1182A11.——*91.*

212 *In Metaphys. Comment.* I. 5. 25 (Arist. *Met.* 985A26)——92.

213 Macr. *Somn. Scip.* I. 5. 17.——*92.*

214 Plato. *Gorg.* 508 A.——*92.*

215 Preserved in Stob. *Flor.* 43, 129; 43, 132, 133, 134; 46, 61. cf. De Latte, *Politique,* p. 71 ff.——*92.*

216 De Latte, *op. cit.,* p. 99.——*93.*

217 *Inst. Arith.* II. 45; De Latte, *op. cit.,* p. 98.—*94.*

218 Dicaearchus in his *Tripoliticos.* He was followed interestingly enough by Cicero in the *De Republica.*——*94.*

219 *V. P.* 130 —— *95*.
220 De Latte, *op. cit.*, 57 ff; Porphyry *de abs.* IV. 18. —— *96*.
221 The story comes from Archytas and is preserved by Arist. *Met.* N. 5. 1092B8. —— *96*.
222 Arist. *Met.* M. 1078B22 (Loeb ed.) trans. Tredennick. —— *97*.
223 Iamb. *V. P.* 200. —— *98*.
224 Strabo VI. 1. p. 252. —— *98*.
225 Speusippus in Diog. Laërt. IX. 21. —— *99*.
226 Plut. *adv. Col.* I. 226a. —— *99*.
227 It is interesting to note that Parmenides keeps the poetical form even though the more rationalistic Ionians are already writing in prose. —— *99*.
228 *Vors.* 28B1. —— *99*.
229 *Vors.* 28B7. trans. Burnet. —— *100*.
230 *Vors.* 28B3. —— *100*.
231 *Vors.* 28B8. —— *100*.
232 *Vors.* 28B8. —— *101*.
233 *Vors.* 28B8, 55. —— *101*.
234 *Vors.* 28B18. —— *101*.
235 *Vors.* 28B6. So we interpret this fragment. —— *101*.
236 *Vors.* 22B80. cf. B8. —— *102*.
237 Diod. Sic. X. 18. 2; Plut. *adv. Col.* 32, p. 1126 D. —— *102*.
238 Diog. Laërt. XI, 25; Strabo VI. 252. —— *102*.
239 *Vors.* 29A1. —— *103*.
240 *Vors.* 29B1, 2, 3 and 4; Arist. *Met.* B. 4. 1001B7. —— *103*.
241 Arist. *Phys.* Z. 9. 239B33; *Vors.* 29A28. —— *104*.
242 E. g. *Theaetet.* 183 c. —— *104*.
243 Diog. Laërt. *Prooem.* VIII. 1, 2; Cic. *Tusc.* V. 2; Diog. Laërt. X. 10. I; Iamb. *Protrep.* I. 9. —— *104*.
244 In Diog. Laërt. VIII. 8. trans. Yonge; Cic. *Tusc.* V. 3. —— *105*.
245 *Varia Socratica* (ed. Taylor), p. 17. —— *107*.
246 Arist. *Met.* A. 987B1-4. —— *108*.
247 Arist. *Met.* M. 1078B17. —— *108*.
248 See introduction, Hippocrates (Loeb ed.). —— *109*.
249 *Varia Socratica,* p. 77 ff. —— *109*.
250 *Varia Socratica, loc. cit.* —— *109*.
251 Arist. *Met.* M. 1078B22. —— *110*.

CHAPTER V

252 See Cochrane, *Thucydides and the Science of History*. —— *117*.
253 *Life of Marcellus*. ch. 17 (Loeb ed.). trans. Perrin. Quoted by Farrington, *Science and Society,* Vol. II, No. 4, p. 439. —— *117*.

254 *Vors.* 11A22 for Thales; *Vors.* 68A164 for Democritus.—— *118.*
255 (Ps.?) Plut. *Strom. Frag.* 2.; *Vors.* 12A10.—— *119.*
256 *Vors.* 12A10.—— *119.*
257 Arist. *Meteor.* B. 1. 353B6; Burnet, p. 66; *Vors.* 12A27.—— *119.*
258 *Vors.* 12A21, 22.—— *120.*
259 Arist. *de caelo* B. 13. 295B10; *Vors.* 12A26.—— *120.*
260 Aët. *Placita* V. 19. 4; *Vors.* 12A30.—— *120.*
261 (Ps.?) Plut. *Strom. Frag.* 2; Plut. *Symp.* 730 f.; *Vors.* 12A30. —— *120.*
262 *Vors.* 13B1.—— *121.*
263 *Vors. loc. cit.*—— *121.*
264 *De. nat. deorum* I. 10, 26; Vors. 13A10.—— *121.*
265 *De civitate dei* VIII. 2.—— *122.*
266 Reading *phykiōn* with Gomperz, *Greek thinkers,* I, 551; Burnet, 136.—— *123.*
267 Hippol. *Ref.* I. 14; *Vors.* 21A33.—— *123.*
268 *Vors.* 21B32.—— *123.*
269 *Vors.* 21B29.—— *123.*
270 *Vors.* 21B33.—— *123.*
271 *Vors.* 21B27.—— *123.*
272 *Vors.* 21B18.—— *123.*
273 *Vors.* 21B7.—— *124.*
274 *Vors.* 21A1, 27.—— *124.*
275 *Vors.* 21B2; cf. *Vors.* 21B12—— *124.*
276 *Vors.* 21B14.—— *124.*
277 *Vors.* 21B15.—— *124.*
278 *Vors.* 21B16.—— *124.*
279 *Vors.* 21B23.—— *124.*
280 *Vors.* 21B24.—— *124.*
281 Diog. Laërt. IX. 24.—— *125.*
282 Arist. *Met.* A. 5. 986B18.—— *125.*
283 *Vors.* 21B1.—— *126.*
284 *Vors.* 21B22.—— *126.*
285 E. g. *Vors.* 22A1, 9 and 10.—— *127.*
286 Plato *Theatet.* 182 C.—— *128.*
287 Plato *Crat.* 402 A.—— *128.*
288 *Vors.* 22B53.—— *218.*
289 *Vors.* 22B80.—— *128.*
290 *Vors.* 22B54.—— *128.*
291 *Vors.* 22B2.—— *128.*
292 *Vors.* 22B40.—— *128.*
293 *Vors.* 22B76.—— *128.*
294 Kern, *Orph. Frag.*, 168.—— *129.*

295 Plato *Soph.* 249 D. (Not B as listed in Ast, *Lexicon Platonicum.*) —— *130.*
296 *Who was Socrates?* p. 27. —— *131.*
297 *Vors.* 22B80. —— *133.*
298 *Vors.* 59B8. —— *133.*
299 *Vors.* 22B126. —— *133.*
300 *Vors.* 59B8. —— *133.*
301 *Vors.* 59B12. —— *133.*
302 *Vors.* 59B12. —— *134.*
303 *Vors.* 59B8, 9, 10. —— *134.*
304 *Vors.* 59B4. —— *135.*
305 *Vors.* 59B10. —— *135.*
306 *Vors.* 59B4. —— *136.*
307 Arist. *Met.* A. 3. 984A11. —— *136.*
308 Lucr. *de rerum nat.* I. 830 ff. and 876 ff. trans. Munro. —— *137.*
309 Euseb. *Chron. Hier.* = Migne, *Patrologia Graeca,* XIX, 478; Apul. *Flor.* 18; Plato *Protag.* 317 B, 328 B, 329 B; *Vors.* 80A4 and 5. —— *138.*
310 Hesych. *Onomatol. ap.* Schol. Plato *Rep.* 600 C; *Vors.* 80A3. —— *138.*
311 Diog. Laërt. IX. 54; *Vors.* 80A1. Aristotle mentions Enathlos, but this seems to be a mistake due to the story that Protagoras and Enathlos, had had a dispute about pay. Diog. Laërt. IX. 56; *Vors.* 80A1. —— *139.*
312 Euseb. *Chron. Hier.*; *Vors.* 80A4. —— *139.*
313 That of Satyros in Diog. Laërt. II. 12; *Vors.* 59A1. In this account Thucydides, son of Melesias, was the accuser. —— *139.*
314 Sext. *Pyrrh.* H. I. 216 ff. *Vors.* 80A74. —— *140.*
315 Sext. *loc. cit.* —— *141.*
316 Herod. III. 38. trans. Macaulay. —— *143.*
317 Euseb. *P. E.* XIV. 3, 7; Diog. Laërt. IX. 51; *Vors.* 80B4. —— *143.*
318 Eur. *Meleager frag.* XX. ed. Dindorf. —— *144.*
319 *de victu* I. 5-24; *Vors.* 22C1. —— *144.*
320 Iamb. *in Nic.* 19, 21; *Vors.* 44B9. —— *144.*
321 Diog. Laërt. II. 16; *Vors.* 60A1. —— *144.*
322 Plat. *Prot.* 337. C. —— *145.*
323 *Pol.* I, 1253B20; cf. *Rhet.* I.1373B18. —— *145.*
324 (Ps.) Plut. *pro nobilit.* 18. —— *146.*
325 *Oxyrrh. Pap.* XI. (ed. Grenfell and Hunt). —— *146.*
326 *Oratores Attici II.* 316. —— *146.*
327 *Frag.* 95. (ed. Koch). —— *146.*
328 Lucr. *de rerum nat.* II. 10. —— *146.*
330 Diog. Laërt. IX. 34; *Vors.* 68A2. —— *149.*

[331] *Vors.* 68B2.—— *149.*
[332] Diog. Laërt. IX. 39; *Vors.* 68A1.—— *149.*
[333] Simplic. *in Arist. Phys.* 330. 14 (Arist. *Phys.* 196B14); *Vors.* 68A68. —— *150.*
[334] *Vors.* 68B118; Euseb. *P. E.* XIV. 27, 4.—— *150.*
[335] *De orat.* I. II. 49; *Orat.* 20, 67; *Vors.* 68A34.—— *150.*
[336] See Lortzing in Bursian's *Jahresbericht,* CXVII (1903).—— *150.*
[337] *Vors.* 68B251.—— *151.*
[338] *Vors.* 68B102.—— *151.*
[339] Hippolyt. *Refut.* I. 13; *Vors.* 68A40.—— *151.*
[340] (Following Leucippus?). *Vors.* 67A1, 6, 7, 8, 10-12, 14, 16, 19, 32; 68A1, 37-38, 40, 49, 51, 60, 80, 93a; 125B156. 125.—— *151.*
[341] *Vors.* 68A1, 37, 38, 43, 47 ff., 49, 50, 56, 80, 93a, 132.—— *151.*
[342] *Vors.* 68B125.—— *151.*
[343] *Vors.* 68A1, 69, 83.—— *152.*
[344] *Vors.* 68A10.—— *153.*
[345] Chalcid. *in Tim.* p. 279 (Wrob); *Vors.* 24A10.—— *153.*
[346] Plato *Phaedo* 96. A and B; *Vors.* 24A11.—— *153.*
[347] *Vors.* 24A5 and 6, with references there given.—— *153.*
[348] *Vors.* 24A5.—— *153.*
[349] *Vors.* 24A10 and 3.—— *153.*
[350] Theophr. *de sens.* 25; *Vors.* 24B1a.—— *153.*
[351] This affinity is most recently questioned by W. A. Heide, *A. J. P.,* Jan. 1940.—— *154.*
[352] *Vors.* 24A1.—— *154.*
[353] *Vors.* 24B4.—— *154.*
[354] Arist. *Met.* A. 5. 986A26, 27. trans. Ross.—— *155.*
[355] Hippocrates—*ab studio sapientiae disciplinam hanc separavit.* Quoted by W. H. S. Jones in Introd. Hippocrates (Loeb ed.) p. XII.—— *156.*
[356] *On Ancient Medicine* XX. in Hippocrates (Loeb ed.) trans. Jones. —— *156.*
[357] *On Ancient Medicine* I. Hippocrates (Loeb ed.) p. 14. (With modifications).—— *157.*
[358] Addison T. Cutler, "The Ebb of Institutional Economics," *Science and Society,* II, No. 4, p. 459.—— *159.*
[359] D'Arcy Thompson, *Legacy of Greece,* p. 142.—— *159.*

CHAPTER VI

[360] Diog. Laërt. III. I.—— *161.*
[361] Andocides *de mysteriis* XVI.—— *161.*
[362] Xen. *Hell.* II. 4, 19.—— *161.*

363 Ariston was not alive at the trial of Socrates in 399. Plato *Apol.* 34 A. We cannot date his death more precisely than this.—— *162.*

364 Anon. *Vita Thuc.* VI; Kirchner, *Prosopographia Attica,* s. v. Pyrilampes.—— *162.*

365 Plut. *Peric.* XIII. Kirchner, *op. cit.,* s. v. Pyrilampes.—— *162.*

366 Plut. *Peric.* XIII.—— *162.*

367 Aristoph. *Wasps* 98; Eupol. *Frag.* 213 ed. Koch; Plat. *Gorg.* 481 C, 513 B; Hesych. s. v. *Demos.*—— *162.*

368 *Who was Socrates?*—— *163.*

369 Thuc. VIII. I.—— *164.*

370 Arist. *Ath. Pol.* XXIX.—— *164.*

371 Arist. *Ath. Pol.* XXIX; cf. Thuc. VIII. 67.—— *164.*

372 Arist. *Ath. Pol.* XXIX.—— *164.*

373 Arist. *Ath. Pol.* XXXII.—— *164.*

374 Grote, *Hist. of Greece* (ed. Mitchell and Caspari), p. 750.—— *165.*

375 Xen. *Hellen.* II. I. 32; Lys. *cont. Alcib.* A. 38; Pausanias IV. 17. 3; Isoc. *ad Phil. or.* V. 64.—— *166.*

376 *Who was Socrates?* p. 66-67.—— *167.*

377 Lys. *cont. Eratos. or* XII. 44.—— *167.*

378 Xen. *Hellen.* II. 3. 39-41; Lys. *Orat.* XVIII. 5.—— *167.*

379 *Who was Socrates?* p. 69.—— *168.*

380 Xen. *Hellen.* II. 3. 35 ff.—— *168.*

381 Plato *Epis.* VII. 324 B-325 A. trans. L. A. Post.—— *169.*

382 *Op. cit.* p. 148 n. 8.—— *169.*

383 Xen. *Hellen.* II. 3. 56.—— *170.*

384 Xen. *Hellen.* II. 4. I; Lys. *Orat.* XII. 97 (*cont. Eratos.*); Lys. *Orat.* XXXI. 8.—— *170.*

385 Aeschines *fals. Leg.* 77; *cont. Ctesiphon.* 235; Isocrates *Orat.* IV. 131; VII. 76.—— *170.*

386 Xen. *Memor.* I. 2. 31; Isoc. *Orat.* XIII.—— *170.*

387 Xen. *Memor.* IV. 43.—— *170.*

388 *Who was Socrates?* p. 75.—— *170.*

389 Plato *Epis.* VII. 325 C.—— *170.*

390 *Who was Socrates?* p 76 ff.—— *170.*

391 Plato *Phaedo* 59 B.—— *170.*

392 Diog. Laërt. II. 5. 41.—— *171.*

393 Plato *Apol.* 38 B.—— *171.*

394 On the social significance of poetry in this period see Christopher Caundwell, *Illusion and Reality,* ch. I and II.—— *171.*

395 Diog. Laërt. III. 1. 29; *Anth. Graec.* VII. 100.—— *172.*

396 *Anth. Graec.* VII. 669, 670.—— *172.*

397 *Anth. Graec.* VII. 99. The tradition in all cases goes back to Aristippus.—— *172.*

398 Diog. Laërt. III. 1. 6.—— *172.*
399 Diog. Laërt. III. 1. 6; II. 103.—— *172.*
400 *Timaeus* 21 E-25 D.—— *172.*
401 Plato *Epis.* VII. 326 B ff. trans. Post.—— *174.*
402 Plato *Epis.* VII. 324 B.—— *174.*
403 Diod. Sic. XV. 7; Diog. Laërt. III. 18-21.—— *174.*
404 Plutarch *Dion.* V. —— *174.*
405 Diog. Laërt. III. 19.—— *174.*
406 Diog. Laërt. III. 7.—— *174.*
407 Plutarch *Dion.* VI (reproducing Timaeus) —— *177.*
408 Plato *Epis.* VII. 327 B and C.—— *178.*
409 *C. A. H.,* VI., 274.—— *179.*
410 Plato *Epis.* VII. 332 C and D. trans. Post.—— *179.*
411 Plato *Epis.* VII. 329 B.—— *179.*
412 Plutarch *Dion.* XI.—— *179.*
413 Plutarch *Dion.* XI; Cicero (*ad Quint. Frat.* II. 13) calls him a "miniature" Thucydides.—— *179.*
414 Plato *Epis.* VII. 329 C. trans. Post.—— *180.*
415 Plutarch *Dion.* XIV. Timaeus is the source.—— *180.*
416 Plutarch *Dion.* XV.—— *180.*
417 Plato *Epis.* III. 16 D. trans. Post.—— *180.*
418 Plutarch *Dion.* XVII.—— *182.*
419 C. A. H., VI, 276 and 277.—— *183.*
420 Diog. Laërt. III. 32. trans. Yonge; Diogenes assigns this incident to the second visit, Plutarch (*Dion.* XVIII) to the third.—— *183.*
421 Diog. Laërt. III. 22. trans. Yonge.—— *184.*
422 *C. A. H.,* VI, 277.—— *184.*
423 E. Bickermann and Joh. Sykutris, "Speusipps Brief an König Philipp," *Berichte über die Verhandlungen der Sächsichen Akademie der Wissenschaften zu Leipzig, Philologisch-Historische Klasse,* 80. Band (1928), 3. Heft.—— *184.*

CHAPTER VII

424 Shorey, *Republic of Plato* (Loeb ed.), Intro. p. VIII; Boeckh, *Kleine Schriften,* IV, pp. 437 ff.—— *188.*
425 See *Who was Socrates?* p. 65 ff.—— *188.*
426 In *Who was Socrates?* —— *188.*
427 This is the position which is caricatured in the famous Melian Dialogue of Thucydides.—— *188.*
428 I am glad to learn that the symbolism of the three figures in the opening pages of the work has also occurred to Mr. David Grene of the University of Chicago.—— *189.*

429 330 B.—— *189.*
430 331 O.—— *190.*
431 337 D.—— *190.*
432 Cf. *Theaetet.* 177 D; *Laws* 714.—— *190.*
433 338 E. It is a small point but significant that the specific examples which Thrasymachus gives, democratic and tyrannical, may both be described as "leftist" in their Greek context.—— *190.*
434 351 A.—— *193.*
435 353 D.—— *193.*
436 Plato *Phaedo* 96 A ff.; see *Who was Socrates?* p. 33 ff.—— *193.*

CHAPTER VIII

437 See Zeller, *Philosophie der Griechen,* II, I. 4th ed. (1899), p. 392. and *Abhandl. d. Berl. Akad. Hist.-Phil. Kl.* (1873), p. 86, quoted by Shorey, *Rep.* p. 145 note.—— *197.*
438 369 B.—— *198.*
439 371 C. Characteristic aristocratic prejudice.—— *198.*
440 Werner Fite has already pointed out that the traditional translation "guardians" for *phylakes* tends to idealize their function. I shall follow him and translate "guards."—— *199.*
441 Cf. among many modern thinkers Mill, *Logic,* VI, 7: Human beings in society have no properties, but those which are derived from and may be resolved into laws and the nature of individual man.

Spencer, *Autobiog.,* II, 543: Society is created by its units—the nature of its organization is determined by the nature of its units.—— *199.*
442 *Laws* 677-680 A-B, i.e., from the family and tribe. The two accounts are hardly compatible, nor are they, as Shorey suggests, "aspects of the subject." *Intro. Rep.* XIV.—— *199.*
443 Francis H. Bartlett, *Sigmund Freud,* p. 33.—— *200.*
444 Arist. *Pol.* 1252B29.—— *201.*

CHAPTER IX

445 419. trans. Shorey.—— *203.*
446 423 A. trans. Shorey.—— *204.*
447 424 C. trans. Shorey.—— *205.*
448 Though, of course, then reciprocally acting on society to influence change.—— *205.*
449 425. trans. Shorey.—— *206.*
450 425 E. trans. Shorey.—— *206.*

451 427 C. trans. Shorey. For the implication of the Greek word *sōphrōn*, see Addendum II at the end of this chapter.—— *207.*

452 431 C. trans. Shorey.—— *209.*

453 432 B. trans. Shorey.—— *209.*

454 433 E.—— *210.*

455 434 E. trans. Shorey.—— *212.*

456 440. trans. Shorey.—— *213.*

457 Cf. *Gorg.* 466 E, where Socrates is made to explain that the tyrant can do what he wishes to do, but not what he wills to do. The will is made into a kind of unitary and unifying power set over against the chaos of desire and impulse.—— *213.*

CHAPTER X

458 401 D. trans. Shorey.—— *219.*

459 Liddell and Scott, s.v. *Euschēmōn.*—— *219.*

460 402 A. trans. Shorey.—— *219.*

461 Nettleship, "The Theory of Education in Plato's Republic," in *Hellenica* (ed. Abbott), p. 100; *Rep.* X. 602 C-605 C; 605 C-606 D; 605 B.—— *221.*

462 424 C. trans. Shorey.—— *222.*

463 522 A. See note on Plato's attitude toward the crafts at end of chapter.—— *223.*

464 414 B. trans. Shorey.—— *223.*

465 414 B. trans. Shorey.—— *224.*

466 *Op. cit.*, p. 300.—— *224.*

467 *Plato: The Man and His Work,* p. 275.—— *224.*

468 Nettleship, *Lectures on the Republic of Plato,* p. 135 n.—— *224.*

469 Nettleship, *Lectures,* p. 162.—— *225.*

470 462 C. trans. Shorey.—— *226.*

471 I. Cor. XII.—— *226.*

472 John XV: 5.—— *226.*

473 Acts IV: 32-34; John XIII: 26 ff.; John XII: 4-6; Luke XIV: 33; John Chrysostom in Migne, Vol. IX, pp. 96-98. See also Kautsky, *Foundations of Christianity,* and Pfluger, *Der Socialismus der Kirchenväter.*—— *227.*

474 See *Apol.* 23 *C.*—— *228.*

475 413 E ff. Nettleship in *Hellenica* (ed. Abbott), p. 124.—— *229.*

476 522 A.—— *229.*

477 477 A-480 A. Quoting Nettleship *ap.* Abbott, *Hellenica,* pp. 124, 128.—— *229.*

478 506 A. Quoting Nettleship *ap.* Abbott, *Hellenica,* pp. 124, 128. —— *230.*

479 564 B and D. Quoting Nettleship *ap.* Abbott, *Hellenica,* pp. 124, 128.—— *230.*

480 522 A. See note on Plato's attitude toward the crafts at end of chapter.—— *230.*

481 525 D ff.—— *230.*

482 525 A.—— *230.*

483 526 D. ff.—— *230.*

484 530 D.—— *231.*

485 Nettleship, *Hellenica* (ed. Abbott) 150. *Rep.* 412 C-413 C; 503 C; 535 C; 537 D.—— *232.*

486 Nettleship, *Lectures,* p. 290.—— *232.*

487 Stob. *Flor.* 43, 49. Cf. above p. 84.—— *233.*

488 535 C-D. Nettleship, *Hellenica,* (ed. Abbott), p. 152.—— *235.*

489 536 B.—— *235.*

490 *Loc. cit.*—— *235.*

491 486 A.—— *236.*

492 Boisacq, *Dictionnaire étymologique de la langue grecque,* 2nd ed., 1939. This derivation is rejected by Brugmann, *Rheinisches Museum für Philologie,* 62 (1907), 634 ff. In this section I have availed myself of the work of Mr. Edwin Eagle.—— *237.*

493 Her. II. 165 ff.—— *237.*

494 Soph. *Ajax* 1121.—— *237.*

495 *Sym.* III. 4.—— *237.*

496 495 E ff.—— *238.*

497 493 B.—— *238.*

498 522 B.—— *238.*

499 590 C.—— *239.*

500 *Theaetet.* 176 C.—— *239.*

501 *Laws* 643 C-644 A.—— *239.*

502 *Laws* 741 E.—— *239.*

503 *Laws* 744 D.—— *239.*

CHAPTER XI

504 444 E.—— *241.*

505 443 A.—— *241.*

506 336 E.—— *241.*

507 451 ff.—— *241.*

508 456 A.—— *242.*

509 457 B.—— *242.*

510 Athen. XII. 561 E.—— *243.*

511 E.g. *Symp.* 184 C, where he links philosophy and homosexuality with virtue in general.—— *243.*

512 468 B ff.—— *243.*

[513] *Pol.* V. 6. 11.—— *244.*
[514] 459 D and E.—— *224.*
[515] 460 A.—— *244.*
[516] 460 B.—— *244.*
[517] 460 C.—— *244.*
[518] Plut. *Lyc.* XV.—— *244.*
[519] 460 D.—— *244.*
[520] 460 E.—— *244.*
[521] 461 C.—— *244.*
[522] 462 A ff.—— *247.*
[523] These suggestions come to me from Professor Karl Heinrich Niebyl of Carlton College, Northfield, Minn., to whom I am extremely grateful.—— *250.*
[524] R. M. Dawkins, *The Sanctuary of Artemis Orthyia at Sparta,* p. 52 ff.—— *250.*
[525] Förster, *Die Sieger in den olympischen Spielen* (Zwickau, 1891).—— *250.*
[526] Alcman. Diels, Vol. II, pp. 11-12; Alc. *Frag.* I. 60 (95) ff.—— *250.*
[527] Her. I. 65. trans. Macaulay; cf. Plut. *Lyc.* IV. 1. —— *251.*
[528] Thuc. III. 112; IV. 3.—— *253.*
[529] Thuc. IV. 80. trans. Jowett.—— *255.*
[530] Arist. *Pol.* II. 9. 14.—— *255.*
[531] Arist. *Pol.* II. 10. trans. Welldon.—— *256.*
[532] This account is drawn chiefly from the study of the Gortynian law code made by Dareste (*Lois civiles de Gortyne*)—— *256.*
[533] Arist. *Pol.* II. 9, 10.—— *258.*
[534] 473 D.—— *263.*
[535] 495 C.—— *264.*
[536] 495 D.—— *264.*
[537] 495 E ff.—— *264.*
[538] 488 B.—— *265.*
[539] 487 A.—— *265.*
[540] 541 A.—— *266.*
[541] 544 D.—— *266.*
[542] 543 C.—— *267.*
[543] 587 E.—— *268.*

CHAPTER XII

[544] *Protag.* 351 ff.—— *273.*
[545] 509 A.—— *274.*
[546] Caird, *The Evolution of Theology in the Greek Philosophers,* p. 83.—— *274.*

[547] 479 D.—— *274.*
[548] Iamb. *V. P.* 200 ff.—— *274.*
[549] 478 C. The whole passage is commended to the student for very careful examination.—— *275.*
[550] Caird, *op. cit.*, p. 112.—— *276.*
[551] 479 A.—— *276.*
[552] 476 C.—— *276.*
[553] See Professor Alister Cameron's valuable study, *The Pythagorean Background of the Theory of Recollection.*—— *278.*
[554] Cf. Xenophanes' famous parody. Diog. Laërt. VIII. 36; *Vors.* 21. B. 7.—— *278.*
[555] *Crat.* 400 C; Kern, *Orphicorum Fragmenta,* 8.—— *278.*
[556] *Vors.* 21. B. 7.—— *279.*
[557] *Vors.* 44 B. 14.—— *279.*
[558] See A. Cameron, *op. cit.*, p. 29.—— *279.*
[559] *Phaedo* 88 D.—— *280.*
[560] *Phaedo* 88 D.—— *280.*
[561] 608 C.—— *281.*
[562] *Phaedr.* 245 C.—— *282.*
[563] *Meno* 80 D.—— *283.*
[564] Caird, *op. cit.,* 90.—— *283.*
[565] Caird, *op. cit.,* 93.—— *285.*
[566] *Meno* 82 B ff.—— *285.*
[567] *Phaedo* 60 A; *Who was Socrates?* p. 40.—— *286.*
[568] 476 C.—— *288.*
[569] *Phaedo* 79 C.—— *289.*
[570] 597 B.—— *290.*
[571] Caird, *op. cit.*, p. 171.—— *291.*
[572] *Who was Socrates?*—— *294.*
[573] 535 A.—— *295.*
[574] 532 A.—— *295.*
[575] 537 E. This passage deserves careful study in its full context.—— *296.*
[576] 537 C.—— *296.*
[577] *Phaedo* 98 C.—— *577.*
[578] Caird, *op. cit.*, p. 127. (Italics ours.)—— *578.*
[579] Caird, *op. cit.,* p. 161 ff.—— *300.*
[580] 509 B.—— *300.*
[581] *Phaedr.* 265 E.—— *301.*
[582] *Soph.* 249 D.—— *302.*

CHAPTER XIII

[1] Cherniss *Riddle of the Academy,* 61.
[2] Gomperz *Wiener Studien* IV, 116.
[3] Wilamowitz-Moellendorf *Philologische Untersuchungen* 1881, 182.
[4] P. M. Schul *Revue des Etudes Grecques* 1946-7.
[5] Magalhaes Vilhena *Le probleme du Socrate* 375 ff.
[5a] Magalhaes Vilhena *op. cit.* 399.
[6] *Who was Socrates?* 69.
[7] Xen. *Anab.* VI, 6, 12; Grote *History of Greece* LXXII, 20.
[7a] Grote *op. cit.* LXXII p. 11; cf. LXXIII, 54 ff.
[8] Thucydides I, 139.
[9] Grote *op. cit.* LXXII, 12.
[10] Grote *op. cit.* LXXII, 15.
[11] Grote *op. cit.* LXXIII, 79.
[12] Xen. *Hellen.* III, 5, 1; Grote *op. cit.* LXXIII, 79.
[13] Xen. *de Rep. Lacaed.* 14; Grote *op. cit.* LXXIII, 57.
[14] Grote *op. cit.* LXXIII, 401.
[15] Pl. *Ep.* VII, 326 b.
[16] Ath. *Deip.* XI, 508 e.
[17] Smith, *Thucydides* note to II, 100.
[18] Pl. *Ep.* V.
[19] Ath. *Deip.* XI, 508 e.
[20] Schul. *op cit.* 49.
[21] Ath. Deip. 506 e after Carystios of Pergamum F. H. G. IV, 356.
[22] Dem. IX, 59.
[23] Gomperz *Wiener Studien* IV, 116.
[24] Diod. Sic. XVI, 2, 3.
[25] Arist. *Pol.* V, 10; Dem. *con. Aristoc.* 659, 662, 674; Plut. *adv Colot.*
[26] Grote *op. cit.* LXVIII, 411 ff.
[27] Grote *op. cit.* LXVIII, 411.
[28] Plat. *Epis.* VII, 336 ff.
[29] Post p. 59; 151 note 35.
[30] *Phaedrus* 246, trans. Jowett.
[31] Skemp *Theory of Motion in the later Platonic Dialogues* 3.
[32] Skemp. *op. cit.* 3, 4.
[33] Cf. Skemp *op. cit.* 7.
[34] Skemp *op. cit.* I.
[35] *Thaetet.* 155 ff.
[36] Taylor *Plato, the Man and his Work* p. 328 ff.
[37] Skemp *op. cit.* 11.
[38] Skemp *op. cit.* 13.
[39] Hardie *A Study in Plato,* 78.
[40] Skemp *op. cit.* 15.
[41] Skemp *op. cit.* 16.
[42] Skemp *op. cit.* 21.

[43] Skemp *op. cit.* 22.
[44] Skemp *op. cit.* 33.
[45] Taylor *op. cit.* 410.
[46] Plat. *Rep.* 509 b.
[47] Skemp *op. cit.* 28, 29.
[48] Skemp *op. cit.* 49.
[49] Taylor *op. cit.* 436.
[49a] Skemp *op. cit.* 49.
[50] Taylor *op. cit.* 441.
[51] Taylor *op. cit.* 445.
[52] Taylor *op. cit.* 454.
[53] Diog. Laert. 111, 46; cf. IX, 65.
[54] Plat. *Leges* 704 c ff. Translation Jowett.
[55] Plat. *Leges* 707 b. Trans. Jowett.
[56] Taylor *op. cit.* 489.
[57] Werner Jaeger *Aristotle* 110 ff.
[58] Jaeger *loc. cit.*

Index

Page references marked with an asterisk indicate brief biographical sketches of the persons named.

Abdera, 113n., 139, 149, 150
Abschnitt as cognate of *temenos*, 27n.
Abstract universal, 109
Academia, 61
Academy, Plato's, 174, 175, 182, 248, 269, 271
Accumulation of property in Homeric family, 35
Achilles, 19, 25, 29, 32, 50
Achilles and the tortoise, 103
Adimantus, 161, 196, 203, 241
Adriatic Sea, 67
Aegean Sea, 66, 69, 70, 71, 78n., 127
Aegean, climate of, 18
Aegina, 71, 174n.
Aegospotami, battle of, 73, 165f., 167
Aeschylus, 28
Aesculapius, 153
Aesthetic training in Platonic education, 234
Aesthetic, Plato's, 220f.
Agamemnon, 29, 30, 56
Agora in Crete, 257
Agricultural progress in Homeric poems, 24, 25
Agriculture, slavery in Greek, 18
Agrigentum, 79, 114n.
Air in Greek cosmogony, 119, 121, 128, 135
Ajax, 26
Akleroi, 31
Akolastos, 217
Alcibiades, 59*, 72, 73, 115n., 146n., 176
Alcidamas, 146
Alcinoüs, 18, 25, 27, 30
Alcmaeon of Croton, 90, 114*, 153ff., 213
Alcmaeonids, 69, 70, 72
Alcman, 250
Alexander of Aphrodisias, 91
Alexander of Macedon, 236
Alexandria, 140n.
"Allies" of Athens, 67f.
Allocation of land, equal, 89
Allotments, land, in Homer, 27
Anarchy, Pythagorean, concept of, 84, 86, 96, 110, 278
Anatolius, 81n.
Anatomy, Greek, 159
Anaxagoras, 62, 77, 113*, 117, 130ff., 137, 138, 139, 144, 193, 220, 296
Anaximander, 63f., 90, 112*, 113n., 118ff., 128, 147, 152, 155
Anaximenes of Miletus, 112*, 121ff., 135
Ancestor cults, origins of, 15
Ancient vs. modern materialism, 116f.
Andrapodon, 18f.
Andromache, 19, 22
Anthropisboi, Socrates' scorn of, 237f.
Antiphon, 146, 188, 189
Antitheses of Platonic philosophy, 63, 129f., 287
Antithesis of body and soul, 48ff., 62f., 86, 110, 121f., 147, 208n., 214, 218, 221, 271, 278f., 287
Apetairoi in Crete, 257
Apollo, 37, 53ff., 57f., 59f., 62, 82, 83, 144, 206f., 216, 251
Apollo and Hermes, 57ff.
Apollo as god of aristocrats, 54ff., 58, 62, 206f.
Apollo, attributes, 54
Apollo, transformation of, 37
Apothetai, 244

A priori categories, Kantian doctrine of, 285
Appearance and reality problem, 101, 277, 285f., 288, 290f.
Arc, reflex, 293
Archē, dualism of, 83, 84
Archelaus, 113*, 137, 144
Archimedes, 117
Archons, Athenian, 161, 164
Archytas, 75f.*, 92, 183, 259, 263
Areopagus, court of, 29
Arete, ambiguity of, 193, 194, 298
Arginusae, battle of, 73, 165
Argonauts, 17
Argos, 70n.
Aristippus, 182f.
Aristocracy, role in Pythagorean philosophy, 82f.
Aristocratic bias, Plato's, 239
Aristocratic expedition to Syracuse, 184
Aristocratic prejudice against manual labor and science, 290
Aristocratic structure of Homeric society, 29ff.
Aristois, 99
Aristokratia sophron, 217
Ariston, 162
Aristophanes, 58, 59, 205, 215f., 221, 243, 294
Aristotle, 46, 61, 63n., 68, 75n., 80, 81n., 90, 91, 94n., 97, 102, 105n., 108, 109, 110, 119, 125, 126, 136, 139, 145, 153, 155, 159, 201, 208, 225, 228, 255, 258, 263, 267n., 292n.
Aristoxenus, 80*, 84f., 88, 95, 111, 233f.
Arithmetic in Platonic education, 230
Arithmetical equality, 94, 209
Arithmetical proportion, 92ff.
Armor, Homeric vs. hoplite, 66
Armor production, 65
Army, rise of professional, 198f.
Army, Spartan, 165ff.
Arrow paradox of Zeno, 103
Art and politics, affinity, 205
Asceticism as outcome of Platonic theory, 214f., 218, 286
Asceticism, Spartan, 254
Asia Minor, 39n., 70n., 122
Askēsis, 106
Asklepidae, 114n., 140n.
Assembly, Athenian, 45n., 115n.
Assembly of the folk in Homer, 33
Aster, 172
Astronomical investigations, origins of, 14
Astronomy in Platonic education, 230f.
Astyanax, 19
Athena, 28, 38, 54, 60ff., 61f., 131, 149
Athena as goddess of reconciliation of class strife, 60ff.
Athena as protector of Athens, 61-62
Athena, attributes, 61-62
Athena, symbolizing state or organ of reconciliation, 62
Athena, transformation of, 38
Athenian and Spartan society, 17
Athenian city-state, 36
Athenian society, 65ff.
Athens, 36, 46, 58, 59, 60, 61f., 65ff., 75f., 77, 85n., 113n., 115, 127, 130, 131, 138, 139, 140n., 164ff., 165n., 172, 173, 175, 176, 177, 181, 182, 183, 184, 206, 249, 250, 259 273
Atomic theory, 104, 116, 118, 137, 142, 147ff., 150, 151f., 159
Attica, 45, 68ff., 71, 75, 126, 127, 161, 176, 252
Augustine, St., 122
Augustus, 55
Authoritarianism, Plato's reactionary, 228
Authority in Pythagorean system, 83, 84, 87
Autos in Homer, 50

Baker, Lynn, VI, 292n.
Banausia, 236ff.
Barbarians, equality of, 146
Barter equivalents in Homer, 22
Barter, Oriental, 17
Basileus, 30, 34

Behaviorists, 293f.
"Being" in Eleatic philosophy, 98, 100, 270f.
Bendis, 194
Bentham, Jeremy, 116
Bifurcation of philosophy in Greece, 77ff., 137
Biology, Greek, 159
Black Sea, 67, 112n.
Black Sea trade routes, 17, 34f.
Blood feud in Homer, 29
Body-soul antithesis, 48ff., 62f., 86, 110, 121f., 147, 208n., 214, 218, 221, 271, 278f., 287
Boehm-Bawerk, Eugen von, 200
Boeotia, 39n., 46n., 65
Boethius, 94
Booty in Homeric poems, 30
Boulé, 69
Breakup of Greek tribal society, 200, 242
Breakup of society and Orphism, 49f.
Brides, purchase of, in Homeric period, 22
Bronze Age, transition to Iron Age, 20f., 28
Brown, Norman O., VI
Bureaucracy in water supply civilization, 14-17
Burnet, J., 80, 88, 104n., 111

Caesar, Caius Julius, 236
Caird, Edward, 283, 284
Calchas, 54
Callicles, 115
Calypso, 56
Canon of the beautiful, Plato's, 221
Canonus, 166
Carthage, 72, 177, 180
Caste, origins in water-supply society, 14f.
Catana, 79, 123
Causes, apparent and real, 277
Celsus, 156
Censorship, Plato's, 221f.
"Centrists" in Athens, 188, 190, 191
Ceos, 113n.
Cephalus, 188, 189, 191
Cereals in Homeric period, 24
Chalcedon, 190
Chalcis, 65, 81n.
Chance, influence of, 152
Change, notion of, 63, 98f., 101f., 127f., 131, 145, 147, 151, 153, 266
Change-permanence antithesis, 63, 16, 221, 287
Change, problem of, in Eleatic school, 98f., 101f., 270
Charmides, 161
Chemistry, ancient, 159
Chersonese, Thracian, 45n.
Chieftains in Homeric society, 31f., 34
Childbearing in Plato's state, 241ff.
Christian Church, early, 227, 262n.
Christianity, self-abnegation, 236
Cicero, Marcus Tullius, 121f., 150
Cimon, 189
Cisalpine Gauls, 177
City-state, conflict of political interests, 13, 62f., 190, 260f., 269
Class conflict, 68ff., 89, 147f.
Class interests and justice, 190ff.
Class structure in Homeric society, 33
Class struggle in ancient society, 89, 147f.
Class struggle in Attica, 68ff.
Classical society and slave labor, 16
Clazomenae, 113n., 130
Cleon, 115*, 188
Clisthenes, 69
Clothes, production of, 65
Clubs, aristocratic, 111, 164, 197n., 248
Clubs, Pythagorean, 81
Clytemnestra, 28
Coin, absence of, in Homeric poems, 25
Coined money, 37, 66
Cold in Greek cosmogony, 119, 121
Collection of tribute, 16
Colonus, 61
Colophon, 112n., 122
Common lands in Homer, 27
Common people in Homeric poems, 29f.

Common possession of women in Plato's state, 244
Communal ownership of land, 22, 26f., 41
Communal Society in water-supply agriculture, 14ff.
Communism, Platonic, 203, 240ff., 249, 259f.
Communism, primitive, of early Christian Church, 227
Conceptualism of Socrates, 105ff., 191ff., 270
Concubinage in Homer, 29
Conservative interpretation of harmonic proportion, 93
Conservation of water as social factor, 14
Constantine, 81n.
Contractual bonds in Greek society, 66
Convention and reality, 144f., 151f.
Convention-nature argument, 78, 241
Copper in the *Odyssey,* 20f.
Copper mines, 65
Corcyra, 89
Corinth, 176
Corrective and distributive justice in Aristotle, 94n.
Cos, 114n., 117
Cos, medical school of, 156
Cosmoi of Crete, 257, 258
Cosmology, Greek, 118ff., 121
Cosmology of Anaximander, 118ff.
Cosmology of Pythagoreans, 86, 87
Council of elders in Homer, 29, 33, 34
Council of Elders, Athenian, 45n.
Council of the Four Hundred, Athenian, 45n., 139, 188
Courage, Plato's definition, 207
Crafts in Homeric society, 25f.
Craftsmanship, pride of, 157, 199
Craftsmen, Plato's prejudice against, 236ff.
Cratylus, 145
Creative role of *NOUS,* 134
Cretan society, 256ff.
Crete, 67, 251f., 255ff., 260, 267, 268
Critias, 146n., 161, 162, 167, 168, 169, 188, 189
Croesus, 112n.
Cronos, 22, 44
Croton, 75n., 78f., 82, 114n., 153
Cyamis, 30
Cyclades, 65
Cyclops, 21
Cylon, 79
Cynical evolution of Sophism, 146f.
Cyprus, 45n., 71
Cyrenaic hedonism, 116, 182f.
Cyrene, 172, 174, 269
Cyrus, 90, 217

Dairy farming in Homeric period, 23
Danubian valley, 21n., 249
Darwin, Charles Robert, 120, 266
Day laborers in Homeric society, 31, 32, 33
Decay of tribal order in Homeric society, 35
Decelea, 176
Definition, technique of, 108f.
Degeneration of dialectics into sophism, 115
Deism in England, 152
Demeter, 49
Democracy and materialism, 77
"Democracy" of special privilege, 68
Democracy, Athenian, 65ff., 115f., 131, 227, 273
Democracy, Democritus' defense of, 151
Democracy, Greek, 113ff.
Democratic constitution of Athens, 184
Democratic imperialism, Athenian, 188, 261
Democratic institutions in Athens, development of, 66, 68f., 70, 71f.
Democratic reforms in Athens, 45n., 71n.
Democritus, 75n., 90, 104, 113*, 116, 117, 118, 132, 138, 141f., 147ff., 159, 199, 296
Demos, 162

Demos, 72, 107, 115, 166, 190, 216
Diaconos, 59
Dialectic in Zeno, 102
Dialectic, degeneration into sophism, 115
Dialectic, material, 147
Dialectical philosophy, 77
Dialectics, 118
Dialectics in Platonic education, 232, 233, 294ff.
Dicasteria, 166
Diels, 105n.
Diké, 39ff., 47f., 62f., 99, 118, 211
Diké, transformation of, 211
Diocles, 177
Diodorus Siculus, 174n.
Diogenes Laërtius, 174n.
Diomedes, 22, 53
Dion of Syracuse, 172ff., 177ff., 181ff., 184
Dionysius I of Syracuse, 172, 174, 175, 177, 178, 179
Dionysius II of Syracuse, 177ff., 182f.
Dionysus, 49, 54, 59f.
Discipline, Spartan, 253f., 286
Disease, treatment of, 109
Distribution of patrimony, equal, 89
Distributive justice, 108
Division of booty, equal, 89
Dogmata, 222
Domestication of animals, 16
Domination of philosophical idealism, 121
Dorians, dominant caste in Crete and Sparta, 251, 253, 256ff.
Doulos, 18f.
Drinking water, scarcity of, in Greece, 17
Dualisms of Pythagorean-Platonic age, 116ff.
Dualisms, Platonic, 129f., 287
Dualistic concept of man, 63

Ear canals, 153
Early Christian Church, 227
Early Greek idealism, Chap. IV
Early Greek materialism, Chap. V
Early Pythagorean thought, 97f.
Earth in Greek cosmogony, 119, 128, 136
Ecclesia, 69
Echecrates, 280
Economics, institutional, 297n.
Economy of scarcity, Greek, 215
Education of Plato's "guards," 198, 201f., 218ff., 230ff., 234ff., 294ff.
Education of women, Plato's, 242
Education, Cretan, 257f.
Education, Pythagorean, 82ff., 202, 233f.
Eëtion, 22
Egypt, 15, 24, 46n., 67, 71, 112n., 172, 237
Eidolon in Homer, 50f.
Elea, 98, 99, 102, 112n., 123
Eleatic school, 47, 98ff., 100, 110, 130, 135, 147, 151, 152, 153, 188, 270f., 272, 287
Empedocles, 92, 114*, 136
Empire, Athenian, 67ff., 72, 149, 188, 206
Empire, Roman, 148, 227
Empire, Syracusan, 173f., 177
Empiricism in medicine, 156ff.
Empiricism, philosophical, 297n.
Engineering, Greek aversion to, 117
England, aristocratic prejudice against trade, 239
English deists, 152
Ens simplex, soul as, 86
Entelechy, 292
Entrepreneur viewpoint in cosmology, 120
Epaminondas, 178
Epanastasis, 82
Ephesus, 113n., 126, 127
Ephors, Athenian, 167
Ephors, Spartan, 253, 257
Ephorus, 174n.
Epicurus, 149, 152, 208
Epitrite, 95
Equality and justice, 210f., 218
Equality, arithmetical and geometrical, 94, 209

Equality concept in Greek thought, 89ff.
Eros, Spartan sacrifice to, 243
Ethical idealism of Socrates, 105f.
Ethical implications of *diké,* 40f.
Ethical universalism, 115
Ethics of sophist thought, 145f.
Ethics, Pythagoras as founder of, 91
Ethiopians, 124
Euboea, 65
Eugenics in Plato's state, 244
Euharmostia of Plato, 229
Eumaeus, 19, 23, 26, 56
Eupatrids, 31
Euphrates, 249
Euphues, 216
Euripides, 130, 144, 217, 221, 243
Eurytus, 96
Euschemosune, 219
Evil, problem of, in Hesiod, 42ff.
Evolution of dialectic into atomism, 159
Evolution of *diké* (custom to justice), 39ff., 41ff.
Evolution of Greek philosophy from Orphism, 48ff., 52f.
Evolution of primitive dialectic, 137f.
Evolution of sophist thought, 145f.
Evolutionary prejudice in history, 13
Exile as substitute for blood feud in Homer, 29
Expedition against Syracuse, 59, 72f., 176
Experience-knowledge antithesis, 287
Experimental method in medicine, 156ff.
Experimental method in psychology, 293
Experimental method in science, 117
Experimental treatment of disease, 109
"Explanation" by numbers in Pythagorean system, 96f.
Exportable goods, production of, 16f.

Fabricius, 81n.
Fall in supply of slaves, 67
Family, patriarchal, 28
Family, Plato's destruction of, 244
Farm laborers in Homer, 31, 32
Favorinus, 175n.
Female captives, fate of, 19
Female slaves in Homer, 18f.
Feminine constancy and private property, 28
Fertilizers in Homeric agriculture, 24
Fire in Greek cosmogony, 119, 121, 128, 136f.
Fish, prejudice against, in Homer, 23
Fleet, Athenian, 65, 66, 165f.
Force and justice, 42ff.
Fossil evidence in early materialist thought, 122f.
Four Hundred, council of, 45n., 139, 188
France, Anatole, 211n.
France, materialism in, 152
Friendship and hatred in Pythagorean system, 84f.
Function of guardianship in Plato's state, 223f.

Galileo, 236
Genos in Homer, 29
Gentile society, breakup of, 18
Geographical position of Sparta, influence on development, 249, 252
Geometrical equality, 94, 110, 209
Geometrical proportion, 92ff.
Geometry, discoveries in, 14
Geometry in conservative philosophy, 93
Geometry in Platonic education, 230
Gerousia of Sparta, 255
Glaucon, 161, 198, 241
Glaukus, 22
Goats as food in Homeric period, 22

Golden Fleece, quest of, 17
"Golden mean," doctrine of, 55
"Good form" as Platonic virtue, 182, 219
Gorgias, 146
Grain imports, 65
Greek cosmology, 118ff.
Greek economic life, conditioning factors, 17f.
Greek idealism and landed property, 81
Greek medicine, 109, 153f.
Greek progressive philosophy, 112ff.
Greek science, 109, 153f.
Greek society, change in, 13
Greek traders in Homer, 26
Gruppe, O. E., 92n.
"Guards," education of Plato's, 198, 201f., 218ff., 230ff., 234ff.
Gyges, ring of, 196
Gylippus, 176
Gymnastics in Platonic education, 218, 222, 229, 232

Halicarnassus, 55n.
Hammurabi, code of, 15
Handicraft industries, 65
Harmonic proportion, 92ff.
"Harmony" in Platonic education, 218, 219, 220, 229ff.
Harmony in Pythagorean system, 87, 279f.
Harmony of opposites, 87, 96f., 155, 158, 270
Harmony, defense of, by Pythagoreans, 116
Harmony, nature of, 128
Harvesting in Homeric agriculture, 24
Hatred and friendship in Pythagorean system, 84f.
Heat in Greek cosmogony, 119, 121
Hector, 22
Hedonism, 116
Hegel, Georg Wilhelm Friedrich, 78, 79f., 127, 129, 267f.
Hegelians vs. Utilitarians, 116
Helots in Sparta, 67, 250, 252ff., 287
Hephaestus, 61
Hera, 78n.
Heracles, 56
Heraclides of Pontus, 104n.
Heraclitus, 101f., 104, 105n., 113*, 117, 118, 125, 126ff., 132f., 135, 141f., 144, 145, 147, 152, 159, 263, 294, 296
Herds in Homeric society, 23
Hermae, mutilation of, 59, 72, 146n., 161
Hermes, 56ff., 62, 274
Hermes and Apollo, 57ff.
Hermes as god of mercantile democracy, 57, 59, 62
Hermes, attributes, 56, 58f.
Hermocrates, 177
Herodotus, 55*, 89, 142f., 149f., 237
Hesiod, 39*, 40ff., 61, 63, 82, 89, 122, 211
"Hide and live," doctrine of, 208
Himera, 79
Hipparchus, 58
Hippias, 69n., 144
Hippocrates, 114*, 144, 153, 156, 199
Hippocratic school, 117, 231
Hippodamus, 85*
Historical materialism of Anaximander, 119
Historical relativism, 142f., 190ff.
History of thought, Socrates' contribution, 108f.
Homeric armor, 66
Homeric society in the Homeric poems, 18-36
Homer's use of "equality," 89
Homœomeria, 136f., 138
Homosexuality as aristrocratic cult, 243, 286
Homosexuality, Plato's, 286
Hoplites, 66
Horace, 55, 76n.
Horses in Homeric period, 22
Household slaves, 18f.
Human nature and the state, 200
Humanistic education, Platonic, 219
Hunting in Homeric period, 23
Hunting societies, early, 15
Husbandry, development of, 16

Hybris, 82, 217, 278
Hyperbolus, 115*, 188
Hyperborean Apollo, 83

Iamblichus, 81*, 95
Ictinus, 62
"Id," Freudian, 200
Idea of the Good, Plato's, 298ff.
Idealism of Socrates, 105
Idealism vs. materialism, 116, 137, 148f.
Idealism, early Greek, Chap. IV
Idealism, origin of, 119
Idealistic criticism of science, 153
Idealistic method in politics, 266f.
Idealistic philosophy and landed aristocracy, 76f.
Iliad, bronze in, 20f.
Iliad, slavery in, 19f.
Immortality, doctrine of, 278f., 280ff.
Imperialism, Athenian, 115f., 148, 188, 261
Improvement in farming in Homer, 21
Individual and state, analogy, 197ff., 226, 270
Individualism and mercantilism, 125f., 148
Individualism, atomistic, 116, 118
Individualism, cosmopolitan, 151
Inductive method, invention of, 108f.
Inequality among Spartans, 252, 255
Inequality and justice in Pythagoras, 88f.
Inequality, development of, in gentile society, 31f., 35, 36
Inequality, "natural," 82, 84, 209f, 214, 269f, 271
Infanticide in Plato's State, 244f.
Infanticide in Sparta, 253
Instincts in vitalist psychology, 293
Institutional economics, 297n.
Integration of personality, Platonic, 213
International law, Greek, 66
Invasion of Hellenic peninsula by Greeks, 17
Ionia, 67, 76f., 112n., 113n., 126f.
Ionian School, 52, 118ff., 121, 122, 124, 125, 129, 130, 132, 159
Iris, 123
Iron Age, transition from Bronze Age, 20f., 28
Iron Mines, 65
Irrigation as social factor, 14
Ismenias, 190
Isolated individual and the origin of the state, 199ff.
Isolation of philosophy, 148f.
Isolationism of Sparta, 255
Isonomia, 90, 154n., 158, 210
Italy, 46n., 72, 75n., 76, 77, 79, 80, 85n., 98, 99, 172, 259
Ivory tower, 118, 146

Jesus and Socrates, 107
Jews in Egypt, slave labor of, 15
John, St., 226, 227
Justice and equality, 210f., 218
Justice and force, 42ff.
Justice as attribute of Zeus, 35, 38
Justice in Homeric period, 35
Justice, evolution from custom, 39ff., 63f.
Justice, problem of, 35, 39, 77ff., 82, 89f., 91ff., 97, 99, 102, 105ff., 128, 132, 145, 188, 189, 190ff., 195, 196ff., 207, 210, 240f., 272

Kallipolis, Plato's, 229, 230, 266
Kaloi kagathoi, 83, 206, 215ff.
Kant, Immanuel, 171
Kings in Homer, 30, 32
Klēros (allotment of land), 27
"Know thyself," 54, 58
Knowledge-experience antithesis, 287
Knowledge vs. opinion in Eleatic thought, 98, 99, 101f.
Knowledge vs. opinion, Pythagorean view, 110

Lacedaemon, 115n., 146n.
Laertes, 19, 25, 34
Lampsacus, 113n.

Land distribution, management of, 14
Landed aristocracy in Sparta, 76, 206, 252ff.
Landed oligarchy, rise of, 66
Landed property and Greek idealism, 81
Landed proprietors and the Pythagoreans, 86, 110, 286f.
Landed proprietors' control of Plato's state, 215
Landholding system in Homeric period, 27f.
Landless in Homer, 31
Landowner, evolution of, in Homeric period, 31
Larissa, 114n.
Lathe biōsas, 208
"Laughing philosopher," 151
"Law and order" in conservative philosophy, 99, 110, 147, 155
Law, Platonic concept, 290f.
Laws of Lycurgus, 251f.
League against Persia, 70
Legal obligations of *diké,* 41
Leon of Salamis, 167
Lesbos, 67
Leto, 53
Leucippus, 104, 113n., 117, 150
Leuctra, battle of, 178, 184
Levels of thought, 292
Lex talionis, 91
Liberal education, Platonic, 219
"Limiting" vs. "unlimited" in Greek philosophy, 86, 110, 125, 147
Livestock as chief form of wealth in Homeric society, 21f.
Logos, 130
"Long Walls," 71, 212
Lucania, 75n.
Lucretius, 99*, 114n., 118, 136
Lycophron, 146
Lycurgus, 93, 251f., 255
Lydia, 78n., 127
Lysander, 165*, 167, 170
Lysias, 188
Macedonia, 69n., 184, 261
Magi, 149
Magna Graecia, 79, 82, 106, 177
Magnesia, 70n.
Male captives, fate of, 19
Male domestics, 19
Malta, 123
Malthakos, 218
Manual labor and experimental science, 117
Many-one antithesis, 63, 103f., 151, 301f.
Many, prejudice against, 285
Marathon, 69f., 139
Marx, Karl, 240
Mater familias, 15
Materialism of Protagoras, 142
Materialism vs. idealism, 116, 137, 148f.
Materialism, ancient vs. modern, 116
Materialism, atomistic, 116, 132
Materialism, early Greek, Chap. V
Materialism, mechanical, of eighteenth century, 152
Materialism, weakness of ancient, 116ff., 132ff., 145
Materialistic concept of strife, 119
Materialistic philosophy and mercantile development, 76f.
Mathematical demonstration of nature of justice in Pythagoras, 88f.
Mathematical explanation of phenomena, 270
Mathematics in Platonic education, 230f.
Mathematics of Pythagoreans, 87ff., 110
Mathematics, discoveries in, 14
Matriarchal family in Homeric poems, 28
Matter, notion of, 118, 135, 137, 141f.
Matter-spirit antithesis, 63, 287, 294
McDougall, William, 292
Medicine, Greek, 109, 153f.
Medism, accusation of, 139
Megacles, 69n.
Megara, 45n., 69n., 71, 172

Megaron in Homer, 29
Melanthius, 20
Melissus, 125
Melos, 68
Meno, 282f.
Mercantile class in Athens, 71f., 116
Mercantile class, rise of, 13, 66, 68ff., 78, 112n., 116f., 125f., 148, 195
Mercantile class vs. landed proprietors, reflection on Olympus, 57ff.
Mercantile democracy and sciences, 231
Merchants, appearance of, in Odyssey, 26
Messenians, 252
Messenian Wars, 250, 252
Metaphysical prejudice of philosophers, 111, 187f.
Metis, 61
Migrations and husbandry, 16
Migrations and Oriental society, 17
Migrations, period of, 21, 249f.
Miletus, 85n., 112n., 113n., 127
Military chieftains, evolution into kings, 31f., 34
Military leaders, rise of, 17, 23
Military training in Platonic education, 232
Mill, John Stuart, 116
Milling in Homeric agriculture, 24
Milo, 79
Mimetic ritual in Orphism, 49ff.
Minar, Edwin L., Jr., V, 86
Mind-body antithesis, 134
Mind-matter antithesis, 294
Mining in Greece, 65, 67
Miracle and change-process, 266
Moderation as an aristocratic tenet, 54f.
Modern state, birth of, 36
Monarchia, 158
Money fine as substitute for blood feud in Homer, 29
Monism in early Greek philosophy, 129, 130
Monogamous family in Homeric poems, 28
Moral training in Platonic education, 234
Mos, 40
Motion in Zeno's philosophy, 102f.
Motion, problem of, 102f., 127f., 133ff., 152, 153
Mousikē, 232
Mules in Homeric agriculture, 22, 24
Munychia, battle of, 161
Muses, 54, 60, 220
Music and politics, affinity, 205, 222
"Music" in Platonic education, 218, 222, 229, 232
Mutilation of Hermae, 59n., 72, 146n., 161
Mysticism and the inductive method, 109
Mythopoesis, 223
Mytilene, 68, 115n.

Napoleon, 236
"Natural" inequality, 82, 84, 209f., 214, 222, 224f.
Natural phenomena and early materialist thought, 120, 121, 122f.
"Natural" subordination in Pythagorean system, 84
Naturalism of Democritus, 152
Nature-convention argument, 78, 241
Nausicaä, 19
Naxos, 69n.
Neoplatonism, 81n.
Nestor, 29
Nettleship, 224, 232, 235
Niceratus, 167
Nicias, 72*, 73, 115n., 167
Niebyl, Karl Heinrich, VI, 15
Nile, 249
Noble lie, Plato's, 223, 224
Noblesse oblige in Platonic code, 236
Nomadic tribes, 21, 249f.
Nomos vs. *physis,* 144f.
"Nothing too much," 37, 54, 58, 217
NOUS, notion of, 132ff., 137, 138

Numbers, significance in Pythagorean system, 88, 96f.

Objective relativism, 115, 192
Odysseus, 18, 19, 23, 26, 27, 29, 30, 32, 33, 34, 50, 56
Odyssey, bronze in, 20f.
Odyssey, slavery in, 19f.
Odyssey, transition to private control of land, 22
Oikeion, 87
Oligarchic opposition in Athens, 71f.
Oligarchical clubs in Crete, 257
Oligarchical constitution of 411 B.C., Athenian, 164
Olive, cultivation of, 17f., 24, 61
Olive oil, importance of, 25, 65
Olympic games, 250
"One and many" problem in Eleatic thought, 103f., 151
One-many antithesis, 63, 103f., 151, 301f.
Opinion vs. knowledge, in Eleatic thought, 98, 99, 101f.
Opinion vs. knowledge, Pythagorean view, 110
Opinion, Plato on, 275f., 285
Opinion, Socrates' contempt for, 272
Opposites, strife of, 102, 119ff., 122, 130, 132, 133, 147, 152, 154, 294
Opposites, unity of, 119ff., 128, 152, 154
Opposition as a philosophical touchstone, 52f.
Optic nerve, discovery of, 153
Optics, Greek, 159
Orchards in Homeric period, 25
Order and symmetry in Pythagorean education, 87, 234
Organic concept in Plato's thought, 296f.
Oriental social organization, 14
Oriental vs. classical society, 16
Origin and validity, distinction between, 201
Origin of idealism, 119
Orpheus, 47
Orphism, 47ff., 53, 62, 83, 86, 118, 122, 125, 129, 278
Orphism as expression of the dispossessed, 62, 125
Ortygia, 177
Otrezok as cognate of *temerros,* 27n.
Overseas expansion, Athenian, 70
Oxen as standard of wealth, 22, 25
Oxen in Homeric agriculture, 24

Paiderastia, 286
Pallas Athena (see Athena)
Pallene, battle of, 69n.
Paradoxes of Zeno, 102ff., 294
Parmenides, 76n., 99ff., 125, 205
Paros, 123
Parthenon's architecture as reconciliation, 62, 220
Particular-universal antithesis, 270, 287, 289, 297, 301f.
Pater familias as guarantor of procreative relations, 15
Pater familias as merchant, 26
Patriarchal family, 28
Patriarchal slavery, 19
Patroclus, 19
Paul, St., 50, 226f.
Peisistratus, 45n., 58, 69*
Peloponnesian War, 71n., 72ff., 73n., 115, 131
Peloponnesus, 65, 253, 259
Penelope, 28
Perdiccas, 190
Periander, 190
Pericles, 59, 62, 71*, 72, 106, 113n., 115, 116, 130, 131, 139, 162, 166, 188, 189, 220
Perictione, 161
Period of migrations, 21, 249f.
Periods of Platonic education, 232f., 233
Perioikoi, 253
Permanence-change antithesis, 63, 116, 221, 287
Permanence in Parmenides' philosophy, 100ff.
Persephone, 284

Persia, 69, 70, 71, 112n., 127, 149, 217
Persian invasions, 69f.
Personal property, Plato's abolition of, 245ff.
Personality, Platonic integration of, 213
Phaeacians, 27
Phaedo, 286
Phaedrus, 172
Pharisees, 227
Phidias, 62, 220
Philemon, 146
Philia, 84f.
Philip of Macedon, 184
Philistus, 179
Philolaus, 75*, 96, 144, 150, 279
Philosopher-king, Plato's, 240, 262f.
Philosophical empiricism, 297n.
Philosophical failure of Sophists, 191
Phlius, 80
Phoenicia, 71
Phoenicians as the traders of Homer, 26
Phratra in Homer, 29
Phylon in Homer, 29
Physis vs. *nomos,* 144f.
Pigs as food in Homeric period, 22
Pindar, 83, 284
Piracy, rise of, 17, 24
Piraeus, 67, 70n., 71, 72, 85n., 177, 188
Plato
  abolition of personal property, 245ff.
  Academy, 174, 175, 182, 269
  aesthetic, 220f.
  affinity of politics with art and music, 205
  and Aristotle, 184
  and Critias, 168f.
  and Dion, 172ff.
  and Hippocrates, 156ff.
  and Homer, 13, 50, 56
  and Jesus, 107f.
  and Phaedo, 286
  and Pythagoreanism, 85, 87, 93, 107, 110, 203, 228
Plato—(*Continued*)
  and Socrates, 107, 150, 163f.
  and Sparta, 250
  and specialization, 199
  and Speusippus, 182, 184
  and the "Thirty," 168f.
  antitheses, 63, 129f., 287
  appearance and reality, 277, 285f., 288
  aristocratic bias, 227f., 229, 239
  arithmetic in education, 230
  as "feminist," 243, 258
  as literary artist, 171
  as poet, 171f.
  asceticism as outcome of his philosophy, 214f., 218, 286
  astronomy in education, 230f.
  atomic basis of his ideal state, 148
  attack on Sophists, 238, 272
  attitude toward manual labor, 27
  attitude toward war, 248
  aversion to change, 205, 288f.
  aversion to mercantile democracy, 205f.
  aversion to plurality, 212
  aversion to relativism, 140
  canon of the beautiful, 221
  censorship, 221
  communism, 203
  debt to Eleatics, 105, 110
  debt to Pythagoreans, 85, 87, 93, 107, 110, 228, 268
  definition of courage, 207
  definition of temperance, 208ff., 216f.
  destruction of private family, 244
  dialectics in education, 232, 233, 294ff.
  disapproval of Homer, 50, 56
  dislike of mercantile democracy, 58-59
  dualisms, 129f.
  education of women, 242
  eugenics, 244
  euharmostia, 229
  faculties of the soul, 212
  fear of revolution, 235
  founding of Academy, 174, 175

Plato—(*Continued*)
geometry in education, 230
"good form," 182, 219
gymnastics in education, 218, 222, 229, 232
harmony in education, 218, 219, 220, 229ff.
his death, 184
Idea of the Good, 298ff.
idealistic monism, origin, 137
idealistic reactionary, 228
infanticide, 244f.
integration of personality, 213
justification of aristocratic state, 209
kallipolis, 229
life, Chap. VI
mathematics in education, 230f.
military training in education, 232
moral and aesthetic training in education, 234
music in education, 229
"natural" inequality, 199, 209
noble lie, 223, 224
noblesse oblige, code, 236
objectives of his philosophy, 160
on Apollo, 60
on art and drama, 60, 221
on Dionysus, 60
on homosexuality, 243, 286
on "innovations," 205
on justice, 48, 82, 145
on levels of reality and behavior, 138
on opinion, 275f.
on piracy, 26
on the state, 47
on wisdom, 207
organism concept, 296f.
prejudice against craftsmen, 158, 203, 207, 264
prejudice against the "many," 273
professional athletes, 219
proportion in education, 218, 219
reconciliation of dualisms, 130

Plato—(*Continued*)
Republic as combination of Spartan and Cretan policy with Pythogorean intellectual achievement, 260
sex in the ideal state, 241ff.
sold into slavery, 174
spokesman for conservatives, 74
unity of personality, 213
unity of state, 226
use of "Sophists" as term of abuse, 272
women and children, 241ff.
Platonic philosophy, antitheses of, 63, 129f., 287
Platonic theory, outcome in asceticism, 214f.
Platonic virtues, 182, 207, 265
Platonism, sources of, 110
Plotinus, 81n., 277
Plowing in Homeric agriculture, 24
Plurality, problem of, 63, 102, 103, 104, 135f., 151, 212
Plutarch, 46*, 117, 174n., 180, 182
Polarization, primary, in Anaxagoras, 134, 136, 137
Polemarchus, 188, 190
Polis, 36, 38, 66
Political conflict in Athenian society, 66ff.
Political role of Pythagoreans, 78ff.
Politics, affinity with art and music, 205, 221
Polus, 115
Polycrates, 78*
Polygamous family in Homeric poems, 28
Polykleroi in Homer, 30, 31
Polyphemus, 23
Poneroi, 215, 216
Pope as philosopher-king, 240
Popular origin of Orphism, 53
Popular origin of religious movements, 47ff.
Population, pressure of, 16, 17
Porphyry, 81n., 95f.
Poseidon, 56
Posidonia (Paestum), 99
Post, L. A., 169

Post-Homeric period, 13, 39, 42, 45ff., 200, 201
Pottery production, 65
Prejudices, Socrates', 273
Pressure of population in Oriental society, 16, 17
Priam, 19, 27, 28
Priest-king, 34
Priesthood in Oriental society, 15, 16, 17
Priests and kings, 17
Primacy of aristocratic ideas among Pythagoreans, 81ff., 85
Primal unity of Orphism, 48, 118
Primary production, processes of, 14, 16, 17
Primitive communism of early Christian Church, 227
Private property, rise of, 27
Probouloi, 164
Process, laws of, 128, 153
Prodicus, 113*
Production for the market, 65f.
Progressive Greek society, 13, 66
Prometheus, 61
Prophet-priest, 34
Prophets, role in Pythagorean philosophy, 83
Proportion, mathematical, in Greek philosophy, 92ff., 218
Protagoras, 113*, 138, 139ff., 151f., 204, 274
Protection of property and the state, 36
Protest of the dispossessed, *dikéas,* 211
Psyche, 52, 118, 121, 122, 124
Psyche, ambiguity of, 193f.
Psychological hedonism, 116
Psychology, modern, 292ff.
Psychology, Pythagorean, 83f.
Ptoliethron in Homer, 38
Puritan and Platonic asceticism, 215
Putsch of Four Hundred, Athenian, 188
Pylos, 254
Pyrilampes, 162
Pythagoras, 75*, 78ff., 83, 104n., 113n., 149, 150, 154, 205n., 218, 220, 225, 277, 279
Pythagorean evolution of Orphic ideas, 86
Pythagorean theorem, 88
Pythagoreans, 47, 52, 53, 75n., 78ff., 80n., 85n., 109ff., 118f., 121f., 123, 125, 143, 147, 153, 154, 155, 172, 188, 193, 205, 211, 213, 222, 228, 231, 233, 234, 248, 259f., 263, 274f., 280, 287, 294
Pythagoreans as originators of Platonism, 109ff.
chaos vs. harmony, 52
cosmology, 118f.
on the state, 47, 52
reconciliation of opposites, 53

Reality in Pythagorean thought, 97f.
Reciprocity as justice in earlier Pythagoreans, 91
Recollection, Platonic doctrine of, 279, 282ff.
Reconciliation of classes, *diké* as, 211
Reconciliation of opposites as a philosophical touchstone, 52f.
Reconciliation of opposites, Platonic, 263, 285, 294
Reflex circle and arc, 293f.
Reform of Athenian constitution, 45n., 68, 71n.
Reforms, Solon's, 68
Reign of terror, oligarchic, 73f.
Reincarnation, doctrine of, 279
Relative scarcity of food in Homeric period, 35
Relativism, historical, 190ff.
Relativism, objective, 192
Relativism, objective vs. subjective, 115
Relativism, philosophical, 139, 140ff., 144f.
Relativism, skeptical, 142, 144f., 150
Relativism, sophistic, 144f.
Religion of Homeric poems, 34f.

Religion, social function of ancient, 15
Renunciation, doctrine of, 277
Repressive institutions in Sparta, 250, 252ff.
Retribution, 63f.
Revolts of Athen's "allies," 70f.
Rewards and punishments, 196f.
Rhegium, 79
Rhodes, 85
Right of bequest in Homer's and Solon's times, 28
Rise of mercantile class, 13, 66, 68ff., 78, 112n., 116f., 125f., 148
River-valley civilizations, 14-17, 18, 21, 249
Rohde, Erwin, 51
Roman empire, 148, 227
Rousseau, Jean-Jacques, 200, 224
Ruling principle in Pythagorean philosophy, 82f., 96

Salamis, 45n., 69n.
Salamis, battle of, 70
Samos, 67, 78, 115n.
Sanctions in totem cults, 15
Science and material development, 117
Science, Greek, 109, 153f.
Science, negation of, by Eleatic position, 104
Self-abnegation of Christianity, 236
Self-interest, 190ff.
Self-sufficiency, agricultural, in Homeric society, 25
Separation of body and soul, 48ff.
Separation of opposites, 118
Separation of opposites in Anaxagoras, 132f., 133f.
Serfdom in Crete, 256
Sex in Plato's state, 241ff.
Sextus Empiricus, 140*, 141, 142
Sexual irregularity, charges of, 243n.
Sheep as food in Homeric period, 22
Shorey, P., 207n., 224
Sicilian expedition, 59, 72f., 149
Sicily, 26, 67, 72, 76, 77, 79, 98, 164, 172, 175, 259
Silver mines, 65, 68
Silverberg, Tom, vi
Simonides, 190
Simplicius, 63f.
Skeptical relativism, 144f., 150
Skepticism, evolution of progressive philosophy into, 146
Skepticism, radical, 132
Skeptics, Greek, 132, 140n., 144f., 146, 150
Slave labor in ancient society, 66f.
Slave labor in Oriental society, 14, 15, 16
Slaveholding state, 250
Slave-owning democracy, 113ff., 117, 145
Slavery in *Iliad* and *Odyssey*, 18f.
Small peasantry and Hesiod, 39
Social affinities between Socrates and Pythagoreans, 111
Social ambiguities as reflected in progressive Greek thought, 116
Social base of mercantile democracy, 211
Social conflict and Greek philosophy, 76ff., 82f., 86, 89ff., 94ff., 104f., 110, 113ff., 116f., 126f., 134, 138f., 147f., 260, 261
Social context of speech, 293f.
Social contract, 198ff.
Social differentiation, signs of, in Homer, 27
Social function of philosophy, 76ff., 82f., 89ff., 94, 104f., 110, 114f., 116f., 147f.
Social origin of ancient materialism, 116f.
Social origin of Pythagorean arithmetic, 96f.
Social position of women in Greece, 242f.
Socrates, 74, 106ff., 130, 131, 137, 139, 150, 166ff., 170, 188, 189, 190ff., 196, 197f., 204, 205, 211f., 220, 225, 237f., 239, 240, 241, 272, 273f., 275, 282ff., 285, 294, 296
Socrates and Christian ethics, 107f.

Socrates and Pythagorean school, 110f.
Socrates and the "Thirty," 167f., 168
Socrates and Xantippe, 286
Socrates as defense attorney of oligarchs, 166f.
Socrates as extreme right-wing spokesman, 188, 189
Socrates on prostitution, 216
Socrates, conceptualism, 105ff., 191ff.
Socrates, philosophy of, 106ff.
Socrates, teleology, 193
Solon, 28, 45*, 46f., 53, 60, 61, 62, 63, 68, 69n., 89f., 90, 161, 211, 236, 252
Soma and *sema,* 278
Sophism, 105, 115
Sophists, 47, 77, 78, 85f., 113n., 115, 138ff., 191, 238, 272, 294
Sophocles, 237
Sōphrōn, 216f.
Sōphronizein, 217
Soul concept of Ionian school, 118f.
Soul, doctrine of, 48ff., 51f., 118f., 193f., 197, 218f., 277f., 280ff., 286, 287
Soul, in Pythagorean system, 83, 86
Soul, separation from body, 48ff.
Soul-body antithesis, 48ff., 62f., 86, 110, 121f., 147, 208n., 214, 218, 221, 271, 278f., 287
Sources of Platonism, 110
Spain, civil war, 227
Sparta, 54, 67, 70, 71, 73, 74, 76, 93, 94, 115n., 165n., 166, 167, 170, 176, 178, 184, 206, 243, 244, 249ff., 253ff., 257, 258, 259, 260, 267, 268
Sparta as center of landed reaction, 54, 204
Spartacus, 236
Spartan army, 165ff.
Spartan society, 17, 250, 252ff.
Sparta's role in Greek politics, 54, 204
Speculators, Athenian wheat, 116
Spencer, Herbert, 158
Speusippus, 181, 182, 183, 184, 205
Spirit-matter antithesis, 63, 287, 294
Square numbers in Pythagorean system, 91f.
State and human nature, 200
State, idealistic vs. relativistic views, 47
State, origin of, 197f.
State, problem of, 77f., 188, 195ff., 213ff.
State, rise of, 60
Status quo, Pythagorean defense of, 82, 84, 96
Stobaeus, 87, 88
Stoics, 130, 236
Strabo, 104n.
Strife in Heraclitus, 102
Strife of opposites, 102, 119ff., 122, 130, 132, 133, 147, 152, 154, 263, 294
Strife, Pythagorean vs. materialist concepts, 119
Subjective relativism, 115
Subordination of opposites, 82ff., 155, 158
Sunium, 65, 68
Suppression of sophists in Athens, 170
Surplus tribute and exchange, 16
Sybaris, 79
Sympathetic magic, 49
Synoikism, 36, 42
Syracuse, 73, 122, 172ff., 176ff., 179ff., 182, 183, 184, 217, 228, 269

Taboos as system of sanctions, 15, 24
Taboos in Pythagorean system, 86
Tarentum, 75n., 80n., 183, 259, 263
Tauromenium (Taormina), 79
Taylor, A. E., 107, 109, 110, 111, 174n., 224
Technique of definition, invention of, 108f.
Technological advance in Homer, 20-21
Telamon, 26
Telemachus, 32

Telis, 79
Temenos, 27
"Temperance," Platonic, 208ff., 216f.
Terror, oligarchical, in Athens, 167ff., 170
Thales, 63, 112*, 118, 129, 135, 189
Thasos, 149
Thebes, 75n., 169, 178, 190, 243
Themis, 99
Themistocles, 70*, 106
Theodorus, 172
Theologizing of justice concept, 82
Theophrastus, 80n., 112n., 153
Theopompus, 174n.
Theory of Creator, germ of, 134
Theramenes, 164, 166, 167f., 169f., 189, 212
Thersites, 33
Thessaly, 69n., 114n.
Thetes, 31
"Thirty," the, 73f., 146n., 161, 167ff.
Thrace, 113n.
Thracians, 124
Thrasybulus, 146n., 166
Thrasymachus, 78, 115, 145, 188, 190ff., 208n., 240, 241
Threshing in Homeric agriculture, 24
Thucydides, 21, 89, 90, 117, 216, 217, 231, 253, 254
Thucydides, son of Melesias, 162
Thumos, 212, 213
Thurii, 85n., 113n., 139
Tigranes, 217
Tigris, 249
Tisis, 63
To ison, 210
To plēthos, 215
Totem cults as systems of sanctions, 15
To thumoeides, 212
Trade, Oriental, 17
Trade, rise of, in Homeric period, 24, 26
Trade routes, 17
Tradition in Pythagorean philosophy, 83
Transition from Bronze to Iron Age in Homer, 20-21, 28
Transition from "custom" to "justice" (*diké*), 41-44, 63
Transition from Homer to Hesiod, 39ff.
Transmigration of the soul, 123f., 278f.
Travel, role of, in Greek education, 149f.
Treatment of disease, 114n.
Trial of Socrates, 170f., 172
Tribal affiliation and slavery, 15
Tribal democracy, twilight of, in Homeric period, 33
Tribal order in Homer, 13, 29
Tribal society, 66
Tribute, collection of, 16
Tribute paid to Athens, 67, 70
Tritogeneia, Athena, 61, 149
Twilight of Athenian democracy, 163
"Two ways," in Parmenides and Plato, 272f.
Tychios, 26
Tydeus, 22, 53
Tyumenev, A. J., 32n.

Unhistorical view of Plato, 187
Unity, nature of, 103, 118, 122, 125
Unity of opposites, 119ff., 128, 152, 154
Unity of personality, Platonic, 213
Unity of state, Plato's, 218, 226, 245ff., 260
Universal in Socrates, 106ff.
Universal, abstract, 109
Universal, Plato's, 287, 289ff.
Upper-class communism, Plato's, 249
Usurers, Athenian, 116
Utilitarians vs. Hegelians, 116

Vine, cultivation of, 17f., 24
Virtue, 197
Virtues, Platonic, 182, 203ff., 207, 265
Vitalism, 292f.

Void, notion of, 151
Vortex, notion of, 152

War, Plato's origin of, 198
War, Pythagorean view, 85, 248
Water in Greek cosmogony, 119, 122, 123, 128, 136f.
Water supply as social factor, 14-17
Watson, John B., 293
"Way," *diké* as the, 211
"Way of truth" in Socrates, 272f.
"Way of truth," Eleatic, 100, 271
Wealth in Homeric society, 30-31
Weltanschauung, Platonic, 296
Wheat and the Golden Fleece, 17
Wine, 65
Winnowing in Homeric agriculture, 24
Women and children in Plato's state, 241ff.
Women in Crete, 258

Xantippe and Socrates, 286
Xenophanes, 112*, 122ff., 279
Xenophilus, 84
Xenophon, 90, 170, 216, 217, 237
Xerxes, 149, 190

Zeno, 76n., 102ff., 153, 159
Zeus, 34f., 37f., 43, 44, 48, 53, 56, 57, 62, 83, 129, 131, 150, 202, 274
Zeus, attributes in Homer, 34f.
Zeus, transformation of, 37f.